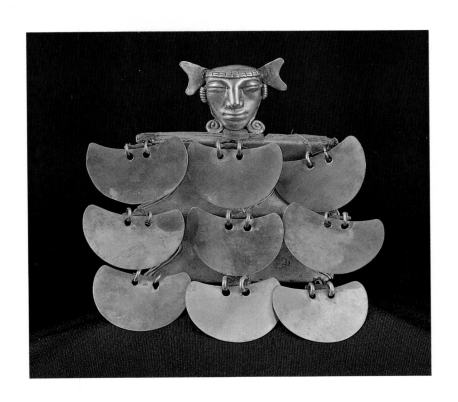

JOHN HEMMING

The Search
for El Dorado

BOOK CLUB ASSOCIATES·LONDON

For Sukie

This edition published 1978 by Book Club Associates
by arrangement with Michael Joseph Limited

This book was designed and produced by
George Rainbird Limited
in association with Park and Roche Establishment

Editor: Mary Anne Sanders
Designers: Yvonne Dedman, Pauline Harrison
Cartographer: Tom Stalker Miller
Production: Jane Collins
Picture researcher: Juliet Scott

Printed in Great Britain by W. S. Cowell, Ipswich, Suffolk
Bound in Great Britain by Dorstel Press, Harlow, Essex

ENDPAPERS The lands of the Muisca lay in high, fertile
valleys of the Andes.

HALF-TITLE The Quimbaya period started only a few
decades before the Spanish conquest. Its warriors were
embellished with gleaming plates of gold.

FRONTISPIECE Quimbaya pendant of cast gold. The figure
is crowned and wears only ear and nose ornaments,
necklace, belt and arm bands. The arms and legs join to
form a pattern of elegant symmetry. Height about 12 cm.

Contents

1 EVERY EXPLORER NEEDS A VISION, SOME GOAL TO KEEP HIM AND HIS MEN STRUGGLING forward. For Christopher Columbus the goal was the Orient. He had seen Paolo Toscanelli's letter telling the King of Portugal that a ship sailing westwards would reach the lands of the Great Khan. Instead of travelling eastwards across Asia as Marco Polo had done, Toscanelli suggested sailing westwards around the globe. He recalled Marco Polo's description of China as 'a country richer than any other yet discovered . . . It possesses gold and silver and precious stones and all kinds of spices in large quantities—things which do not reach our countries at present.' He mentioned the fabulous city of Quinsay (Hangchow) with its ten marble bridges, the province of Cathay (around Peking) where the Great Khan resided, and the famous island of Cipangu (Japan), an unknown place 'very rich in gold, pearls and precious stones, with temples and palaces covered in gold'.

This was Columbus' inspiration when he put Toscanelli's theory to the test in 1492. His purpose was thus a practical one: to explore a new sea route to the wealth of Asia. He was naturally elated when his three small ships made their famous landfall in the Bahamas. Disappointed at finding only simple, naked people, he was not daunted. He called the natives 'Indians' and the misnomer has persisted. In the Journal he wrote for his royal patrons, Columbus said: 'I wish to leave for another very large island, which I believe must be Cipangu, according to the signs made by these Indians I have with me. They call it "Colba" [Cuba]. They say that there are ships and many very good sailors there. . . . But I am still determined to proceed to the mainland and to the city of Quinsay, to present the letters from Your Highnesses to the Great Khan . . . ' When he reached Cuba a week later, Columbus noted that it took large ships of the Great Khan ten days to sail there from a mainland.

Columbus clung to the conviction that he had reached India, long after he himself had found the continental mainland. It was on his third voyage, on 5 August 1498, that Columbus sailed past Trinidad and anchored off the coast of South America. He found the land to be 'the loveliest in all the world, and very populous' and contacts with the natives were friendly. They indicated that they called their country Paria. 'They came out in hordes to the ship, and many of them wore pieces of gold at their breasts and some had pearls round their arms. I rejoiced greatly when I saw these things, and spared no effort to find out where they obtained them. . . . Both sides were sorry that they could not understand one another: they because they wished to ask about our country, and our men because we wanted to learn something about theirs.'

Columbus was most impressed to see the volume of water being discharged by the mighty Orinoco river into that gulf of Paria. 'I have come to believe that this is a vast continent, hitherto unknown. I am strongly supported in this view by the great river . . . ' Although he suspected that he had discovered a continent, and although on his fourth voyage he explored hundreds of miles of the coasts of Central America, Columbus was reluctant to accept that this was not Asia. A series of explorers who followed Columbus were less obsessed, and the Asiatic illusion slowly faded.

There was an extraordinary burst of maritime exploration during those final years of the fifteenth century and the first decades of the sixteenth. Spanish and

Ordás reported that the rapids thundered through a defile 'with sides of smooth rock, extremely high'.

5

In August 1498 Columbus made the first landfall on the mainland of South America, at the gulf of Paria opposite Trinidad. The size of the Orinoco river convinced him that he had discovered 'a vast continent'.

Portuguese sailors took their small ships along thousands of miles of uncharted coastlines. They made their way past the northern and eastern seaboards of South America, around the islands of the West Indies, and along the edges of the Caribbean. They rounded headlands, investigated rivers, sounded bays and anchorages. They observed endless coastlines—the bleak cliffs or bare pampas of the Argentine, the steep wooded hills of southern Brazil, the reefs and surf of the Brazilian north-east, mangrove swamps of the mouths of the Amazon and Orinoco, dense rainforests of Darien, dunes of northern Venezuela and the majestic peaks of the snowy mountains of Santa Marta. They mapped and charted as they went, and the outline of the Americas emerged with remarkable accuracy on European maps.

Those early voyagers frequently made contact with many hundreds of tribes living along the American coastlines. Each tribe in turn experienced the shock of meeting an alien race from over its horizon. There were bartering sessions and canoes full of Indians were often grabbed to be interrogated about any possible wealth in their lands, or kept to be taught Spanish and used as interpreters. But there was growing disappointment. These new lands contained little obvious wealth. There were some pieces of gold or pearl necklaces among the primitive tribes, but none of the rich cities or saleable spices that would have been found in Asia. The first rush of explorers and adventurers began to dwindle and the Indies were acquiring a poor reputation. Some protagonists of the New World were reduced to inventing fantasies to rekindle enthusiasm: Columbus spoke of a river near Santo Domingo full of gold nuggets 'of such quality it was a marvel' and Bartolomé de las Casas claimed that men used nets to fish gold from the rivers of

Darien. But the first inspiration, the riches of Asia, was gone; and there was no new attraction to replace it.

The breakthrough came in the second decade of the sixteenth century. In September 1513, Vasco Núñez de Balboa, guided by local Indians, hacked and fought his way to the watershed of the Isthmus of Darien and gazed down on the South Sea, the Pacific Ocean, which he claimed for Spain a few days later. In 1516 the Pilot Major of Spain, Juan Díaz de Solís, explored the estuary of the River Plate in an attempt to find a sea passage to this newly-discovered ocean. This search was accomplished by the man who has been described as the greatest of all explorers: Fernão de Magalhães. Magellan, as he was known to his Spanish employers, left Spain in 1519 and forced the passage of the Straits of Magellan next year, on the start of the first circumnavigation of the world. There was now a new objective for South American explorers: the discovery of a passage to the South Sea easier than the fearful strait at the tip of the continent. In that same year 1519 the Spaniards founded the settlement of Panama, across the Isthmus of Darien, as a base from which to explore the Pacific coasts. A new wave of exploration was thus geographical, concerned with reaching the seas and spices that lay *beyond* the Americas.

It was also in 1519 that Hernán Cortés landed on the coast of Mexico at the start of the most amazing adventure of all. The following year his 450 men marched along the causeway into the Aztec capital Tenochtitlan, modern Mexico City. The great chronicler of Cortés' expedition, Bernal Diaz del Castillo, could only compare such marvels with the splendours of antiquity. 'When we saw so many cities and villages built in the water and other great towns on dry land, and that straight and level causeway going towards Mexico, we were amazed and said that it was like the enchanted houses described in the legend of Amadis, on account of the great towers and buildings rising from the water, all built of masonry. Some of our soldiers even asked whether the things we saw were not a dream? It is not surprising that I describe it here in this way, since there is much to ponder and I do not know how to tell it; for we saw things never before heard of or seen or even dreamed!' After such a discovery and the conquest of an empire of such magnitude—for Mexico was as large and as populous as Spain itself—anything was possible. There was now a thrilling new inspiration for explorers: conquest of kingdoms of unimagined wealth that might lie beyond the most unpromising coasts.

There was a third type of expedition to attract conquistadores. This was to

LEFT A native view of the Spanish ships that appeared on the American shores.

RIGHT Hernán Cortés landed in Mexico and conquered the Aztec empire in 1519.

discover fertile fields for colonial settlement. Seeing such vast land masses peopled by tribes whose military technology was inferior, Europeans thought in terms of permanent acquisition. It was the start of the colonial era, the centuries of European expansion. From the outset, explorers and conquistadores staged ceremonies taking possession of other people's lands. Balboa even strode into the waters of the South Sea with a royal standard and claimed the entire Pacific Ocean for the King of Spain. The problem was to follow up these theatrical gestures with lasting occupation. Towns had to be founded, with living conditions attractive enough to induce Spaniards to take up permanent residence. This could be achieved most easily if there was a mine, a natural resource, or a lucrative crop. Seeing the gold objects that were proud possessions of native chiefs, the Spaniards naturally wanted to find the source of the gold itself. Bernal Diaz explained why Cortés' men scattered throughout Mexico after the overthrow of the Aztecs: 'In Montezuma's tribute books we looked for the districts from which he was brought gold, and where there were mines, or cacao, or cloth for cloaks; and . . . we wanted to go there.' The ultimate dream of every conquistador was to discover a gold or silver mine that would yield a steady flow of treasure.

Diego de Ordás marched with Cortés into the Mexican capital, Tenochtitlan.

There were thus three main motives to lure expeditions into the interior: a search for passes to the South Sea and the spice trade of the Orient; the hope of finding hidden kingdoms of fabulous wealth; and the wish to discover mineral deposits or fertile land for settlement. All the early expeditions started with one of these objectives—although it was quite possible for them to change direction, to be diverted to a different purpose while on the march.

The north coast of South America—then known as Tierra-firme, 'the mainland', or to foreigners the Spanish Main—had few obvious attractions for colonists. When Columbus first landed in 1498 he was impressed by the pearls and gold objects worn by the Indians of Paria. The source of the pearls was soon found. They came from the waters of the barren island of Cubagua, just off the coast of eastern Venezuela. A pearl fishery was established, but it had to obtain firewood and even water from the mainland. A small settlement was therefore established on the continental coast, at a place called Cubagua. Dominican friars tried to establish a mission there—the conversion to Christianity of American Indians was the ostensible moral justification for the invasion of their lands. But the proselytizing efforts of the missionaries were nullified by a new scourge: slave raids by Spanish ships to seize people from the coastal tribes.

An Italian called Girolamo Benzoni took part in one of these slave raids, and described it in his *Historia del Mondo Nuovo*. 'All along the coast, the Indians come down from the hills to the shore to fish. We therefore used to land and hide ourselves in places where we could not be seen. We often used to wait all day hoping to take prisoners. When the Indians arrived, we jumped out like wolves attacking so many lambs and made them slaves. We caught over fifty in this way, most of them women with their small children. In the end we went so often to one place and another that we were discovered by our enemies, who were fishing. They immediately started hollering to warn the rest that we were there, so that they all ran from the beach, and we on the shore caught some fish drying on a reed grill over a slow fire . . . Our captain then . . . turned back and led us to the house

8

of a poor chief, a friend of the Spaniards, and giving him a jug of wine, a shirt, and some knives, with civil words entreated him to lead him to a place where slaves could be caught. The chief went off with a party of his men, and returned the following day bringing sixteen Indians, with their hands tied behind their backs.'

The pearl oysters of Cubagua were fished by divers enslaved in the Bahamas. To pay for them, the Spaniards of Cubagua raided along their coast and shipped slaves north to work on the plantations of the island of Santo Domingo. The Indians naturally suspected the Dominican missionaries of complicity in this traffic. So in 1512 and again in 1519, tribes who had initially welcomed Christianity rebelled 'either because of their natural wickedness—or because they were forced to labour in the pearl fishery'. All Spanish settlers and friars on the mainland were killed. The Europeans retaliated with punitive expeditions authorized to enslave any captives as 'rebels'. As a result of this ugly fighting a Spanish town was founded at Cumaná in 1521, the first colonial municipality in South America.

The foundation of Cumaná was followed by the establishment of three other tiny settlements along the two thousand kilometres of coast between the Orinoco and the Isthmus of Panama. In 1524 an unruly town called Santa Marta was founded on the coast of Colombia, below a range of snow-clad mountains; in 1528 the Spanish authorities established Coro on the dry coast of Venezuela, as a base for the suppression of coastal slave raids; and in 1533 a town was founded at Cartagena, at a part of the Colombian coast where natives had previously repelled Spanish landings. These were the bases, the orifices through which the conquistadores' deadly expeditions were to spread destruction deep into the heart of the continent.

Three expeditions left the coast of Venezuela between 1530 and 1531. Each was inspired by a different motive for exploration, but the one that had the most lasting effect was an expedition up the Orinoco led by Diego de Ordás. His expedition became a precursor of the searches for El Dorado. Diego de Ordás had been one of Cortés' captains, one of the men who marched down the causeway into the Mexican capital before its destruction. Cortés sent Ordás back to Spain to announce his conquest, immediately after the *noche triste*, the 'sad night' in which the Aztecs tried to annihilate their invaders. Ordás was in Spain again in 1528 when Cortés returned in triumph. Francisco Pizarro was also there, reporting that he had found traces of another advanced civilization in a place he called Peru on the Pacific coast of South America.

Diego de Ordás was like most modern explorers or mountaineers: no sooner was he returned from one expedition than he began planning another. He was impressed by the relative ease of Cortés' conquest, and longed for the fame of leading his own campaign. He contemplated asking the Emperor for a licence to explore the hinterland of the River Plate: Ordás studied reports of Sebastian Cabot's explorations there and concluded that 'it is a very good business and it is hoped that it will be the best yet discovered. . . . I have the report they brought, which tells marvels and of much wealth, especially silver.' He noted that Cabot's men had brought back 'sheep'—llamas—of better quality than those brought from Peru by Pizarro. The Crown was ready to grant Ordás the province inland of the Plate and Paraguay; but in the end the conquistador asked for a different

9

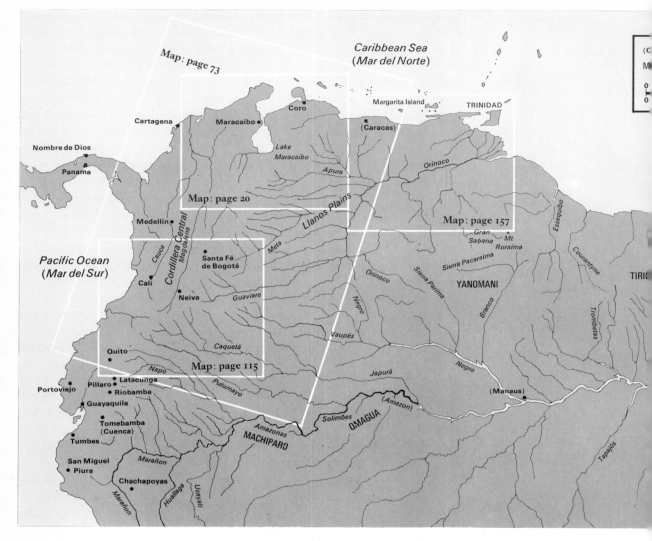

Map: page 73

Map: page 20

Map: page 157

Map: page 115

Caribbean Sea
(*Mar del Norte*)

Margarita Island

TRINIDAD

Cartagena

Maracaibo

Coro

(Caracas)

Nombre de Dios

Panama

Lake
Maracaibo

Apure

Orinoco

Medellin

Cordillera Central

Magdalena

Santa Fé
de Bogotá

Llanos Plains

Meta

Gran
Sabana

Mt
Roraima

Essequibo

Pacific Ocean
(*Mar del Sur*)

Cali

Cauca

Neiva

Guaviare

Orinoco

Sierra Pacaraíma

Sierra Parima

YANOMANI

Branco

Courantyne

TIRIO

Negro

Vaupés

Quito

Caquetá

Napo

Putumayo

Japurá

Negro

Portoviejo

Pillaro

Latacunga

Riobamba

Guayaquila

Tomebamba
(Cuenca)

Marañon

Solimões

(Amazon)

(Manaus)

Tapajós

Amazonas

OMAGUA

Trombetas

MACHIPARO

Tumbes

San Miguel
Piura

Chachapoyas

Marañon

Huallaga

Ucayeli

grant. He opted to explore the region between the Amazon and the Orinoco.

Diego de Ordás was apparently convinced that gold 'grew' better near the equator. There was an obvious link between the colour of the most precious metal and the golden glow of the sun. Silver, the moon's colour, was cooler, and Ordás saw a connection between the Plate (the Silver River), at 35 degrees from the equator, and an abundance of silver. Ordás became convinced that he would find the source of American gold near the headwaters of one of the great rivers, the Amazon or Orinoco, both of which apparently rose near the equator and behind the Andes mountains. The idea that gold would be found near the heat of the equator was widely held. The Jesuit naturalist José de Acosta believed this. He also felt that it was God's design to place mineral wealth in the remotest parts of the world among the most primitive peoples. 'God placed the greatest abundance of mines . . . [in such remote places] so that this would invite men to seek those lands and hold them, and in this way to communicate their religion of the true

Key map of northern South America: the Orinoco, Magdalena and Amazon rivers and the northern Andes.

Towns of recent origin

Tribes in text

200   300   400 Miles

400   600 Kilometres

tlantic Ocean
(Mar del Norte)

(Cayenne)

Oyapock

Marajó Island

(Belém)

God to those who did not know them . . . A father with an ugly daughter gives her a large dowry to marry her; and this is what God did with that difficult land, giving it much wealth in mines so that by this means he would find someone who wanted it.'

Diego de Ordás, one of Cortés' first conquerors of Cuba and Mexico, was an important man, a knight of Santiago with an income of 6–7,000 *pesos de oro* a year from his Mexican property. The Emperor therefore granted his request for the governorship of Marañón (the Amazon), and he had little trouble in recruiting a large force. He took soldiers, artisans, farm labourers, some minor nobility, horses and mares. He found men in Spain and in the Canaries, and in the end his force sailed across the Atlantic in five ships, ranging from the flagship carrying 320 men and 27 horses, to a small caravel with only 30 men: 600 men and 36 horses in all. The flotilla scattered in storms. The flagship struck South America some miles north of the mouth of the Amazon. The second ship, commanded by Juan Cortejo, never appeared: there was a persistent rumour that it ran aground in the river's shallows and its men took refuge among the tribes of the Amazon. Ordás wanted to establish a settlement from which to strike inland. His ship sailed north-westwards along the coast of the Guianas, for forty days, unable to find a suitable place amid its reefs and mangrove forests. In the end, water and fodder for the horses were found on the island of Trinidad, and the expedition landed on the mainland opposite—in the same gulf of Paria seen by Columbus 33 years before.

Ordás was eager to pursue his conviction that the Orinoco led inland to the source of gold. He soon prepared brigs and a sailing barge to take his men and horses up the river. The expedition moved into the swampy, forested mouths of the Orinoco. Its brown waters were 'so flat, broad and deep and navigable that it seemed . . . as if the water was hardly moving'. But the lack of any breeze forced Ordás to put most of his men into the brigs, where they rowed, towing the unwieldy barge against the current. Progress was imperceptible. The Spanish soldiers complained bitterly at the hard labour of rowing. 'This region was so terrible and the vapours that congeal on this river are so corrupt and heavy, that if someone . . . was bitten by a vampire or got a small cut . . . he immediately became cancerous. There were men who, from one day to the next, had their entire feet consumed by cancer, from the ankle to the sole. Men were dying one by one from such diseases, and from hunger: for the land there was very flooded and covered by the river, and there was nowhere for the brigs to seek food.'

The expedition finally emerged from the delta and reached the large Aruak village of Huyapari, 'a famous place, praised by the Indians of that coast'. The Spaniards found it imposing, with 200 large thatch huts and nine chiefs presided over by the 'chief priest' Naricagua, 'the only one among all those people who had a beard on his face'. The Indians' farming was impressive: they grew manioc in lands flooded by the Orinoco, planting as the waters receded and harvesting in front of the rising flood. 'Their food is manioc and the wine they make from it, and much good fish which they kill with arrows or in great basket traps, into which manatees also fall. There are enormous quantities of shrimps: they dry these for use as a staple when they are surrounded by the flooding river. They grind and drink them, and do the same with other dried fish which they keep for the same purpose. They mix these into the beverage they make from fermented manioc . . . which, when they drink it clear, looks like new white wine from Castile.'

The weary Spaniards were excited by the sight of Aruak women, who were naked apart from 'a rag in front of their private parts, which is loose and just long enough to cover them . . . Thus when they sway, or in a wind, everything is revealed.' As in most South American tribes, the women—the fertile sex—were responsible for agriculture; but the men guarded them while they farmed, and fished while they did so. Both sexes were industrious, with the men busy making arrows, nets, hammocks or fishtraps. It was a fantasy world for men: with many more women than men in the tribe, the men could be polygamous. The tribe provided an attractive woman to sleep with any stranger; and when he left, the woman was free to go with him. The godlike bearded strangers doubtless enjoyed this privilege. It surprised their Spanish sense of honour to learn that, if a woman who had slept with a stranger chose to remain with her husband, 'she was not disapproved of, or treated any the worse for this. Instead, her husband felt . . . obliged to love her more, both because she had slept with his friend the guest, and because she had not denied [her husband] in favour of the new acquaintance.'

The Europeans soon shattered the welcome given them by the Aruak. They had brought some thirty pigs and sows, and kept these near the Indian village. Some soldier said that the natives were planning to kill the pigs and their swineherd: the upshot was a night skirmish in which the Aruak defended themselves well with their bows and arrows. The Spaniards were forced to retreat into the village; but the Indians removed their women and children and set fire to the place. They preferred to lose their entire food supply than have it sustain the uncouth foreigners. Desperate for food, Ordás decided to leave his sick men, defended by a rampart and with the larger boats, and to take the rest of his force across to the south bank of the Orinoco. The Warrau tribe lived there in a village called Baratubaro. The chroniclers agree that the Warrau welcomed the Spaniards, but that something then went wrong: either they refused to give food or they were suspected of treachery. Diego de Ordás decided on a savage reprisal. He lured as many as he could into a hut with promises of a distribution of trade goods. He then had the unarmed tribesmen put to the sword. 'And because some had hidden themselves among the dead, to escape his fury, he had the hut set on fire—to satisfy his suspicion and ensure that none remained alive. Thus over a hundred Indians were burned. He took their wives to make manioc and distributed them among the houses and Indians of the other town of Aruacay, where they were taken as prisoners.' Pedro de Aguado condemned this as 'an abominable form of punishment . . . more like the cruelty of the barbarians themselves than the laws of equity of [Ordás'] King.'

Ordás was still determined to reach the source of the Orinoco. He had sent one of his captains on a twenty-day exploration into the Guayana foothills to the south, and the officer returned with reports of a good land, full of game and fish. But Ordás was not interested: he 'wanted . . . only to pursue his original plans, which were to follow the river upstream'. When his men demurred, the governor told them that although 'it was uncertain where they were going, the [success of] the expedition was considered certain'.

The vast llanos of Venezuela, flooded during the rains and dusty during the dry season, with the Orinoco river and the Guiana hills in the distance.

The expedition set off up-river, with some 200 men and 18 horses in a special launch. The men suffered terribly, 'continually heaving cable after cable, a work of intolerable rigour'. They managed to drag the boats up one set of rapids. The Orinoco was flowing across Venezuela's famous plains, the *llanos*. The banks of the river itself were forested, but beyond stretched the savannahs, flooded in the rainy season and hot and dusty, covered in low scrub, during the dry months. These endless plains are broken only by occasional *mesas* or tablelands. Today this is cattle country, but it is not an easy place: during the floods the cattle have to be driven from one *mesa* to the next, and when the grasses become parched and inedible at the height of the dry season, the animals have to be herded on to the soggier areas near the rivers or the coastal valleys. But the cattle were introduced by Spaniards. Before the European invasion, the *llanos* were empty except for deer, egrets, game birds, and a few native villages, perched on knolls above the floodwaters or baked and windswept during the summer months.

Ordás' men toiled up the Orinoco for hundreds of miles. They finally reached the confluence of the Meta, the largest of the many slow rivers that flow across the *llanos*. The Indian guides pointed on up the Orinoco and imitated water hammering on rocks. 'Each man interpreted this according to the desire he nourished' but the more obsessed hoped that it signified goldsmiths beating golden metal. The expedition therefore chose to follow the main river. A hundred kilometres above

the Meta junction progress was blocked by the mighty Atures and Maipures rapids. 'The water falls more than 2½ or 3 estados (about 20 feet) like a mill race and is almost a crossbow-shot wide, [in a rocky defile] with sides of smooth rock, extremely high. It was impossible for any man on foot or in a small or large boat to go up it.' The Indians explained that the upper river beyond this barrier could be reached only by a long detour up the Meta and behind some hills.

Unable to reach the source of the Orinoco, Ordás was forced to turn back. As the expedition sailed down the river it had ascended with such difficulty, it was attacked by Carib archers. Spanish conquistadores had learned that a swift, savage response often demoralized native warriors. The camp-master Alonso de Herrera landed the horses. The Caribs replied by setting fire to the parched savannah, one of their favourite hunting techniques. But as the flames raced towards them, the Spaniards lit a counterfire and charged through the smoke on to the burned plain. The sight of charging horses—the first time this tribe had seen such animals—caused the usual panic: the Caribs were routed and two were captured. The prisoners were carefully interrogated. One was asked whether his land contained any of the materials used by the Spaniards. He responded only when shown the governor's gold ring. 'He said that there was much of that metal behind a mountain range that rose on the left bank of the river. There were very many Indians and their ruler was a very valiant one-eyed Indian: if they sought him they could fill their boats with that metal.' The Indian warned the Spaniards that they were too few to attempt such a conquest. He also indicated that the people of those rich mountains rode on animals like llamas. It all corresponded exactly to Ordás' dream: a ruler of fabulous wealth, deep in the mountains, who used the llamas that Pizarro and Cabot had both associated with hidden wealth. But Gonzalo Fernández de Oviedo knew that Indians normally tried to give answers that a questioner wanted to hear. He wrote: 'Those Caribs were shown gold and silver. They said that there was no silver, but that they would find much gold; and they would obtain it in the province of Meta . . . Whether they were understood well or badly, those Indians continually praised that land of Meta.'

Diego de Ordás had abandoned his idea of finding gold deposits at the source of the Orinoco, but he now had a far more exciting prospect: the capture of the ruler of Meta, a second Moctezuma. Ordás himself wanted to attempt the Meta river immediately, but it was December and the waters were falling alarmingly. An attempt to move up a small tributary was abandoned after a few miles. The trouble was that where Cortés had been fed and helped by native allies, the Orinoco was almost empty. During hundreds of miles of ascent the Spaniards had found only one Carib settlement, Cabruta, and that was a few miles from the river. The Orinoco itself was dropping so fast in the dry season that the Spaniards saw that trees they had cut on the way upstream were now a lance length above the water. Their flagship had been left anchored in a backwater. They now found it 'on dry land, over $2\frac{1}{2}$ leagues inland on a savannah or plain, with the ship scarcely visible in the grass—and yet to reach that place they had sailed over the tops of guava trees.' Ordás ordered the stranded boat to be unloaded, broken up and burned. He finally agreed with his officers that they should return to the mouth of the Orinoco, equip a new expedition, and attempt to reach Meta from an entry further west along the coast. 'So those men turned back, . . . leaving eighty or more dead from the labour of taking the boats up-river or because many of them entered it already ill or injured. After any died, they were thrown into the river.'

Back on the Caribbean, Ordás became embroiled in litigation. The owners of the Cubagua pearl industry resisted Ordás' wish to build a western base for his attempt to reach Meta. He decided to return to Spain to extend his concession. 'He set off, loaded with affidavits and testimonies . . . and ill. His only gain from that expedition was that most of his followers lost their lives; and those who escaped alive were left poor and sick, without property in that wilderness. Ordás himself was very unpopular with them all because his enterprise had such a bad outcome.' Diego de Ordás never reached Spain: he died at sea from his illness. But his venture into the heart of the continent opened a chapter of exploration: the search for Meta and its one-eyed chief.

These anthropomorphic figurines of cast gold show variations on a common theme: each holds two maces and has wings, a bat-like nose, crown of double hemispheres and broad flat legs.

2

THE TWO OTHER EXPEDITIONS THAT MARCHED INLAND IN 1530 AND 1531 LEFT FROM Coro, the small settlement that was the seat of government—and the entire European occupation—of Venezuela. Both were led by Germans, for Venezuela itself had been granted to the German banking house of Welser. Perhaps German efficiency and toughness could achieve more than Ordás' romantic illusions.

It is worth pausing to trace the events that led to the German presence in Venezuela. The Welser were merchant adventurers in the best sense of the word. Their fortune had been built during almost two centuries, in the south German cities of Nuremberg and Augsburg. In 1473 four Welser combined to found a trading company, and in 1490 Anton Welser married the daughter of the owners of a silver mine in the Tyrol. The banking and trading empire was soon established in the busiest commercial centres of Europe. The Welser had long traded in oriental spices, and their Fondaco dei Tedeschi, built in 1441, still stands on the Grand Canal in Venice. They had agents in cities from Danzig to Rome and from Zurich to Seville. Their house in Antwerp was the imposing 'De Gulden Roose' near the Cathedral. Their man in Zaragoza dealt in saffron, and in Lisbon they traded in the highly-prized spice pepper. The Welser invested heavily in an expedition from Portugal to India in 1505, and they bought land in the Canary Islands to grow sugar cane. Their agents kept them well informed of developments in the new discoveries of America.

The presence of German merchants in Spain—a country intensely suspicious

RIGHT The Fondaco dei Tedeschi, the Welser office in Venice, still stands on the Grand Canal.

OPPOSITE Darien style figures have themes that are found throughout Central America and may have links with Mexican art. A fine pendant, height 12 cm.

of foreigners—and eventually in the conquest of America, stemmed from the actions of the beloved Queen Isabella of Castile, the Queen who had licensed and helped finance Columbus. Isabella ensured good marriages for all her children. She married her daughter Juana to the Habsburg Philip the Handsome of Austria, son of the Holy Roman Emperor Maximilian. When the Queen died in 1504 her son-in-law arrived as King of Spain with a retinue of Flemish courtiers and a guard of German troops. Philip died twelve years later—from overindulgence in Spanish food followed by a game of tennis—and his queen Juana, already eccentric, became distraught. Their son Charles therefore succeeded as King Carlos I of Spain, even though he had been educated entirely in Flanders and did not yet speak Spanish. He was still in the process of visiting the different courts of his Iberian kingdom, when in 1519 news came of the death of his grandfather Emperor Maximilian. It was known that Francis I of France and Henry VIII of England were interested in the vacant throne of the Holy Roman Emperor. Charles had to find the vast sums needed to bribe the German electors. There was no money to be had in Spain. It was therefore to the German bankers that he turned for funds, borrowing 300,000 ducats from the Fugger and 141,000 from the Welser. He pledged almost the entire royal property of Castile as collateral; but he duly gained election as Emperor Charles V, with a magnificent ceremony in Charlemagne's capital Aachen.

A few weeks later, when the new Emperor was at Ghent, two members of Cortés' Mexican expedition reached him with presents that the Aztec emperor Moctezuma had given to Cortés. There was a golden sun the size of a cartwheel, covered in engraving, and an even larger silver disc representing the moon. Bernal Díaz recalled that the sun was of the finest gold and weighed over 20,000 *pesos de oro*. There were also 'twenty ducks made of gold, very natural looking, and some dogs of the kind they have, and many pieces of worked gold shaped like jaguars, lions or monkeys'. Albrecht Dürer, who was the son of a goldsmith, happened to see these treasures when they reached Europe. He described them just as Bernal Díaz had done, and exclaimed that 'never in all my life have I seen things that delighted my heart as much as these. For I saw among them amazing artistic objects, and I marvelled at the subtle ingenuity of the people of those distant lands.'

It was the weight of the gold in Moctezuma's treasure that most delighted the Welser—who were among Dürer's patrons. So when the Emperor approached them about a further loan, they obtained as collateral the governorship and licence to explore the American territory of Venezuela. The name Venezuela means 'Little Venice'. The first explorers to enter Lake Maracaibo were surprised to find its Onoto and Pemeno Indians living in huts raised above the water, with canals running through their villages. Calling their land 'Venezuela' was a lighthearted allusion to the Italian city, with all its canals, but the name stuck. It seemed very possible that this lake or lagoon of Maracaibo might lead to a passage to the South Sea, for it was thought that the land barrier of South America was no broader than in Central America.

The Welser had already established a 'factory' (a factor and a trading depot) at Santo Domingo on Hispaniola in 1527, and they planned to send German miners and black African slaves to work the island's gold. The licence granting them

ABOVE Queen Isabella of Castile financed Columbus and married her daughter to the son of the Habsburg Holy Roman Emperor.

RIGHT Dürer's drawing of Isabella's grandson, King Charles I of Spain and Holy Roman Emperor Charles V, the ruler who awarded Venezuela to the Welser and whose subjects conquered South America.

Venezuela was signed by the King-Emperor at Madrid on 27 March 1528. It spoke of fifty German miners to be sent to find the continental goldfields. It granted the Welser extensive trading rights, to extract and trade in 'metals, herbs and spices' between the Indies and Spain and the rest of the world. The licence also defined the Welser jurisdiction as extending from coast to coast, from the North Sea (Caribbean) to the South Sea (Pacific). The Welser clearly placed great importance on this link with the Pacific: it was doubtless the hope of reaching it through Lake Maracaibo that made them ask for the territory of Venezuela. Maps of this period showed a second lake joining Maracaibo to the south, with the Pacific Ocean not far beyond.

The Welsers' first choice as governor of their Venezuelan colony was a rich young man called Ambrosius Dalfinger from the city of Ulm, not far from Augsburg on the upper Danube. The Dalfinger family had made its fortune from cloth, merchant factoring and banking, and Ambrosius had already shown his interest in America by giving financial backing to Sebastian Cabot's voyage of 1526 to the

River Plate. Dalfinger reached the tiny settlement of Coro in February 1529, with three shiploads of handsomely dressed Spanish adventurers. They were dismayed to see the Venezuelan capital. Coro was a dusty little place, with a few dozen thatched houses, one of which was the church and another the municipality. Coro itself was watered by the small Coro river, but the surrounding countryside was desperately dry—sand dunes and barcanes, sparse scrubby vegetation of cacti, agaves and stunted trees.

Dalfinger had no doubt about his first duty: to explore Lake Maracaibo and try to find an outlet towards the South Sea. He soon sailed along the coast and built a base of cane and thatch huts, at what was to become the town of Maracaibo. He then spent a year exploring the lake with German thoroughness. He took his brigs and canoes into every inlet and marched his men up every tributary. The numerous tribes living on the lake had been victims of Spanish slave raiders. Many were by now filled with 'deep-rooted hatred and enmity against the Spaniards. They preferred to die than be subjected or dominated by them, because they received

Early explorations from Venezuela, 1530–33.

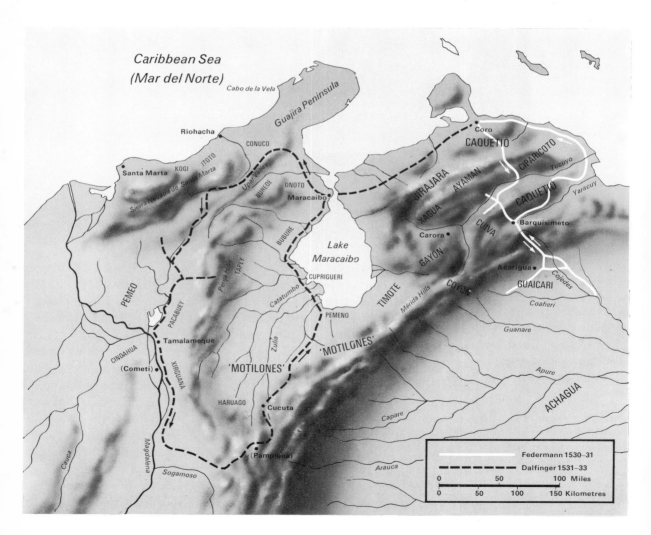

The native Indians carried ornaments of brilliant feathers and kept macaws and other pets.

excessive, intolerable abuse to themselves and their children, wives and property.' Some tribes therefore harassed Dalfinger's explorers, so that he lost men, killed or wounded in Indian skirmishes or from disease. It was all in vain. Esteban Martín, one of Dalfinger's captains, sadly recalled how they explored the southern end of Maracaibo 'where we thought there was a sea strait leading inland, but there is none'. When Dalfinger finally returned to Coro he was greeted by a parade and sung mass. But he had lost a hundred men during the eight-month expedition.

The Germans were not daunted by Dalfinger's failure to find a passage from Maracaibo to the Pacific. They rapidly organized two further expeditions of pure exploration, neither of which began with any notions of mysterious kingdoms or veins of gold beneath the equatorial sun. Soon after Dalfinger's return, on 12 September 1530, another young German, the 24-year-old Nicolaus Federmann, left Coro leading 126 men of whom 16 were mounted. Federmann was an ambitious, red-bearded man; the Spaniards described him as short for a German, but well proportioned. He was calm and serious, 'a man of exceptional intelligence, an admirable and excellent captain; . . . all the men went contented with Federmann.' The Federmanns were from Ulm, like the Dalfingers. Nicolaus' father was a businessman with a grinding mill, and the Federmann family was reasonably prosperous and distinguished. One cousin published a German translation of Petrarch and a description of the Netherlands. Young Nicolaus had served the Welser in Italy and Spain before sailing for the New World as second-in-command of a Welser ship. He reached Coro in March 1530, when Dalfinger was still exploring Maracaibo, and helped to arrange the parade to greet the governor when his battered expedition returned to Coro.

The interior of Venezuela was still a mystery. Dalfinger shared the Welser conviction that the South Sea was not far away, and so, having himself failed to find a link, he sent young Federmann to explore due south from Coro. Federmann himself wrote: 'Our main purpose was to reach the South Sea.'

Nicolaus Federmann was the only conquistador leader to write a full account of his expedition. It was not a very long expedition but it was very exciting—for this was first exploration, with every hill or river unknown to Europeans and every tribe having its first contact with the alien civilization. For the first few miles Federmann was crossing the lands of known tribes—the coastal Caquetió and beyond them the Jirajara, where the chief and his people were living well-ordered lives, with plenty of food 'and some small gold objects that they gave us, receiving us very well'. It took five days to cross the high, dense forest of this tribe, towards the site of the modern town of Churuguara.

By the end of September the explorers entered the lands of the Ayoman, a hitherto unknown tribe. Federmann felt that contact must be abrupt: he attacked the first Ayoman village 'for fear that they would flee, being a timid people who knew nothing about us and had never seen nor heard of horses or of clothed and bearded people'. Having surprised this village, Federmann resorted to the one tactic that has always—and still does—win the friendship of American Indians: he gave presents of beads and iron tools. For a people still largely dependent on stone axes, the cutting power of iron knives and axes was miraculous. Suddenly the men's labour of felling forest clearings, hollowing dugout canoes or carving bows becomes

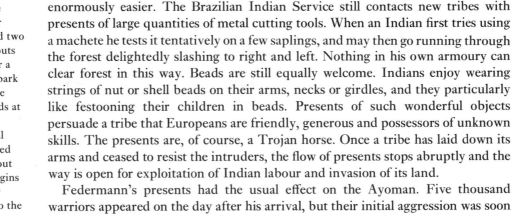

The Indians of Lake Maracaibo and other American rivers used two types of canoe: dugouts and bark canoes. For a bark canoe, a tree's bark was heated over a fire until it curled inwards at either end. The introduction of metal tools greatly facilitated manufacture of dugout canoes. A dugout begins as a felled tree; after hollowing is rolled to the water by the author (below left) and companions; and rides in the river beside a forest camp.

enormously easier. The Brazilian Indian Service still contacts new tribes with presents of large quantities of metal cutting tools. When an Indian first tries using a machete he tests it tentatively on a few saplings, and may then go running through the forest delightedly slashing to right and left. Nothing in his own armoury can clear forest in this way. Beads are still equally welcome. Indians enjoy wearing strings of nut or shell beads on their arms, necks or girdles, and they particularly like festooning their children in beads. Presents of such wonderful objects persuade a tribe that Europeans are friendly, generous and possessors of unknown skills. The presents are, of course, a Trojan horse. Once a tribe has laid down its arms and ceased to resist the intruders, the flow of presents stops abruptly and the way is open for exploitation of Indian labour and invasion of its land.

Federmann's presents had the usual effect on the Ayoman. Five thousand warriors appeared on the day after his arrival, but their initial aggression was soon changed by his show of friendship. Federmann distributed presents to the Ayoman chiefs. He told them about the Spanish Emperor and Christianity and had them accept some form of submission to these incomprehensible alien powers. They told him about a terrible epidemic of smallpox or measles that had struck them some years before. A large part of the tribe had been killed, and the remnant had started to intermarry with neighbouring tribes to recover its numbers. Federmann here encountered another of the great forces that have changed the destiny of American Indians. Columbus and the explorers and conquerors who followed him carried a range of diseases that were unknown on the far side of the Atlantic. Europeans and Africans had survived a series of epidemics and diseases—smallpox, plague, measles, influenza, tuberculosis—and each individual had acquired genetic defences against these scourges. There was no such immunity among the Americans. Indians in perfect health and physically fit will sicken and die in a matter of days from imported diseases against which they have no resistance. Every tribe must expect to lose most of its members within a few months or years of its first contact with the aliens. Disease is the main reason why the lowland native population of the Americas has declined by about 95 per cent since the sixteenth century—a period when the rest of the world's population has increased explosively. A year or two before Federmann's expedition, a strange epidemic had struck the court of the last paramount Inca Huayna-Capac when he was at Quito. The disease killed the Inca himself, his heir and many of his important officials. Francisco Pizarro was to sail from Panama in December 1530, a few months after Federmann left Coro, on his third voyage that was to lead to the conquest of the Inca empire. That conquest was greatly facilitated by the confusion following the death of the Inca, and it is now thought that the strange epidemic was one of the diseases brought across from Europe. It could have been smallpox, striking from tribe to tribe across Colombia and Ecuador in advance of the Spaniards themselves.

The Ayoman lived in forests on either side of the Tocuyo river. Won over by Federmann's presents, they gave his expedition a warm welcome, cutting a trail for the horses and sending many men to help as porters. Various villages provided food for the strangers. The expedition crossed the Tocuyo river on rafts, with the horses swimming. Federmann then decided to make a detour into the dense forests of the Matatere hills, solely out of curiosity to see a tribe of dwarfs. A Spanish raiding party was sent to capture some of these curiosities: after a stiff fight in which many natives were killed, it returned with 150 men and women. These really were small, not more than 30 inches high, 'but well proportioned in relation to their height. We could make no use of these people [as porters] owing to their small size.' Federmann released the captives and gave them presents. In return, a dwarf chief came with three hundred followers and gave Federmann some gold objects. 'The chief presented me with a girl dwarf, four spans high, beautiful and with fine proportions and figure. He said that she was his wife—for [such a gift] is normal among them as a confirmation of peace. I accepted her, although she was distressed and crying much, for she believed that she had been given to devils.'

The tribe living beyond the Ayoman was their bitter enemy the Gayon. Federmann tried to make friends with these people but was rebuffed because his expedition was seen as too friendly to the Ayoman. Federmann's comment was a typical expression of conquistadores' hypocrisy—and their awareness of the colonial advantages of divide-and-rule: 'All this was basically indifferent to me. I was interested only in convincing them of our loyal friendship and of the fact that our permanence among them was for their good. In another sense we could have been pleased to see them enemies of one another, for this meant that we had to concern ourselves less about the danger to us from alliances between them.'

After an initial exchange of presents, the Gayon suddenly abandoned their village. Federmann took this to be a declaration of hostility. He sent fifty men, four of them mounted, to attack a native village 'by night, three hours before dawn

All Spanish expeditions forced Indians to carry their baggage. Thousands of natives died from the weight of their loads and from oppression by the explorers.

24

Federmann's expedition moved through the hills and valleys separating Coro from the Venezuelan llanos.

when all are asleep and an enemy is least expected.' Eighty men and women were captured. A similar attack on the chief's village met with a fierce resistance in which seven Christians were wounded and one killed. The explorers were well aware of the psychological benefit of their novelty and semi-divinity: 'The other Christians buried [the dead man] in a secret place where nobody went. We did not want the Indians to see this, or realize that we were not immune to death—for they believed us to be immortal.' Many Gayon were killed in this battle, and the chief and 43 of his people were captured. Federmann chained him to the rest of his slaves, 'for he was a man who had failed to keep his promise. I divided the rest of the prisoners from both villages among my men, to carry their loads and equipment. We needed this urgently, for many of the Indians we had brought with us had fled.' The expedition had left Coro with many coastal Caquetió as porters and auxiliaries. Federmann wanted to preserve what remained of these, since they were valuable as scouts and warriors. They were now considered reliable: they were too far from home to return except as part of the Spanish expedition.

Beyond the Gayon, the expedition had to spend three days wading down a river. 'Throughout this time we did not leave the water, except at midday and nightfall when we found some clearing on the bank where we could rest to eat or spend the night.' Federmann tried the same tactic with the Xagua tribe that had succeeded with the Ayoman. He launched a night attack on a small village, and even he felt sorry for the shock this caused to the sleeping inhabitants. 'Astounded by the unexpected assault of unknown people, whom they considered demons rather than men, they gave no thought to defending themselves.' By releasing prisoners and giving presents the tribe was won over.

The explorers had been moving across forested hills, past five separate cannibal tribes. They were now delighted to find the forest give way to the flat plain of Barquisimeto, 'one of the most beautiful that had been seen in the Indies'. They were also pleased to find that the inhabitants of this plain were a rich and populous tribe of Caquetió—another branch of the same people that lived on the Caribbean coast near Coro. Up to now Federmann had been having great difficulty over interpreters, for each new tribe he had added another interpreter, and his messages eventually had to be translated five times. 'There is no doubt that before each could understand the other and transmit to the fifth what I had ordered, each would have added or omitted something. Of every ten words I spoke, scarcely one would arrive exactly as I desired. I considered this a great hindrance. It often impeded our discovery of many secrets of the land—the principal object of our journey.'

The numerous and warlike Caquetió occupied the entire plain of Barquisimeto, having driven other tribes into the surrounding forests. The Spaniards camped at the edge of the plain and sent gifts to the nearest village. 'Our position there was advantageous because we could use our horses, which were our best weapons. The Indians greatly fear them, for they make the greatest slaughter among them.' The Caquetió villages were impressive. Federmann reckoned that the first village contained 4,000 people and that there were about thirty thousand fighting men in all the 23 villages along the river. Some of the villages were a mile long, but consisting of only one or two streets. Up to eight families would live in each hut. The men were tall and well built and 'the women in particular are very beautiful: because of this we called this province . . . The Valley of the Ladies.' Federmann was particularly pleased to find that these Caquetió were 'rich people who treat, work, elaborate and sell gold'; and they gave him gold presents worth 3,000 *pesos de oro* and were happy to exchange gold for iron tools.

'In this province I heard tell of the other sea, the South Sea, which was precisely what we hoped to reach and which was the main purpose of our journey. For it was there that we hoped to find, more than in any other place, great wealth of gold, pearls and precious stones . . .' The Caquetió said that they knew about this sea but had never been there themselves—in this way they avoided being forced to guide the explorers.

Many men on the expedition had fallen ill, and they thought that this might have been caused by the humidity of the Barquisimeto valley—it was common in the sixteenth century, before knowledge of germs or infection, to suppose that 'bad air' caused disease. So the expedition moved on, with the sick men carried in hammocks by porters or riding horses. Federmann did not want the Indians to know that Europeans could fall ill, so he pretended that the sick being carried in this way were particularly important. The Indians must have been unimpressed by this charade, for it was they who deceived the Christians: two hundred Caquetió porters accelerated ahead of the main expedition and then ran off, abandoning their loads in the middle of a plain. There were no Indians nearby who could be pressed into service. The explorers had to bury all inessentials, hoping to recover them on the return journey.

Federmann's men were now marching down the deserted Cojedes river, which flowed on to the *llanos* and joined the Guanare and the Apure before entering the Orinoco. The men were hungry and worried that there were no Indians ahead for them to pillage. One consolation was that the plains contained deer which 'do not run quickly because they have never been frightened by the Indians, who have

Spanish explorers relied on food received or stolen from Indians. A newly-contacted Asurini woman with a catch of fish and a turtle.

neither horses nor dogs. They can therefore easily be hunted by horsemen.' Finally Indian villages were sighted. After the customary difficulties, the expedition managed to make friends with the Cuiba tribe, which then provided porters and an escort. For five days the expedition was fed by successive Cuiba villages as it crossed the tribe's lands.

In mid-December 1530 the explorers reached a large town called Hacarigua, stretching for a quarter of a mile along the banks of a river 'two-arquebus shots wide'. Federmann reckoned that the chief of this town controlled sixteen thousand warriors and their families, in a cluster of villages. The population was a mixture of Cuiba and Caquetió, and the two tribes combined to provide a good diet of fish and farm produce. The Europeans were lodged in the town, near the river. They were wary: they guarded their precinct well at night, and often sent pairs of horsemen through the town to ensure that the women and children were still there—for they knew that Indians would never attack before evacuating their families. Federmann also tried to keep the chief with him as a hostage. He pretended that this was an honour and 'he appeared to be convinced. We conversed and I talked to him about the exploration of the land and especially about the South Sea.'

The Cuiba begged the Spaniards to help them attack their enemies the Coyón, who lived to the west at the foot of the Andes. Federmann reluctantly agreed and sent 35 of his men, leading a force of 800 local warriors. The inhabitants of a Coyón village ran into their huts when attacked by the Europeans. To force them out, the Spaniards set fire to the entire village. 'They thus captured about six hundred people—men, women and children. Many were burned to death although they could have saved themselves: they preferred to let themselves be burned alive than to fall into the hands of enemies.' Two Spaniards and one horse were killed in this battle, various Spaniards wounded and many of their Cuiba and Caquetió allies were killed. Federmann wrote: 'I was displeased with this result, both because of the damage suffered by my men and also that of the enemy.' He did not hesitate, however, to keep four hundred of the fittest Coyón as porters, and to distribute the other two hundred among his allies. A royal treasurer called Antonio de Naveros was shocked by the way that Federmann accepted gold presents without keeping a proper financial record. Naveros also protested at the burning of Indian villages without giving due warning to the wretched inhabitants. Because of these complaints Federmann 'ordered me put in irons, which I wore for over two months until I entered this city [Coro]!'

Federmann was still obsessed with the discovery of the Pacific Ocean, which was in fact thousands of miles to the south. The expedition pushed on through Cuiba territory, and then past deserted villages to the large Coaheri river. The riverine Guaicari tribe was thickly settled along this river's banks. These were fishing people, with elaborate basketwork fish traps and large markets at which they traded their fish with the Caquetió. There was a rumour that bearded strangers had already penetrated the rivers ahead in a floating house, but had been killed by the local tribes. Federmann noticed that one chief had European cocks and hens, which the Indians said they had traded from a neighbouring tribe. This convinced Federmann that Sebastian Cabot had been nearby on his exploration of the Paraguay—a geographical error of gigantic proportions, ignoring the entire

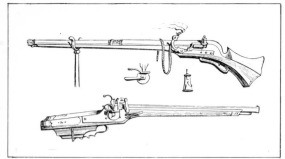

Firearms were used only rarely during the early conquests. Arquebuses were fired by a lighted wick or, later, by a flint-lock mechanism. These guns were heavy to carry and cumbersome to fire.

Amazon and Orinoco basins that lay between. So when Federmann and some of his companions climbed a small hill one morning and gazed out over an expanse of water, he was sure that he was looking at a lake near the Pacific. The morning mist prevented him from seeing the lake's dimensions. It was, of course, the edge of the *llanos*, flooded by the annual rains.

Nicolaus Federmann decided to turn back, with many men sick and his progress southwards blocked by the floods. The return journey was more brutal. It is worth telling some of the incidents on it, as they illustrate the toughness and savagery of these explorations. The Guaicari assembled 1,500 plumed warriors for a surprise attack, but the Spaniards were ready: they drove the attack back to the river, and succeeded in killing some natives with their arquebuses. Firing these was a cumbersome business that involved applying a lighted fuse to a train of powder connected to the charge and shot rammed down the muzzle. It is surprising that Federmann's men had carried arquebuses this far into the interior of Venezuela, for firearms were rarely used in the early American conquests. They were designed to penetrate armour and were far too unwieldy to be effective against agile, naked warriors. But the bang of the gunpowder had a strong psychological effect. After the battle the expedition tended its wounded in a deserted village. 'We stayed there that night and at dawn we set fire to the village. We did the same to all the villages or places we passed that belonged to that chief. We continued in this way with much difficulty and hardship, with men and horses wounded, looking more like gypsies than fighting men.'

28

The expedition had left its sick at a village called Corahao. When Federmann returned to them, they reported that they had felt menaced by the local tribe during the entire time he had been absent. Federmann immediately took the chief of that village and another who had been guiding his reconnaissance. 'I ordered . . . that they be tied up and taken to a forest, and there tortured to tell us their intention in coming to meet us armed for battle, and refusing food to my men . . . When the chief was tormented, he suffered many tortures without betraying himself or confessing anything. I therefore had him killed in the presence of the other prisoner, to serve as a horrible example. . . . And I had *him* locked in a chain with the rest . . .'

Beyond the village, the expedition met eight hundred Guaicari armed for battle. Federmann parleyed with them, arguing that they should lay down their weapons. 'But, while I distracted them with words . . . I arranged that they should be surrounded by the horses, which would attack them—for we were on a beautiful plain that could not have been better suited for this purpose. We took them by surprise and killed five hundred. They did not suspect us since we were conversing with them and calmly discussed peace, and they had no time to use their weapons. We stabbed many on the ground and put the rest to flight. The horsemen charged into the thick of them, knocking down as many as they could. Our footsoldiers then slaughtered these like pigs. They had no recourse but flight, and the speed of our horses prevented this. In the end they tried to hide in the grass, or the living hid beneath the dead, but these were found and many of them beheaded after we had finished with those who were fleeing.'

Federmann's expedition nearly died of starvation and thirst, when lost in impenetrable forest.

After this treacherous slaughter, the expedition thought it best to cross the river in darkness, with the horses swimming and the men who could not swim pulled across on their wooden shields. They marched back past deserted villages, occasionally catching natives in surprise raids. The captive men were led back to Coro in chains 'and I distributed the women among the Christians to serve them'. Federmann himself was now struck by a malarial fever 'which made me alternately cold and hot' and the expedition waited for sixteen days in the hope that he might recover. They had hoped to strike southwards on higher ground, through Coyón territory, in another attempt to reach the Pacific. But by the end of February 1531 they decided to return to Coro. The Cuiba welcomed them again, and so did some of the Caquetió near Barquisimeto. The expedition wisely decided to return to the coast by the Yaracuy river instead of the direct route across the forested hills. But the advance was slowed by illness and by attack from some Caquetió. On one occasion the Europeans wanted to rest in a captured village 'because,' wrote Federmann, 'I had suffered such a violent attack of fever that I could scarcely sustain myself on my horse.'

At another village, all seemed peaceful until Spanish horsemen reported that the women and children were secretly leaving. Federmann summoned the chief and reproached him. 'I ordered brought before me the Indians I was leading bound in chains, whom I had captured during this journey . . . [The chief] supposed that we were going to seize, enslave and chain him . . . and suddenly jumped from the seat on which he was sitting opposite me, to flee. I ordered him held . . . but he began to shout loudly calling to his people for help. Therefore, to avoid worse developments, I ordered a Christian to run him through with a sword. We had a sharp skirmish with the inhabitants of this village, killing and capturing many before we made them flee from it.'

After the skirmish, the weary and wounded Spaniards returned to rest in the chief's hut. They had not noticed that a dozen warriors had hidden on the barbacoa, the raised food storage platform in the middle of the hut. These suddenly opened fire on the Christians, wounding five, including Federmann who was hit on the shoulder by an arrow. Federmann ordered his men to knock down the platform, since 'we could not set fire to the hut with the Indians inside it, because we had to save our belongings that we had there'. Federmann rushed up and cut one of the platform supports. It collapsed and the warriors fell to the ground. 'Protected by my shield, I jumped on to an Indian to run his body through with my sword. But he gave me such a powerful blow with his *macana* (as they call their wooden swords) that he knocked a piece two inches wide off my shield, which was made from the bottom of a barrel. I was giving him another stab and had not noticed the defect in my shield, which no longer protected me adequately. He struck me a blow on the head that made me fall to the ground in front of him. He would have taken my life had others not come to my rescue and killed the Indian. I was unconscious for almost two hours. . . . Those Indians on the barbacoa, although there were only twelve of them, did us more harm and wounded more of my men than all the rest.'

Instead of following the Yaracuy as far as the sea, the expedition tried to move northwards across jungles inhabited by the Ciparicoto tribe. Some chained Indians

The Spaniards found the Coanaos to be 'spirited and truthful people'. A modern woman from the Guajira peninsula.

guided the Europeans by little-used forest paths. The men ate all their supply of food, but they encountered no villages or even streams. They were thoroughly lost in dense forests. 'We had been deceived by the Indians. We could obtain no information from them, either by good treatment or by torture. So we travelled all that day without food and even without water . . . I had two Indians quartered to terrify the rest, but it was no use—they preferred to be dead than remain as our prisoners. They had brought us along this path in order to lose us, so that we should die of hunger, which we were close to doing, and they could thus have vengeance on us. We were frightened. We did not know whether to go forward or backwards, for we were all exhausted by hunger from lack of food and especially of water.' In the end the men were saved by killing a large tawny jaguar and eventually finding a small stream. After another day cutting through dense forest, they came upon a small village with plenty of food. 'This had been the greatest hunger we suffered. Had it lasted just one more night and had we not found that creek, very few of us would have reached Coro.'

Federmann's brutal explorers found their way back to the Yaracuy, near its mouth. They then followed the coast around to Coro, which they reached on 17 March 1531. Federmann made his way back to Europe and made sure that the Emperor received a report of his adventure.

It was now the turn of the governor, Ambrosius Dalfinger, to make another attempt to find the elusive passage. Dalfinger left Coro on 1 September 1531, first westwards to Maracaibo and then to strike south on the far side of the lake. He wanted 'to see the secrets and features of the other [ocean], the South Sea, so that all the land should be contacted and known from sea to sea'. Dalfinger had the advantage of taking an officer called Esteban Martín, an excellent soldier and something of an interpreter of native languages. This Martín wrote a report of the expedition that has survived, and it is an admirable document, written by an efficient but modest man with a sympathy for the Indian tribes he encountered. Beyond Maracaibo Dalfinger's expedition—170 men, of whom 40 were mounted —marched across the coastal plain behind the Guajira peninsula. They passed across the territories of successive tribes: the 'very domestic and unwarlike' Bugures, naked apart from a calabash that a man wore on his penis and a small vine leaf worn by the women. 'We made peace with them, but they did not trust us much.' Then the Buredes, speaking a similar language, but tonsured like friars and with no body covering whatsoever; beyond, at the foot of the mountains, were the Conucos; and beyond them the Coanaos, 'a very numerous and spirited people . . . From what we saw and learned they were truthful people.' The Spaniards were impressed by the Coanaos' sack-like cotton mantles and cotton bonnets—clothing still worn by a few surviving Chaké Indians near this part of Colombia. They were also interested to note that the Coanaos farmed extensively and went inland to trade sea salt for gold. The route used for this trade was the pass between the northern tip of the Andes, the Sierra de Perijá, and the Sierra Nevada de Santa Marta that towered above the Spanish settlement of that name. This pass opened to the south and was an obvious avenue for Dalfinger's exploration towards the South Sea.

Moving into the pass, the expedition found that the Indians either fled or tried

The Tolima style comes from gold-rich streams flowing eastwards into the upper Magdalena valley, near the region where Benalcázar's men found native gold dust.

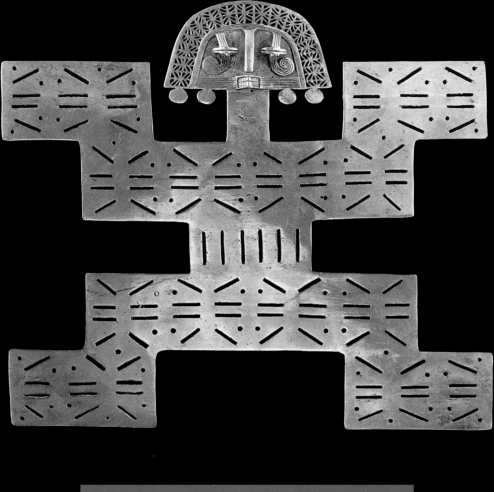

RIGHT The Pacabueyes
were an ideal tribe from
Dalfinger's point of view:
hospitable and rich in
gold. Modern Indians
from the Sierra Nevada
de Santa Maria still wear
traditional cotton mantles.

OPPOSITE Tolima goldsmiths
reduced the human body into
outlines of brilliant simplicity.
A cast gold pectoral with an
openwork headdress of skilled
workmanship; pendants of
human figures, one playing a
pipe.

to placate them with small offerings of gold. This was because Spaniards from Santa Marta had already penetrated here, and had seized people and 'we learned that they used to ransom them for gold, for 50, 80 or 100 castellanos a head; but after they had no gold left, they carried them off as prisoners.' The expedition pressed on through this valley, past the Xiriguana, whose women tattooed their breasts and arms 'with very beautiful black paintings' that were fixed for life; then to the deserted villages of the Zamyrua, where 'we found traces of the Christians of Santa Marta: old sandals, and headstalls, horseshoes and halters of their horses.'

Dalfinger's men now met the sort of tribe that all conquistadores hoped to find. The Pacabueyes welcomed the strangers: ten or twelve villages came in peace. Their land was very fertile. The Spaniards rested for a time at a village called Pauxoto and then moved on thirty miles to Tomara, a town of over a thousand huts. 'This town is the best we had seen in that entire land. It is on a height and very airy, with many savannahs and small hillocks round about it. The town has some very handsome tall trees like oaks that the Indians plant by hand. There are also many oranges, not as perfect as those of Spain, but they suck them and they have a fine taste. There are also many guavas, and plenty of game—deer, partridges and iguanas.' But the greatest attraction of the Pacabueyes was their gold. 'In some eight days we obtained, by gifts or by raiding, over 20,000 castellanos [91 kilos] ... All the Indians of this town of Tomara work gold. They have their forges and anvils, little hammers, and scales with which they weigh gold. The hammers are of a black stone or metal like emery, the size of eggs or smaller. The anvils are like average-sized cheeses, and the scales are made of a bone like ivory or of a black wood. They are notched like our balances, and they can weigh from half a castellano to fifty castellanos on them.' They used long reeds as bellows.

Esteban Martín's account made the months spent among the Pacabueyes sound harmonious and idyllic. Other writers paint a more sombre picture. Juan de Castellanos had a friend called Captain Salguero who told him that Dalfinger's

33

LEFT Near Tamalameque
Dalfinger's expedition
was attacked by a
colourful flotilla of canoes
full of Indian warriors.
Indians still use canoes to
fish the lagoons beneath
the Sierra Nevada de
Santa Marta.

BELOW LEFT Dalfinger's
men emerged from Upar
to the valley of the mighty
Magdalena river, then
forested but now cleared
for agriculture.

progress through the Upar valley had been a bloodbath. 'He came through it destroying and ravaging with bloodthirsty fury, even burning chiefs; and he had fierce engagements against Guanaos, Itotos and Aruacos. . . . After ranging across the lands of Upar and collecting a small mountain of gold, he moved on . . . to the savannahs of Guatapori and Garupare, putting many Indians to the sword: he annihilated the Pacabueyes, the tribe with pale skins, and the Chimila.'

Castellanos also knew Fernando de Alcocer, a member of the expedition who told the chronicler-poet about it. When Dalfinger moved down to Tamalameque he was welcomed by its people. The expedition was lodged and fed by chief Cumujagua in a village surrounded by lagoons. These Indians gave the Spaniards plenty of gold; but, greedy for more, they seized and tried to ransom the chief. Furious at this betrayal of its hospitality, the tribe assembled a flotilla of canoes full of three thousand magnificently plumed warriors. Fernando de Alcocer vividly remembered the brilliant spectacle of these Indians, painted for battle in red and black dyes, glistening with gold ornaments, and with headdresses and feather ornaments of bright green, red, blue or white feathers from the parrots, macaws and egrets of their forests and marshes. Their canoes and finery were reflected in the lagoon waters under the Caribbean sun. The Spaniards, on their side, draped their horses with deerskins or quilted cotton armour, festooned them with rattles, and then hid them and the horsemen. Dalfinger tried the same treacherous tactic that Federmann had used so successfully against the Guaicari. He parleyed with the Indians after they had landed and while talking launched the concealed horses in a murderous surprise attack. But the natives stood their ground and managed to escape to their canoes. Dalfinger's men immediately moved against another village, of a chief called Nicaho. They waded across its defensive waters. Instead of resisting the weary and soaked Spanish attackers, Nicaho's people surrendered and laid down their arms. 'Those who were present describe it as a marvel. The quantity of weapons that those Indians were carrying was so great that they formed a heap so high that a mounted man could not be seen on its far side.'

Dalfinger's expedition was taking a new dimension. From mere geographical reconnaissance, it was becoming a successful treasure hunt. It had also stumbled into an area that seemed ripe for conquest and settlement. Dalfinger decided to spend some months among the hospitable Pacabueyes. He sent his most trusted lieutenant Iñigo de Vascuña to take the expedition's gold back to Coro and bring reinforcements for a conquest or colony.

Vascuña left on Epiphany, 6 January 1532, taking 24 picked men, including the brother of the King's inspector Pedro de San Martín. Unfortunately, Dalfinger also gave Vascuña a task connected with the original geographical exploration. Instead of retracing the expedition's route, Vascuña was sent due east, across the Perijá hills 'to discover a lake of which he had news from these Indians: after discovering it and taking full note of how it was, he should return to the town of Maracaibo.'

While the expedition awaited Vascuña's return it rested in the Pacabuey towns of Pauxoto and Tomara. A sortie was made westwards against the Aruacana, apparently one of the Muisca-speaking peoples living on the forested southern

35

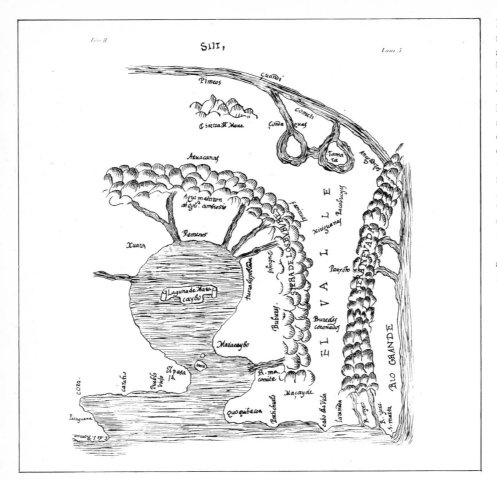

slopes of the Sierra Nevada de Santa Marta. These were enemies of the Carib-speaking Pacabueyes. They were thoroughly unattractive to the Spaniards: they had no gold, and they defended themselves stoutly, using poisoned arrows. Esteban Martín and another man were hit by these arrows: the other man died and so would Martín had he not known 'how to mend myself'.

At the beginning of April, Dalfinger moved his men from the attractive town of Tomara, back to the lakes and lagoons of Tamalameque. They had in fact reached the great Magdalena river; but they were convinced that they had been marching due south and therefore supposed this to be some unknown river running from east to west. It was an excusable mistake, for the Magdalena does run almost westwards at this point. They were unable to cross this mighty river, which was 'a quarter of a league [more than a mile] wide and running like a wind, so that a canoe could scarcely cross its great current'. But the Indians told them that the Cindahuas people on the far bank were very rich, living in 'a country of great plains and many creeks from which they extract the gold'. Friendly Indians were sent across the river. They returned next morning accompanied, as if by magic, by nine Cindahua bringing the governor a present of 'nine pounds of gold, all of the finest quality'. It was enough to excite even the most hardened conquistador.

All conquistadores were obliged to preach the Requirement to their American victims: a native view of a Spaniard brandishing a cross.

Vascuña had been gone for three months and Dalfinger was becoming anxious. He decided to send Esteban Martín back with twenty men to investigate. Martín left on 24 June and, following the expedition's outward route, took only 34 days to reach Maracaibo. Martín accomplished his mission successfully, bringing some reinforcements back to the expedition; but there was no sign of Vascuña and the gold.

There had been reports of a rich native town called Comiti, up the large river and on the near bank. The united expedition therefore pushed up the right bank of the Magdalena, moving south along its flooded banks. The Magdalena valley is still humid and uninviting. The Spaniards found it a place 'in which many insects and mosquitoes of all sorts breed. These were a plague and heavy torment to them. They were forced to endure them; but their bites caused sores and swellings on the soldiers' legs, hands and other parts of their bodies.' The expedition investigated the territory of the Chocó-speaking Pemeos and then met a tribe of Xiriguaná living in flooded forests. These Xiriguaná were hostile: they refused to listen to the Requirement, an extraordinary document that all Spanish explorers were supposed to read to newly-contacted tribes whose territory they invaded.

The Requirement was the product of a debate that had long been raging in Spain over the moral and theological right of Spaniards to conquer foreign lands. Some Spanish ecclesiastics told the King that his soul was endangered by these conquests in his name. Fighting infidel Moors was a valid crusade; but the occupation of lands of innocent tribes that had never heard of Christianity was not. The answer was the Requirement. This proclamation was to be read aloud, through interpreters if possible, before the Spaniards launched an attack. The Requirement contained a brief history of the world, with descriptions of the Papacy and

The natives of the northern Andes kept the bodies of dead ancestors in their homes.

'We marched all day across a moor in the greatest cold and rain and wind'. Desolate scenery of the sierras crossed by Dalfinger's men.

Spanish monarchy. The native audience was required to accept the King as its ruler, on behalf of the Pope. It must also allow the preaching of Christianity to its people. Failure to comply immediately made the listeners liable to Spanish attack, enslavement of wives and children, and looting of property, and—in the words of the Requirement—'we protest that any deaths or losses that result from this are your fault...' This absurd document was read in strange circumstances: to empty villages, to Indians already enslaved, or from the decks of ships approaching unknown shores. Bartolomé de las Casas confessed that he did not know whether to laugh at its ludicrous impracticability, or weep at its injustice.

Unimpressed by the Requirement, the Xirihuaná defended their forests, wounding four Christians and one horse, all of whom died of their wounds. Ambrosius Dalfinger decided to stop struggling against the flooded river and to turn into the mountains towards Maracaibo. The expedition struggled upwards. Esteban Martín was sent ahead to reconnoitre a route for the horses. He soon found himself fighting hard against an 'unknown tribe' that used long lances of black wood, clubs, slings and bows and arrows. Its men and women wore long painted cotton mantles. The expedition fought its way through this territory, but never

38

managed to learn about its opponents. Beyond lay three days' march across rough hills devoid of food or pasture. Some horses fell from the hillsides or dropped dead, 'and we ate them right down to their hides, roasted and boiled: anyone with a piece of tripe or hide made something good to eat from it.' They came upon a poor mountain village and seized some captives 'to carry our gold and other things forward, for we had great need of porterage.'

Esteban Martín was again sent forward, with seventy men. Striking into the mountains, he came upon a town of fifty huts called Elmene. His men pushed higher and spent a night on a pass, presumably near the 4,200-metre peak El Viejo. 'We all thought we would die of cold there. When dawn came next morning we found most of the sierra covered in snow, and we were almost frozen and frost-bitten.' Martín returned to the main expedition after a ten-day reconnaissance. The army was near starvation, cold and dispirited. It staggered forward into the mountains, but as the Spaniards approached Elmene they saw its inhabitants set the town on fire. 'This made us very sad, for we greatly needed the huts as it was a very cold land and we had many sick men.' The unknown tribe had fine planta-tions of maize, yams, celery and 'earth truffles'—potatoes. But when the invaders went to loot these fields they were ambushed and three men were swiftly beheaded with razor-sharp cane knives. 'These Indians have a custom of keeping, as ornaments in their houses, the heads, arms and legs of dead Indians, with the bones removed, stuffed with grass and with the fingers and nails [still attached]. We did not know whether these were Indians whom they had eaten or dead members of their own people.'

Had the expedition made peaceful contact or interrogated captives from this unknown tribe, it might have learned that it was only a few days' march from the northern edge of the territory of the Muiscas—the Chibcha people whose wealth inspired part of the El Dorado legend. But Dalfinger's men suspected nothing of this. Such is the irony of exploration. No Spaniard had yet heard about the golden man, El Dorado, and no one knew that there was a rich native culture in these mountains. Dalfinger's expedition saw the Andes only as a terrible obstacle separating it from its bases at Maracaibo and Coro.

The expedition moved on, over a pass on to a high plateau. 'We marched all day across a moor in the greatest cold and rain and wind. We spent the night on that moor. The Governor was in the van with twenty-five men, and the rest slept scattered along the route, each as best he could. The best sleeping place any man could find was with his feet in cold water, sitting shivering like a dog, without eating a mouthful for we had nothing with us.... Eight Christians remained there, dead from the cold or from hunger. Among them lay [Johannes] Kasimir [of Nuremberg], a captain of horse who had been very ill and swollen for many days. Alongside the Christians on that moor, there also lay one negro and one mare and 120 dead Indians. Chains and many pieces of equipment were also left, because there was no one to carry them.' The wretched Indians who were forced to work as porters came naked from their tropical valley: they died of exposure and starvation, with no fires to warm them on that wet, treeless pass. Dalfinger's expedition was notorious for keeping its native porters chained at the neck, in a train of human misery. If one person flagged or died, it was customary to behead

39

the corpse so that the body fell and there was no need to undo the neck shackle.

The expedition moved from one burned village to another. The men stole native food. The Indians attacked often, but their fear of the horses stopped them from pressing home their attack. The expedition entered the populous territory of the Haruago, then turned north-east into a region with large villages of 400 or 600 huts. Early one morning, Esteban Martín was breakfasting before scouting forward. To his surprise, Governor Dalfinger decided to accompany him. Martín recorded their conversation: ' "Ride off, Esteban Martín. Let us go forward." [To which Martín replied] "Where is Your Honour going so early in the morning? Sir, you should march with the men, and I will go forward right away." [Dalfinger:] "I want to go with you. Let us take five or six soldiers with us." "It would be better if a dozen went." ' After this small party had advanced for some distance, it entered a defile out of sight of the main force. Suddenly, 'without knowing how or whence [they came], we found ourselves surrounded by Indians who were already shooting arrows at us from all directions. When I saw this, I put spurs to my horse and charged towards the largest group of Indians. The Governor came behind me. We began to lance some of them and they at once took to flight. But when we turned back we found another battalion of them shooting arrows at us from behind. We attacked these but they wounded one of our corporals and another who had gone after the Indians. When I looked round I saw him surrounded, with an Indian hitting his horse with a club. I attacked there. I was lancing that Indian, but they hit my horse with five arrows—it died as soon as we reached the camp. When we returned to the camp we found that we were all wounded by poisoned arrows—something we had not found anywhere else in the mountains.' Ambrosius Dalfinger had been hit on the neck by an arrow. The Welsers' first governor of Venezuela survived for only four days before dying, delirious and raving from the poison, in the deserted village of the tribe that had killed him. He was buried there, on the upper Zulia river at a place that was later known as Ambrosio's Valley. The expedition elected the royal official Pedro de San Martín as leader. Esteban Martín was desperately ill. The expedition waited a week 'because I was incapable of travelling further and we thought that I would never leave there. Had it not been for the strict diet I took—for I went fifteen days without drinking a drop of water—I would also have died from the poison. Once I was feeling somewhat better we began to march down that valley.'

The remnants of the expedition made their way towards the southern end of Lake Maracaibo. There were more skirmishes with tribes whose territory they crossed, more natives seized as porters, more Spaniards killed, and more food stolen. The explorers crossed the land of the Pemones, a tribe with well-ordered villages of thirty or forty communal huts. Most villages were abandoned, but at the last the Spaniards managed to catch twenty people. Esteban Martín found that he could understand something of the Pemones' Carib speech. He asked them why they had tried to run away. They told him that there was a man like them living in a village a few miles away: they feared that the expedition had come to find him and would kill them for having him. Martín told his leader. It seemed highly improbable, but it was decided to investigate. An officer called Francisco de Santa Cruz took some men and swam a river to reach the village. As he approached

'he met a Christian, stark naked as he was born, with his genitals exposed, and dyed, with his beard plucked like an Indian and his bow and arrows and lance in his hand. His mouth was full of *hayo*, a herb that prevents thirst, and he carried a *baperón*, which is a gourd in which Indians keep a type of lime that removes hunger when they chew it. Not looking closely, he took him for an Indian. But the man came straight to Santa Cruz and rushed towards him, for he recognized Santa Cruz before they embraced . . . With open arms they went to one another and embraced and kissed one another on the cheeks many times with great delight, because they had been friends in the past, and because of the novelty of the situation and the Christian's relief.'

The Indianized Spaniard turned out to be one Francisco Martín, sole survivor of the twenty-five under Iñigo de Vascuña sent back by Dalfinger with the expedition's gold over eighteen months previously. He told a horrifying story. Dalfinger had sent this group eastwards to explore an unknown region on the way back to Maracaibo. But 'they had struck an empty land and had all lost their way.' They had crossed the territory of the poor Tapeys tribe, but failed to catch any as porters. They divided the gold among them, with each Spaniard carrying 10–12 pounds. Having no food, they were reduced to eating bitter palm hearts, so tough that they broke their swords on them. They were growing weaker, hungry, and often barefoot or lame. They came to a broad river and attempted to descend it in rafts, but one of the rafts capsized with its load of gold in the first rapids. Some men pushed ahead on land, but one group tried to remain on the raft: they were found next day riddled with arrows or vanished leaving only bloodstained clothing. The men had by now eaten their horses and a dog. 'They were very exhausted and starving, cutting a path with pieces of their swords, most of which were broken.' Some of the men wanted to leave the gold, which was becoming an intolerable burden. But Vascuña persuaded them to stagger on for a further week. In the end they were forced to leave their beloved gold, burying it in a basket beneath a tree and blazing all the surrounding trees with their swords.

The expedition was beginning to disintegrate. It spent three days going down a stream gully, but this led only to swamps; it took four days to stagger back, with Captain Vascuña limping from a wounded heel. Three men and a boy attempted to take a different route, but the boy returned alone. 'He told them that his father Juan Córdero and the other two had killed an Indian woman they were taking with them, and had eaten her. They were carrying part of her for their journey; and the boy showed a piece of her.' This murder and cannibalism shocked the chroniclers: Gonzalo Fernández de Oviedo exclaimed: 'Oh, diabolical plan! But they paid for their sin, for those three men never reappeared: God willed that there should be Indians who later ate them.' The dying men were still obsessed with the gold: they returned to its burial place, and spent some of their remaining strength digging it up and reburying it a crossbow shot away, under a towering tree beside a creek leading to a red earth bank. The men were dying one by one, too weak from hunger to continue. The treasurer Francisco de San Martín had his face swell until he was blinded. 'He said that he could not possibly move from there, so he sat on the ground, and was left there.' Vascuña's foot was much worse. He begged his men wait for it to heal. But after a few days' wait in a place devoid even of palm hearts, and after an attempt to carry him, he agreed that he must be abandoned. Two other sick men stayed with him, as did his servant Francisco. To assuage their hunger they killed and ate a friendly Pacabuey boy who was with the expedition. The rest marched back to the river and had the good fortune to meet eighteen canoes full of Indians, armed and in full plumed regalia. The meeting was friendly, with the Indians giving food and weapons to the Spaniards. Seven Indians remained with the explorers and the rest said that they would return to guide them to the Lake. But some Spaniards suspected treachery and it was decided to try to seize the seven sleeping Indians. In the event, the Spaniards were too weak even for this mad plan and all but one Indian escaped. 'They took that Indian, bound, and reached a gully that enters the river, and killed him and divided him among them. They made a fire and ate him and slept there that night. They roasted what was left of his meat for their journey.'

Francisco Martín was by now too lame to walk, with 'his feet eaten by worms . . . able to move only on his belly or pulling himself along seated'. His companions had to abandon him and he crawled to the river bank. He caught a log and drifted downstream to some Indian huts, to which he crawled on all fours. The Indians picked him up, carried him to a hammock and tended him for three months while his foot healed. Some canoes of Cuprigueri Indians from Lake Maracaibo came up the river, trading their salt for maize, and Martín slipped away from his tribe in the Cuprigueri canoes. He spent a month in the Cuprigueri village, on stilts over the Lake; but instead of returning him to Maracaibo, these Indians sold him for a golden figurine to the Pemeos. It was a two-day canoe journey to the Pemeo village at the southern end of the Lake. Francisco Martín spent a year there, living entirely as an Indian. The tribal medicine-men taught him their arts and he became a shaman. 'His medicines were to roar and suck and apply wads [of herbs]; and with this practice he lived among them and was highly regarded.' He had been given an Indian wife. On three occasions he was bound to a stake and was apparently about to be killed, 'but his wife got him released and saved him from death each time, and he was alive thanks to her.' He dared not admit that he was a settler from Maracaibo, one of the ruffians who had so often seized and enslaved Pemeos: he claimed instead that he was a Pacabuey Indian, despite his telltale beard. When, by extraordinary good fortune, the survivors of Dalfinger's expedition happened to come so close to this Pemeo village, Martín had to pretend that they were his enemies. In this way he was able to get near enough to embrace Santa Cruz. The expedition then moved off, with Francisco Martín again dressed as a Spaniard, and reached the Lake at the end of June.

The men marching overland reached Maracaibo on 29 August 1533; after resting, they returned to Coro on 2 November. The expedition had lasted over two years and cost the lives of hundreds of Indians and Spaniards. It failed to find a route to the South Sea, and the excitement over the rich lands beyond the Pacabueyes proved to be a delusion. It did yield 40,436 pesos (184 kilos) of gold. An expedition naturally set off the following year taking Francisco Martín to try to locate the tree under which Vascuña's men had buried their gold. It was never found by those or later seekers. It is presumably still there, somewhere between the Catatumbo and Santa Ana rivers to the west of Lake Maracaibo.

3 WHILE AMBROSIUS DALFINGER WAS EXPLORING THE NORTHERN TIP OF THE ANDES, another Spanish conquistador was enjoying far greater success two thousand kilometres further south in those same mountains. Francisco Pizarro's third expedition left Panama at the end of 1530, while Federmann was on his exploration south of Coro. Pizarro landed on the coast of what is now Ecuador and took many months to reach Peru. He founded a town, San Miguel de Piura, at the northern end of the Peruvian coastal desert. With only 170 men, Pizarro then marched down the coast and into the mountains to meet the Inca Atahualpa.

On the day after the Spaniards' arrival at the Inca provincial capital of Cajamarca, 16 November 1532, Atahualpa came to meet Pizarro. The Inca and his retainers crowded into the square of their city. Pizarro launched a surprise attack so typical of Spanish conquistadores everywhere. At a prearranged signal his horsemen and footsoldiers charged out of the buildings surrounding the square. In two terrible hours, as night was falling, his men slaughtered six or seven thousand Peruvians and captured the Inca Atahualpa. Pizarro's secretary exclaimed: 'It was an extraordinary thing to see so great a ruler captured in so short a time, when he had come with such might.' The audacious conquistadores then ransomed their prisoner, promising to free him if he filled a chamber once with gold and twice with silver. 'Certainly an offer of vast proportions!' This treasure, the masterpieces of Inca gold- and silversmiths, gradually reached the Spaniards' camp from all parts of the great Inca empire. By June 1533 there was enough treasure at Cajamarca for the invaders to organize an official melting and distribution. The King of Spain normally received taxes of a fifth, 20 per cent, of such loot, and Pizarro sent his brother Hernando back to Spain with this princely tribute.

Hernando Pizarro's progress towards Spain was sensational. Everywhere his ships landed—Panama, Santa Marta in Colombia, Santo Domingo—he brought the news that another empire, richer even than Mexico, had been discovered. More ships came with more treasure during the ensuing months. The governor of Panama wrote that 'the riches and greatness of Peru increase daily to such an extent that they become almost impossible to believe . . . like something from a dream.'

At Santa Marta the governor García de Lerma was preparing an expedition to explore the Magdalena river. He had previously written to the King that the Magdalena is 'very important. I firmly believe that Your Majesty will get greater service from it than from all the rest of the Indies together . . . It will prove to be a very rich affair. For if one goes 150 leagues up that river one comes under the [equatorial] line and is in the same place as Francisco Pizarro is now in Peru.' But when the ships arrived with news of Pizarro's fantastic success, the object of this expedition changed: its purpose was not 'to strike the South Sea and the land of Peru'. One of the ships with the Inca treasure spent five days at Santa Marta 'during which time the people there saw what it was bringing from [Peru] and became very excited and restless.' The governor calmed them with presents, and promised that his expedition would lead them to Peru. 'No one could take the men anywhere except towards Peru . . . To encourage them, the governor promised that if it did not go well, he would let them go [to Peru] on their return.' In the event, the expedition made little progress up the Magdalena. The governor him-

Carib Indians of the Guianas. Spaniards and Caribs fought unmercifully on the lower Orinoco.

45

self became so 'moved by the greed of Peru' that he sailed off to join Pizarro with a boatload of his men. There was a similar stampede from other Spanish settlements. The royal officials on Puerto Rico lamented that 'the news from Peru is so extraordinary that it is making old men move and youths even more so . . . there will not be a single citizen left unless they are tied down.' The governor there caught some men trying to escape to Peru and had them flogged and their feet cut off.

Hernando Pizarro's ship reached Seville in January 1534. He had brought a few Inca works of art: 38 objects of gold and 48 of silver. They included silver eagles, a golden idol the size of a small boy, two small drums and two huge gold and silver urns 'each of which could hold a dismembered cow'. The Emperor showed no interest or delight in these lovely objects from a remote civilization. He ordered that they be melted down and immediately turned into coins. When the royal officials begged the King at least to see the artefacts, he agreed that they might be put on public display for a few weeks before being destroyed. One visitor who saw them was Pedro de Cieza de León, who was later to march on the first expedition across Colombia from the Caribbean to Peru and who became one of the most perceptive chroniclers. He wrote that he always remembered 'the magnificent specimens brought from Cajamarca and exhibited in Seville'.

There was nothing like the sight of gold to galvanize Spanish adventurers into action. The royal officials at Santo Domingo had previously been contemptuous of treasure-seeking expeditions. Now gold fever seized even these civil servants. They pompously wrote to the King that 'according to the altitudes and graduations of cosmographers' the richest lands should be inland from Venezuela and near the equator. It was the old theory that had sent Diego de Ordás up the Orinoco. These same officials wrote 'to the governors of Venezuela and Cartagena, telling them about the discovery [of Peru] so that they might be prepared. For they have horsemen and could arrive very close to that land. They should try to enter inland as far as they can—for they cannot possibly fail to find great secrets and riches!' It was the start of a new wave of exploration. Expeditions would soon be leaving the coasts of Venezuela, Santa Marta, the Orinoco, and Peru itself to strike deep into the heart of South America.

Jerónimo Dortal had been royal treasurer on Diego de Ordás' expedition up the Orinoco. Having survived this ordeal, his first ambition was merely to become treasurer of the small and almost bankrupt pearl island of Cubagua. He then decided to try to succeed Ordás as governor of Peru. But his petition was modest: he asked only for a small stretch of coastline opposite Trinidad, and he was scornful of 'those who come from Spain and whose imaginations are far more than anything the land contains'. He assured the King that his only plan was to colonize a stretch of the coast and trade peacefully with the Indians. Then Dortal's plan suddenly changed. Instead of a humble trading venture, he equipped three ships and hundreds of men. Instead of taking trade goods he filled his vessels with weapons and armour-plating for river boats. It is obvious what changed Dortal's mind: the arrival of the Inca treasure. Dortal remembered Ordás' vision of gold at the source of the Orinoco, and he became obsessed by the Caribs' description of the golden land of Meta. Dortal obtained permission to buy horses in the

Sebastián de Benalcázar and Hernando Pizarro confront the Inca Atahualpa at Cajamarca.

Canaries and to trade in slaves in the Indies. He had no trouble recruiting men: adventurers from all parts of Spain flocked to join the American gold rush. There had been unexpected empires of fabulous wealth in Mexico and now in Peru, so why should there not be more? Dortal left Spain in a hurry, with part of his force to follow later. Dortal was already racing other conquistadores to be the first to pillage the kingdom of Meta.

Jerónimo Dortal reached Paria in October 1534. He wrote to the King that his force was 'so good and so well armed that I think that no better for this purpose has ever left Spain'. He boasted that: 'I think that in a short time I will do for Your Majesty more service than any man has done in these parts . . . I am certain that when we went up the river with the late Diego de Ordás, we were not 150 leagues from where Captain Pizarro found Atahualpa. I tell you that the Indians themselves gave reports of [Atahualpa], hearing it from other Indians, and of the brothers he killed to usurp and rule over them. Among the Indians whom Your Majesty ordered me to assemble on this island [Cubagua] as interpreters there are two Caribs who declare all this and more, for they are from the province of Meta, to which they are going to guide me.' These Caribs 'give great reports of the gold and what they do with it after they extract it from a mountain. It would clearly seem that all the gold of Peru comes from this region.' This was a return to Ordás' original theory that gold 'grew' better near the equator, and that the gold of Peru came from behind the Andes. 'I believe that the greatness of gold is under the equator,' said Dortal.

Jerónimo Dortal had to await part of his force, but he decided to send Alonso de Herrera up-river to establish a base. Herrera had been one of Ordás' leading officers. Oviedo described him as 'a valiant man and experienced. He had been with Hernando Cortés in the conquest of New Spain [Mexico]. But he knew more about killing Indians than caring for them.' Herrera set off with 130 well-armed men, in nine brigs and one seagoing caravel for the horses. The journey through the Orinoco delta was agonizing. The caravel proved too unwieldy for the men to sail or row: in the end they had to row its anchor upstream, and then winch the ship up by its capstan. This task took weeks, during which the men were short of food and suffering from insects. The land was flooded and the soldiers had to make their cooking fires on logs projecting above the waters. They finally reached the town of Aruacay, but were dismayed to find it abandoned because of Carib attack. Herrera took his expedition across to the north bank, to seek the town of Carao. Its inhabitants vividly remembered how Ordás had slaughtered them less than four years previously. They fled, but left enough manioc to feed Herrera's men during the coming months. The Spaniards therefore set about building a flat-bottomed barge for the horses, and Herrera sent some gold down to Dortal. He warned Dortal to hurry, as his men were impatient to see the secrets of Meta.

For a time the natives returned, to make wary contact with the invaders occupying their homes and eating their crops. Herrera's men were busy sawing wood and building the barge, and they pressed, roasted and ground the manioc themselves. They were trying to accumulate enough manioc for the Meta expedition. One night the hut containing this store caught fire; a Spanish sentry extinguished the blaze, but it was suspected that it had been caused by an Indian fire-arrow.

47

Herrera decided to exact reprisals. He ordered his men to pretend to go about their business among the natives next day, and then suddenly pounce and seize as many unsuspecting Indians as they could. This treachery worked smoothly: the Spaniards took over three thousand men and women. Herrera 'put iron shackles on Indians who looked fit for battle and who could harm them if they escaped . . . and he tied the rest by the necks with ropes, as was usually done in such cases.' An Indian attempt to ambush the Spaniards and free the prisoners ended in a bloody battle. Herrera sent most of his captives downriver for sale as slaves, but they managed to open the caravel's hatch one night and many swam to safety. The men at Carao were becoming increasingly restless. A group of five Italians was caught practising sodomy and Herrera had them all burned to death, despite their entreaties and attempts to bribe him. The barge was complete and the manioc ready. The local tribe was furiously hostile. Alonso de Herrera therefore decided to await his governor Jerónimo Dortal no longer: early in 1535 he and his men embarked alone on the conquest of Meta.

The journey up the Orinoco went smoothly. With a following wind the brigs and barge took only twenty days to sail or row the 700 kilometres to the mouth of the Meta river. This was not far from the rapids on the main river that had defeated Ordás. On the upward journey the expedition surprised a raiding party of Caribs returning with captives and human flesh from tribes upstream. The Caribs fought hard, but were finally all killed, after killing three Spaniards. 'When this fight was over, the Spaniards scattered across the field, both to enjoy themselves at seeing so many bodies dead by their hands, to search for any gold and useful things, and to witness the carnage of other Indians that those Caribs had there for food.' They found plenty of hammocks and arrows, and were able to release some captives who promised to entertain them in their tribe up-river. At Cabruta (a place that still exists on the north bank of the Orinoco near the mouth of the Apure) the inhabitants had fled leaving no food. The Spaniards were plagued by vampire bats. One mulatto woman almost died from loss of blood from the vampires. As always, the expedition was itself parasitical, relying on food stolen from Indian villages. There were raids and skirmishes to capture food, but this was never easy: tribes do not build villages in exposed locations on main rivers, but hidden up backwaters. The Orinoco itself was full of fish and the men were continually fishing. They caught one fish that is common in the streams of the Venezuelan *llanos*, but when a soldier pulled it from the water 'he started to tremble, and his arm and entire body almost lost their force, until he let it go'. Anyone who handled this fish trembled 'as long as it lived, but once dead it had no power or poison and was very good and tasty to eat'. This mysterious creature was, of course, an electric eel.

Herrera's men finally turned into the Meta river, giving thanks in a special mass as they did so. The going now became much harder. The river was low, so that rapids were an obstacle. But with the start of the rainy season the current strengthened, and the winds were adverse. It took forty days to cover only twenty leagues, 110 kilometres. 'They did all those leagues by towing. Those pulling on the ropes had water up to their chests, and with extreme effort they would cover half a league or a little more in a day. I do not believe,' wrote Fernández de Oviedo, 'that many of them would have endured such fatigue to reach paradise itself!'

A Tolima pendant perhaps inspired by a bat. These flat, schematic figures have silhouettes of great beauty. Lost-wax casting, height 19 cm.

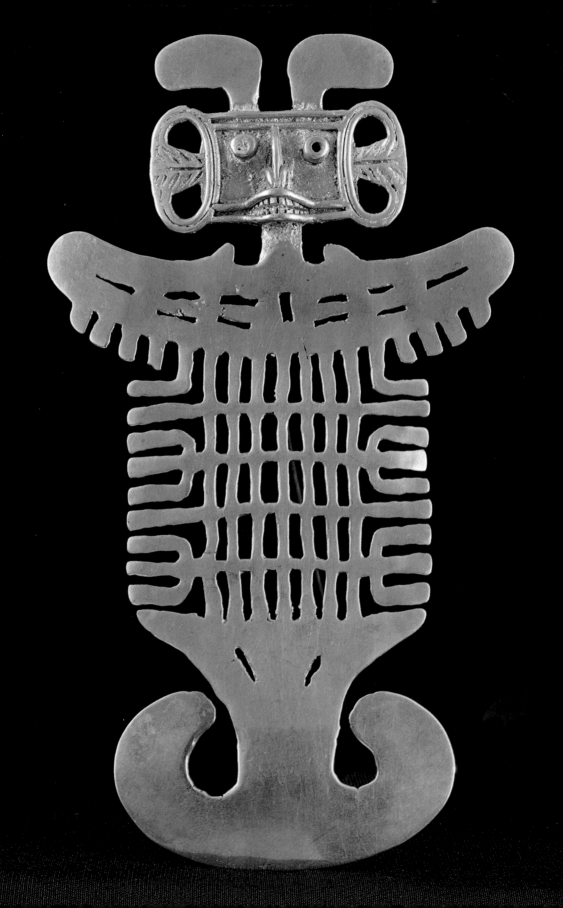

Herrera decided that he must try to find an easier route. He left some men who were ill or particularly exhausted, to guard the boats. The hundred best men were divided into two groups and sent scouting across country. They were desperate to find villages to plunder. One group managed to catch an Indian woman. She guided them 'from place to place, lost, lying to them in many ways. Because of this, finding themselves deceived and wishing to reward her for her efforts, they hanged her from a tree.' Herrera finally found better land with plenty of Indian crops, about a hundred kilometres from the river. The two squadrons of Spaniards met and occupied a village of twelve huts. 'One day most of the Christians were out picking maize that they had not planted, and a few had remained in the huts with Captain Alonso de Herrera. Some hundred Indian archers approached without being observed. They attacked the village with much violence, especially the hut containing the Captain. He quickly ran to saddle his horse. But he did not have time, for they wounded him with five or six arrows, one of them through his mouth. They wounded most of the Spaniards before they could make use of their horses.' One Spaniard managed to mount, and rallied the men in the maize fields. The Indians were driven off, but with the loss of a number of Spaniards who died from poisoned arrows, as did most of the horses. 'Before the third day after being wounded, [Herrera] began to rage and lost his reason, biting his hands. He died after three days, raving, for that is what happens to those who are wounded by that poison that the Indians use on their arrows.' Before dying, Herrera had appointed Diego de Ordás' young nephew Alvaro to succeed as leader, and the men were pleased to accept him. The expedition returned to the boats on the Meta. It was now reduced to ninety men and one horse. The exhausted men all decided to abandon the attempt and return to Paria. It took only a few weeks to glide down the rivers that they had ascended with such anguish. The survivors of this disastrous expedition staggered back to the Caribbean in mid-1535. It was the second failure to reach Meta, and the second expedition to lose its leader to a poisoned arrow.

The men who went on these ventures were not mercenaries: they received no pay from the expedition's leader. They were adventurers who took passage to the Americas in the hope of making their fortunes. In the early days of the conquests, any reward for these desperadoes had to come from the Indians themselves. They were predators hoping for easy plunder. Their food and personal service came from the Indians they hoped to rob. Gonzalo Fernández de Oviedo had been on various expeditions in his youth before settling at Santo Domingo and writing his famous history; he therefore saw a great many shiploads arrive from Europe. 'They are the sort of men who have no intention of converting the Indians [to Christianity] or of settling and remaining in this land. They come only until they get some gold or wealth in whatever form they can obtain it. They subordinate honour, morality and honesty to this end, and apply themselves to any fraud or homicide and commit innumerable crimes . . . In the course of these histories of new discoveries, there have been and will be mutinies, ruinations and ugly deeds, mixed with treachery, disloyalty and inconstancy in some of the men who come here.' Oviedo reminded his readers that, although the leadership was Spanish except in Venezuela, the rank and file came from many places. 'No language from any part of the

Cast gold Tolima pin heads show inventive fantasy. The pins, up to 45 cm. long, were used to fasten cotton mantles.

49

Christian world is lacking here—they come from Italy, Germany, Scotland and England, and [include] Frenchmen, Hungarians, Poles, Greeks and Portuguese...'

Although Christian Spain had just completed the reconquest of its land from the Moors—with the fall of Granada in the same year as Columbus' first discovery—the country was by no means exhausted. It was in fact one of the most heavily populated parts of Europe. Castile alone had $1\frac{1}{2}$ million households in 1482, which would mean a population of seven or eight million. To this were added Aragon with a million, and then Roussillon and Navarre with a further 150,000. Seville, with some 150,000 inhabitants, was one of the largest cities in Europe. There was thus considerable demographic pressure for colonial expansion. This was heightened by the aridity of much of Spain, and by the country's appalling social inequality. The aristocracy, nobility and knightly classes comprised less than 2 per cent of the population; but they and the church owned 98 per cent of the land. The urban proletariat, of artisans, peons, vagabonds and beggars accounted for about 12 per cent of the population; but the rural peasantry, at 83 per cent, was the vast majority of Spaniards. To give an idea of the staggering inequality, the grandee Marquis of Villena had annual rents of some 100,000 ducats, whereas the annual pay of a specialized worker was about 48 ducats, of a carpenter 22, and of a day labourer 17 ducats. A rural worker might receive a total of only 1 ducat in a year. There was thus widespread misery in Spain, as elsewhere in Europe. The Americas were a potent lure for these people with so little to lose; and those who went were accustomed to hardship.

Many men who went to the American adventure were from a floating population, ranging from younger sons of the lesser nobility to dispossessed peasants or failed artisans. They tended to be socially resentful, violent and rebellious. There were arrogant gentlemen 'de capa y espada'—who tried to keep up appearances even if they owned little more than their cape and sword. There were semi-professional soldiers who had fought in the battles of Italy or Flanders. Oviedo called them 'heartless braggarts' and the saintly Las Casas complained that even men born to servile condition shunned any manual labour as soon as they set foot in the New World and wanted to be 'elevated with a staff in their hands, to be persecutors of the tame and humble Indians, and to command!'

Groups of men could not simply march off into the interior of the New World. They had to attach themselves to an authorized leader, a 'governor and captain-general' or his recognized lieutenant, who held a royal licence to 'conquer and settle' some stretch of coastline. These licences or *capitulaciones* were highly one-sided in favour of the Crown. The governor had to provide all the initial finance, for ships, arms, trade goods, horses and food supply during the transatlantic journey. Columbus' first voyage cost 3,000 ducats to finance, and the rate of interest on loans for risky American ventures rose sharply. A new governor's territory was often ill-defined, by royal cosmographers unsure of the geography of the new lands—many savage feuds (notably that between Pizarro and his partner Almagro) arose because the boundaries between concessions were ambiguously drafted. The licensee had to accept considerable bureaucratic interference from royal legal or financial officials in one of the *audiencias*. He was liable to a *residencia*, an enquiry into his conduct in office that could easily result in disgrace or imprisonment. The grant of governorship was normally only for the recipient and one heir: two lifetimes. The governor was supposed to provide clergy and missionaries, and he had to enforce a stream of royal legislation that was often irrelevant to the Americas. He was also, of course, expected to develop his area, explore it, found municipalities, discover mines and (in theory at least) turn the natives into loyal and contented Christian subjects. In return for all this, the King provided nothing—no naval protection, no territorial defences, no churches, and very little administration. If anything valuable was found—precious metals, jewels, pearls, slaves—the royal share was a fifth, and that was a fifth of the *gross* value without any allowance for the costs of obtaining it. If the loot came from a tomb this royal share rose to half. Despite this, there were always eager candidates for these licences: the royal documents were tremendously important, occasionally forged, and often brandished during legal disputes.

Anyone who obtained one of these licences and organized an American enterprise had to be a gambler, a mad visionary. He pawned everything in order to sail off to the unknown at the head of a band of cut-throats. He was prepared to face incredible physical hardship, and he had to keep control of a gang of adventurers, each of whom had gone at his own risk and owed allegiance to none. The inspiration for all this was the lure of the unknown, a gold-rush mentality fuelled by discoveries as fabulous as the empires of the Aztecs and Incas. This was the eldorado spirit, even though the legend of El Dorado itself had not yet taken shape in conquistadores' imaginations. The Spanish adventurers were like packs of hounds, roaming the interior to pick up a scent of gold. They sailed across the Atlantic full of bravado and ambition and then filled the tiny coastal settlements, hoping to grow rich as parasites on the native population, or waiting to be led inland by their authorized commanders.

In the mid-1530s the Spaniards were to embark on a series of expeditions of conquest and exploration that must rank as one of the most dramatic bursts of European discovery. A succession of expeditions plunged deep into the interior of South America. For sheer endurance, mileage walked, and tribes, hills and rivers 'discovered', these exploits far exceed the famous travels of the nineteenth-century African explorers.

The expeditions set out from a few settlements in a broad arc across the north and west of South America. Because they were marching inland from an arc they were all moving towards the same central objective. None was quite sure about what it would find—but that is the nature of true exploration. They groped forward, hoping to find signs of wealth; or accelerated, marching headlong towards an illusory goal. In the end, three expeditions turned into a form of race towards the land of the Muisca or Chibcha, the richest native kingdom after the Aztec and Inca empires. But it was a race in which the participants did not know they were competing. We shall see how different motives led each expedition towards the Chibcha. Some missed the goal of this eldorado entirely; others found their way to it almost by chance.

The starting points for the second round of exploration were, from east to west: Paria at the mouth of the Orinoco; Cumaná and the nearby gulf of Maracapana; Coro and Maracaibo; Santa Marta; Cartagena; the gulf of Urabá at the end of the

Isthmus of Darien; Puerto Viejo on the coast of modern Ecuador; and San Miguel de Piura, Pizarro's first settlement on the north coast of Peru.

Sebastián de Benalcázar, conqueror of Quito

At the southern end of this arc, Francisco Pizarro had collected most of the Inca Atahualpa's fabulous ransom, but like other kidnappers, he reneged. On 26 July 1533 he had the captive Inca garrotted on the same square of Cajamarca where he had been captured eight months before. The decision to execute Atahualpa was hurried and panicky, based on rumours that an Inca army was coming to free the hostage. The death of the Inca was expedient: it allowed Pizarro to march south towards the Incas' capital city Cuzco. He entered Cuzco on 15 November 1533 and his men had another orgy of pillage, melting down tons more gold and silver treasures—a very different result to that of Dalfinger's expedition, whose survivors staggered back to Coro in that same month.

When Pizarro marched south from Cajamarca, he sent a lieutenant called Sebastián de Benalcázar to accompany some treasure back to the port of San Miguel de Piura. That port was soon filled with shiploads of adventurers who had sailed to Peru to join the scramble for Inca plunder. It was not long before these men persuaded Benalcázar to march north into the Andes, towards the Incas' northern capital Quito. Everyone knew that Quito had been Atahualpa's base and that the Incas had planned to develop it into a second Cuzco. It seemed likely that there would be great treasures there. Benalcázar also knew that one of Atahualpa's generals, Rumiñavi or Rumiñahui, had a sizeable army at Quito: he wanted to crush this potential threat. But most alarming of all, Benalcázar heard the electrifying news that Pedro de Alvarado, one of Cortés' most important captains in the conquest of Mexico, had landed on the coast of Ecuador in order to march on Quito. Alvarado was the conqueror and governor of Guatemala. He had no proper royal licence to invade Quito; but Pizarro's title to this northern capital was by no means certain. Benalcázar therefore marched out of San Miguel, early in 1534, on the conquest of Quito.

Geography favoured Benalcázar. He advanced along the line of the Andes, where the Incas had built a fine road along the intramontane valleys. The native armies fought hard to defend their homeland, but Spanish horses, swords and armour were too strong. The Spaniards defeated Rumiñavi's Inca armies in a series of pitched battles, and reached Quito by June 1534.

Pedro de Alvarado was an old friend of Diego de Ordás and may therefore have shared Ordás' views that gold grew better near the equator. He therefore landed on the Ecuadorean coast at Manta, almost on the equator itself. After landing, Alvarado learned more about the 'greatness of the treasures of Quito'. But Alvarado's route inland was very difficult. It involved crossing the forested lowlands of Ecuador, then moving northwards up the jungles of the Macul river, and finally scaling one of the steepest and highest passes in the Andes. The expedition was as cruel as any in the Americas, with a dismal succession of destruction of villages, setting trained dogs on to chiefs or hanging them, and the enslavement of hundreds of innocent lowland Indians. 'They repeatedly burned and tortured Indians to be told the route.' After the hunger and hardship of the jungle crossing, Alvarado's men were in no shape to tackle the high Andes. A combination of exposure, starvation and altitude sickness killed eighty-five European men and women, with the dying huddled together in the deep snows of the pass. 'Almost all the Indians whom Alvarado took with him perished, even though there had been many of them.' It was all in vain, for when the survivors finally reached the Andean valleys they found the tracks of Benalcázar's horses, which had already passed on the way to Quito. After a near-confrontation between the two groups of conquistadores, Alvarado admitted defeat: he sold his fleet and equipment to Pizarro and allowed most of his men to join Pizarro in Peru or Benalcázar in Quito.

Both armies had been obsessed with finding the wealth of Quito. When Alvarado's men heard about it, they forced their leader to reach it by every possible means. In one lowland town they found much gold, silver and emeralds, and called the place 'pueblo de oro' (town of gold). 'They also found armour, of plates of gold, to arm four men, nailed with nails of the same gold . . . and helmets with many emeralds. But it all seemed little compared to the quantity they hoped to find in Quito.' Benalcázar's men had similar expectations. All were bitterly disappointed when they reached Quito in June 1534 and found it devoid of easy plunder. There were frantic raids to try to find treasure in nearby towns. Rumiñavi and other Inca generals were still at large, and Benalcázar sent expeditions to defeat and capture each of them. Rumiñavi escaped a Spanish attempt to capture him in a fortified retreat near Píllaro; but he was caught and taken, after a hand-to-hand combat, in a pass near Panzaleo. Rumiñavi himself and all the Inca generals of Quito were tortured to death or executed in a vain attempt to locate their treasures. Benalcázar was convinced that they had hidden Atahualpa's gold. But the tortured chiefs 'behaved with great composure and left him with nothing but his greed. He had them killed inhumanely because he could not rid his mind of his first impression' that there must be treasure to be found.

An officer called Luis Daza led the campaign that captured Rumiñavi: Benalcázar sent him to catch the Inca general and also a native chief whom the Spaniards knew as *el indio dorado*—'the golden Indian'. This was the first mention of a chief called 'dorado'. He was apparently a chief from the gold-rich tribes of southern Colombia who had allied himself to the Inca army. This 'golden Indian' was captured by Daza and brought back with other prisoners. Benalcázar interrogated him, and he inspired an expedition north to conquer his homeland. One of Daza's companions said that it was 'from the report of that *dorado* Indian—when we went to discover the route to his land—that the provinces and captaincy of Popayán came to be discovered.' The chronicler Alonso de Herrera confirmed that this *dorado* chief came from a land twelve days' march north of Quito. Benalcázar dispatched a series of small expeditions north into the lands that the Incas knew as Quillacinga because their inhabitants wore golden nose pendants. But there was no great excitement about finding any land called El Dorado. It was over a year before Sebastián de Benalcázar himself set out, in 1536, to conquer Pasto, Popayán and Cali in what is now south-west Colombia. Even then, his motive was not to find a land of gold, but the geographical aim 'to discover what lay between Quito and the North Sea [Caribbean]'.

4 WHILE BENALCÁZAR WAS STARTING TO PENETRATE COLOMBIA FROM THE SOUTH, another group of conquistadores was marching into what is now Colombia's eastern region. The Welser had appointed another German to replace the dead Ambrosius Dalfinger as governor of Venezuela. They did not choose the ambitious young Nicolaus Federmann, but rather Georg Hohermuth, a 27-year-old soldier from a prominent family of the imperial city of Speyer on the Rhine. Hohermuth had briefly studied theology at Heidelberg, but turned to the more congenial world of finance and warfare. After his selection, the Welser sent him to recruit his expedition in Seville. A young German in the party, Hieronymous Köler of Nuremberg, recorded every detail of the preparations. His manuscript lay unpublished for centuries until Juan Friede discovered it recently in the British Museum. Köler painted the expedition as it marched to the ships on the Guadalquivir: first musicians playing trumpets and tambourines, then Franciscan and other friars with candles, followed by the expedition's leaders. These were big men mounted on massive war-horses. They had long oval shields on their left shoulders and wore powerful Toledan swords. Some carried spiked battle maces. All were heavily bearded—with black, red, even grey beards. They wore plumed helmets or caps, fine damask breeches, and long leather boots sometimes to thigh length. They all used the long stirrups of medieval knights, rather than the short stirrups and crouching seat that came to be used by Spanish *jinetes* fighting naked Indians. Behind the leaders came lancers with their long weapons shouldered, handlers with hunting dogs, arquebusiers, and specialists such as shoemakers, smiths, armourers, masons and tailors. It was a cosmopolitan army, for besides Spaniards and Germans there were Flemings and even English, Scots and Albanians.

RIGHT The young German Köler painted the flagship of the Welser expedition that reached Venezuela in 1535.

LEFT Caripuna of the Río Branco with a tapir, the largest animal of the South American forests.

Hohermuth's expedition reached Coro in January 1535—to the merriment of the bedraggled veterans already there. Much of the finery that had looked so splendid in Spain was considered ostentatious and inappropriate for the heat and hardship of the American wilds. Nicolaus Federmann reached Coro a few weeks later, bringing a shipload of two hundred much-needed horses from Santo Domingo. Prices of horses, saddles and bridles fell, to the delight of the men of Coro. The Germans now started to organize expeditions to pursue the findings of Federmann and of Dalfinger. It was decided that Hohermuth himself should strike south-

55

wards 'to follow where Nicolaus Federmann had discovered', while Federmann himself should pursue the golden lands of the Pacabueyes seen by Dalfinger: he should wait for the dry season so that he could 'pass the great river in search of the [gold] mines'.

Governor Georg Hohermuth left Coro with a mighty expedition on 12 May 1535. (The Spaniards found Hohermuth's German name unpronounceable: they tried calling him Formut and then settled for Jorge Espira, meaning 'George of Speyer'. His second-in-command Andreas Gundelfinger caused an even more hopeless tangle in Spanish palates: he was known simply as Mister Andreas.) Hohermuth took 400 men and 80 horses. He had Esteban Martín, the veteran explorer who had described Dalfinger's expedition, and 'some Spaniards expert in the land and skilled in Indian wars' who had been on the Orinoco quests for Meta. This was to be a great exploration. One German, Tito Neukomm of Lindau, wrote that they planned to be gone for two and a half years, and he added, excitedly, that 'we all believe in [the expedition's] good fortune and great wealth of treasure and gold: for we already know very well here that the land in the interior is full of gold!' Hohermuth's real hope was to conquer the rich kingdom that had eluded Ordás and Herrera. He was 'overcome by the great fame of Meta, which was the general objective that explorers pursued in those days.'

The coastal plain near Coro was by now denuded of Indians. Hohermuth therefore planned to capture his native porters from the populous tribes of the cordillera. The first months of the expedition were spent in ugly manhunting. After the coastal desert, where 'it was very hot and the horses and men cannot quench their great thirst', the expedition turned into the Tocuyo valley—the valley that Federmann's men had named the Valley of the Ladies because of its beautiful Caquetió women. There were raids on any village that seemed sufficiently weak. Philip von Hutten, a young German nobleman who wrote an account of the expedition, described a typical raid on a village called Oytabo: 'We invade that village, lance some people and capture about sixty captives. One horse and three Christians were wounded.' At a larger village, the chiefs brought tribute of two golden eagles for the governor, who condescended to enlist the tribe as subjects of Spain. Hutten wrote that 'we stayed there for six days, neither in peace nor in discord: for although the Indians did nothing against us nor we against them, there was no true, legitimate peace.' This was hardly surprising, for Hohermuth was still sending out slave raids. He sent a captain called Sabalas with sixty troopers and they 'bring back a hundred prisoners, who are divided among the Christians'. When the expedition finally moved on it took the chiefs themselves in chains as porters. By the time the two parts of the expedition reunited in the Barquisimeto valley, 'we found no Indians at all, for our infantry had descended from the [Carora] forests and had totally destroyed and devastated them.' Esteban Martín, the laconic chronicler and Indian linguist, was frequently sent off on slave raids during the ensuing weeks.

By 20 June 1535 Hohermuth's men reached the village and river of Acarigua, near the southern point reached by Federmann in 1531. One Spaniard called Orejón rode too far into the plain in pursuit of deer. The governor had arquebuses fired to try to guide him back to the camp, but in vain: Orejón had to spend the

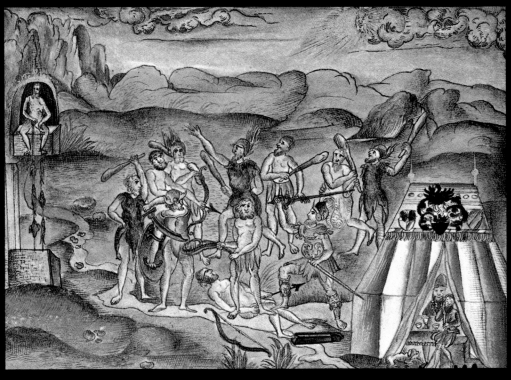

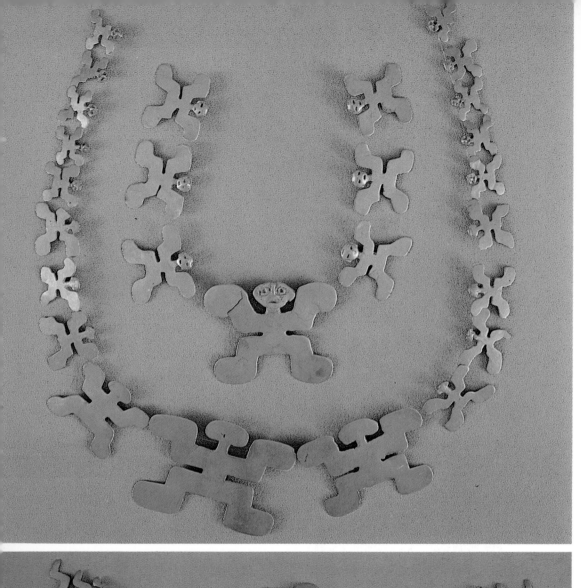

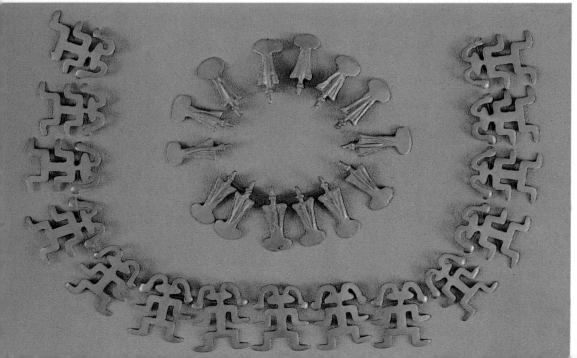

night sleeping in an isolated Indian hut. While he was asleep, the Indians crept up and cut off his head with his own sword. Meanwhile the expedition sent search parties: Esteban Martín, who returned with Orejón's riderless horse, and Juan de Cardenas, who brought the Spaniard's sword and equipment and thirty captives 'among whom were some who had witnessed the death of the Christian. [Hohermuth] had these eaten by the dogs in the presence of the rest; and the others were divided among the Christians.'

The expedition was now on the far side of the mountains, at the edge of the endless expanses of the *llanos*. From now on, for months and even years, the expedition would advance south-westwards, always keeping the Andes above them to the right and the broad horizon of the *llanos* to their left.

Hohermuth's men were now moving into unknown territory, the first alien invaders seen by its tribes. They were, as usual, wholly dependent on the Indians for food, porterage, and information. They caught one chief who 'told us something about great riches, but we later found that it was all lies.' The Guanare river was crossed in mid-September. The expedition was now on the far side of the Mérida cordillera, south of Lake Maracaibo. The advance party rested in a village and 'almost all the Christians fell ill there. When the [Coyon] Indians saw that there were few of us and that we were also very ill, they attempted to expel us with much violence from their land. Between five and six hundred Indians appeared one morning amid great shouting. But although they attacked seriously, they soon fled.' The fearful sight of warhorses succeeded again. 'The horsemen rode out and began to wound and lance those people, naked in body but not in courage.'

Sickness raged in the camp. 'Not only were the Germans ill, but also all our Indians and the horses as well.' It was thought that 'bad air' was to blame. So, on 3 November, 'we set off with over eighty Christians ill. It was necessary to carry thirty of them across the saddles of the horses, tied on like sacks, which was lamentable to see. Four died before reaching the next camp.' But any sympathy for explorers is dispelled by their slaving. Philip von Hutten's journal records a wretched litany of captives, torn from their homes by these outlandish invaders: on 27 June Andreas Gundelfinger came in with 53 captives; on 30 June, Martín brought 70; on 21 August, Santa Cruz brought 28; 21 October, Esteban Martín returns with 'only ten Indian captives'; in November Gundelfinger and Cárdenas both go raiding, but between them catch only eighteen captives . . . and so the depredations continued, throughout the duration of this cruel expedition. An acute shortage of food prompted Hohermuth to send Francisco de Velasco into the Mérida hills with a powerful force of two hundred men. He returned after a month with 2,500 bushels of maize, the contents of one tribe's food stores, carried by sixty Indian men and women captives. It was Christmas, and 'the Governor distributed these things among the Christians with his own hand.'

The hills entered by Velasco were east of the passes crossed by Dalfinger two years before. Had either Hohermuth or Dalfinger penetrated the Andes farther south, they would have stumbled upon the rich kingdom of the Muisca. But Hohermuth was now advancing rapidly across the *llanos*, despite sickness and hunger. A typical entry from Hutten's journal was: 31 December: 'We could not stay for lack of food. We set off, short of everything and with great fatigue. We

Typical Tolima silhouettes create delightful necklace beads of human beings or birds with folded wings.

57

arrived with many sick.' In mid-January, Hohermuth decided to divide his force, leaving behind 150 sick men, and continuing the advance with 199, of whom 49 were mounted. The expedition crossed the Apure river in late February, and the Arauca on 2 March 1536. Tribes who were having their first sight of Europeans brought presents of maize and fish, with customary Indian hospitality. The expedition was now on the plains below the northern end of Muisca lands. At a village called Sarobai, 'all the Indians said unanimously that the riches were on the far side of the mountains. [A chief called] Waikiri said that he knew this, not just from hearsay, but had seen it with his own eyes. We took that chief with us, intending to cross the mountains; but we could find no pass through which the horses could pass.' The mighty Sierra Nevada de Cocuy prevented the conquistadores from finding this eldorado.

Hohermuth clearly had no prior knowledge of the wealth of the Muisca in their mountain valleys. Had he known this, he would not have given Federmann the task of following Dalfinger's old Upar route into these mountains. He would also have tried far harder to penetrate the mountains from the *llanos*. The expedition in fact reached the Upía river in April 1536 and spent eight months on its banks, waiting for the rains to cease. 'During all this time the poor Christians suffered great privation and lack of food, from which many died.' They had no idea that they were immediately below Tunja, Bogotá and the sacred lake Guatavita.

Many of the Aruak-speaking tribes on the edge of the *llanos* had been friendly to the explorers. But one tribe speaking a different language, possibly Guahibo, tried to attack the Spaniards when they dismounted in its village. During the engagement, the tribe 'burned a large hut containing a chief and over a hundred of our Indian slaves'. The captives were chained and unable to escape from the fire. Hutten commented that 'we had to leave promptly because of the smell of the dead . . .' Beyond the Upía, the expedition failed to establish peaceful relations with the Waipis tribe. At Christmas 1536 the Spaniards found some gold and silver in a village and were told that it came from across the mountains. Esteban Martín was sent to investigate, but again failed to find a pass. The dry season had returned, and the expedition pushed ahead across more rivers, fighting or pillaging more tribes. On 19 January 1537 the hungry men invaded a village and were overjoyed to find it well stocked with maize. This was by now such an important event that 'the Governor entertained all the camp to a banquet: 102 Christians ate at table with him. First he had a mass sung, with solemnity demanded of necessity. A procession was made. We promised 500 pesos to Our Lady and also swore that henceforth we would not march on Sundays or holy days, but would rest.'

There was a final attempt to investigate the sierra. An Indian chief told Hohermuth that his tribe's salt and ponchos came from very rich people living in the mountains. Juan de Villegas was sent to explore with forty men, but reported that the ascent was too difficult for horses. Writing with hindsight, Pedro de Aguado remarked sadly: 'Thus, by their laziness, they allowed that piece of prosperous land virtually to slip from their hands.' But Juan de Castellanos said that Diego de Montes—a man whom Hohermuth respected, but a subscriber to Ordás' theory of equatorial gold—urged that the expedition continue southwards across the *llanos* to reach the equatorial zone. Hohermuth was therefore delighted when, a few weeks later, he 'ordered the altitude of the sun to be measured and it was found that we were at 2¾ degrees above the equator: we no longer saw the pole star.'

The decision to push on southwards towards the equator was a sorry mistake from the adventurers' point of view. Ironically, they now had a sight of a Muisca building, in an isolated trading post where the mountain people bartered their salt, textiles and gold jewellery for food and even children of the plains Indians. The Muisca hut was 'of admirable size, two hundred yards long and with two large doors on either side. It was later learned that this hut was a temple of those barbarians, where they performed sacrifices to the sun, which they worshipped as a god. They used to keep many maidens cloistered in it, to be offered as a sacrifice by their parents. There was an aged Indian with these girls—a form of priest [supervising] their offerings. It was his duty to instruct those women in the conduct required of them by their precepts. . . . In this hut they kept a quantity of all manner of food for the support of the confined maidens.' The children and food were more probably being kept ready to trade with the Muisca: references to cloistered holy women were an echo of the Peruvian mamacona, the holy women of the Inca who reminded the Spaniards so strongly of their own nuns. Instead of following the

Hohermuth's expedition found a hut full of women and children to be traded for Muisca gold. A Yanomani hut on the border between modern Brazil and Venezuela.

trade route into the hills, Hohermuth tried to encourage his men by 'founding' a Spanish municipality in this remote corner of the *llanos*. With some ragged ceremonial and appropriate legal documents on deer-hide parchment, the Muisca outpost became the town of Nuestra Señora, a name later changed when it was refounded as San Juan de Los Llanos.

When they were marching along the edge of the *llanos*, Hohermuth's men were often among the simple, nomadic Guahibo and Chiricoa tribes—hunter-gatherers who had learned to survive and multiply in the harsh grasses and swamps of those plains. The Guahibo were naked, with little decoration beyond black genipapo or red anatto dye. To exist in that difficult environment, they had to keep moving, living in small groups of a few families and never occupying their straw thatch huts for very long. They hunted deer, peccary and tapir, surrounding the game with a ring of beaters and then killing it with clubs or arrows. Some hunters stalked deer behind hides of branches and attracted the game with a resin they smeared on their bodies. But the Guahibos' favourite animal food was armadillos, which were very plentiful on those plains: the Indians would drive them into their burrows and then kill them with pointed sticks after burning off the savannah grass. When a group of Guahibo reached a new location, the men would hunt or fish and the women would go in search of edible roots, notably the guapo which was also a favourite of the routing peccary. There were also wild pineapples. From April to June the tribe gorged itself on palm fruit: the date-like fruit of the becirri and the fruit-like olives from the cunama. This was the happiest time of year for the nomads, the months when they wandered from palm grove to palm grove with their stomachs filled with fruit. These simple, amiable tribes were a great disappointment to the Spaniards. They had none of the food stores that the conquistadores needed to loot in order to feed their parasitical expedition.

Hohermuth's men were now marching to the headwaters of the Guaviare, another great tributary of the Orinoco. They crossed the Ariari and entered a higher, more populous region with large native villages. Six days' march south of the Ariari, they turned westwards on the advice of local Cauicuri Indians who 'told us that if we were seeking gold it was better for us to pass to the right.' There was a rich province twenty or thirty days' march to the west: presumably the upper Magdalena around Neiva. 'The chief said that his father had been there and had brought back some sheep [llamas] and gold'—the two commodities that symbolized the wealth of Peru in conquistadores' fantasies.

The expedition duly turned westwards, to reach the Papamene river, probably the Güejar, another headwater of the Guaviare. There were battles against various tribes during all these marches. The Guayupa tribe attacked fiercely, protected by tapir-hide shields and firing slingbolts with such force that they frightened the horses, who balked at charging them. The Indians of the Papamene appeared, in hundreds of canoes, and confirmed that there was a land rich in gold and silver beyond the source of their river. 'It was as if they had entered into the hearts of our men: for they depicted in words exactly what our men were seeking. . . . The Spaniards and their Governor were in no doubt about it, but took four or five of these same Indians as guides, struck their tents, crossed the Papamene river, and marching where the Indians guided them arrived at a province called Choques.'

A Gorotire Indian girl holding a peccary, the South American wild pig.

A royal official who wrote an account of the tribes of Venezuela described the Choques as having reasonable villages in hilly, forested country. 'They fight in a squadron like soldiers. Their battle technique is with wooden shields, well made and painted with suns and stars, and with javelins. They are far too expert with these weapons'—for each shield had a razor-sharp cane attached to its side for slitting an enemy's throat or severing his head. The Choques had stockaded villages surrounded by pit traps and protected by swamps and dense forests. As with so many other tribes, their resolute battle order was easily broken by a cavalry charge.

The mangroves and undergrowth of the Choque hills proved too dense for Spanish horses. Hohermuth therefore ordered the redoubtable Esteban Martín to reconnoitre with fifty men on foot. Even Martín was hesitant to enter those forests without the protection of cavalry. But he went, advancing for four days through the forest in constant rain. He found an Indian trail and followed this for a further two days before coming upon a fortified Choque village of thirty large thatched huts. Martín ordered his men to attack, although they were torn and exhausted by a night march. The defenders were initially confused. 'They suddenly found strange people and weapons attacking them. They were wounded and mistreated by the Spaniards. They cried out, shouted to warn the rest of the village.' There was heavy hand-to-hand fighting. At one stage the Spaniards set fire to part of the village. Martín tried to withdraw in darkness, but his column was attacked on a path near another Choque village. 'The leader, Esteban Martín, emerged from this battle wounded by seven dangerous lance thrusts. He concealed them, so that his men would not lose heart . . .' But Martín and three other badly wounded men had to be carried in litters on the return march. One of their Indian auxiliaries offered to guide them by night, and they crept out of the Choque village, leaving a tied dog to bark and howl all night. 'They were separated from the Governor by over twenty leagues of very bad paths, dense and swampy and often under water at that time, for it hardly stopped raining by night or day. . . . Each of them blasphemed and cursed the mad determination of that foreign [German] governor, whose ill-considered obstinacy had placed them in such difficulties, refusing to be guided by those who knew more about that type of warfare.' The paths were steep and slippery. Streams were flooded and had to be crossed on rotting logs or creepers. Two of the badly wounded had to be abandoned and another died, 'which somewhat lessened their labour'. But, despite every effort, Esteban Martín died from his wounds. His loss demoralized the entire expedition. Philip von Hutten shared the grief, for Martín 'had managed the camp and was also a man of the greatest importance, highly valued in these regions because, having spent almost his entire life among Indians, he knew how to treat them.'

Hohermuth rallied the dispirited men and tried to push forward into Choque territory. Everyone begged him to turn back. He managed a hard march around some swamps. 'Our men were beginning to fall seriously ill because of the heavy winter and the humidity of the region, and also because they had suffered great hardships and much hunger.' It rained unceasingly. 'It was almost as if one did not know when it was summer in that country. During those months the greater part of his men grew ill and died, with men dying on him every day. The horses also died: since they enjoyed no good pasture, a great quantity of worms grew in their guts, and this killed them. The death of the horses was a very serious loss, regretted almost as keenly as that of the Spaniards themselves.' Hohermuth made a last despairing effort to explore ahead to the rich land of his dreams. He took twelve horses and forty men—the only healthy men left in the camp—but was defeated by a broad river that proved impassable.

Back at the camp there was near mutiny. Philip von Hutten described how 'once again everyone demanded of the Governor that he turn back—even though the majority had lost hope of ever returning to Coro. We did not have enough healthy Christians to guard the camp, nor for the vanguard nor the rearguard. We were 550 leagues [over three thousand kilometres] from Coro, about forty horsemen and a hundred footsoldiers; but among these scarcely forty were fit, and the greater part without a sword or other weapon. We had no arquebus or crossbow, which are very necessary for fighting Indians—although we had left Coro with over sixty arquebusiers and twenty crossbowmen: on the long expedition they had all died or stayed behind . . . So, on 13 August 1537 we turn back, suffering as much misery and privation as, in my opinion, any Christians had ever previously suffered.'

The return march was reasonably fast—as fast as weary men could march across the sunbaked plains. Each swollen river presented a barrier that delayed the expedition for months at a time. There were now no Indians to be exploited. 'We found that almost all the villages through which we had passed were burned and devastated, as Indians are accustomed to do. We had to seek food far from our route.' The Wangari river held up the retreat for two months, and the Spaniards were saved from starvation only by the generosity of river Indians. 'We suffered from an almost complete lack of food, but finally made peace with the Indians. They then arrived in canoes and brought us maize and fish with which the camp was sustained during those days. A plague struck our horses, so that almost all fell ill and many died.' By Christmas 1537 Hohermuth's men were back at the Upía river.

From Upía to Coro took the expedition six months, marching as fast as possible towards the settlement that many had doubted they would ever see again. There was a curious episode between the Dacari and Apure rivers: local Indians reported that there were other Christians nearby. Hohermuth did not believe them. It was only a few weeks later that there were clear signs of the passage of horses heading south, and tribes said that it was Nicolaus Federmann 'bringing help'. Philip von Hutten was sent back to try to overtake Federmann, but the Apure had now risen to such an extent that 'the water on the trail where we had passed dry was now up to the height of a man.' So the governor returned to his base—and Federmann managed to lead his own expedition south without meeting Hohermuth's survivors returning along the same route. Hutten rejoined Hohermuth and entered Coro with him on 27 May 1538. The expedition had lasted three years and had been a disaster. Of the 130 sick men left behind during the expedition, only 49 had reached Coro. Hohermuth now led back a further 110 men and 30 horses. 'We were no better clothed than the Indians who go naked. Thus, of the four hundred men who had left here [Coro] with the Governor, only 160 of us were alive. Only God and those who experienced it know how much privation and misery, hunger

Hohermuth's expedition was saved by fish brought by riverine tribes. A Tucano Indian of the Caquetá river of southern Colombia using a long arrow to shoot fish.

and thirst, hardship and effort the poor Christians suffered during those three years. It is amazing that the human body could endure it for so long. It is horrible [to consider what] the poor Christians ate on that expedition: all the vermin such as snakes, frogs, lizards, vipers, worms, herbs, roots and other food always of the same sort and without any value. Some, contrary to nature, ate human meat: one Christian was found cooking a quarter of a child together with some greens. Horses killed by [arrow] shots or plague were also eaten—they sold [in the camp] for 400 pesos de oro or more. I myself joined some other Christians in buying a dog for a hundred pesos. Many deer hides . . . were soaked in water, cooked and eaten. With such bad, insipid and unnatural food, and from the rigour of exposure to rain and wind, we Christians were consumed and emaciated. God dispensed his grace to those of us who managed to save our lives!'

These great treasure-hunting expeditions were a wild game of blind man's buff, a game in which Georg Hohermuth's expedition had blundered past great riches— the land of the Muisca—and hurried off into oblivion. The leaders immediately started trying to plan a new expedition. They were convinced that the expedition had only just failed to find its promised land. The young Philip von Hutten wrote to his father that 'the Governor is already preparing to make another expedition. I hope to go with him, as long as God gives me health. For while I am here, I want to see what we can reach.' To another friend he wrote: 'We learned about a rich land, and I believe that we were not more than thirty leagues from it . . .' And he told his father about the powerful curiosity that lured him into these harrowing adventures. 'God knows that it was not avarice that impelled me to undertake that journey, but a strange desire I have harboured for a long time. I believe that I could not have died in peace without having seen these Indies.'

Governor Hohermuth himself wrote to the King that when he turned back from the Choques, 500 leagues from Coro, 'according to the Indians' report, [I was] only 25 leagues from that for which I had been searching for three years with so much hardship and deaths of Christians. But I found myself so debilitated in men, horses, weapons and everything needed to complete my journey that I could do no more. I was simply forced to return to this city [of Coro], to re-equip myself in what was needed, and immediately return to that place.'

Before Hohermuth had left Coro in May 1535, he wrote detailed instructions for his lieutenant Nicolaus Federmann to follow up Dalfinger's exploration beyond Maracaibo. He wanted Federmann to establish a settlement beyond Cabo de la Vela, so that the Guajira peninsula would belong to Venezuela rather than to Santa Marta. Federmann was then to follow Dalfinger's route through the Upar valley and across the great river to the gold-rich peoples of Cuandi and Cometi.

Federmann sent his men ahead by land and himself sailed to Santo Domingo to bring more horses. He rounded up four or five hundred peaceful Caquetió Indians from near Coro, and led them off in chains to act as porters. Royal officials protested to the King that 'all or most of them were peaceful baptized Christians. Because of this, six Indian villages near this city have been depopulated.' Federmann rejoined his men at Cabo de la Vela early in 1536 and set off on his mission. There had already been heavy losses on this expedition: one camp full of sick men was left to winter on the Macomite river, but when their companions returned they 'found very few alive, for with the diseases and hunger and heat all the rest had died and were dead in their own beds and hammocks. The living, who were very few, could not bury them . . .' Things grew worse as Federmann marched inland. The expedition was effectively harassed by Indian ambushes. Many men were lost from hunger, disease and particularly thirst. 'Some soldiers whom thirst tormented most, went off to seek water. They plunged inland into the interior, which was very flat in some parts of that land. They easily became foolish: they lost their direction and could never again strike the path along which they had entered. They marched like madmen from place to place, until overcome by exhaustion and lack of strength they could no longer move from one side to the other, and they remained there, wherever this sad siren voice had summoned them, self-important, and dead.'

When Federmann finally reached the land of the Pacabuey at the far end of the Upar valley, he was sadly disillusioned. There was no gold left in the province that had been so thoroughly ransacked by Dalfinger and by men from Santa Marta. It was also evident that the large river that Dalfinger had imagined running east to west was none other than the Magdalena. The governor of Santa Marta made it quite clear that if Federmann tried to cross he would be trespassing: he had obtained a ruling from the Audiencia in Santo Domingo that the Pacabuey valley was the boundary between the two jurisdictions. Anyone who attempted an expedition into another governor's zone would lose all possessions, titles and rewards. Federmann therefore turned back, sadly, leaving some of his men camped in the Carora hills east of Maracaibo and himself returning to Coro in September 1536. Bishop Bastidas of Venezuela wrote to the King that Federmann's expedition had been a disaster: 'He found that land uninhabitable for settlement, but also because of ill-treatment, and because he delayed to await his appointment as governor, some two hundred men died.'

Gold-rush fever was gripping conquistadores at the eastern end of Venezuela during these months. Alonso de Herrera's disastrous attempt to ascend the Meta river did nothing to dampen belief in the Meta legend. If anything, it seems to have inspired others: if the quest for Meta caused so many deaths, the goal must be worth striving for. Jerónimo Dortal, Herrera's governor, decided that there was no need to sail upriver to reach the middle Orinoco: it was now known that the great river ran almost due east towards the gulf of Paria. Dortal therefore obtained an extension of his jurisdiction to include the gulf of Maracapana, between Cumaná and Cape Codera. He built himself a base at the mouth of the Neverí river near Codera and soon plunged inland. His geographical reasoning was correct, and he was lucky to find that this is an area where no coastal range separates the Caribbean from the *llanos*. So Dortal moved rapidly, enjoying the magical experience of being the first European to visit uncontacted tribes. His expedition received customary Indian hospitality, not yet soured by European outrages. Dortal's men saw the Patigurato valley with over two thousand huts; they visited the town of Anoantal surrounded by a triple rampart, whose chief Guaramental was widely obeyed in the surrounding districts; they entered the rich provinces of Chaygot and Maulera. Well pleased by this reconnaissance, Dortal returned to the coast to organize a larger expedition.

The Calima style of gold objects were found near Popayán and date from a brief period in the fourteenth century A.D. – bonnetted human figurines and a jaguar with an articulated head, itself decorated with feline symbols.

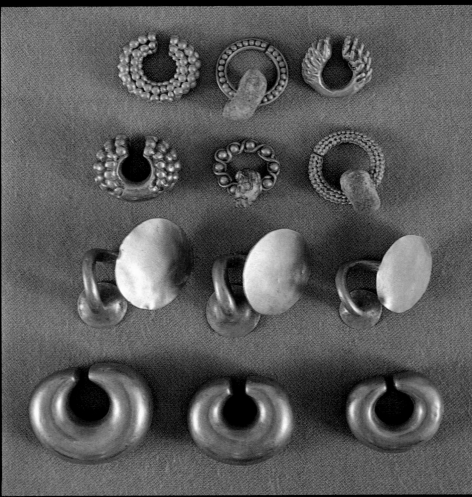

The lure of Meta had by now become an obsession with another Spanish conquistador, Antonio Sedeño, who was technically governor only of the island of Trinidad. For a time it looked as though the two governors might organize a combined expedition. But, as Fernández de Oviedo drily remarked: 'With this hope they spent two or three months thinking how to deceive one another.' Months were spent in legal wrangling, clandestine expeditions, and attempts to seize or subvert one another's men and horses.

Finally, in about March 1536, Jerónimo Dortal led an expedition inland, marching due south towards the Orinoco. He moved across fertile open plains that were well inhabited. He sighted a range of hills beyond the Orinoco that were the mountains that had halted Ordás. He was sure that he was now nearing the equator. And, like Ordás, he received beguiling reports from the Indians. While his men sat out the rains at a place called Temeurem, its chief Chapachauru gave Dortal a golden eagle and offered to lead him a few days' march to a province called Tihaos where all the table service and ornaments were of gold. 'The Governor and Spaniards were delighted at this news! They treated that chief very well, clothed him and gave him things of little value but good appearance—objects of glass or brass such as beads or bells, and some knives and mirrors.' Perhaps they were finally near their elusive goal. Or were the Indians practising the oriental courtesy of telling a questioner what he wishes to hear? Gonzalo Fernández de Oviedo had been in the Americas long enough to know that 'Indians promise Christians what they see they want: namely, gold.'

The excitement of being so near the golden land was too much for the adventurers. A brawl broke out between two factions in the camp, and when Dortal tried to punish the ringleaders the brawl turned into a mutiny. Fifty men under Juan Fernández de Alderete and the overseer García de Aguilar rejected Dortal's leadership. 'They began to proclaim their intentions, calling for liberty. Losing all sense of shame, they said that they wanted neither governor nor royal officials: they wanted to serve the King without such ministers and would serve him much better!' So Jerónimo Dortal was sent packing by his own men: he was expelled from the camp and rode back to the coast with a few companions.

The mutineers then tried to find their promised land. They moved westwards from river to river and tribe to tribe, continually seeking news of Meta. They never found the land described by chief Chapachauru. They suffered from strange diseases. In one valley all the horses succumbed to a disease in which they were apparently crazed for salt: they refused maize or grass but wanted only to eat clothing or saddles that were soaked in sweat. The men also suffered. 'That land was full of a disease of fevers and dysentery. (Although it was free of foot sores, for it does not have the humidity of other parts of these Indies.) . . . Those fevers caused a form of drowsiness that made them unconscious. . . . I heard some of those who came from Jerónimo Dortal's expedition tell that they were very inhuman to one another. When a man was ill, if he was a footsoldier he was given to a horseman to carry on his horse so that he would not be left behind. But the sick man would keep falling, unable to stay in the saddle because of his illness. The horse's owner would put him across the saddle like someone throwing a sheep, tying his hands and feet to the girths on either side with cords. But when the rest

Calima objects excavated from the Cauca valley: a magnificent mask, and a series of nose ornaments generally for clipping to the septum.

had moved forward, the owner of the horse would arrive a few hours later without his cargo, saying that the sick man he was carrying had died and that the negroes must go and bury him. Three or four men died in this way—not without suspicion that those carrying them had finished them off, or helped them to die with some blow.'

The survivors of Dortal's mutineers eventually marched along the southern edge of the mountains, south of the future site of Caracas, and into the Welser jurisdiction of Venezuela. They were disarmed by Federmann's men near Barquisimeto. But they brought with them a bacillus: the conviction that they had been close to the long-sought golden land. Juan Fernández de Alderete, one of the leading mutineers, said that he had gone 'in search of the province of Meta and . . . had marched for over two hundred leagues. Sixteen of his men and twenty horses had died. In view of this, and because he had lost his interpreter, and so that they would not be finally ruined, he decided, with the consent of all his men, to return to this province [Venezuela] to join its captain-general who was also going in search of it [Meta].' When he met Federmann, Alderete 'told him that he was coming with [some sixty] men, to join him, in order to make the expedition under his banner to the province of Meta, which was rich.'

This search was the exciting prospect that sent Nicolaus Federmann marching south in December 1536, ostensibly to take help to Governor Hohermuth. Federmann is an enigmatic figure. Some chroniclers and contemporaries admired the short, red-bearded German: they said that he was calm and decisive, a fine leader loved and admired by his men. His own chronicle revealed that, although interested in tribal societies, he was as ruthless in killing Indians as any other conquistador.

He certainly appears to have been ambitious. Federmann was determined to become governor of Venezuela and he evidently resented the Welser sending a man of his own age to replace Dalfinger. Bishop Bastidas and the historian Gonzalo Fernández de Oviedo—both shrewd judges of men—considered Federmann to be devious and dishonest.

When Federmann himself returned to Coro in September 1536 he left most of his men in the hills of Carora, where they had a hard time resisting attack by Jirajara and Xagua Indians. He may have left them there to intercept any news from the missing Hohermuth: if the governor had died on his expedition, as Dalfinger had done, Federmann wanted to ensure that he himself would be the first to know. The men at Carora were now conveniently positioned to embark on a search for Meta. The arrival of Dortal's mutineers gave Federmann important reinforcements of seasoned veterans with knowledge of the *llanos*. Some of the new arrivals had been with both Herrera and with Dortal. They brought the idea that the golden land should be sought in the mountains, just as the Aztec and Inca empires had proved to be on high ground far from the sea. Federmann left Coro hurriedly, without seeking permission from the Welser who would certainly have forbidden another long expedition before Hohermuth's return. Federmann probably had some such venture in mind all along, which was why he had not brought his men back to Coro after the failure of the Cabo de la Vela mission. So, at the end of 1536 Federmann led an expedition 'to enter the llanos in search of news of Meta'. No one was yet searching for El Dorado for, as Pedro Simón said, 'that name had not yet been invented in the world'; but Meta was the equivalent legendary goal.

Federmann's expedition set off along the edge of the *llanos*, following the route taken by Hohermuth two years before. As we have seen, the two expeditions failed to meet. Hohermuth, returning toward Coro with his shattered men had no idea that anyone would be coming to relieve him. At the time when they should have met, near the Apure river in early 1538, Federmann had veered off into the plains, returning to the edge of the sierra only after Hohermuth was safely past. Most Spaniards assumed that this was done on purpose. Aguado said that Federmann knew from Indians that Hohermuth was approaching and therefore, without telling his men, 'he left the route that led along the flank of the cordillera and deceitfully advanced in the interior of the llanos.' In a testimony in 1539, Federmann said that for 200 leagues he marched southwards along the mountains, but 'on some occasions he veered to the south-east' into the *llanos*. In a letter to a friend he said that, after three months' march, he had rested his men in a province called Aracheta 'inhabited by many people, richer in arrows than in food'. But, with food low, he could no longer continue along Hohermuth's route. The Indians led him for eight days across uninhabited land and 'seeing the lack of remedy for the privation they were suffering, he determined to take another path, along which no Christians had passed, but where he also suffered great lack of food.' It was not until April 1538 that Federmann returned to the edge of the mountains and saw fresh tracks of horses moving northwards. But, he claimed, there seemed so few tracks that he assumed it was merely a small group sent back by the governor. When some Indians later confirmed that Governor Hohermuth had been with this group, the Indians said that there were more Spaniards waiting inland—this was apparently said in order that Federmann would push ahead and not spend the rainy season with that tribe. So Federmann did continue southwards. We cannot know for sure whether his detour into the *llanos* at the crucial time was fortuitous; but it is difficult to see how Federmann, alone of his men, could have guessed that Hohermuth was approaching.

Federmann's men 'wintered' during the rains from May to November 1538 on the banks of the Meta itself. After a few months his men were desperate for food. 'They were without bread on most days, eating roots from the ground and fruit from the trees. Their hunger became so acute that they determined to turn back, even though they had left the land very threadbare. It seemed better to return for leftovers than to live in a wilderness during that harsh winter.' They eventually found their way to the land of the Waipis, in the foothills, where there was still ample food despite the fact that Hohermuth had previously wintered there. When the rains cleared, Federmann pushed on south. He reasoned that Hohermuth, who had all the best guides and who had entered a virgin country, would not have gone so far south had he not 'had a report of a rich land ahead'. It was not until Federmann had gone as far as the future San Juan de los Llanos that the Guayupa tribe convinced him that their gold came from the mountains. This coincided with the theories of the men who had previously been with Herrera or Dortal. So Federmann turned westwards up into the Andes. But he climbed into the mountains with far greater determination than the reconnaissances sent out by Hohermuth ...

5 ON 6 APRIL 1536 THE LARGEST OF ALL THE EXPLORING EXPEDITIONS MARCHED INLAND from Santa Marta. This one was to be different from the others. It was organized and led by distinguished men, newly arrived in the Americas. It had more men, supplies and equipment and it was amphibious, going partly by land and partly in special river boats. It was a return to the rational unromantic venture with a geographical purpose: to explore the mighty Magdalena river (then still known simply as the Río Grande, the Large River) to its source. The hope was that this would lead to Quito and the South Sea, the Pacific Ocean.

There was a new governor of Santa Marta, don Pedro Fernández de Lugo, governor of the island of Tenerife and son of the man who had conquered the Canary Islands for Spain. Most transatlantic expeditions sailed from the Canaries to take advantage of the favourable current. Fernández de Lugo was thus in touch with many explorers and mariners who visited the Canaries, and he was soon seized by the excitement of joining the American adventure. For a while he was interested in the River Plate—just as Diego de Ordás had been—and he questioned Sebastian Cabot about this southern region. He probably talked to Ordás when he was in the Canaries and may have heard his ideas about gold mines being found near the equator. Otherwise it may have been the Italian merchant bankers Francesquini and Geraldini who influenced Fernández de Lugo's change from the Plate to the Caribbean, for these Italians financed the expeditions of both Ordás and Fernández de Lugo. Doubtless the arrival of Pizarro's Inca treasure affected the decision. Whatever the reason, Pedro Fernández de Lugo applied for and received the governorship of Santa Marta and sailed with a fine expedition in November 1535. His geographical interest was revealed by the fact that, before setting sail, he referred to himself as governor of the province of 'Santa Marta and the South Sea' or of 'Santa Marta from sea to sea'. He clearly wished to discover the passage to the Pacific that had eluded the Welser explorers.

When the time came to launch his great expedition up the Magdalena, the cautious Fernández de Lugo chose a 36-year-old lawyer, Licentiate Gonzalo Jiménez de Quesada, as its leader. Jiménez, himself the son of a government lawyer from Granada, had gained his degree (becoming a 'licentiate') at Salamanca University and then sailed to Santa Marta as a prospective magistrate. Fernández de Lugo had evidently been watching his officers during some expeditions against tribes near Santa Marta. His choice of Jiménez de Quesada was all part of his careful planning of the exploration. It took the army by surprise; but it turned out to be a brilliant selection.

The governor issued elaborate instructions to his lieutenant. One clause described an optimistic way in which gold could be removed from the Indians. 'You will take every care to make the peoples by which you pass peaceful, giving good treatment to the Indians . . . As soon as they are at peace you will ask them for gold, as much as you estimate that they can give according to their quality and quantity. Tell them how badly I need it to pay for the ships and the food of the Christians or for whatever else you see fit.' If Indian generosity was aroused by this ludicrous appeal, Jiménez de Quesada was to avoid vexing or mistreating them, 'so that, after giving it, they remain happy and contented, so that they will be at peace henceforth and will willingly give more gold later.' But if the tribe

On the road from Bogotá to Neiva, Jiménez de Quesada probably crossed the natural stone bridge over the Sumapaz river.

refused to part with its treasure, the lieutenant was to read the Requirement through interpreters and, if that failed, 'wage war of fire and blood on them . . .'

All contemporary sources agree that Jiménez de Quesada marched out of Santa Marta with most of his men on 5 April 1536, but reports of the number of men on the expedition varied between five hundred and eight hundred. The plan was that the overland contingent was to march due south to rendezvous with the six river boats at the mouth of the Sompallon river. But even this simple plan went awry. A storm struck the fragile river brigs as they sailed towards the mouth of the Magdalena. Two boats were swept to Cartagena; another was wrecked and its survivors staggered ashore, unarmed and half-drowned, into a cannibal Carib tribe that exacted swift revenge on the invaders, all of whom 'were miserably and cruelly killed at the hands of these barbarians and buried in their stomachs.' The boat commanded by Diego de Urbina was wrecked but rescued by friendly Indians, so that the survivors reached Cartagena; but Urbina's men then decamped for more enticing adventures in Peru. The two remaining brigs managed to enter the river and awaited the rest of the flotilla, harassed continually by hostile riverine tribes. The governor Fernández de Lugo tried to make good these early losses by sending an officer to Santo Domingo for more supplies, but even this miscarried: when the man landed he was promptly arrested for bad debts and for a breach-of-promise action by a girl he had jilted. It was some months before the boats finally started up the Magdalena.

Jiménez de Quesada's early progress overland was equally disastrous. For the first forty leagues the army was crossing a land 'sterile in water and gold'. This country inland from Santa Marta is still barren, a dry wasteland of stunted trees, sandy soil and periodical floods that leave mosquito-breeding lagoons. One of these floods caused the expedition of 1536 to march higher on the slopes of the Sierra Nevada de Santa Marta, but this meant that it had to cross turbulent mountain streams with ropes and cables, losing much equipment in the process.

During this part of the journey, the Spaniards were under attack from indomitable Chimila Caribs. These Indians avoided set battles and adopted more effective guerrilla tactics. They also used the one native weapon that really frightened Europeans: poisoned arrows. Anyone seriously wounded by a fresh poisoned arrow died, raving, within a few days. Pedro de Aguado said that if the arrow drew blood, 'the poison flows along the bloodstream and reaches the heart within twenty-four hours, where the herbal poison reigns with greater force. It causes trembling and convulsions of the body, and loss of reason that makes men say bold, terrible things of dubious faith for dying men. In the end they die in such a desperate state that the living are often prompted to kill them themselves rather than await such a death.' Spaniards hit by poisoned arrows took drastic measures, cutting away chunks of flesh around the wound, cauterizing it with burning brands, or taking supposed antidotes that were often fatal. Some soldiers tried to protect themselves by completely covering their bodies and their horses in quilted cotton padding. 'A man seated on a horse, protected by such armour, looks like the most deformed and monstrous thing you could imagine, for he is swollen with the thickness and lumps of the cotton. It turns a trooper into a tower, a misshapen object that fills Indians with great terror, when they see the grandeur and

Gonzalo Jiménez de Quesada, the lawyer chosen to lead the exploration of the Magdalena river.

ostentation of a man on a horse armoured in this way.' Oviedo wrote that the main ingredient in this curare was manzanilla, a form of camomile, whose tempting red fruit is highly poisonous; to this were added poisons from snakes and other venomous animals.

Beyond Chimila, Jiménez de Quesada trusted his Spanish guides to lead him across another desolate region towards Tamalameque. The guides took the wrong route across this wilderness of low, dry woods. After twelve days the expedition was thoroughly lost and men were dying of hunger. Salvation came, as it so often did, from the natives. 'Guided by almighty God, who did not wish so many men to perish, they came across a small Indian settlement.' Indian guides led the expedition to Tamalameque in three days.

Tamalameque was the chief town of the Pacabuey, the village surrounded by lagoons where Ambrosius Dalfinger had confronted a colourful native army four years previously. The Pacabuey had earned the undesirable reputation of being rich in gold. Raiders from Santa Marta had already ransacked the area, and it was only a matter of weeks since Federmann's expedition from Cabo de la Vela had passed by there through the Upar valley. The people of Tamalameque, who had once been so hospitable to Europeans, now mounted a stiff resistance. They defended the causeway into their village, and Jiménez de Quesada's men had to fight hard to force their way into the town. Their reward was a three-week rest, consuming the tribe's food stores.

The expedition moved down to the main Magdalena river, crossed the César tributary, and then moved painfully upstream towards the Sompallon where it was to meet the boats. Although the route to Sompallon had previously been explored, this was a gruelling march. Many men newly arrived from Spain had fallen ill. For some unknown reason, Jiménez de Quesada had set out on his expedition at the start of the rainy season. The dying men suffered terribly in the heat and humidity of the Magdalena valley. By the time the boats finally arrived, after the army had waited for some months at Sompallon, no less than a hundred men had died. There was jubilation when the two parts of the expedition finally reunited. The sickest men were embarked on the boats, with an escort of able-bodied to protect them from attacks by the canoes of the river tribes.

Jiménez de Quesada now led the remainder of his expedition upstream along the banks of the swollen river. Even today, the unsurfaced road that runs down this bank of the Magdalena is treacherous, thick with glutinous pink mud during the rains, and dusty, pot-holed and rocky during the dry months. The modern road runs well to the east of the river. The Spaniards in 1536 tried to keep close to the flooded river that contained their boats. There were no trails: the local Indians moved entirely by canoe. The men had to hack their way with axes and machetes, often through dense undergrowth or jungle. They were continually crossing flooded, swampy land. Captain Jerónimo de Inzá led the squad of machete men at the head of the column. They cut through thick woods of ivory palms or dwarf cedars, or expanses of tough nacuma grass. Each tributary river presented a formidable obstacle that had to be crossed by makeshift bridges or rafts. Some men were even killed by caymans while wading in chest-high reddish waters. At one crossing, a soldier just managed to stop a raft full of the expedition's weapons from being captured by Indians. 'Those sinners and soldiers suffered in many ways, on the water and on land: from fighting men, from illnesses, from hunger and thirst, from heat, from cold, from nakedness and lack of clothing, shoes and equipment. . . . There was so much vegetation and forest, brambles and other plants. Cutting their trails by hand, it was a very good day's march if they covered two leagues. . . . There were dead and more sick every day, and there was no way to succour or relieve them, without beds and in heavy rains.'

There were many jaguars, and some men were killed by them. The mosquitoes, black flies, ticks and other insects were appalling. The men suffered from a worm called barros that entered the skin and grew without being felt, until it reached the size of a cattle worm. Pedro de Aguado advised his readers: 'You kill these by putting a patch of turpentine on top of them.' Another worm caused the terrible furunculosis disease. The expedition's horsemen often rode on to higher ground to try to hunt deer for the hungry expedition. But during the march, Jiménez de Quesada and the other officers walked, leaving their horses to carry the sick. The expedition's two friars, one a Dominican and the other of the Order of St Peter, were kept busy giving absolution to the dying.

The expedition finally emerged from this ordeal, on to slightly higher ground at an Indian village called La Tora (now the town of Barranca-bermeja, 'Red Ravine'). The place seemed a paradise, with its thirty large huts—deserted by their inhabitants—and surrounding plantations of manioc and maize. Some of the Spaniards called the village the Town of Four Arms, for four rivers joined the Magdalena near it.

Jiménez de Quesada was still determined to complete his mission, by reaching the headwaters of the Magdalena and finding either that he gazed down on the Pacific or that he was close to Quito. But when he sent boats to explore upstream they reported that the river soon became impassable—narrower, faster-flowing and with densely forested banks devoid of native habitation. Jiménez de Quesada explained his predicament: 'The waters now bore down with such force that we could not continue forward. . . . I was horrified to think that the route had stopped so that I could ascend no further up that river.'

Many of the men lost heart and wanted to turn back. The expedition's losses had already been appalling, perhaps the worst in a short space of time of any American exploration. Jiménez de Quesada seized on one small detail to provide some hope in his predicament. He had noticed that, whereas the tribes of the lower Magdalena used sea salt, those at La Tora used cakes of rock salt. The cakes were shaped like sugarloaves. Their efficiency indicated that they were the produce of an advanced society, and that there was a trade route between the Magdalena and the source of the salt. Before admitting defeat, Jiménez de Quesada tried sending another reconnaissance of 25 men in six canoes up one of the tributaries, the Opón, which flowed into the Magdalena from the south-east.

The reconnaissance returned after two weeks. Its leader, Captain Juan de San Martín, reported that he had gone upstream until the current became too strong. Rounding a bend in the river, his boats had surprised an Indian canoe. A soldier called Bartolomé Camacho dived in and swam with his sword in his mouth to capture this native canoe: it proved to be full of trade goods, coloured cloaks and

Expeditions converging on Bogotá in 1539 and (inset) the lands of the Muisca.

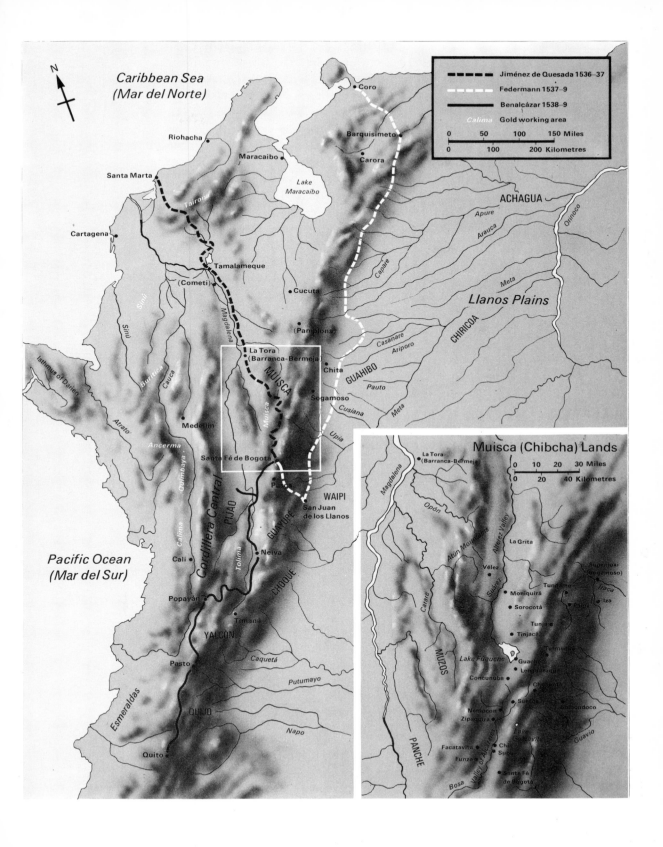

N

Caribbean Sea
(Mar del Norte)

Riohacha

Maracaibo

Lake
Maracaibo

Coro

Barquisimeto

Carora

Santa Marta

Tairona

Cartagena

Tamalameque
(Cometi)

Magdalena

Cucuta

(Pamplona)

La Tora
(Barranca-Bermeja)

MUISCA

Sinú

Sinú

Buriticá

Cauca

Atrato

Medellín

Ancerma

Quimbaya

Santa Fé de Bogotá

Muisca

Chita

Sogamoso

GUAHIBO

Pauto

Cusiana

Upia

ACHAGUA

Apure

Arauca

Meta

Llanos Plains

Casanare

Ariporo

CHIRICOA

Meta

Orinoco

Isthmus of Darien

Cordillera Central

Calima

PIJAO

Tolima

Cali

Popayán

Timaná

YALCON

Pasto

Esmeraldas

QUIJO

Quito

Neiva

CHOQUE

GUAYUPE

Pasto

WAIPI

San Juan
de los Llanos

Caquetá

Putumayo

Napo

Pacific Ocean
(Mar del Sur)

Jiménez de Quesada 1536–37
Federmann 1537–9
Benalcázar 1538–9
Calima Gold working area

| 0 | 50 | 100 | 150 Miles |
| 0 | 100 | 200 Kilometres |

Muisca (Chibcha) Lands

La Tora
(Barranca-Bermeja)

| 0 | 10 | 20 | 30 Miles |
| 0 | 20 | 40 Kilometres |

Magdalena

Opón

Carare

Atún Mountains

Alférez Valley

La Grita

Vélez

Suárez

MUZOS

Lake Fúquene

Moniquirá

Sorocotá

Tunja

Tinjacá

Suganasxi
(Sogamoso)

Tundama

Itaca

Iza

Paipa

Turmequé

Guachetá

Lenguazaque

Chocontá

Suesca

Simijaca

Suta

Guavio

PANCHE

Nemocon

Zipaquirá

Concunuba

Lake
Guatavita

Facatativa

Funza

Bosa

Chia

Suba

Valley of Alcázares

Santa Fé
de Bogotá

the curious salt cakes. San Martín noticed huts on the river banks, landed, and struck inland. Following Indian trails, he came upon deserted villages and finally a storehouse full of cakes of salt and painted mantles. Jiménez de Quesada was delighted. 'They gathered from this that those must be salt markets, and that this was the route by which salt reached the Río Grande [Magdalena] . . . When [Jiménez de Quesada] heard this he decided to go himself to explore the mountains. He took as his objective to ask for the cake where that salt—so different from that eaten by the coastal Indians—was made. He suspected that wherever this salt was made, there must be much commerce with the people of the South.' Having failed in his main objective, Jiménez de Quesada now recalled the rumours he had heard about the rich land of Meta. He later said that he hoped, by striking eastwards into the mountains, to find a route to the 'powerful and rich province called Meta, which, by the route indicated by the Indians, must have been towards the source of the Río Grande [Magdalena].' But he may have thought that Meta lay in the plains *on the far side* of the mountains—which was where explorers from the Orinoco or from Venezuela had sought it. Aguado said that he sent the reconnaissance to find 'some road or people or clearing that would guide them to pass to the far side of the mountain range, which he so greatly desired'.

Jiménez de Quesada took sixty healthy men on his exploration of the Opón river. They were too many for the available canoes, so they had to go by land, cutting a trail for fourteen leagues (eighty kilometres) to the storehouses. It was another terrible ordeal. The rains fell continuously. The river was flooded and forced 'our men to advance like fish through the water by day and climb into trees to sleep at night'. The few surviving horses had to sleep with water up to their bellies. The men carried their own supplies, and the daily ration was 40 grains of roast maize per man. A single dog had followed the explorers, and this was eaten by the leaders. 'Some who were present confirm that the feet, legs, head, tripes and even the skin of that dog were consumed as if it had been the most tender lamb.'

Having reached the salt shores, Jiménez de Quesada sent two young hidalgos (gentlemen, literally 'hijos-de-algo' or 'sons of someone important') called Juan de Céspedes and Antonio de Lebrija forward on another reconnaissance. They took their men up steep hills in dense forest, following Indian paths but knowing nothing of what lay ahead. After fifteen leagues they came upon some Indians wearing the painted mantles, self-confident men 'who remained unperturbed in their hammocks even though the Christians came up to them. They had much food and were pleased that the Christians ate it.' After a further fifteen leagues, there was a small village with some signs of an advanced civilization: more fine mantles and some worked gold. The village was deserted and the explorers chased through the woods trying to catch some Indians. They finally hunted down one man who, when he recovered from his terror, agreed to guide them forward. After three days they reached a valley in the forests called Opón. They managed to capture a chief, when the poor man was in the middle of his marriage ceremony. At first the Spaniards tried to behave well, telling him about Spain and about the presents they intended to bring him. 'They told him that they had not come to harm anything, but greatly valued his friendship.' But they showed their true colours when, a few days later, they suspected him of planning an attack on them. 'At which one soldier, with the officer's consent, gave him a swipe with the flat of his sword and knocked him to the ground.' The chief was forced to guide them forward, with a rope around his neck. They followed a 'very perverse and steep path' for three days, to a valley they named after the ensign who entered it first. It was a populous place, but they pressed on. The men of this reconnaissance were now shod, having emerged barefoot from the floods of the Magdalena: 'The officers and men worked for two days without stopping, to make themselves rope-soled sandals out of some cotton hammocks or sheets they found there. Some made soles, others the uppers and other the lacings. In this way they remedied that need, which was no small one.'

Finally, after three more days through forested hills, the trees ended and the men suddenly emerged on to high, flat uplands. There were paths in all directions and populous villages. A raid to the nearest village yielded some gold and emeralds. They had clearly stumbled on to the edge of an advanced civilization; for they were in fact near the northern limit of the lands of the Muisca. The conquistadores were overjoyed. This valley came to be called Grita, the Valley of the Shout, because of the rapturous shouting with which Jiménez de Quesada was greeted when he emerged on to these uplands a few weeks later.

The scouting party made its way back, down the forest paths to Opón and then down to report to Jiménez de Quesada at the salt stores. The general then went back to the main camp at La Tora on the Magdalena. He narrowly missed capture by a flotilla of five hundred canoes of river warriors that were attacking the camp. As his canoe approached, it was fired on by a cannon mounted on one of his expedition's brigs. The men were delighted to see their leader back after an absence of fifty days.

La Tora was a pestilential place. Two hundred men had died during the march up the river from Santa Marta and almost as many died at La Tora. Jiménez de Quesada himself fell sick immediately after his return, and came close to death. He took a roll call, challenging his men to follow him up into the mountains. An officer called Gallegos was left in charge of the boats, with 25 healthy men and 35 sick: his instructions were to wait for eight months and then return to Santa Marta—in the event Gallegos ran out of food and returned sooner, limping into Santa Marta in May 1537 with only three boats and forty men. Jiménez de Quesada himself set off with 170 men, 30 of whom were mounted, and 70 horses. They left La Tora on 28 December 1536. Sixty of the men were so ill that they had to move with walking sticks, and by the time the general reached the top of the forests 'he was in such a state that, unless he was carried bodily, he could not remain standing upright or on a horse.' With this small force of battered, emaciated, sickly and half-naked men, he hoped to conquer the kingdoms of the Muisca. By coincidence, he had almost exactly the same number of men as Pizarro had had on the conquest of the Incas.

The expedition toiled up from the Magdalena valley. They started up the Opón river and then through swamps and flood to reach the lower slopes of the Andes. From there the ascent must have seemed interminable. They were climbing the steep, densely forested slopes of the Atún mountains. Castellanos described them as 'thick forest and muddy ground: I believe that this is the worst in the New World, a place where light is never seen, to give relief, and where the rigour of the rains [continues] without pause.' It was extremely difficult to haul the horses up these mountain sides. Paths had to be cut for them, and there were places where they had to be pulled up in cradles of creepers. Men could clamber along fallen logs or slip under forest obstacles, but the horses could not. Twenty men died during this ascent, but it was a triumph that only one horse was lost—it fell off a precipitous mountain trail. The reward came when the explorers gazed down over open upland valleys full of villages and fertile farmlands. To their left were rows of hills covered in vegetation and with spectacular limestone cliffs; behind lay the deep canyon of the Opón and the humid abyss of the Magdalena valley; to the right was a range of mountains, with the snow-capped peaks of the cordillera shining against the deep Andean sky. Gonzalo Jiménez de Quesada knelt down to give thanks to God for this rich, well-ordered land that he could conquer. His men knelt beside him.

The invading expedition veered right, southwards, as it left the forests. The Grita valley (Valley of the Shout) where they emerged was probably the place now called Aguamiel, near the modern town of Vélez. After four days' march past native villages, Jiménez de Quesada sent horsemen to scout ahead and they reported that 'those towns were getting larger and were always greater'. They had seen a valley with five hundred houses, and then, scouting further, had sighted a valley of two thousand houses. The main expedition then advanced, fording the fast-flowing Saravita river, which they called the Suárez after an officer who lost his horse during the crossing. A village beyond was deserted but full of food, including a row of freshly-slaughtered deer, apparently an offering to these god-like strangers. A few days later the expedition acquired Indian porters and every man was wearing an Indian poncho—even Jiménez de Quesada and the other captains, who wore them over their chain mail. The men who looked so desperate a few weeks earlier were now rapidly regaining their health, restored by the plentiful food and the invigorating mountain air and in high spirits at the prospect of plunder that lay ahead.

One of the most important items on any of these plundering expeditions was a log of all gold or treasure taken from the natives. No man was allowed to keep anything to himself. Everything was deposited in chests of gold kept at the door of Jiménez de Quesada's lodging, where all could see them. When the expedition started acquiring emeralds and other stones, these were placed in a box that hung from the rafters of the general's quarters. Both Jiménez de Quesada and the royal officials kept ledgers of all the treasure placed in these well-guarded chests. One of these record books has recently come to light. It showed that the expedition obtained some gold at the outset, near the mouth of the Magdalena. There was then a lull of ten months until March 1537 when the entries come thick and fast. Each 'town of the sierra' added its quota of gold, all of which was carefully weighed and graded.

As the expedition marched into Muisca (or Chibcha) territory, the two races keenly observed one another. We have no contemporary account by a Muisca—nothing to compare with the Mexican codexes or the chronicles of Titu Cusi

Jiménez de Quesada's coat of chain mail. During the conquest, he wore a Muisca mantle over it.

Yupanqui Inca or the Inca mestizo Garcilaso de la Vega. The Muisca were like all American Indians in having no writing, although they were fine orators with a tradition of verbal history reminiscent of the bards of Homeric Greece. We can only try to imagine what they thought of this mysterious and menacing column that had suddenly emerged from the forests and was advancing into their lands. 'The Indians said to one another—as was later learned—that our men must be sons of the sun and must have been sent to punish their shortcomings and sins. They began to call the Christians *usachies* meaning "sun-moon" ', since they regarded the sun and moon as the creators of their world. The Spaniards had the advantage of knowing their own origins and their intentions: they were simply waiting to find the extent of this civilization before deciding how to conquer, loot, destroy and occupy it. They suffered from the lack of a good interpreter. They had captured an Indian in the Opón valley who spoke some Muisca as well as the Carib language of the Magdalena tribes, but he knew little about Muisca society and had learned no Spanish. 'The Christians went like dumb men, asking by sign language and being answered by signs, so that they had to divine what fortune would dispose.'

The Spanish column passed the populous town of Moniquirá and moved along its beautiful river. They paused at Tinjacá and were given more gold and emeralds by its chief. They were guided only by asking for the source of the salt cakes, following good native roads that seemed to be leading into the heart of their kingdom. They crossed the *páramo* or moor of Merchán and gazed down on the lovely lake now called Fúquene. Their route lay alongside the waters of the lake, and they could see a great temple on an island in its midst. On 12 March 1537 they reached Guachetá, a large town of two thousand houses that impressed the Spaniards with the good order of its plan. Their priest called it San Gregorio as it was entered on that saint's day.

We can judge something of the perplexity of the Muisca by the behaviour of the people of Guachetá. The townspeople had retreated into a fortress on a crag above their town, but the invaders found one old man and a cooking fire abandoned among the houses. They concluded that he had been left as an offering, in case they were gods who liked human meat. When the Spaniards passed by this victim, the Indians assumed that they had rejected him 'because he was old and rotten meat, so they sent other, fresher meat, making some of their own children go down to be eaten. The Christians made them signs that this was not their type of food.' The Indians gave them presents of mantles, and some fine emeralds. The Spaniards doubtless made it abundantly clear that this was the sort of present they *did* appreciate. 'So peace began to be established between the two parties; although it did not last long, but only for a short time.'

It was now possible for the Spaniards to observe much of the country they hoped to invade, even if they were still unable to talk to its inhabitants. The Muisca occupied a series of flat highland valleys, sloping gently away from a central watershed. Most of the settlements were situated between 2,500 and 2,800 metres (8,200 to 9,200 feet) above sea level, a good altitude for Andean farming—low enough for maize to flourish and high enough for the best potatoes and quinoa. This was above the line of tropical forest but below the treeless *páramo*. At a

latitude of only 5° north, the best farm lands tended to be at this altitude, in Andean valleys where the climate was temperate and often quite cool and misty. Modern Bogotá often has overcast skies and rainy drizzle.

What most impressed the explorers was the orderly farming and the abundance of produce. The Muisca did not have large cities, but their land was intensively cultivated and supported a large population—at least a million inhabitants in an area smaller than Belgium. The countryside had frequent villages, farms and market centres, connected by a network of good paths—not really roads, as there were no pack animals, no wheeled vehicles, not even llamas that occurred farther south in the Andes. The Muisca were great traders, with busy markets. All the crops were strange to Europeans. It is difficult to grasp how isolated the Americas had been from Eurasia and Africa before the conquests: almost every plant, animal and disease had evolved quite differently in those separate land masses. With the single exception of cotton, all the Muisca plants were novel. There was a wide variety of potatoes: white, yellow, even pink—for, unknown to the conquistadores, the humble potato was the greatest treasure of the Andes: the world's annual potato harvest is worth many times the value of all the precious metals looted from the Muisca and Inca empires. Maize was the food staple of the Aztecs, a nourishing plant evolved by human husbandry. There were plants that have not been exported from the Andes: cubio tubers, protein-rich quinoa that looks like a foxglove and grows in rich autumnal colours from russet to purple, arracacha, and camote sweet potatoes. There were tomatoes, broad beans, squashes and chili peppers; and a wide variety of fruits, ranging from pineapples to avocados, guavas, pitahayas and cherimoya custard-apples. The Americas were generally worse endowed than Europe in foods: there were none of the cereals that provided the European daily bread, and almost no domestic animals—no cattle, pigs, sheep or chickens. The only meat easily available to the Muisca was cavies, a species of guinea-pig that was also the Incas' main source of meat protein. There were also plenty of deer, but these seem to have been reserved for the chiefs and nobility. Once the Spaniards were in Muisca lands, they never fell ill and were always amply fed by the Indians. Fernández de Oviedo wrote that 'it was noteworthy that during the two years of that conquest, there was not a single day when food of all [local] varieties failed to arrive in the Spaniards' camp in great abundance. There were days of a hundred or 150 deer, and at the very least thirty deer in a day. There were a thousand or less guinea-pigs a day.'

The Spanish expedition advanced from Guachetá to Lenguazaque, where it saw the splendid panorama of the gorge of Peña Tajada, with the Lenguazaque river plunging through sheer rock outcrops. There were more presents of gold, emeralds and food from the awed natives. Jiménez de Quesada wanted to preserve this peace that was proving so rewarding. He issued strong orders that there must be no looting or abuse of the Indians. One soldier called Juan Gordo ('Fat John') was caught stealing a poncho from a Muisca, and the general ordered him hanged. The sentence was carried out, despite pleas for clemency from the officers and clergy: Jiménez de Quesada knew that he must enforce good behaviour at all costs.

Beyond Lenguazaque the Spanish column crossed a low watershed into the valley of Suesca, a rich town whose name meant 'macaw's tail'. The local reception still appeared friendly. There were more presents for the strangers at Cocunubá. The Spaniards had their first look at a salt factory and discovered that it did not come from a lake, but from saline wells. They were learning more about the Muisca. They observed that both sexes wore cotton mantles, with the inner garment belted and the outer cloak loose. Some of these were vividly painted, but rarely woven or embroidered. The people wore coloured garlands on their heads, often with a flower of their favourite colour in front. Chiefs wore conical cotton bonnets.

The Spaniards had not yet experienced Muisca fighting methods, apart from a brief skirmish near the Grita valley. Unknown to them, the chief of Suesca had sent to advise his paramount ruler, the Zipa of Bogotá, about the intruders and their animals. The Bogotá had an army ready to attack his traditional enemy, the Zaque of Hunsa (Tunja), and he decided to launch this against the Spanish column. While the van of Jiménez de Quesada's column was entering Nemocón, the Muisca approached behind the cover of a hill called Perico to ambush the Spanish rear. They attacked in full battle array, with the mummified bodies of the previous Bogotá and other heroes carried in litters at their head. This was just the sort of fighting at which the Spaniards excelled. They could easily deploy their horses on the open plains of the Muisca. It was for this moment that they had marched their horses through the floods and swamps of the Magdalena and Opón valleys, and heaved them up the mountains of Atún. The horses were the tanks of the conquest. In battle a mounted man has an overwhelming advantage over a man on foot, using his horse as a weapon to ride down the enemy, more manoeuvrable, less exhausted, inaccessible and continually striking downwards from his greater height. It is for these reasons that police still use horses to quell crowds. The horses of the conquest were the more fearsome because they were completely new: terrible creatures larger than any animal in South America.

The conquistadores were using a new method of riding. They had no need of the heavy metal armour with which medieval knights confronted pikes and cross-bows. Instead of riding with legs stretched out to stand the shock of jousting, troopers in the Americas adopted a new style called 'a la jineta'. The rider used short stirrups, with his legs bent backwards, almost kneeling on top of the horse. 'With the high Moorish saddle, the rider used the powerful Moorish bit, a single rein, and always rode with rather a high hand. The reason was that the horses were all bitted on the neck, that is to say they turned by pressure on the neck and not by pulling at the corners of the mouth . . . As the bit had a high port, and often a long branch, the raising of the hand pressed the port into the palate . . . and a horse turned far more rapidly and suffered less [than under] the modern system.' This system of riding left one hand free for fighting, and it made horses very agile, easily able to wheel or charge in the heat of battle. Horsemen used long lances, thin and light, with a leaf-shaped metal point. The rider could charge with his lance held down by his thigh, parallel to the galloping horse; or he could stab down with it. His sword and daggers were also readily available and always filed to razor sharpness. Toledan steel swords were famous throughout Europe for their quality: each blade was tested by being bent into an S and struck against a hard surface, before being sold. And the Spaniards themselves were the most successful and respected

BELOW 'There were a thousand guinea-pigs a day' to feed Jiménez de Quesada's expedition. Guinea-pigs and cavies were the main source of meat for the Muisca and the Incas.

soldiers of Europe in their day. Those who crossed to the Americas were seasoned veterans, the toughest and most adventurous of their breed.

The Muisca response to these formidable conquistadores was a pathetic array of biblical weapons. They had sharp wooden sword-maces. They used fire-hardened javelins hurled from spear-throwers—a throwing stock with a heel at one end that gave more impetus and accuracy than an unaided throw. Muisca warriors defended themselves with wooden shields. They did not use bows and arrows, perhaps because they lacked the necessary woods. And they did not use curare or other poisons that the Spaniards feared so much. Nicolaus Federmann described the Muisca as 'hardly a warlike people, with weapons of little offence: lances and throwing sticks'. And Benalcázar dismissed them as 'very spineless, cowardly and feminine people, badly armed and without poison'.

In this first pitched battle, the Muisca attacked with only five or six hundred warriors. Although they attacked the Spanish rear and took it by surprise, they were easily outclassed. Many were killed and the rest were routed. All the Spaniards joined in the pursuit, riding down fleeing Indians for many miles. The paramount chief of the Muisca, the Zipa of Bogotá, was watching the battle from a distance, but the Spanish horse came close enough to threaten him—his followers had to rush him to safety in his litter. Some defeated warriors fled to the lagoons of the Hunza river. Others took refuge in a fortress called Busongotá. When the Spaniards approached this fort, one brave Muisca came out, apparently to challenge them to single combat. But one of the toughest Spanish captains, Lázaro Fonte, galloped up, grabbed the man up by the hair, and rode off, half-dragging and half-carrying him. Disheartened by this final humiliation, the Muisca abandoned Busongotá, which proved to be defended by a maze of earth ramparts and a stockade of wooden uprights, woven canes and thick cotton canvas, to a height of 5 metres and two thousand metres in length.

A few days after this battle, on 22 March 1537, the victorious Spaniards entered the valley of Bogotá, the heart of the Muisca territories and the seat of its most powerful ruler. 'They began to see beautiful and magnificent buildings, houses and palaces of wood, more ornate and better than all they had seen before.' Each chief had a tall building surmounted by a high, conical thatched roof. Above this projected a central mast, dyed red with anatto and adorned with sail-like vanes. These palaces were wooden, with walls of woven cane and daub, sometimes surrounded by square or circular containing walls. The windows were closed by reed shutters like jalousies. They were well built, particularly imposing from a distance as they towered above the flat savannah. Antonio de Lebrija said that, 'although thatched, they could be considered as some of the finest seen anywhere in the Indies.' To Jiménez de Quesada they were 'like a fortress or citadel, surrounded by many curtain walls, outside and within, in such a manner that they almost resemble those paintings commonly called labyrinths. There are many notable features in these buildings, which belong to their lords . . .' They reminded him of the tiered battlements of Moorish castles. As he gazed across the broad valley, with these palaces rising from it as in the background of a renaissance painting, he gave it the romantic name *Valle de los Alcázares*, Valley of the Castles.

The invaders were now aware that the paramount ruler of the Muisca was called

Calima goldwork from the upper Cauca valley – (left) circular pectoral decorated with a face, (right) a repoussé breastplate and (below) a feline mask.

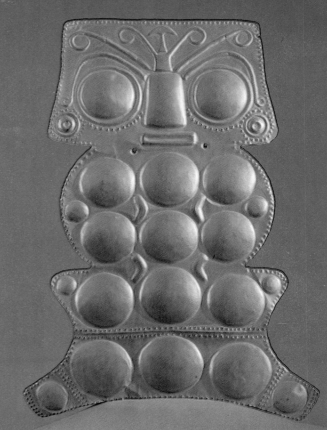

the Zipa of Bacatá (which name became Bogotá). His court was a palace compound called Muequetá, at a place now called Funza a few kilometres north-west of modern Bogotá. The Zipa of Bogotá had many semi-independent chiefs who owed him allegiance, and the Spaniards reckoned that he could assemble an army of fifty thousand or even a hundred thousand warriors. The Spaniards did not yet appreciate that this Bogotá was only one of two or even three paramount rulers: his traditional enemy was the Zaque of Tunja, a ruler able to muster forty to fifty thousand fighting men. Ignorant of this rivalry, Jiménez de Quesada failed to exploit internecine native feuds in the way that Cortés or Pizarro had done. 'Had the Christians had an interpreter, and information about the stupid and perpetual enmity that existed between these two princes, the land would have been conquered quicker and with less danger or effort—and it would have yielded many more benefits and great treasures . . .' As they moved down the valley, the Spaniards tried to negotiate with the Zipa, through native embassies. There were sporadic skirmishes and ineffectual attempts to stop the invasion. But the Spaniards advanced inexorably towards their goal. On 23 March they were at Chía, traditional seat of the heir to the Zipa. Easter was celebrated there. By 5 April they were at Suba, and finally, on about 21 April 1537, they reached the palace of Muequetá, residence of the king they had come to conquer.

The conquest of the Muisca or Chibcha homelands took more than a year. During that time the Spaniards learned about the society they were invading, marched on expeditions to explore its valleys and surroundings, fought many battles, visited many towns, and above all looted. The Zipa himself escaped their clutches, fleeing to the mountains and removing his fabulous treasures. The invaders spent a month at Muequetá, warding off native attacks and desperately trying to find the missing treasures. Two expeditions were sent to explore the forests that lay beyond Muisca territory: both returned to report that below the Muisca lived a formidable nation of naked, forest-dwelling Indians called Panches, who were skilled archers, used curare poison, and were far more dangerous adversaries than the more civilized and regimented Muisca. Jiménez de Quesada continued to try to meet the Zipa Bogotá, but native cunning prevented his discovering the ruler's whereabouts. Whenever the Spaniards tried to attack him they were confronted by masses of Indian levies. During one night battle, the Indians set fire to the invaders' lodgings, and the Spaniards had to hurry from the fighting to extinguish the fire.

In mid-May, the Zipa lured the Spaniards away from his lands by sending embassies, that pretended to come from a rich region to the north and always brought fabulous presents of emeralds and gold. Such a bait soon had Quesada hurrying north. By 20 May his force was at Chocontá, a rich town with a large garrison defending a pass to the lands of the Zaque of Tunja. Besides amassing a growing horde of treasure, the conquerors were forcing Indian women to serve and sleep with them. Unknown to their captors, these girls would put a hallucinogenic herb called tectec, a form of datura, into the cooking pots and 'once the men were mad, they could safely run off that night, for since their masters were senseless they did not know and could not prevent their flight. It was amazing, when the Christians first entered that land, that each morning many Christians would wake

The Muisca made hundreds of triangular votive figurines called *tunjos*. The entire pieces are of cast gold, including wire-like features, ornaments, genitals and limbs.

The Funza river falls from the plateau near Bogotá in the spectacular Tequendama falls.

up crazed and do foolish things at which everyone was horrified. Some even attributed it to a miracle, or to a punishment by God.' One girl finally explained what was happening and showed the conquistadores how tectec looked.

The expedition passed through the low, barren hills that form the watershed between the Magdalena and Meta-Orinoco basins. They had crossed into the lands of the Zaque of Tunja, but were still on the plateau of the Muisca homelands. They camped at Turmequé, where they were worshipped with the obeisances, incense and offerings due to gods. Instead of continuing north-eastwards to Tunja, Quesada sent an expedition to investigate a rumour that there were mines producing the magnificent emeralds that they kept acquiring. Emerald mines were a new concept, 'a great novelty . . . for up to then there had been many opinions in the world concerning emeralds, but no Christian or infidel prince was known to have such a thing [as an emerald mine]!' But the emerald mines *did* exist, on a mile-long spur of the Cerro Negro. The Spaniards watched in fascination as skilled Indian miners prised the emeralds loose with long sticks and flushed them out with a system of water channels. Only a few chosen Indians from the Somondoco tribe were permitted to observe the mines or work them. Diviners inspired by hallucinogens located the richest veins.

When the reconnaissance returned on 14 July, to tell Quesada about the mines, its leader also described some vast, apparently fertile plains that he had glimpsed beyond the mountains. When Quesada had left the Magdalena valley at La Tora, he had hoped to reach the rich land of Meta *beyond* the mountains. He was therefore fascinated by this report of 'very great plains that were a marvel . . . [which] appeared to be inhabited.' An expedition was sent to try to find a route down to these enticing plains. Juan de San Martín spent forty days clambering down rocky defiles, past plunging rivers, down into the barren lands of a tribe so primitive that it ate only crushed ants. He failed to find a passage. So also did another determined expedition sent by Quesada the following year. The plains remained a mirage that tantalized Jiménez de Quesada. He did not realize that he was looking out over the *llanos*, those same plains whose drought or floods were tormenting Hohermuth and Federmann.

It was inevitable that the conquerors would learn about the powerful Zaque of Tunja. Once they heard about his wealth they moved fast, determined not to be deprived of this loot. One group crossed a pass so cold that one officer was frozen so numb that he did not feel his clothes on fire from the camp fire. The Zaque tried to assemble levies to resist, but the speed of the Spanish advance took him by surprise. As the flying column approached Tunja expecting a battle, it was met by an embassy of aged dignitaries. The old men brought presents and invited Quesada to camp in a nearby village. He suspected that this was a delaying tactic to give time for the Zaque to escape and hide his treasure. So, as night was falling on 20 August, the Spaniards swept towards the palace compound of Tunja. Some officers advised caution 'since it was already late and because he was a great lord. In the end they proceeded forward. It was amazing to see the innumerable warriors they encountered, for [the Indians] were off guard and the roads were full of men going towards the principal town where Tunja resided.' The Spanish commander ordered his men to ignore their flanks and fight only forwards. They thrust along the road like a column of tanks.

At the gate of the Zaque's palace, Jiménez de Quesada was asked to dismount and enter to meet the ruler. He complied, advancing into the palace with only ten arquebusiers and crossbowmen. 'The palace was large and, apart from the main gate it had many doors through which many Indians were entering—so many that the General ordered his men to allow no more to enter. So he went in with six men to where Tunja was.' Quesada confronted the aged chief and delivered a version of the Requirement, that arrogant and incomprehensible statement about the supremacy of the King of Spain and the church of Rome. The Zaque of Tunja invited the strangers to lodge in a corner of his palace. Jiménez de Quesada then went out, leaving some men to observe what happened in the palace, richly adorned with intricate cotton mantles, plumes and gold patens. 'All the Indians were so agitated that it was suspected that some outbreak might occur.' Night had now fallen. At one point a fat native official called Qhimuinchatecha managed to shut the compound gate, so that the ruler and his treasure could be removed by another exit. The Indians tried to evict the soldiers left by Quesada. Captain Antón de Olaya galloped up and cut the ropes of the gate with his sword, so that the horsemen could charge into the compound. Olaya rushed into the main building, past a shouting throng, and grabbed the Zaque by the arm to arrest him. There was confused fighting in the darkness. Spanish horsemen patrolled the compound throughout the night. The Muisca failed to re-enter, 'leaving their lord inside, a prisoner in the General's power; and the Spaniards camped inside the palace itself.' As dawn appeared over the crests of the Andes, many Indians attacked, but in vain. The jubilant conquistadores were able to ransack the Zaque's chambers. They threw his precious objects into a courtyard until they formed a pile the height of a mounted horseman. There were patens, figurines, bracelets, breastplates, eagles, diadems and a great golden funerary urn shaped like a lantern. The booty amounted to 136,500 pesos (621 kilos) of fine gold, 14,000 pesos of base gold, and 280 emeralds.

The Muisca or Chibcha are famous for their gold. In a sense this is correct, for pre-conquest Colombian goldsmiths were brilliant by any standards. Judged by the tiny fraction of their work that has survived, they produced masterpieces. They had evolved almost all the known metallurgical techniques, and they carried them to perfection. They melted metal in moulds of refractory clay; and they frequently used the lost-wax process, in which figures were shaped out of wax which was melted away to leave a cavity for the molten metal. They were skilled at hammering, embossing and engraving. They understood annealing, tempering, soldering with gold, and gilding.

One of the most exciting recent discoveries, from examination of objects in Bogotá's famous Gold Museum, is that some pieces were shaped from cold metallic gold. Precipitated gold was reduced from an auriferous solution, to form fine granules or simple crystals. Gold in this state, mixed with a glutinous substance, could be worked when damp almost like clay. It could be moulded directly by hand, pushed into moulds or worked with spatulas. Once dry, it became hard enough to be heated and thus given the appearance of cast gold. This amazing technique baffled modern observers, who could not explain apparent finger marks on Colombian gold objects. The Quimbaya of the upper Cauca valley were particularly skilled in this technique. It explains the marvellously fluid curves of the waists, shoulders and buttocks of their most delicate figures.

But among the various peoples and districts of Colombia that worked gold, the Muisca were not outstanding. The Quimbaya and Calima of the upper Cauca, Sinú of the hills south of Cartagena, and Tairona of the Sierra Nevada de Santa Marta all produced finer golden objects than the Muisca. Spanish conquistadores in other parts of Colombia were discovering some of these treasures, for, unlike the Muisca, other tribes buried gold objects with their dead. When Captain Francisco César from Cartagena explored the middle Cauca valley, the Indians showed him a temple. 'Digging in a certain place they found a vault, very well built and with its opening to the east. In it were many pitchers full of jewellery of very fine gold, all of it of 20 or 21 carats. It amounted to over forty thousand ducats.' He was told that many other tombs existed in that valley, and the Spaniards found a series of wonderfully rich tombs in Sinú. Pedro de Cieza de León, who marched across western Colombia a few years after Quesada's conquest of the Muisca, said that there were gold mines and gold-rich streams in the mountain of Buriticá near Ancerma and at Corome near Antioquia on the middle Cauca. 'It is a fact that from this mountain came most of the riches that were found in the great tombs sacked in Sinú. I myself saw very rich burials sacked . . .' Near Ancerma, chief Cauroma had many idols 'which looked like wood but were made of the finest gold. They confirm that there was a great abundance of this metal: that chief obtained as much as he wanted from a river.' And when Cieza de León's expedition moved south to Arma, he found its people 'marvellously rich in gold . . . When we first entered this province with Captain Jorge Robledo, I recall Indians coming armed from head to foot in gold . . .' Could this be the land of Benalcázar's *indio dorado*, twelve days' march from Quito? The geographical location tallies, and it would be logical to describe a man wearing such armour as a 'golden Indian'.

Cieza de León tried to justify the tomb robbing: he lamented that 'great treasures have been lost [to us] in these parts. Had we Spaniards not taken what has been found, it would certainly all have been offered to the devil and to their temples and burials. For these Indians do not want it or seek it for any other purpose. They do not pay wages to their fighting men with it nor trade in cities and kingdoms. They want it only to deck themselves when alive and to take with them after death.' Spanish theologians had greater scruples about sacking tombs. The royal attitude was ambivalent, if not downright hypocritical. A royal decree worried that tomb robbing was contrary to Christian morality, since biblical kings had buried treasure in their tombs and it was still normal for gold coins to be placed in graves in Spain. Desecration of tombs also violated the rights of the descendants of the dead. It was therefore declared to be mortal sin to rob any tomb, however old. On the other hand, the royal tax on loot taken from tombs was raised to half, compared to the fifth required of treasure stolen from living Indians. If there was to be mortal sin, the tax man wanted his share of the proceeds.

The problem for the Muisca was that they had no source of gold. They had to acquire raw gold from neighbouring tribes by trading their salt or cotton cloth for it. Possibly because gold was rare on the Muisca highlands, it was buried less lavishly with the dead. Muisca goldsmiths made the greatest possible effect with the metal: they tended to beat it out into thin plates or shape it into flat figures. A favourite Muisca piece was a *tunjo*, a flat triangular human figure, broad at the shoulders and tapering at the feet, with details of limbs, facial features and ornament depicted by wire-thin rolls of gold. It looks as though these features were a form of filigree or were soldered on to the triangular base. But the entire objects were in fact made by the lost-wax process, with the limbs shaped of thin rolls of wax before the molten gold was poured into the mould. Surviving Muisca gold thus compares unfavourably with the masterpieces from other parts of Colombia. But we must remember that most Muisca gold objects were easily available on the surface and thus fell into the conquistadores' hands. Everything acquired by the Spaniards was melted down, with complete disregard to artistic value.

Golden objects from other cultures, that are now the glory of Colombian museums, came from tombs that escaped the frenzied searches of the first conquistadores. The intensity of those searches emerges from contemporary complaints about appalling tortures inflicted on chiefs suspected of knowing the location of tombs. A report of 1560 complained that 'there are great robberies, looting the sanctuaries and the tombs of their ancestors from the Indians. This is so common that there are many men who live from nothing else.' Indians became aware of the Spaniards' mad lust for gold: the last thing they wanted was for gold deposits to be discovered near their homes. 'The Indians refuse to reveal [gold mines]. Indeed, if they learn that one of them is about to say where these are . . . the others kill him with some poison. For they say that if [mines] are revealed they will all perish by being forced to work in them, just as all Indians are finished in any places where [mines] do exist.'

Jiménez de Quesada's men spent a few days at Tunja, digesting the treasure they had looted from its palace and receiving tribute from neighbouring chieftains. Then someone told them about another wealthy ruler, the Sugamuxi (Sogamoso) of Iraca, a town a few days' march north-east of Tunja. This Sugamuxi was also the spiritual leader of the Muisca, custodian of their most holy temple. So, like burglars hurrying to grab valuables, Quesada pushed northwards with twenty horsemen and thirty footsoldiers. They advanced by forced marches, worried that some treasure would be hidden if they delayed. On the first night they reached the plain of Paipa, a chief who tried to appease the invaders with presents but whose town was invaded none the less. The men of Tundama tried to stop the Spaniards by crushing them with boulders rolled from hilltops. Advancing along the Chiticuy river, Quesada's men entered the broad, fertile plain of Iraca. A determined resistance was easily defeated on that open plain, a perfect place for cavalry manoeuvre. So the conquistadores pressed on to capture the magnificent holy city of Sugamuxi, 'the Rome of the Chibchas'.

The Indians managed to remove many treasures during the night, but they left the temple of Sugamuxi intact. They imagined that the invading demi-gods would respect the sanctuary of the god Remichinchaguai A naive hope: the Christians could hardly wait to ransack this rival holy place. Two soldiers called Sánchez and Rodríguez were so eager that they went to look at the temple that very night. They contemplated its great treasures in the flickering light of straw torches. They saw thick plates of gold cladding on its great columns of guaiacum wood brought up from tropical valleys. There were mummies of famous warriors, suspended from barbacoa platforms and decked in golden regalia. The temple's floor was covered in matting of white esparto grass. The two soldiers could not wait until morning. They immediately started to dismantle the gold of Sugamuxi, resting their torches on the floor to do so. The result was as predictable as it was tragic: a conflagration that quickly spread from the matting to the walls and soon engulfed the entire temple, despite Spanish efforts to extinguish it. Castellanos said that the sanctuary of Sugamuxi burned for five days. Despite the fire, two officers who were royal officials wrote that forty thousand pesos of fine gold were found 'hanging in some shrines' at Sogamoso. Nicolaus Federmann felt that this temple represented the 'house of Meta' that so many explorers had sought in vain on the *llanos*. He reported that the temple of Sugamuxi 'no longer has any saints [effigies] because the men from Santa Marta carried them off in sacks', while Jiménez de Quesada's own comment was that, by stealing the treasures of 'the sanctuaries and houses of prayer in the town, our men learned how devout the people of that land were in their idolatries.' The chief of Sugamuxi, with his temple destroyed and his palace sacked, accepted Christian baptism with the name Alonso.

The invading force returned to Tunja with its loot. Their successes at Tunja and Sugamuxi made them realize what an opportunity they had missed in failing to capture the Zipa of Bogotá. The most powerful and richest of all the Muisca rulers had escaped with all his treasures. It was tantalizing for such successful invaders to have missed such a prize. Jiménez de Quesada said ruefully: 'He has put his gold and treasure in some safe place and not with himself, so that it has not appeared up to the present; and it is said to consist of innumerable riches!'

The Spanish general decided to return to Bogotá by forced marches, hoping to take the Zipa Tisquesusa by surprise. He took a fast contingent, mostly horsemen. But the Muisca had an efficient system of early warning of attacks from Tunja: the Zipa learned by smoke signals of the Spaniards' approach, and went to hide in a mountain stronghold. Efforts to communicate with the Zipa were again rebuffed. There was constant but ineffectual skirmishing against the invaders. Quesada finally learned from captured Indians the location of the Muisca ruler's retreat. A night raid was immediately organized and the horsemen covered the four leagues to the fort or pleasure house in a few hours. They attacked at once, in darkness. 'Since it was not yet daylight [they failed] to recognize the Bogotá or lord of the Indians. They climbed a stockade to attack the hill. This caused the Bogotá to emerge with others fleeing from the house. He was later found on the hill, dead from two wounds. It is believed that, since he was heavy and elderly, they wounded him as he jumped from that stockade.' Two Spanish officers said that he was killed by mistake among the fugitives 'because he was not recognized. They even say that he was wearing worse clothes than the rest. But at that time we did not know of his death; for he went off to die on a hill without our knowing or seeing him.' Such was the conquistadores' incompetence: within a few weeks of accidentally burning down the Muiscas' main temple, they inadvertently killed their most powerful ruler.

The Bogotá treasure remained an obsession. Although Quesada withdrew to Tunja and other raids, he returned to Bogotá and the Valley of the Castles in 1538. The natives were overcome by the murder of their Zipa, on top of all the bewildering and terrible disasters that had suddenly struck their land. They chose a chief called Sagipa to succeed as Zipa of Bogotá, and rallied a force to resist from the mountains. Other chiefs tried to accommodate with the Europeans. Jiménez de Quesada held an assembly of friendly chiefs and was delighted to find that one of them, the lord of Chía, claimed that he was the rightful heir of his uncle the dead Zipa. Various expeditions were sent to try to capture Sagipa. He eluded them; but there were evidently anxious debates in the Indian camp. Sagipa was finally persuaded to try to reach an understanding with the small force of invaders, and to enlist these brilliant warriors against the Muiscas' traditional enemies. To the surprise of the Spaniards, Sagipa suddenly emerged to parley with Jiménez de Quesada. The Spanish general readily agreed to a request to organize an expedition against the fierce forest-dwelling Panches—a venture that involved the Spaniards in difficult fighting, with heavier losses from Panche arrows than from all the weapons of the Muisca.

Back from the successful Panche campaign, in late 1538, Quesada decided to interrogate Sagipa about the missing treasure. Sagipa said that he had never had it: the old Bogotá must have buried it somewhere. Jiménez de Quesada was a lawyer, and he decided to stage a 'trial' of the Muisca chief. Gonzalo de Inzá was appointed as prosecutor, the general's brother Hernán Pérez de Quesada as defender, and Jiménez de Quesada himself acted as judge. This tragic farce was recorded by the legalistic conquistadores and the document, although damaged, has survived in the Archive of the Indies in Seville. Sagipa was formally accused of having 'rebelled' against the Spaniards and of concealing the treasures of the dead Bogotá. Through interpreters, he protested that 'he had none of the gold or jewels of that Bogotá: what he had was maize and manioc, and he knew nothing of the gold of Bogotá or of the many other things demanded of him.' This defence failed. Jiménez de Quesada delivered sentence: 'I condemn the said Sagipa to a session of torture . . .' Because they were far from home and without other means of torture, Sagipa was condemned to a rope torment: his hands were tied behind his back with a vine and he was lifted up by them from a beam. Released from this painful ordeal, Sagipa promised to produce some gold.

Some greedy Spaniards suggested that they might ransom Sagipa in the way that Pizarro had done to Atahualpa five years before in Peru. Sagipa rashly agreed. According to Gil López, he told Quesada 'that he would give him a hut full of gold within twenty days, and that he would give them [the gold objects] tied in an agave [sisal] rope—the Licentiate [Jiménez de Quesada] should send one of his officers every day to cut one. If, when these [days] were over he had not given the hut full of gold, they should kill him and cut off his head.' The chief did persuade his lords to bring much gold, although it was not Bogotá's treasure; but he failed to fill the promised hut. His chiefs also brought rare feathers, ornate mantles and other objects valued by the Muisca, and Sagipa said 'that he considered these as gold, and therefore they should not kill him.' There was another session of the 'rope torture'. Sagipa bought release by saying that he would try to find Bogotá's treasure. He was hurried off, guarded by an escort under Captains San Martín and Suárez, to the mountain retreat where the Zipa had been killed. Sagipa indicated a likely place to dig; but nothing was found. The conquistadores were very angry. 'Since Sagipa had lied to them and made them dig where there was nothing, the footsoldiers and horsemen, seeing themselves tricked and because he had caused them so many days and months of effort, took him and gave him two or three very severe tortures.' 'They threw the Indian on to his back and put burning fat on his belly. They struck a shackle on to each foot . . . and thus put fire to his feet . . .' 'They repeatedly scored the soles of his feet, applying large quantities of fire so that, because of those tortures, his feet immediately turned, as if fallen. They also gave him other forms of torture, two or three times; so that, a few days later, after they had brought him back to the camp, he died.' This was another blunder.

OPPOSITE ABOVE Conical thatch huts of the Kogi (Arauaco), in the Sierra Nevada de Santa Marta, have creast combs similar to the places of the Muisca.

OPPOSITE BELOW A Cuiva hunter resting in the long grasses of the Colombian llanos.

OVERLEAF LEFT Yanomani or Waika Indians of the Parima hills on the border between Brazil and Venezuela. (Above) A child carries her baby brother in a head band, and (below) a mother decorates herself with feathers glued to her hair, quills in her lips and nose, and parrot feathers in her ears.

OVERLEAF RIGHT Indian body painting may have inspired the legend of El Dorado, the Golden Man. The most common vegetable dye are red annatto and black genipap (Top left) A Yanomani mother has decorated her face, (top right) Kamayura men anoint one another for wrestling, (below left) Yanomani archers from the Parima hills, a region approached by Philip von Hutten in 1543–44, and (below right) Kogi of the Sierra Nevada de Santa Marta wear traditional cotton mantles and use gourds full of lime for chewing coca.

Jiménez de Quesada was lawyer enough to realize that the King of Spain would not approve of his men torturing to death a fellow monarch. The divine right of kings was jeopardized and Catholic moral values were offended by such conduct. Quesada therefore promptly organized an inquiry, the purpose of which was to establish that *his* torture had not killed Sagipa. Witnesses declared under oath that the rope torture 'was a very trivial affair from which he could not have received [permanent] physical detriment or damage, certainly not enough to die from it . . .' Jiménez de Quesada later claimed that his rope torture was given 'so mildly that even a child of five or six could not have died or been maimed by it'.

The conquerors spent the last month of 1537 and the year 1538 in various expeditions. There was a serious battle against the warriors of Duitama, near Sogamoso, who assembled a force of twelve thousand men and prepared pit traps for the Spanish horses. Oviedo said that this group fought better than the men of Bogotá or Tunja, and they used long lances that were effective against cavalry. At one moment Quesada himself was hit on the thigh, knocked from his horse, and just rescued from the mêlée by the lance thrusts of a horseman called Baltasar Maldonado. But the invaders were victorious again. There were excursions to the Sáchica and Zaquencipá valleys, each of which yielded more gold. There was treasure from the lagoon now called Tota.

Someone said that the Muisca obtained their gold by trading with the people of the Neiva valley, far to the south along the line of the Andes. Jiménez de Quesada decided to investigate. From Tunja and Suesca he marched south to Pasca and the desolate moors of Sumapaz. He probably crossed the Sumapaz river by a spectacular natural bridge of rock. His force then descended into the upper Magdalena valley, to the fertile region of Neiva, not far from the site of the earlier culture that produced the famous monolithic sculptures now called San Agustín. Although Neiva *did* produce alluvial gold dust, the Spaniards found little. They were disappointed by Neiva and called the place the Valley of Sorrows. By mid-February 1538 the men from this sortie were back with their comrades at Bogotá.

Then, in June 1538, came the moment of which every adventurer dreamed: the melting down and division of the expedition's booty. Here again, the legal documents have survived. They give a fascinating insight into the way a group of would-be conquerors organized their venture. The conquest was clearly a common enterprise, with no prior contract and few formal preconditions defining the men's relationships to one another. The first step was to compare the records of treasure kept by Quesada and by the royal officials. All the conquistadores were then searched for hidden gold or jewels. The next stage was to identify and pay common debts, for medicines, trade goods, or horses killed during the final part of the conquest. The army was then divided into three parts: captains (or officers), horsemen, and soldiers. Each part named its assessor: respectively Juan de San Martín for the captains, Baltasar Maldonado for the cavalry, and Juan Valenciano for the footsoldiers. These men placed values on such things as the surgeon's salary, medicine, lead, crossbow cord, axes, mattocks, whetstones, nails, sandals, etc. A trifling 200 pesos was set aside for alms in the two churches of Santa Marta, to provide masses for the souls of five hundred men who died during the first months of the expedition.

There were two types of Muisca *tunjo*: flat triangular figures, or small rounded figures whose arms and legs may have clasped offerings. Heights generally 5–10 cm.

Next day, the three royal officials (three of the most prominent captains) presented the booty to Jiménez de Quesada. The royal fifth was formally extracted from both the gold and the emeralds. This tax amounted to 38,259 pesos (175 kilos) of fine gold, 7,257 pesos of base 9-carat gold, 3,690 pesos of the copper-gold alloy tumbaga, and 363 emeralds. Some gold was reserved for premiums to reward outstanding valour. But it was decided to omit completely the men left with the boats at La Tora on the Magdalena river, and the heirs of the hundreds of men who had died on the expedition. The treasure was then divided into 289 'parts'. These were assigned as follows: 10 parts to the governor of Santa Marta; 9 to Jiménez de Quesada; 4 to each captain; 3 to the sergeant major; 2 or 3 to each lieutenant or subaltern; 2 parts to each cavalryman or clergyman; 1½ parts to arquebusiers and crossbowmen; 1 part to ordinary swordsmen or soldiers. A 'part' was calculated as 510 pesos (2.320 kilos) of fine gold, 57 pesos (260 grams) of base gold, and five emeralds. Such was the reward of the tiny handful of adventurers who conquered an American eldorado.

Most conquistadores were ignorant, uneducated men. Only the most ambitious, foolhardy or romantic optimists crossed the Atlantic for the American adventure. In their wild gold-rush camps, so remote from any stabilizing influences of wives or families, rumours and fantasies could flourish until, by repetition and wishful thinking, they gained the stature of accepted truths. Who was to say that anything was impossible? These desperadoes had already made discoveries and conquests beyond the dreams of their fathers. They were in a new hemisphere where every plant, animal and insect was novel. They had already found and conquered the realms of the Aztecs, Maya, Inca and Muisca. Nothing in history has equalled the sheer tonnage of gold, silver and jewels looted from these civilizations and sent off to disrupt the economies of Europe. It seemed reasonable to seek the exotic creatures of classical or medieval legend in a continent that had already produced armadillos, tapirs, three-toed sloths, manatees, peccaries, llamas and other strange beasts.

One of the most persistent fantasies was that Amazons (whose home in the classical legend was near the Black Sea) would be found in the Americas. In his Journal entry for 16 January 1493, Columbus had spoken of the island of Martinino, south-east of Española, where women lived without men, importing men at certain times of year for procreation, and keeping only daughters. In his letter to the King of 15 October 1524, Cortés had the same notion about a tribe of women living in the Colima region south of Panama. In 1536, when Jerónimo Dortal was marching towards the Orinoco, he visited a chieftainess called Orocomay 'who was a great friend of the Christians: she was served only by women, and there were no men in her town or society, apart from those whom she summoned to fulfil some command or to send into battle.' A year later Hohermuth and Philip von Hutten heard rumours of Amazons living on the Papamene river deep in the Colombian *llanos*. In 1538 Jiménez de Quesada's men had the same idea. 'When the camp was in the valley of Bogotá, we had news of a tribe of women who live on their own with no Indian men living among them; because of which we called them Amazons. Those who told us about them said that these women become pregnant from certain slaves whom they purchase. If they give birth to a

The monolithic sculptures of San Agustín, near Timaná on the upper Magdalena, date from about a thousand years before the Conquest. An owl catching a snake (above) —reminiscent of the symbol of the Aztecs and of modern Mexico.

son they send him to his father; but if it is a daughter they rear her to augment their republic. . . . And they were very rich in gold . . . of the same gold of this land or that of Tunja.' The Amazons' queen was called Jarativa. The Spanish general therefore sent his brother Hernán Pérez de Quesada off to conquer these rich ladies. He failed, because the route was across thickly forested hills; but he believed that he had come to within a few days' march of their territory. He returned to the camp at Bogotá on 12 May 1538.

Two other persistent rumours were about the elusive kingdom of Meta, and about a House of the Sun, a sun temple like the fabulous Coricancha in the Inca capital Cuzco. Towards the end of 1538, Jiménez de Quesada started home, to descend to La Tora, the Magdalena river and return to Santa Marta. He then heard about 'a province, on the slopes of the llanos to which [his men] had failed to emerge, which is called Menza [Meta?]. The Indians say that in that province there is a very rich people and that they have a house dedicated to the sun . . . and that they keep in it an infinite quantity of gold and jewels, and live in stone houses, go about dressed and booted, and fight with lances and maces.' This report sounded so interesting that Quesada decided to return to Bogotá and then investigate. There were men in Quesada's camp who had been involved in the Orinoco expeditions—which could explain why this Menza sounded so like the Meta that had been sought in the same area.

New fantasies were taking shape among the conquistadores in Quito, 750 kilometres south-west of Bogotá along the line of the Andes. During and after his march on Quito, Sebastián de Benalcázar had sent captains to round up the remaining Inca generals. On one of these sorties, the Spaniards captured a chief they called the *indio dorado*, who evidently came from the gold-rich tribes of southern Colombia. He indicated that his homeland lay twelve days' march to the north. He may well have referred to the lands of the Calima and Quimbaya, on the upper Cauca river—the region that has produced the most magnificent specimens in modern Colombian gold museums. The capture of this Indian caused no great excitement. Benalcázar sent some reconnaissance expeditions to the north. But it was not until 1536, after various campaigns in other parts of what is now Ecuador, that he himself marched north. He founded Spanish municipalities at Popayán and Cali, close to the Calima region; but by mid-1537 Benalcázar was back in Quito.

Francisco Pizarro, the conqueror and governor of Peru, had always been suspicious of Benalcázar, his lieutenant who had conquered Quito without orders. It appears that Benalcázar was saved only by the patronage of Gaspar de Espinosa, the rich governor of Panama who had also financed Pizarro's own expeditions. Pizarro was angry with Benalcázar for his unauthorized venture into southern Colombia, and sent an officer called Pedro de Puelles to replace him as lieutenant-governor in Quito. When Benalcázar returned in 1537 he had to hurry south to Peru, where he was reconfirmed in his Quito post thanks to the intervention of his protector Espinosa.

Back in Quito, Benalcázar started planning a long expedition into the Quillasinga region around Popayán. The plan was very unpopular among the conquistadores who had started to settle at Quito: they feared that Benalcázar would remove hundreds of Indians who were serving them. There was near mutiny in the town council, which consisted of the leading conquistadores. The mayor of Quito, Gonzalo Díaz de Pineda, was sent off to complain to Pizarro. At this time, in August 1537, Benalcázar's protector Espinosa died after an illness while visiting Peru. Pizarro again decided that Benalcázar had led too many unofficial ventures. In January 1538 he named Díaz de Pineda as lieutenant-governor in place of Benalcázar; a few weeks later, the new appointee was marching north armed with an order to arrest Benalcázar and send him back to Peru. Benalcázar apparently learned about this warrant. In March 1538 he hurriedly marched north from Quito, taking his supporters and even some men, such as Pedro de Puelles, who were pressed on to his expedition against their will.

Benalcázar must have been bitter about the reversal in his fortunes. He was deprived of Quito, and he now knew that the King had awarded the region he had penetrated in southern Colombia to Gaspar de Espinosa. Following Espinosa's death, Pizarro was also claiming that this area lay within his jurisdiction. Thus, despite his conquests, Benalcázar had no administrative title of his own, and he was running from an arrest warrant by Francisco Pizarro. He decided to round up the men he had left in Popayán and Cali, and strike out with them to the east. 'Learning that Licentiate Espinosa was Governor of that northern territory [of Popayán, Benalcázar] depopulated it . . . and went from there towards [the east].'

When Benalcázar reached Popayán, in May 1538 according to Castellanos, he found the settlement threatened by attack from tribes in the hills to the east. It seemed appropriate to march against them, since this was the direction in which he hoped to find rich lands. Benalcázar had in his force a number of veterans from the Orinoco expeditions and these would have told him Ordás' and Dortal's theories about the land of Meta. When he had been in Peru he met Captain Juan de Alderete, the firebrand who led the mutiny against Dortal and whom Federmann had refused to take on his expedition into the *llanos*: Alderete evidently told Benalcázar about Federmann's and Jiménez de Quesada's ventures into the interior, for Benalcázar exhorted his men: ' "We are fit, and our band is well equipped with swift and spirited horses. Let us go to investigate these riches before some who are coming on their trail snatch them from our hands! For, as you know, explorations and searches are under way by many other groups." '

Benalcázar therefore plunged into the wild hills of the Cordillera Central, climbing into the uplands of Puracé, with their volcanoes, sulphur deposits, and primeval coniferous forests. It proved to be a tough expedition. The tribes fought fiercely and effectively. In a testimony the following year, Benalcázar said that his expedition travelled for eight months, crossing snowy mountains and continually meeting native tribes. One of his horsemen, Cristóbal de Segovia, recalled that at one time 'the men being in a state of great weakness from hunger', he and thirty other men had gone foraging for food but had been routed, 'in consequence of which the expedition endured much suffering'. Pedro de Puelles said that they left Popayán to explore 'snowy mountains and some forests, [a land] of bad trails and bad Indians'.

When, after four months of 'continual misfortune . . . amid obscure woods, dense undergrowth, volcanic land, and marshes', they emerged into the open valley of the upper Magdalena, it seemed like paradise. In their excitement, some called it 'another Mexico'. They were near Neiva, and they found some of the gold dust that the local tribes traded with the Muisca. To their dismay, they also came upon 'traces of horses and Christians'—the tracks of Jiménez de Quesada's reconnaissance to Neiva earlier that year. Having no interpreter, Benalcázar could not ask about the Europeans who had left these tracks. He sent a captain to follow them, but this man returned after doing so for twenty leagues. Benalcázar correctly surmised that they were the tracks of Jiménez de Quesada's men from Santa Marta.

The Quitan expedition then moved northwards, marching down the Magdalena valley. There is no hint in any of their movements that they were aiming for Bogotá. From Popayán they had gone eastwards; and although they now turned north, they started along the eastern bank of the Magdalena but then, after eighty leagues, they *crossed* back to the left or west bank and continued down river for a further seventy leagues. They entered the territory of the formidable Pijaos, a tribe that later resisted Spanish occupation with great determination. Pedro de Puelles said that they came to 'mountain slopes with tiny villages and bad, poor people [armed] with much poison, where our men were being killed every day'. So Benalcázar went off 'to find a route to cross the snowy mountains to return to Popayán and Cali', leaving Puelles with the rearguard in the Magdalena valley. They had given up and were looking for a route back. This was hardly the behaviour of an expedition aware of the wealth of the Muisca or searching for some eldorado.

At this juncture, one of Jiménez de Quesada's captains called Lázaro Fonte was south of Bogotá in the land of a Mosca chief called Pasca. The Indians told him that there were Christians in the Magdalena valley, and they drew pictures of the horses and pigs brought by Benalcázar's men. Fonte returned to tell Quesada, who sent his brother Hernán Pérez de Quesada to investigate. He took a dozen men, descended the forests to the Magdalena, crossed the river, and cautiously approached the Spanish camp. Such was the suspicion between rival Spanish commanders that Hernán Pérez de Quesada actually laid an ambush to capture some unsuspecting Spaniards. Two men were caught, while fishing, and brought to tell Hernán Pérez about their expedition and its leader. They explained that 'the route they were taking was to explore towards the North Sea [Caribbean]' and Quesada's brother told them that they would have terrible difficulty trying to descend the Magdalena. Benalcázar himself was summoned next day, and there was an amicable meeting between the two expeditions. The men from Quito were amazed to see those from Santa Marta dressed in Muisca clothes, for 'apart from the horses and their own persons, swords and lance heads, they could no longer claim to carry or possess anything from Spain.' Benalcázar sent some men back up the river to 'found' municipalities at Neiva and Timaná in order to stake a claim to the region in which he had seen the gold dust. A week later, he crossed the Magdalena and started up towards Bogotá, to meet Gonzalo Jiménez de Quesada.

This was amazing news for the conquerors of the Muisca. They were wondering whether they could keep control of their prize against another better-armed expedition. Then came more alarming news. 'We learned that, from the direction of the plains to which we had been unable to emerge—which is towards the sun rise—other Christians were coming, and that there were many of them, with many horses! We were considerably amazed by this and could not think who it could be.' The Indians said that the strange force was only six leagues away, in the lands of Pasca. It turned out to be Nicolaus Federmann's expedition from Venezuela: the men who had entered the *llanos* at the end of 1536 and had failed to meet Hohermuth's returning survivors.

After the rains, at the end of 1538, Federmann had pushed south from the Meta to the future site of San Juan de los Llanos. It was here that the Guayupa Indians finally persuaded him that, if he wanted gold, he must strike up into the Andes. With characteristic efficiency Federmann had brought the parts of a forge on his expedition: these were now assembled at San Juan, to repair tools, machetes and horseshoes for the journey ahead. Advancing into the foothills, Federmann captured a stockaded village of Operigua Indians. But while he was gone his expedition's porters managed to escape. Captains were sent out in three directions to try to capture people to replace these, and they duly returned 'well provided with natives'. Pedro de Limpias surprised a village on the Ariari river when its men were away fishing: he had to content himself with the women and older children whom 'he strung together in his neck shackles'. Back at the camp, all these victims were divided among the men of the expedition to carry their loads.

Pedro de Limpias scouted ahead, up the Tegua river. He climbed into bleak uplands, sometimes having to hack a path for the horses. At times it was necessary to cut a path around rocks; and in places where this was too difficult, the horses had to be hauled up obstacles in rope slings. In one defile a tribe set fire to the grass, and flames swept down on the Spanish column. The horses could not be turned or unloaded in time. Limpias lit a counter-fire, which checked the danger to the horses. But 'this fire burned many of the Indian porters with the loads and clothing they were carrying, as well as a sick Spaniard who was being carried in a litter: he was abandoned by those carrying him, to save their lives, and was roasted there.' Another Spaniard called Bibanco was too frightened to jump through the line of flames, and fell to his death. There is no record of how many shackled Indians were burned to death.

Federmann recalled that the worst part of the journey came high in the Cordillera. It took twenty-two days to cross 'an extremely cold, uninhabited moor, so bad that sixteen horses died of pure cold, frozen to death'. This bleak mountain is still called 'Fredreman' in garbled honour of the German conquistador. They reached Fosca in the territory of the Mosca Indians and then moved to Pasca, a few miles from Bogotá. Messengers were exchanged with Jiménez de Quesada's men, who described the Venezuelans as 'wearied and exhausted by much travel and bad country, and also from some uninhabited moors and frozen wastes they had crossed, so that with a little more hardship they might all have died. In our camp they found all the welcome, and the food and clothing they needed to restore themselves . . .'

Suddenly, in February 1539, there were three expeditions camped in a triangle, a few miles from one another, in the homeland of the Muisca. It was a celebrated meeting, a famous moment in South American exploration. Quesada's officers

94

exclaimed: 'We considered it a great marvel for men from three governorships—from Peru and Venezuela and Santa Marta—to join up in a place so remote from the sea!' They referred, of course, to Benalcázar (from Pizarro's Peru), Federmann (from Hohermuth's Venezuela), and Jiménez de Quesada (from Fernández de Lugo's Santa Marta).

Jiménez de Quesada needed all his skills as a lawyer and diplomat. His ragged veterans were heavily outnumbered by the new arrivals. Each of the other expeditions was better armed and had more horses; each had endured great hardships to reach Bogotá; each was led by an ambitious lieutenant-governor; and each thought that, on geographical grounds, the rich lands of the Muisca lay within its governor's jurisdiction.

Quesada shrewdly decided to win over Federmann's men first, since they were exhausted and without gold. They contained some men originally from Santa Marta; and some of them were xenophobically hostile to their German leader. On 7 March 1539 a pact was signed between Jiménez de Quesada and Federmann. The two leaders agreed to travel together to Spain and to accept arbitration by the Council of the Indies. Federmann agreed to sell his equipment, including some cocks and hens he had brought from Spain. His men would remain in the Muisca lands, where they would settle as colonists. He himself accepted a rich encomienda —a grant of the Indian subjects to a native chief, who would henceforth be obliged to work for and pay tribute to the Spanish holder of the encomienda. A few days later, Jiménez de Quesada reached a similar agreement with Benalcázar. The conquistador from Quito agreed to sell his horses and pigs to the Muisca colonists. Some thirty of his men would remain as settlers, but the rest would return to colonize the new towns he had founded in other parts of Colombia. Benalcázar also agreed to travel to Spain with the two other leaders, and to accept royal arbitration. Jiménez de Quesada thus skilfully avoided any junction between the two new arrivals, so that their men could not unite to evict his from their conquest.

The three conquistadores moved down to the Magdalena valley, built boats and sailed downstream—at one point shooting the Honda rapids that caught them by surprise. In June 1539 they reached Cartagena and prepared to sail to Spain. A local official seized this opportunity to interrogate the three great explorers and some of their leading officers. He asked them about the wealth and fighting qualities of the Muisca and neighbouring tribes. The three explorers testified under oath, and their fascinating statements have survived. Each leader made the geographical case whereby he claimed that the Muisca lay within his governor's jurisdiction. Jiménez de Quesada argued that it was his by right of prior discovery and because the Magdalena river was its easiest access to the sea. Benalcázar maintained that, by keeping to the unforested mountains, it was easier to reach the Pacific across his lands. And Federmann claimed (wrongly) that Bogotá lay south of Lake Maracaibo and therefore within Venezuela.

The three generals sailed for Spain with high hopes. Each was ambitious for royal rewards and the governorship of his territory. Fernández de Oviedo, who hated Federmann, wrote sarcastically: 'Nicolaus Federmann believed that he would be made governor of Venezuela, just as Georg Hohermuth had been, by the

German Welser Company—as a reward for having left many Spaniards and many more Indians dead!' Instead, he found himself facing legal action by the Welser, who imagined that he had enriched himself at their expense. Fernández de Oviedo gloated: 'If justice is done, the legal action will have a very different outcome to that imagined by this captain. In truth, he was never esteemed here as a man faithful to his masters; . . . and he was even rumoured to be a Lutheran!' The Welser attack on Federmann brought a tough response from the man who had marched so many miles and destroyed so many natives. Wronged and bitter, Federmann launched a bogus counter claim that the Welser had defrauded the royal treasury. The legal wrangles moved from Flanders to Spain and dragged on through 1541. They ceased only with the sudden, unexpected death of Nicolaus Federmann, still only in his mid-thirties, in February 1542.

Gonzalo Jiménez de Quesada also returned to a cool reception. He had brought hundreds of emeralds for the King and an advance consignment of royal gold. But there was a moral climate at Court opposed to American conquests. The royal fiscal was also highly suspicious of all conquistadores, and of the rich Jiménez de Quesada in particular. So, instead of a hero's welcome and a grant of the vacant governorship of Santa Marta, the lawyer-conquistador found himself faced with an avalanche of law suits. Various members of his expedition who had been left on the Magdalena river sued him for a share of the Muisca treasure. The fiscal charged that Quesada had declared only a fraction of the amount due to the Crown. An interim governor of Santa Marta went up to Bogotá and launched a series of inquiries against both Quesada brothers. Jiménez de Quesada was accused of having caused the death of the ruler Sagipa with his tortures. (He had foreseen some such accusation and armed himself with testimonies to show that later tortures caused the death.) The conqueror of the Muisca defended himself for a time and then vanished, apparently going to France to find a better market for his emeralds. He returned to Spain in 1545 and faced his accusers. He defended himself with great determination and legal brilliance. Accusations and counter-accusations flew. Old soldiers were tracked down to testify for or against Quesada. In the end the conquistador triumphed. In 1547 the man who had faced ruinous fines and had bail fixed at 15,000 ducats, was fined a mere 50 ducats each on two counts, one of which was the torture of the Bogotá Sagipa. He was soon loaded with honours: the title of Marshal and of alderman and then mayor of the new town of Santafé de Bogotá. We shall meet him again later, for Jiménez de Quesada eventually returned to the scene of his early triumph and embarked on a last desperate expedition.

The only conquistador to have a good reception in Spain was Sebastián de Benalcázar. The conqueror of Quito had a useful audience with the King. He told Charles of his plans to lead a venture to find and extract the cinnamon that he believed lay in the forests of the Amazon. He was soon on his way back to South America, with a patent of governor, not of Bogotá but at least of Popayán, and a royal licence to market cinnamon.

A Muisca breastplate of a figure whose arms and body form a shape of fine simplicity and movement. Height 18 cm

6

THE LEGEND OF EL DORADO, THE GOLDEN MAN, WAS BORN IN QUITO AT THE BEGINNING of 1541. It was a beguiling story and it quickly caught the imagination of the conquistadores. It spread fast, gained momentum and credibility, and evolved in detail during the ensuing century. It became one of the most famous chimeras in history, a legend that lured hundreds of hard men into desperate expeditions. Such is the conclusion of the distinguished Venezuelan historian Demetrio Ramos Pérez, who traced the genesis of the legend through elaborate detective work in documentary and chronicle sources. His painstaking research led him to fix the time and place of the birth of the legend, and to conclude that it was entirely unconnected with the Muisca. If he is right, he refutes the accepted version, an attractive story told by the chroniclers within a few decades of Jiménez de Quesada's conquest.

What exactly was the legend? Fernández de Oviedo was surprised by it and, with his usual diligence, interrogated men who could advise him. 'I asked Spaniards who have been in Quito and have come here to Santo Domingo . . . why they call that prince the "Golden Chief or King". They tell me that what they have learned from the Indians is that that great lord or prince goes about continually covered in gold dust as fine as ground salt. He feels that it would be less beautiful to wear any other ornament. It would be crude and common to put on armour plates of hammered or stamped gold, for other rich lords wear these when they wish. But to powder oneself with gold is something exotic, unusual, novel and more costly—for he washes away at night what he puts on each morning, so that it is discarded and lost, and he does this every day of the year. With this custom, going about clothed and covered in that way, he has no impediment or hindrance.

In Oviedo's version of the El Dorado legend, a naked ruler was coated in powdered gold every morning.

OPPOSITE The Muisca, having no source of gold in their territory, flattened their figures to make the greatest effect with the precious metal.

South American Indians regularly paint their bodies with resins and vegetable dyes—a possible derivation of the gold applied to El Dorado. Men and women paint one another every few weeks, or on festive occasions, with red anatto or black genipapo dyes.

The fine proportions of his body and natural form, on which he prides himself, are not covered or obscured, for he wears no other clothing of any sort on top of it.' The chronicler marvelled at the thought of such waste: 'I would rather have the sweepings of the chamber of this prince than the great meltings of gold there have been in Peru or that there could be anywhere on earth! For the Indians say that this chief or king is a very rich and great ruler. He anoints himself every morning with a certain gum or resin that sticks very well. The powdered gold adheres to that unction . . . until his entire body is covered from the soles of his feet to his head. He looks as resplendent as a gold object worked by the hand of a great artist. I believe that, if that chief does do this, he must have very rich mines of fine quality gold. On the Mainland, I have in fact seen plenty of the gold that Spaniards call placer gold, in such quantities that he could easily do what is said.'

Fernández de Oviedo told this legend in the context of events at Quito in mid-1541. He told the story in full because it was new, and he was careful to warn that it was based on hearsay from Indian sources. But, as a good historian with an open mind, he did not dismiss El Dorado as pure fantasy. He had been told it on good authority, and he reasoned that a region rich in gold mines could easily produce enough for this magnificent custom. His vision of a handsome naked prince, gleaming with the brilliance of gold, was not utterly impossible. The sun temple of the Incas had yielded a garden of life-size golden statues of llamas, maize and other plants and attendant figures. It was—and still is—very common for American Indians to paint their naked bodies.

A Jesuit called José Gumilla lived among the tribes of the Orinoco in the seventeenth century. He observed that 'with very few exceptions, all tribes of those lands anoint themselves from the crowns of their heads to the tips of their feet with oil and *achote*. Mothers anoint all their children, even those at the breast, at the same time as they anoint themselves, at least twice a day in the morning and at nightfall. They later anoint their husbands very liberally. On special days a great variety of drawings in different colours goes on top of the unction . . . The ordinary daily unction is a mixture of oil and anatto that we call *achote*. It is ground and kneaded with oil of cunamá or turtle eggs. It serves not only as clothing but as a sure defence against mosquitoes, which abound in such a great number of species. It not only prevents mosquitoes from biting them', but the insects stick in the gum. It is also cool, a protection against the heat of the sun. Amazon tribes still do this regularly, painting their bodies with scarlet anatto or black genipapo vegetable dyes. So, if naked tribes painted themselves red or black, why not gold also?

The next chronicler to mention El Dorado was Pedro de Cieza de León, a soldier historian who wrote an incomparable account of the conquest of Peru. He was the only contemporary chronicler to visit Quito, passing through that Andean city in the late 1540s. He said that Gonzalo Pizarro, youngest brother of Francisco, the conqueror of the Incas, went to Quito in 1541 'and observing in that city many [unemployed] men, either youths or veterans, he became eager to discover the valley of El Dorado.' According to the recent story, this land lay beyond the mountains east of Quito. An expedition had just returned from an attempt to find cinnamon in those wild hills, the territory of the Quijos Indians. 'The Indians said that further on, if they advanced, they would come to a wide-spreading flat country, teeming with Indians who possess great riches, for they all wear gold ornaments, and where there are no forests nor mountain ranges. When this news spread in Quito, everyone there wanted to take part in the expedition.' Gonzalo Pizarro himself wrote to the King that 'because of many reports which I received in Quito and outside that city, from prominent and very aged chiefs as well as from Spaniards, whose accounts agreed with one another, that the province of La Canela [Cinnamon] and Lake El Dorado were a very populous and very rich land, I decided to go and conquer and explore it.' This letter of 1542 was the first time that the legend of the Golden Man was linked to a lake.

Gonzalo Jiménez de Quesada never mentioned El Dorado in those early years— although it later became an obsession of his brother and of himself in old age. In his Logbook of the conquest of the Muisca he spoke of many fabulous places—the country of the Amazons, the rich land of Menza, the House of the Sun and the enchanting plains visible from the high Andes—but he never spoke of the Golden Man. Nor did he do so in the interrogation at Cartagena in July 1539. It was only in the *Epítome*, an account of the conquest apparently written by him in 1550, that he suggested that the Meta or El Dorado that everyone had been seeking for the past nine years was the rich land of the Muisca that he himself had conquered in 1537: 'All the reports . . . which set everyone's feet marching from the North Sea so excitedly . . . later appeared to be the same thing, namely this kingdom of New Granada [the lands of the Muisca].' This was a wonderfully tidy solution. All the expeditions had been moving towards the same goal, which was why Quesada, Benalcázar and Federmann had all met so dramatically in 1539. It was an explanation developed and repeated by later chroniclers. The only trouble was that it was not true: we have seen how each of those three expeditions reached Bogotá for different reasons, and none of them in search of El Dorado.

Jiménez de Quesada was also interested in the idea of rich lakes. On the journey up from the Magdalena valley, he thought that his men would find a lake that produced the salt cakes traded by the Muisca. This was 'the lake of the salt, in which, as they were assured by the Indians, there was a very large town of many huts and many golden effigies as big as pitchers.' In the event, the salt came from saline wells. But there *were* many lakes in Muisca territory, as well as large towns and gold objects. Quesada later said that the Muisca 'have many woods and lakes consecrated to their false religion . . . They also go to do their sacrifices in these woods and they bury gold and emeralds in them . . . They do the same in the lakes which they have dedicated for their sacrifices. They go there and throw in much gold and precious stones, which are thus lost for ever.'

Sacrifice in a sacred lake was the theme of Juan de Castellanos, the next serious chronicler to deal with El Dorado. Castellanos was the vicar of Tunja, a careful author who checked his facts and knew most of the participants in the conquest. His main failing was to see himself as an epic poet rather than a historian. He wrote long elegies to famous men, modelled on classical heroic verse and sometimes allowing poetic licence to overrule historical accuracy. Castellanos composed his verse epics between 1570 and the late 1580s, a time when El Dorado was long established as a lure for successive expeditions. Castellanos wanted to follow Quesada in establishing that the elusive El Dorado was his own homeland of Bogotá. He wrote that rumours were rife in Quito after its first discovery. 'Benalcázar interrogated a foreign, itinerant Indian resident in the city of Quito, who said he was a citizen of Bogotá and had come there by I know not what means. He stated that [Bogotá] was a land rich in emeralds and gold. Among the things that attracted them, he told of a certain king, unclothed, who went on rafts on a pool to make oblations, which he had observed, anointing all [his body] with resin and on top of it a quantity of ground gold, from the bottom of his feet to his forehead, gleaming like a ray of the sun. He also said that there was continual traffic there to make offerings of gold jewellery, fine emeralds, and other pieces of their ornaments. . . . The soldiers, delighted and content, then gave [that king] the name El Dorado; and they spread out [in search of him] by innumerable routes.' But Castellanos went on to warn his readers that 'El Dorado does not and never had any foundation, beyond what I have declared . . . I know for sure that it does not certify news of any rich land.'

These few authors—the chroniclers Fernández de Oviedo, Cieza de León and Castellanos, and the conquistadores Gonzalo Pizarro, Jiménez de Quesada and Sebastián de Benalcázar—were the only primary sources for the original El Dorado legend. All later writers embellished these early accounts. Pedro de Aguado, a friar who wrote a valuable contemporary history, never told his version of the origin of El Dorado: this part of his history was removed by an ecclesiastical censor. Antonio de Herrera, who published an official history of the Spanish conquests in 1615, based his account on Cieza de León and Castellanos. He said that the 'itinerant Indian' was an ambassador from the ruler of Cundinamarca who had gone to request military help from the Inca Atahualpa. According to Herrera, Luis Daza captured this envoy near Quito, and Benalcázar interrogated him. He told of the great wealth of his land, which lay twelve days' march away. All this tallies well with Daza's official contemporary report of his capture of the 'indio dorado' in 1534. It could well have referred to the rich Quimbaya lands of the Cauca valley. Herrera made no mention of Bogotá or of sacrifices on a lake; but he commented that the story 'has been the cause of many men undertaking the discovery of El Dorado, which until now seems an enchantment'.

The legend of El Dorado really took shape in the writing of Father Pedro Simón. His *Noticias historiales de las conquistas* was written in 1621–3 and shamelessly plagiarized Castellanos—Simón simply turned Castellanos' verse into prose, and added corroborative details apparently derived from his own common sense. Simón wrote that the Indian in Quito called his land Muequetá and its chief Bogotá. He gave a lyrical description of the raft, lake and gold dust ceremony, which took place on a clear morning with the sun shining brilliantly on the radiant chief. Father Simón then connected the Indian's account with the Muisca custom of making sacrifices to lakes. He located the ceremony at Lake Guatavita, an eery, perfectly round lake on desolate hills 50 kilometres north-east of Bogotá. He also told a dramatic story of an adulterous chieftainess. His legend was that the unfaithful wife of a chief of Guatavita, unable to endure her husband's scorn, threw herself and her daughter into the lake. She remained in its depths, living with a monster. There were apparitions of the chieftainess, which led to a cult, with offerings to gain her protection. The chief himself started to gild his body, to sublimate his own offerings; and when the Spaniards invaded, the Indians threw treasures into this sacred lake.

The story evolved further with the next chronicler, Juan Rodríguez Fresle, who wrote the *Conquest and discovery of New Granada* in 1636. In his version, the gilding ceremony became the ancient ritual of investiture of the successor to the Zipa of Bogotá. The heir was stripped of his Muisca cloaks, anointed with gum and gold dust, and launched on to the lake on a raft with four other chiefs and a pile of gold and emerald offerings. As chanting and liturgical music from the shore reached a climax, the prince and his attendants cast their tribute into Lake Guatavita. 'From this ceremony was taken that famous name "El Dorado" that has cost so many lives and fortunes . . .'

A later history of the conquest, by the astute Bishop Lucas Fernández Piedrahita, sought to reconcile the various earlier stories. He implied that the Indian captured by Benalcázar at Quito directly inspired the march towards Bogotá—although there was in fact a gap of four years. He said that the 'indio dorado' of Quito came from a people who were fighting *against* the Muisca or Chibcha, and he prudently omitted any detail of the offerings or investiture ceremonies.

A final version of the legend, by the eighteenth-century author Basilio Vicente de Oviedo, located El Dorado on the Ariari river, near the Orinoco. It was a land so rich that tufts of grass pulled from the ground had gold dust on their roots. Every year a young man was chosen by lot, and then offered as a sacrifice to their idol. 'They open him up and salt him with gold dust, and offer him as a sacrifice in their church. Because of this they call him El Dorado.'

So the legend of El Dorado evolved from a vague notion of a rich, flat land east of Quito, to Fernández de Oviedo's prince anointed daily, to the offerings of Castellanos, the penitent chief of Simón, the investiture of Rodríguez Fresle, and

The mysterious Lake Guatavita, north-east of Bogotá, as depicted by Alexander von Humboldt, which may have been the location of the El Dorado ceremony. There have been repeated attempts to drain the lake and find its treasures (*see page* 195).

the sacrifice of Basilio de Oviedo. The constants in all these versions are: the Indian messenger at Quito, the lake, and the anointment with gold dust. By analysing these elements, Ramos Pérez has shown how difficult it is to accept that the El Dorado of the legend was the ceremony at Lake Guatavita.

Could the 'indio dorado' captured near Quito really have been an envoy from the Muisca? It seems impossible. The Incas had conquered the region of Quito and what is now southern Colombia only a few years before the arrival of the Spaniards. The Muisca were not an expansive military empire, and they were under no threat that would justify seeking help from such a distant source. The Incas were fighting on their northern marches when the civil war between the Incas Atahualpa and Huascar broke out. There were hundreds of kilometres of mountain and forest, and innumerable hostile tribes separating the two rich Andean peoples. It is hard to imagine how a single Muisca could have survived such a journey to seek an Inca alliance.

Another theory is that the 'foreign itinerant Indian' was a trader—for the Muisca were above all accomplished traders. They had a lively commerce, exchanging salt and finished cotton textiles for gold or raw cotton, with tribes of the Magdalena valley or the eastern *llanos*. But these commodities were too bulky to trade as far afield as Quito; and there was no Quitan produce that they would want in return. Perhaps he was an emerald merchant—for the Spaniards found many emeralds on the coast of Ecuador? It is an ingenious theory, until a careful reading of Garcilaso de la Vega and other Peruvian chroniclers shows that the Ecuadorean and Muisca emeralds were of quite different quality: Garcilaso was interested in precious stones, and he wrote a long account of the differences between emeralds from these two regions. No conquistador found any sign of trade or other contact between the Muisca and Inca—apart from the one wishful remark in Castellanos and, following him, Simón.

The concept of El Dorado as a lake is intriguing. Gonzalo Pizarro *did* say that he was looking for 'Lake El Dorado' in his letter to the King in 1542—although no other early source connected El Dorado with a lake, not Cieza de León, Fernández de Oviedo, Benalcázar, Jiménez de Quesada or his brother Hernán Pérez de Quesada. It is also true that the Muisca venerated lakes. Jiménez de Quesada described their offerings in woods and lakes, in his *Epítome de la conquista* of 1550. This was a small element in Muisca religion, whose main worship was of the sun, moon and stars. They had idols in their temples. Castellanos, who as a Christian priest was concerned to destroy these rival manifestations, described Muisca idols: 'Some [were] of gold and others of wood or fibre, large and small, all with hair and badly sculpted. They also make idols of wax or of white clay. They are all in pairs, male with female, adorned with mantles placed on them in their infamous sanctuaries . . .' Water entered into many Muisca rituals, such as the washing of the dead or the puberty rites of girls. The chief of Chía used to bathe ceremonially in the fountain of Tíquisa, and the chief of Bojacá bathed in Lake Tena. Guatavita was one of a series of sacred lakes, which included Guasca, Siecha, Teusacá and Ubaque.

One of the questions in the Catholic inquiries designed to eradicate pre-conquest 'idolatry' was: 'Have you worshipped in the lakes?', and Muisca artefacts have occasionally been found on the beds of old lakes. One of the most fascinating of all such finds was a golden replica of a raft with a tall central figure and four attendants. This amazing discovery was made at the edge of Lake Siecha. It convinced Ernst Röthlisberger, Eduardo Posada, Liborio Zerda and many others that this was proof of the Guatavita legend of El Dorado. The golden raft certainly looks like a religious ceremony, although Vicente Restrepo Tirado thought that the two tiny tubes of gold held by the central figure represented trophy heads, the skulls of Panche or other enemies being offered to the lake deity. The raft is only 19.5

A ceremony on a raft depicted by Muisca goldsmiths. The discovery of this fascinating object in Lake Siecha convinced many historians that the El Dorado legend referred to a ceremony on a Muisca lake.

centimetres long, but beautifully detailed, with six outer rows of logs curving inwards at the ends and enclosing a central section covered in matting. There are ten attendants on the raft, all flat, triangular figures with features and limbs of wire-thin gold, in typical Muisca style. They wear diadems that probably represent feather headdresses. The central figure towers above the rest, although his height is only 10 centimetres. All the figures face forward. Their careful grouping and static postures leave no doubt that they are performing a ritual.

It is important to place this raft in perspective. It evidently portrays a ceremony on a lake. But it is only one of thousands of surviving gold Muisca artefacts. Worship of lakes was only one element in Muisca religion. The first observers of Muisca society wrote much about its religion but scarcely mentioned the importance of lakes, for the Muisca worshipped mountains, celestial bodies, ancestors, and the magnificent rock gorges and outcrops that make the scenery around Bogotá so exciting. The Muisca did not produce gold: they traded it from other tribes, and their gold objects tended to be small as a result. They could not have afforded the prodigal waste of gold dust described in the El Dorado legends. Thus, although there was religious significance in the mysterious Lake Guatavita, it was not central to Muisca beliefs. It is difficult to see how it could have given rise to the powerful El Dorado legend, so far away in Quito, when contemporary conquerors of the Muisca had not heard of it.

A third element in the different versions of El Dorado was powdered or ground gold. Jiménez de Quesada had heard that the Muisca obtained raw gold from the

Neiva region of the upper Magdalena: he hurried off to investigate in a disappointing mission, early in 1538. Sebastián de Benalcázar's men emerged into the same valley a few months later, after their harrowing crossing of the Cordillera Central, and were delighted to find its Indians in possession of gold dust. Benalcázar himself and two of his leading officers testified about their trip, at Cartagena in July 1539. Benalcázar and Pedro de Puelles made no mention of El Dorado, although they told about the gold of the Neiva region and the wealth they later saw in the Muisca lands. But Benalcázar's royal treasurer Gonzalo de la Peña made a surprising remark. He said that the expedition left Popayán 'in search of a land called the golden [el dorado] and Paquies, of very great fame in gold and jewels'. Peña went on to describe the towns and temples of the Muisca 'where they offer gold and jewels and make their sacrifices'. He never again used the words 'el dorado'. His use of this expression was its first appearance in any source; it does not recur until 1541, after which it was on everyone's tongue. Demetrio Ramos Pérez thought that Gonzalo de la Peña was simply using this as an adjective, calling the valley of Neiva a golden land (although the adjective should then have been 'dorada' and not 'el dorado'). Possibly the El Dorado legend had just begun to take shape at Quito, so that Peña mentioned it; but it was still too insignificant an idea to be repeated by Benalcázar or any other contemporary.

Nicolaus Federmann wrote to a friend that Benalcázar told him that 'he had come 500 leagues in search and demand of' the lands of the Muisca. But this was a typical claim by Benalcázar who, on seeing the wealth of Bogotá, liked to think that this was what *he* had been seeking all along. He had left Popayán to escape arrest by Francisco Pizarro. Doubtless, like any conquistador, he hoped to strike some rich land. But he was clearly not aiming for Bogotá. He moved eastwards to Neiva rather than northwards; and when his men did turn north, to descend the Magdalena, they were looking for a route to the Caribbean. They had no inkling of the rich land in the mountains to their right. When Hernán Pérez de Quesada came to meet them, Benalcázar himself was already looking for a route *back* to Popayán, and his men were on the far side of the Magdalena from the Muisca homeland.

Benalcázar himself never claimed that he had been looking for the lands of the Muisca or for El Dorado. He did not do so in the testimony at Cartagena in July 1539; or in a meeting with the King in Spain later that year; or in a conversation with Gonzalo Fernández de Oviedo in Santo Domingo in 1540; or in his letter to the King from Cali in March 1541. This was not from any false modesty. Benalcázar was one of the most ambitious and pushing of all the conquistadores, and his letters show that he was a forceful, eloquent writer. It was only after mid-1541, after he had received reports about events in Quito, that Benalcázar suddenly started talking about reaching El Dorado. In his subsequent letters he often mentioned it, and he and his lieutenants made strenuous efforts to reach it. From then on he sought to establish a prior claim on El Dorado, for he believed that it could be reached from his new governorship of Popayán. He and his men were convinced that El Dorado lay in the mountains south of Neiva and Timaná, the towns he had founded on the upper Magdalena.

It was apparently Benalcázar's son Francisco who persuaded Juan de Castellanos that his father had been seeking El Dorado when he reached Bogotá. The young Francisco later marched with his father on abortive attempts to explore for El Dorado south of Timaná. He then became convinced that his father had not received due recognition among official historians of the Spanish conquests. He applied to the Council of the Indies for permission to examine its records, so that he could write a justificative biography of his father's exploits. He also organized a *probanza*, a judicial inquiry, about his father's 'merits and services'. This Francisco de Benalcázar was in Bogotá in 1569 when Castellanos was gathering information for his *Elegies of Illustrious Men*. The diligent vicar Castellanos interviewed anyone who could help him, and he would certainly have questioned this son of such a famous conquistador. One of Castellanos' epic poems was about Benalcázar; and in the preamble Castellanos echoed Francisco de Benalcázar's view that his father's exploits needed to be brought out of obscurity. So it was almost certainly Francisco de Benalcázar who persuaded Castellanos that his father had been seeking El Dorado in Bogotá—a view repeated by Pedro Simón and many later writers, but not confirmed in contemporary sources.

So how did the idea of El Dorado begin? All sources show that it started in Quito; and contemporary sources leave no doubt that it took shape there in late 1540. The story seems to have been brought back by Spaniards returning *from* Bogotá. It was the creation of the Spaniards themselves and not of any 'itinerant Indian'. All Benalcázar's men had been impressed by the gold dust of the Neiva-Timaná region, and of course by the wealth of the Muisca. The men who were left as settlers at Timaná, near the famous archaeological sites of San Agustín, soon found themselves fighting very hard against Yalcones Indians. Benalcázar's lieutenant Pedro de Añasco brought the son of a Yalcon chief back to Popayán and had him baptized Rodrigo. It may have been this boy who inspired the legend; for Cieza de León attributed it to reports by Añasco. Pedro de Añasco returned to Timaná and was soon killed, with most of his men, by the Yalcones. A punitive expedition by Juan de Ampudia, at the beginning of 1540, suffered a similar fate, with its fat leader riddled by Yalcones lance thrusts. The Spaniards became convinced that the Indians were defending Timaná so fiercely because it was the gateway to greater riches. But the man who was probably the final catalyst in originating 'El Dorado' was Pedro de Puelles. He had gone down the Magdalena with the three leaders in 1539; in his testimony at Cartagena he stressed the 'fine gold and gold dust from mines' of the upper Magdalena, and he hinted that there was more to be found, since his expedition had only '*begun* to find some rich settlements'. Puelles returned to Quito just before Gonzalo Pizarro arrived there at the end of 1540.

The idea of gold dust, so fine that it could be anointed like the dyes used by the Orinoco Indians, seems to have combined with earlier notions that the rich lands should be sought 'behind the mountains' and in the gold-bearing lands close to the equator. The region east of Quito or south of Timaná would fit this location. A report written in 1541 was quite specific. It said that Timaná was situated in an 'armpit' of two mountain ranges, one of which held the source of the Magdalena and Cauca rivers, and the other led to Bogotá, 62 leagues to the north-east. It also stated: 'From the province of Timaná to the province of El Dorado, which . . . is considered a rich affair, there are about 36 leagues of road, according to information I have received. [El Dorado] has a large [lake] with certain islands . . . and appears [to be] on the equator or very close to it . . .' So, when Gonzalo Pizarro, youngest and most impulsive of the four Pizarro brothers, reached Quito to replace Benalcázar as its governor, he was immediately excited by all these reports. He heard that the men of Popayán and Timaná were about to march south to conquer El Dorado. He became 'greedy to discover the valley of El Dorado' and decided to race to reach it first.

There was another element connected with the legendary land of El Dorado. It was the spice, cinnamon. Ever since the Spaniards first conquered Peru they noticed that the Incas used a form of cinnamon, which they obtained from forest tribes east of Quito. Spices were very highly prized in Europe in the days before refrigeration: they helped preserve food and hid the taste of rotting meat. The Portuguese made vast profits with their spices from India and the East Indies (Indonesia); Columbus himself had crossed the Atlantic hoping to find a fast route to the gold and spices of the Orient. Francisco Pizarro was therefore eager to discover the source of the Incas' cinnamon. When Pizarro sent Gonzalo Díaz de Pineda to Quito to replace Benalcázar in 1538, he urged this mayor of Quito to search for the cinnamon. Pineda set out, but after reaching the high mountains of the eastern Andes and descending to the 'Cinnamon Valley', his expedition was repulsed by Quijos Indians. These were the Indians who told Pineda's explorers that, farther on, there was a broad, flat land full of Indians who all wore gold ornaments. This news, coupled with the thrilling reports coming back from Timaná and Bogotá, galvanized Gonzalo Pizarro into action. 'When this news spread in Quito, everyone who was there wanted to take part in the expedition. The Governor Gonzalo Pizarro began to make presentations and collect men and horses. In a few days he assembled 220 Spaniards, horse and foot . . .' From then on, Gonzalo Pizarro always said that he set out to find the province of Cinnamon (La Canela in Spanish) and El Dorado.

Sebastián de Benalcázar was also keen to find this cinnamon. He told the King about it when he was in Spain, and on 31 May 1540 the King granted him a licence to search for and extract cinnamon, 'since you gave me a report that you have news of some lands that contain spices or at least cinnamon'. When Benalcázar was back in the Americas later that year, he met Fernández de Oviedo, who wrote: 'He had many reports of cinnamon, and he told me . . . that his opinion was that he would find it towards the Marañón [Amazon] river, and that this cinnamon should be taken to Castile and Europe down that river, for the Indians had given him information about the route. He thought that he could not fail . . . He considered his information to be certain, [obtained] from many Indians.' A few months later, in March 1541, when he had reached his new governorship of Popayán, Benalcázar wrote to the King about the exciting news of wealth beyond Timaná. 'Since coming to this land, I have great reports of rich lands of far greater dimensions than what I told Your Majesty there [in Spain] about the Cinnamon, which Your Majesty awarded to me. . . . For Indians have come [to Timaná] to say that they want to give and show the Christians rich lands, beyond there.' Benalcázar had not yet heard the El Dorado legend; but he connected the land of cinnamon with reports of rich country south of Timaná—exactly as Gonzalo Pizarro was doing at that same moment in Quito.

When Benalcázar finally did learn the El Dorado idea, he immediately claimed that this was the land he had always been planning to conquer. He wrote to the King again in 1542: 'I have decided to make this expedition called El Dorado and Cinnamon, of which I have news for so many years. [I am financing it] of my own person, although poor and wasted and more in debt. I discovered the entry to it via the town of [Timaná]. To the great content of the explorers and with all speed, I am preparing and have prepared a quantity of men and horses and cattle and other necessary things. God willing, I shall be ready four months from now to fulfil what I have agreed with Your Majesty. I am certain that Your Majesty will be well served by it, and your royal patrimony increased. I plan to run on towards the [Caribbean] and find a port on it, so that there may be trade with all places, specially of the cinnamon which we have seen in such quantity.' Having often spoken about his cinnamon plans, it was easy for Benalcázar to couple these with the new concept of El Dorado in that same region. He wanted to establish a prior claim to this El Dorado. From then onwards, Benalcázar frequently talked about El Dorado, and he managed to connect himself with the origin of the legend in the minds of two important chroniclers, Cieza de León and Castellanos. It was this that led Castellanos (who wanted to locate El Dorado in his own homeland near Bogotá) to say that when Benalcázar found his way to the Muisca lands in 1538–9, he was looking for El Dorado. We now know that he had never heard of it at that date.

7

1541 WAS A YEAR OF GREAT EXPEDITIONS. IN A CURIOUS WAY IT MIRRORED 1538-9 when Jiménez de Quesada, Benalcázar and Federmann had converged on Bogotá. For the three expeditions of 1541 were led by a Quesada, a Pizarro, and a German lieutenant of the Welser. But by 1541 the El Dorado legend had been born: El Dorado fever was starting to send men marching into the depths of South America. And their target area was the eastern foothills of the Andes, 600 kilometres south-west of Bogotá—one of the wildest places in all the tough interior of South America.

The first to leave was Gonzalo Pizarro. He assumed office as governor of Quito on 1 December 1540. Within a matter of weeks he had decided to seek El Dorado and the land of Cinnamon. By February 1541 he had assembled 220 Spanish adventurers and had rounded up four thousand wretched mountain Indian porters. The city council tried to order the governor to release these people from the shackles in which he was holding them before departure. Pizarro assembled almost two hundred horses, arquebuses, crossbows, ammunition, llamas as beasts of burden during the early stages, over two thousand live swine, and a great pack of hunting dogs who were also trained to attack hostile Indians. This army marched out of Quito at the end of February, in high spirits at the prospect of great wealth ahead. 'Each man carried only a sword and a shield, with a small sack of food beneath it.' The llamas and Indians carried all the heavy loads.

Gonzalo Pizarro was the epitome of a conquistador: brave, handsome, magnificently dressed when the occasion was appropriate, a fine horseman and swordsman, but, according to his cousin, rather mean. He was also cruel. In the conquest of Peru he had been a scourge of the Incas, and his physical abuse of the Inca Manco led to a native rising there in 1536-7. He had just pursued Manco into the forests of Vilcabamba, beyond Machu Picchu, before marching north to Quito. In the wooded hills east of Quito he found no convenient Inca roads. The expedition crossed high mountains where many Indians died of cold, and then plunged down into the jungles, cutting a path for the horses with axes and machetes. Pizarro ordered a rest when the expedition reached a fertile valley called Zumaco, a mere thirty leagues east of Quito, because 'both the Spaniards and the horses were all quite exhausted from the great hardships which they had endured, climbing and descending the great mountains, and because of the many bridges that had been built to cross rivers.'

The expedition began to find some cinnamon trees, which reminded them of large olive trees, with big flowers and pods. 'This is cinnamon of the most perfect kind, and of much substance.' The only trouble was that the trees were scattered among dense, hilly forests. The local Indians were primitive and few in number, and it was quite obvious that these cinnamon trees could not be farmed commercially. Gonzalo Pizarro kept asking the Indians how soon he would emerge into open country and rich, populous provinces. The natives said that they knew nothing but other forest-dwellers like themselves. Cieza de León wrote that 'Gonzalo Pizarro was angry that the Indians had given no reply in conformity with what he wanted. He went on to ask them other questions, but they always answered in the negative.' He ordered cane platforms to be built 'and the Indians to be put on them and tortured until they told the truth. The innocent natives were promptly

Gonzala Pizarro plunged into dense rainforests east of Quito in his search for El Dorado.

stretched on those frames or barbecues by the cruel Spaniards, and some of them were burned. . . . The butcher Gonzalo Pizarro, not content with burning Indians who had committed no fault, further ordered that other Indians should be thrown to the dogs, who tore them to pieces with their teeth and devoured them. I heard that there were some women among those who were burned or eaten in this way, which made it worse.'

Desperate to find an exit from the jungle hills, beset by heavy rains, and short of food, the expedition divided. Gonzalo Pizarro explored ahead with eighty men on foot, leaving the horses and others at Zumaco under the second-in-command Francisco de Orellana. Gonzalo Pizarro wrote that 'we endured great hardships and spells of hunger on account of the roughness of the country and dissension among the guides; as a result of which hardships a few Spaniards died.' This was true exploration: hacking forward blindly into the endless forests, never knowing what lay ahead, trying to gauge the slope of the forest floor in order to find streams and water. It is a dark world, dank with the smell of rotting leaves. Sometimes the forest opens into the gloomy majesty of a cathedral, with fallen trees lying like great tombs. In such places the going is easy and the danger is of losing direction — for the sun is visible only filtered through the canopy far overhead, or striking down in rare shafts of blinding brilliance, with huge blue morpho butterflies hovering over the leaves that it illuminates on the forest floor. More often, the jungle is lower and denser. There are lush fans of spiny ferns and cascades of creepers, mosses and bryophytes hanging from the trees. Explorers have to hack a path through the foliage. Thin saplings can be severed easily with a blow from a machete, but creepers dance aside when struck and have to be pinned against a tree and chopped. The cutting seems easier in the morning, when machetes are sharp and cutting arms are rested; but by the afternoon, when it is hotter, it takes two or three frustrating blows to clear something that could have been cut with a sharp 'ping' in the morning. The dead leaves seethe with ants, ticks and jiggers. There are swarms of biting blackfly, *pium* and *borrachudo*, during the day, and mosquitoes at night. Men cutting trails must wear broad-rimmed hats, for a blow at a creeper will bring down a shower of insects, twigs, scorpions or tree snakes. The cutting might disturb a nest of fierce forest hornets. By the end of a few weeks of such toil, men are pale and thin, with their clothes torn and boots disintegrating. Their skin is covered in bites, thorns and festering scratches; and the glands that filter insect poison from the arms and legs are sore and swollen. Gonzalo Pizarro's men were moving in the wet season, when the forest is dripping with rain, there is danger from falling trees and branches, and the ground rapidly turns to slimy pink mud, or swamp, or flooding. This is the season when mosquitoes are most active.

Gonzalo Pizarro covered much territory on his reconnaissance, cutting across hills and finding new rivers. At one camp on a river bank, a flash flood during the night carried off many of his expedition's supplies. 'Gonzalo Pizarro was much distressed at finding that he could not reach any fertile or abundant province beyond such rough country . . . He frequently deplored having undertaken this expedition.' The advance party came upon a broad river, presumably the Napo. They were inspected by a local chief called Delicola, who 'decided to go himself to see what manner of men had invaded his country'. But when he learned of the

The beauty and menace of South American wildlife: (above left) a vampire bat, (above right) a morpho butterfly, and (below) a rear-fanged Venezuelan snake.

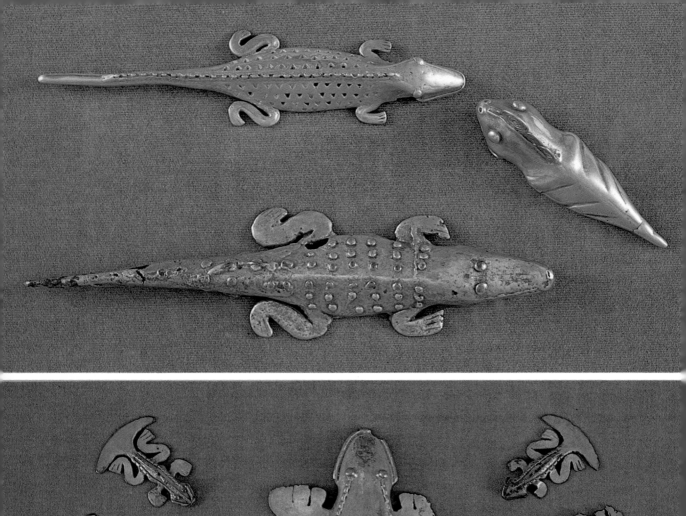

expedition's cruelties to other tribes, Delicola decided to try to rid himself of them. 'So he determined to tell them that there were very great populations further on and very rich regions full of powerful lords. Gonzalo Pizarro and his followers were delighted to hear this, believing it all to be true.' But further exploration beyond the river was disappointing.

The expedition reunited at Zumaco and another officer was sent out on a further exploration. There were meetings with various forest tribes, skirmishes in which the natives were frightened off by arquebus fire, and more interrogation and torture of captives. The Spaniards eventually had the chiefs of four different tribes locked together in their chains and shackles. The months of 1541 went by in these fruitless explorations. At one time, Pizarro thought that he had news of the rich plains he was seeking. But instead of finding El Dorado, 'I set out and reached a province that is called Omagua, passing through great marshes and crossing many streams.'

The expedition reached another broad river, possibly the Coca, one of the main sources of the Napo. Gonzalo Pizarro and his men were well aware that these rivers to the east of the Andes flowed into the Atlantic—although they had no conception of the width of the continent or magnitude of the Amazon river. Every one of their Andean Indian forced labourers had died or fled. Therefore, 'reflecting that of all the servants they had brought from Quito not one remained, and none could be found where they were, the Spaniards came to the conclusion that the best plan would be to build a craft, on which their supplies might go down the river, with the horses following by land, in the hope of reaching some region of plenty, for which they all besought Our Lord.' Gonzalo Pizarro was determined, 'if we did not find any good country in which to found colonies, not to stop until I should come out in the North Sea [Atlantic]'. Francisco de Orellana thought that they should continue to explore overland, seeking the elusive fertile plains. But Pizarro was sure that their salvation lay in building a river boat. There was no shortage of timber, lianas for cordage, or resin for pitch. The camp was scoured for metal that could be turned into nails. 'In this manner, and with the labour of all, the boat was built.'

The expedition moved off down-river, with the sick and heavy equipment on the new brig, some of the men in canoes, and the rest struggled along the banks with the horses. The undergrowth is thickest near Amazonian rivers, the ground nearby is marshy or flooded, and the rivers themselves tend to meander in infuriating loops. The advance was arduous. The horses had to be swum across innumerable streams. The swamps were too deep for the Indian men and women porters to cross on foot. Bridges of logs or creepers were improvised for some rivers; others had to be crossed on logs or canoes. The expedition laboured downstream for 43 days. 'They found little food and no inhabitants, and they began to feel the pangs of hunger—for the herd of five thousand swine they had brought from Quito had all been eaten.' The men were threatened with starvation and death in that remote forest. The shackled Indian chiefs managed to swim to safety, after having told the desperate invaders that there was a prosperous country up a river to the east. Captain Orellana volunteered to take the brig with sixty men to try to find this land.

The Quimbaya evidently revered the creatures in their rivers and lakes: an alligator, lizard, tadpole, and necklace shaped as frogs.

It was the turning point of the expedition. For Orellana and his men did not find food, but sailed on down the entire length of the Amazon to the Atlantic, leaving Gonzalo Pizarro to struggle back overland towards Quito. Was it treachery on Orellana's part? Pizarro was convinced that it was. 'Being confident that Captain Orellana would do as he said, because he was my lieutenant, I told him that I was pleased at the idea of his going for food . . . and gave him the brig and sixty men. . . . But instead of bringing food, he went down the river without leaving any arrangements, leaving only signs and blazes showing where they had landed or had stopped at the junctions of rivers . . . He thus displayed towards the whole expedition the greatest cruelty that faithless men have ever shown. He was aware that it was left unprovided with food, trapped in a vast uninhabited region and among great rivers. He carried off all the arquebuses and crossbows and munitions and iron materials of the whole expedition.'

Orellana's excuse was that he was swept further and further downstream in search of food. His men were desperate from hunger. They were reduced to eating hides or the soles of their shoes cooked with herbs. Many were too weak to stand. When they crawled into the forest to search for food they often ended by eating poisonous roots. Seven died of starvation. 'They were like madmen, without sense.' The river led them forward enticingly, with the hope of finding settlements beyond each bend or rapid. They sailed for a week 'and as the river flowed fast, we proceeded at the rate of from twenty to twenty-five leagues [a day], for the river was now high and swollen by many other rivers which emptied into it . . .' An attempt to send a canoe back to Pizarro failed, and the unwieldy brig could not possibly sail up against such currents. 'Although we wanted to return to the expedition where the Governor [Pizarro] had remained behind, it was impossible to go back because of the fact that the currents were too strong . . .'

Orellana's men finally came upon a tribe of prosperous Indians who loaded them with food when they claimed to be sons of the sun. They remained there for a month, waiting to see whether Gonzalo Pizarro might follow. They were now becoming eager to explore this river, to see whether it did flow into the Atlantic. So they built a second ocean-going boat, and they eventually set off on a voyage of pure discovery. None of them suspected that they were attempting the world's largest river—for the Amazon dwarfs any other rivers in the breadth and depth of its channel, the size of its basin and the immense volume of its water. One fifth of the fresh water that enters the world's oceans comes from the Amazon river. But, once past the rapids of Napo, the voyage was relatively simple. For, despite its enormous length, the Amazon drops very little before reaching the Atlantic. It is thought that the mighty river once flowed westwards into the Pacific, long before continental drift caused the Andes mountains to be uplifted.

Orellana and his fifty men descended the Napo towards the Marañón and Amazon. They were the first white men seen by the many tribes and innumerable villages along its banks. Tribe after tribe experienced the profound shock of first contact with men of another race. It was a terrible experience in store for every tribe in South America, one to which each group reacted differently. Some Indians ran away in terror and allowed the famished Spaniards to eat the food in their village. Others greeted the strangers in full plumed regalia. Some submitted to

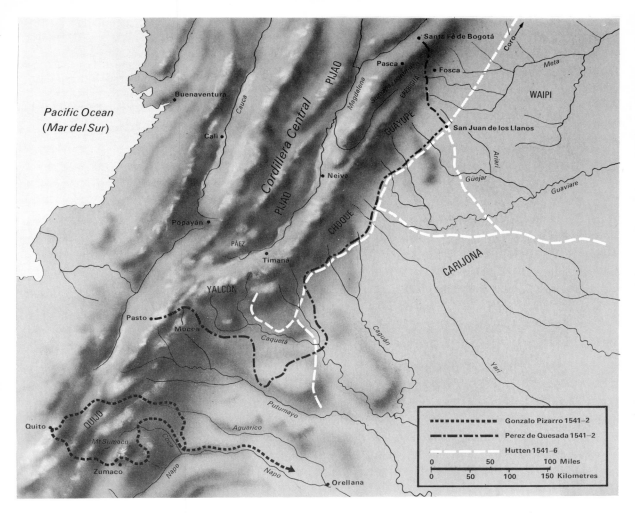

Map labels:

Pacific Ocean
(Mar del Sur)

Buenaventura
Cali
Popayán
PÁEZ
YALCÓN
Pasto
Mocoa
Quito
QUIJO
Mt Sumaco
Zumaco
Napo
Coca
Aguarico
Napo
Orellana
Putumayo
Caquetá
Caquetá
Cauca
Cordillera Central
PIJAO
PIJAO
Neiva
Timaná
Magdalena
Suaza
PIJAO
CHOQUE
Pasca
Fosca
Santa Fé de Bogotá
Sumapaz
Uraricuera
Fusagasugá
GUAYUPE
San Juan de los Llanos
CARIJONA
Caguán
Yari
Guejar
Ariari
Meta
Guaviare
WAIPI
Coro

Legend:
- - - - - - Gonzalo Pizarro 1541–2
- · - · - · Perez de Quesada 1541–2
– – – – Hutten 1541–6

0   50   100 Miles
0   50   100   150 Kilometres

Expeditions seeking El Dorado east of Quito, 1541–46.

ceremonies of annexation by the representatives of the King of Spain.

On the main stream of the Amazon, Orellana met the powerful Machiparo branch of the Omagua nation. Indians paddled out in canoes to inform the expedition that their chief wished to meet them. The Spaniards landed and advanced towards the village in battle order, with the fuses of their arquebuses lit and the strings of their crossbows cranked back ready to fire. The chief was courteous and allowed the bearded strangers to occupy part of his village. The Machiparo had plenty of food: maize, manioc, yams, beans, peanuts and gourds. They raised thousands of turtles in ponds beside each house and they had vast stores of dried fish. All this was too much for the hungry Spaniards, who ran amok and started pillaging the huts and turtle tanks. The Indians concluded that they were not deities but greedy mortals, and suddenly attacked. They came at the disorganized Spaniards with clubs and spears and were protected by long shields of crocodile or manatee skin. The invaders managed to rally and drove off the attack, capturing some of the shields and killing many Machiparo; but they suffered sixteen wounded and two dead.

Downstream lay the rich villages of the great Omagua tribe. The Spaniards were impressed by their 'numerous and very large settlements and very pretty country and very fruitful land'. They noticed 'many roads that entered into the interior of the land, very fine highways'. These broad paths later caused much excitement, particularly when Orellana followed one for a couple of miles and saw that it widened like a royal highway. But the roads probably went no farther than to plantations behind each village. For although the Omagua and Machiparo were very populous, with great villages stretching for kilometres along the banks of the river, they probably did not live beyond the fertile flood plain. They depended on the river's fish and turtles, and they had developed a successful technique of leaving manioc and other food buried beneath the flooding river each year. They were sufficiently numerous and warlike to survive in such exposed locations.

The explorers were also impressed by the fine glazed pottery of these Indians— pottery that is still found by archaeologists on the sites of Omagua villages, and is the pride of museums in Belém at the mouth of the Amazon and in Río de Janeiro. They saw huge jars capable of holding a hundred gallons, plates, bowls and contorted objects like candelabra, all superbly decorated with geometric designs and expertly glazed. Toribio de Ortigüera said that these pieces were 'thin and smooth, glazed, and with colours shading into one another'. Orellana's men found the colours of these ceramics brighter and the designs more sophisticated than Málaga ware. They failed to mention two further peculiarities of the Omagua: that they flattened children's heads so that they bulged sideways like bishops' mitres or hammerhead sharks; and that they were the first people in the world to use wild rubber, making boots and syringes from it. The visitors did observe some gold objects in the Omagua huts, but refrained from taking these as they wanted to escape alive. It was later learned that the tribes of the upper Amazon obtained their gold from a trading tribe called Manaus, who lived on the middle Negro river but could move down to the Amazon through flooded forests in the rainy season. The Manaus evidently obtained the gold from the headwaters of the Negro, which rose not far from Neiva and the lands of the Muisca. An earlier Spanish expedition of 1538, that struck eastwards from northern Peru, had reached the edge of Machiparo lands and had noted their wealth and gold objects.

An expedition down the Amazon in the seventeenth century observed how the Omagua pursued manatees in their light canoes and harpooned them with shell-tipped lances. Hidden Indians would watch when turtles laid their eggs on the river's beaches, and then flip the creatures on to their backs as they walked back to the water. Holes were drilled in their shells and the turtles were towed back to the Omagua villages behind canoes. They were kept in their thousands, in tanks enclosed by wooden railings. They were fattened on foliage and killed when needed: 'Thus these barbarians never know what hunger is, for one turtle suffices to satisfy the largest family.' The Omagua made an intoxicating brew from manioc and loved to hold drunken parties. 'With the help of this wine they celebrate their feasts, mourn their dead, receive their visitors, sow and reap their crops: indeed on any occasion on which they meet, this liquor is the mercury that attracts them and the riband that detains them.'

Orellana's expedition entered the main Amazon or Marañón in mid-February

Orellana's men were impressed by the native pottery they saw on the upper Amazon. Such pots were always shaped without potter's wheels, for American Indians had not invented the wheel.

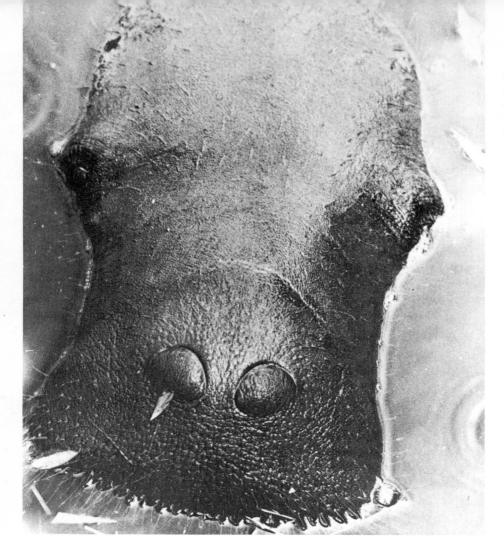

1542. They cruised down its swirling waters for weeks on end. The Amazon near the Omagua lands is as broad as a lake, and its mass of gently flowing water is the colour of an Indian's skin. The banks are unbroken walls of dark green vegetation, with the great trees masked by a screen of undergrowth. These endless lines of treetops are now interrupted only by the occasional mud bank; but in Orellana's day there were frequent Indian villages, with long lines of huts along the water's edge. The monotony of the river and its banks is compensated by movement in the skies. Immense formations of clouds pile up or race across the heavens, soaking up the moisture of the Amazon forests or turning purple-black with tropical storms. At dawn and sunset the surface of the river mirrors a dazzling spectacle of colour, from silver to golden orange or violet. There are occasional floating logs or islands of grass, a fish breaking the surface, tributaries making brief openings in the curtain wall of trees, or flights of macaws, herons, toucans or eagles watching the edges of the river. Otherwise, for day after day, there was only the immensely broad, placid river and the unbroken lines of trees.

The expedition had various adventures with the many tribes along the two

M. Australis. ———— American Manatee.

thousand kilometres of river they descended. Their uncouth behaviour made them less welcome as they passed from the territory of each successive tribe. They were frequently attacked by colourful flotillas of native canoes. They landed to steal food from the smaller settlements, and often had to fight off the angry inhabitants. On 2 June 1542 they passed the mouth of the Negro and gave it the name that has survived, because its black, clear waters—draining the geologically ancient and heavy eroded Guiana shield—make such a sharp contrast with the sediment-laden brown water of the Amazon. Eight days later they passed the mouth of the Madeira, another huge river, entering from the south.

It was below the Madeira that the expedition passed the gleaming villages of 'the excellent land and dominion of the Amazons'. When native canoes menaced the Spanish boats and rejected their peaceful overtures, the explorers decided to fight. They rowed their brigs against a village defended by masses of warriors. Spanish guns and crossbows took a heavy toll of the defenders, but these fought on, firing a barrage of arrows, dancing and shouting, heedless of their losses. The Spaniards protected themselves with manatee-hide shields from the Omagua. Their boats were hit by so many arrows that they looked like porcupines. Five Spaniards were struck before reaching the shore. One victim was the expedition's chronicler, the Dominican friar Gaspar de Carvajal, who was hit by an arrow that pierced his rib cage. 'Had it not been for the thickness of my habit, that would have been the end of me.' The invaders jumped into chest-high water and fought for an hour, slashing a landing against waves of native warriors. Carvajal was convinced that the defenders' determination resulted from being subjects of the Amazons. 'We ourselves saw ten or twelve of these women, fighting there in front of all the Indian men as female captains. They fought so courageously that the men did not dare turn their backs. They killed any who did turn back, with their clubs, right there in front of us, which is why the Indians kept up their defences for so long. These women are very white and tall, with very long braided hair wound about their heads. They are very robust, and go naked with their private parts covered, with bows and arrows in their hands, doing as much fighting as ten

Fast-growing manioc or yucca is the staple food of the upper Amazon. (Left) An Andoke woman rasps manioc root; (below left) a Tukano mother sieves manioc flour; and (right) a Yanomani woman roasts manioc loaves over a smoking fire.

Indian men.' The Spaniards reckoned that they had killed seven or eight of these Amazons before escaping to their boats. They drifted off with the current, too exhausted to row.

An Indian captured during the battle was interrogated about the Amazons. He said that he had often visited their villages, a week's march to the north of the river. He evidently agreed with all the preconceived ideas put to him by his captors: for the picture of the Amazons that emerged was an exact replica of the classical legend. All the details about having intercourse only once a year, keeping only daughters, and cutting off the right breast to facilitate drawing a bowstring, were included. The sceptical chronicler Francisco López de Gómara commented a few years later: 'I do not believe that any woman burns or cuts off her right breast in order to be able to shoot with a bow: for they shoot very well with [that breast].' The land of the Amazons, as portrayed by this captive Indian, was just like Peru, with stone buildings, llamas, and the inevitable wealth of gold and silver objects. López de Gómara angrily recalled that other explorers had heard tales of Amazons in the Americas. 'No such thing has ever been seen along this river, and never will be seen! Because of this imposture many already write and talk of the "River of the Amazons".' But the world's largest river continues to be named after this elusive tribe of sexually-liberated women.

Orellana's veterans survived many more skirmishes. In one attempt to raid a village, friar Carvajal had an eye pierced by an arrow. 'I have lost the eye from this wound, and am still not free from suffering or pain.' By late July they were near the mouth of the river. They spent some weeks refitting their boats for a voyage up the Atlantic coast, and this went remarkably smoothly: summer winds and currents carried the two brigs past the Guianas and Trinidad, to reach the island of Margarita, off Venezuela, on 9 and 11 September 1542. They had achieved one of the world's greatest explorations—one that Fernández de Oviedo described as 'something more than a shipwreck, more a miraculous event'.

Meanwhile, far away across the continent, Gonzalo Pizarro's battered explorers tried to survive after what they regarded as Orellana's treacherous betrayal. They were lost in trackless forests. The rains poured down ceaselessly night and day. The swamps grew worse as the Spaniards pushed wearily eastwards. 'To enable them to proceed and bring along the horses, the strongest young men went ahead, opening a trail with axes and machetes, never ceasing to cut through that dense wilderness in such a way that all the camp could pass.' They ate some of the remaining horses and dogs, wasting no part of the entrails or skin. Alonso de Mercadillo, the captain who had led the first expedition to sight the Machiparo in 1538, was with Gonzalo Pizarro, who sent him to scout ahead in canoes. He returned empty-handed. Another sortie, by Gonzalo Díaz de Pinea, descended to the Napo (where they saw Orellana's blazes on the trees) but then went up that river. They finally chanced upon an abandoned Indian manioc plantation. 'They went down on their knees and gave thanks to our Lord God for his great mercy. They then began to pull up [the manioc roots] and load the two canoes, returning with these full to where Gonzalo Pizarro was waiting with Spaniards who had given up all hope of escaping with their lives. When they saw the canoes and learned what they brought, they all wept for joy . . . Gonzalo Pizarro had been there for twenty-seven days with his party, eating nothing but some horse and dog meat with herbs and leaves from trees. They had also eaten the saddle and stirrup leathers, boiled in water and then roasted over ashes. . . . The Spaniards were very sick and sore, wan and wretched, in such an afflicted condition that it was very sad to look upon them.' They all moved to the enormous manioc plantation and recovered some strength—although eating nothing but manioc gave the men bad diarrhoea. They wandered for many more leagues, through forests and up rivers. Most were barefoot, suffering terribly from the thorns and broken roots of the forest. 'In this condition they went on, nearly dead with hunger, naked and barefoot, covered with sores, opening the path with their swords. Meanwhile it rained, so that on many days they never saw the sun and could not get dry.' After months of suffering, they finally saw a line of mountains in the distance, and moved towards them. Gonzalo Pizarro wrote a harrowing account of it all to the King. He told how they finally returned to Quito, in June 1542, bereft of everything they had taken with them, 'with only our swords, and each with a staff in his hand'.

When Sebastián de Benalcázar heard about Gonzalo Pizarro's return, he also wrote to the King. He blamed Orellana for treacherous desertion and urged the King to give him 'exemplary punishment'—he did not want Orellana to return with a rival bid for El Dorado. He also discredited Gonzalo Pizarro, who had 'returned with a hundred men on foot, lost and defeated, with no horse or other thing, having failed in an attempt to reach the land he had gone to seek . . .' He carefully omitted to mention Gonzalo Pizarro's goal: for Benalcázar wanted to reserve the discovery of El Dorado for himself.

Although the El Dorado vision was causing such excitement in Quito and Popayán, it had not yet crossed the Andes to Venezuela and the Orinoco. Far away at the mouth of the Orinoco, Jerónimo Dortal was still doggedly looking for the land of Meta, and fighting off the rival pretensions of Antonio Sedeño. The two men fought each other like rival cattle barons of the American West: stealing one another's horses or men, issuing legal warrants against one another, and continually complaining to the King. In 1538 a judge called Frías was sent to arrest Sedeño; but the conquistador simply persuaded the judge to follow him on yet another venture into the interior—such was the lure of Meta and the fanatical conviction of its seekers. Sedeño died on this expedition, deep inside the Venezuelan *llanos*. His officers pushed on, and when further royal emissaries came to arrest them, they convinced these that they would 'rapidly come upon another affair far better than Peru'.

In 1540 Jerónimo Dortal plunged inland to punish yet another group of mutineers. Insubordination was endemic among the hard men of those hot, dusty plains. Dortal managed to surprise the renegades at the Guarico river, and executed the ringleaders. He advanced to explore more rivers, Tisnados (where Sedeño had died) and Carranca, and mapped the way in which they flowed into the Orinoco. He then 'passed forward, crossing many rivers, and reached the mouth of the Meta. At the very place where his lieutenant Alonso de Herrera had been killed [in 1535] they found a bell for summoning to mass and a tin jar, which had lain there since the Indians defeated that lieutenant.' Dortal later explained the geography of the *llanos* and Orinoco to his friend Gonzalo Fernández de Oviedo, who included a fine sketch map in his monumental history, 'because a painting clarifies much, and better explains these matters of geography'. Jerónimo Dortal returned from the middle Orinoco without finding the legendary Meta, but with a clear picture of its geography. There were more legal complications and a brief arrest on his return to the coast. Then, 'tired of struggling and labouring in vain, and wishing to employ better what was left of his life', he married a rich young heiress and settled down as a prosperous citizen of Santo Domingo. Jerónimo Dortal was the only one of these explorers to reach a contented old age. He was the only man to survive being seized by the lure of Meta or of El Dorado.

Captain Pedro de Reinoso, one of the survivors of Sedeño's last expedition, took his men across to Venezuela to avoid arrest in his own captaincy. He reached Barquisimeto at the end of 1539 with 86 men. One morning a smaller force, led by the young German nobleman Philip von Hutten, crept up to Reinoso's camp and disarmed his explorers before they awoke. It was not long before Hutten had persuaded these new arrivals to join a new venture he was planning.

Philip von Hutten was the young optimist who returned from Hohermuth's disastrous expedition convinced that it had almost succeeded. It was Hutten who wrote to a friend in Germany: 'I believe that we were not more than thirty miles from . . . a country richer than Peru.' Most people in Coro were disheartened by the losses and failure of Hohermuth's expedition—apart from that German governor himself, who planned energetically to repeat it, until he died of disease in June 1540. All this opposition changed dramatically with news of Federmann's reaching Bogotá and the golden lands of the Muisca. Philip von Hutten wrote to his brother that 'such reports arrive from Federmann, of the great riches

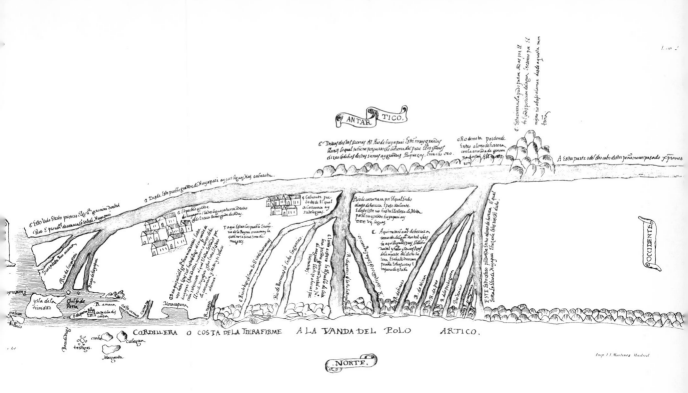

discovered by him, that not only people who are [already] here think of nothing but going, but all Santo Domingo and part of Spain want to come here!' When Hohermuth died, Philip von Hutten was determined to lead the next expedition. It was Hutten who wrote to his father: 'God knows that it was not avarice that impelled me to undertake that journey [with Hohermuth], but a strange desire that I have harboured for a long time . . .' He was now convinced that 'this new expedition will not be as difficult or long as the other: for we now know for sure where we must seek. He whom God allows to survive will receive the reward for his effort!'

The problem for Philip von Hutten was that he could not march inland without proper authority from a governor of Venezuela. Hutten himself hoped to be appointed: he urged his influential brother to press his claim in Germany. He was worried that other expeditions would reach the rich land before him: he knew that Dortal had gone inland from Maracapana, and that Sebastián de Benalcázar was back in the Americas and planning a similar quest from Popayán and Timaná. His men were becoming increasingly restless. Some of the uncertainty ended when Bartholomeus Welser, eldest son of the head of the Welser merchant bank, reached Coro in February 1541. Hutten knew that this young Welser would be the next governor; but the two aristocratic young Germans became good friends and energetically planned their expedition together. In November 1540 Hutten had also been joined by Pedro de Limpias, one of the roughest and most experienced of all the explorers, a man who had been with Dalfinger and then with Federmann on his Muisca expedition.

Hutten's plans suffered a serious reverse when the bulk of his men, exasperated by all the delays, deserted Venezuela and moved to New Granada. They were led by Hohermuth's favourite captain, Montalvo de Lugo, who was 'compelled by all the soldiers' to cross the *llanos* and climb into the Andes. His men managed to climb the Casanare valley. When he reached Bogotá, Montalvo de Lugo rapidly became a close friend of Quesada's brother, Hernán Pérez de Quesada, who was acting lieutenant-governor there. The two friends soon planned an expedition to reach the 'rich land' before Philip von Hutten.

Gonzalo Jiménez de Quesada tried to leave some semblance of government in the Muisca lands, or New Granada as he called them. He founded municipalities at Santa Fé (Bogotá), Tunja and Vélez. When he left for Spain he requested the royal authorities to send charters to these towns, and to endow churches and build forts in them. He left his brother Hernán Pérez de Quesada in charge of New Granada, with detailed instructions on how to administer it. The two brothers awarded encomiendas—the labour and produce of thousands of natives within a defined area—to their friends. The government of New Granada was soon disputed, first by Jerónimo Lebrón and then by the son of Fernández de Lugo. Each new governor undid the work of his predecessor and awarded the encomiendas to new recipients. The result was anarchy. The docile Muisca, who had been such admirable farmers and traders, suffered appallingly. Each Spaniard tried to extract as much wealth as he could from the wretches under his control. Jiménez de Quesada himself wrote that 'it is notorious that much ill-treatment of the Indians has been committed by conquistadores and other Spanish settlers. There have been murders, robberies and cutting off of members, in order that they will give gold and jewels, to such an extent that it is a scandal to tell it all. Because of this many towns have been depopulated and a great infinity of Indians killed. The governors and justices have taken little care to punish such crimes . . .' The lawyer Jiménez de Quesada was particularly concerned that there was no definition of how much tribute an encomendero could extract from his Indians. He also worried about the suffering of Indians forced to carry loads up from the Magdalena, along the route of his own conquest, toiling up the steep slopes of the Opón valley with enormous cargoes.

When they became aware of the catastrophe of their defeat, some Muisca tried to resist or rebel against the European conquerors. They fought with more determination than during the confused months of the conquest, but they were still completely outclassed in battle. The sporadic outbreaks of resistance were unco-ordinated. The country was now full of Spaniards who had fresh horses and adequate weapons.

We learn something of the cruelties of the conquistadores from many legal accusations during those turbulent years. There was Juan de Arévalo who sacked the town of Cota because its chief would not give him enough gold. 'He went to that town and destroyed it, killing many Indians in it, cutting hands or noses off others or breasts off the women, and cutting the noses off small children.' One witness said that this Arévalo was 'known as a cruel butcher in the Indies'. He placed the chief of Chía in an iron collar said to be so heavy that it would have killed anyone: that chief died after forty days of this torture. The Indians of Suta and Tausa, near Suesa, rebelled because the houses of their chiefs had been burned. They killed a Spaniard and then took refuge in a hilltop redoubt. Juan de Arévalo was sent as leader of the punitive campaign. He surrounded the Indians and closed in on their retreat. 'Since the Christians were attacking them from both sides, the Indians gathered in the middle of the hilltop. At this point the Christians paused, exhausted from killing a great quantity of Indians.' Arévalo demanded the surrender of the remainder, and they duly laid down their arms. Arévalo then 'ordered that [his men] should attack them with fire and sword and throw them from the cliff. So they threw them from that crag, and people who were below said that they saw seven hundred [dead] Indians in the valley below the crag.' Others were pursued through the forests. Fifty prisoners were burned to death in a hut, and others were thrown to the dogs. 'This resulted in the deaths there of three or four thousand souls, small and adult, men, women and children, breaking the peace and making an enormous and cruel punishment. It was said openly in that land that Herod's cruelty was no greater than that of Juan de Arévalo against these innocent people.'

It was said that Hernán Pérez de Quesada depopulated the area around Guatavita with his extortions, burning huts and sacking native crops. The Indians fled to the forests. Captains Pineda and Olalla were later sent to Guatavita to suppress its rebellion, and they killed over 1,500 men and women, burned villages and looted. Martín Pujol was accused of having his dogs kill Indians of Guasca and Suba; to which he protested that he had had them baptized before execution. Captain Rodríguez Zorro was in trouble for mutilating and setting dogs on Indians of his encomienda of Simijaca and Chía, and Francisco Sánchez Alcobaza was accused of sodomizing people of both sexes on his encomienda. A favourite punishment for Indians was impaling: Lope Montalvo de Lugo defended this because Indians 'never have feared and do not fear being hanged or beheaded, but fear only the punishment of impaling'. This impaling consisted of inserting a stake 'from between the legs to emerge at the head'. The legal records are full of such atrocities, including hanging victims upside down over a fire, burning with hot oil, killing infants so that their mothers could carry heavier loads, and using dogs trained to kill.

A leading captain and horseman of the conquest was Lázaro Fonte. He fell foul of Jiménez de Quesada, who disliked him intensely and ordered his banishment from New Granada for crimes against Indians. Legal actions between the two leaders were full of horrible accusations. Lázaro Fonte was charged with killing and mutilating many Indians 'all in order to get gold and emeralds from them against their will'. He was further accused of seducing small Indian girls. One witness, Simón Díaz, testified that 'he saw Lázaro Fonte put a girl of seven or eight years in his bed, a daughter of the Bogotá, and he kept her there and raped her, for I heard her cry and scream that night and next day I saw the blood spilled by that child in Lázaro Fonte's bed. I said to Juan de Gómez and to other captains: "Look what a great wickedness Lázaro Fonte has done by raping that child!"—for she was so tiny that the Indians carried her in their arms because she could not walk. She was an Indian, but I do not know whether she was a Christian. When I protested to Lázaro Fonte how bad it was to fornicate with such small girls, he said: "Just wait and see!" and he removed a hooded helmet he was wearing and threw it at the girl and hit her with it, and said: "Since she does not fall over from that blow, I can certainly sleep with her!" '

After Jiménez de Quesada left Bogotá, his brother Hernán Pérez de Quesada set off to try to find a place known as the House of the Sun. This imaginary temple, with a name like the great Inca enclosure Coricancha at Cuzco, had been an obsession of the Orinoco explorers for several years. Pérez de Quesada heard a rumour that it lay in the Andes north of Bogotá and the other Muisca lands. So he marched north from Tunja, past Sogamoso to the valleys of Chicamocha and Servitá. He entered the valley that now contains the town of Pamplona. But at this point some veterans who had been with Ambrosius Dalfinger recognized the place: this was the same valley they had reached after crossing the mountains, shortly before Dalfinger's death from poisoned arrows. Pérez de Quesada therefore desisted and returned to Bogotá. During the remainder of 1540 and early 1541 he made no expeditions other than punitive raids against Muisca resistance. He also warded off an attempt by the interim governor of Santa Marta, Jerónimo Lebrón, to assert his authority in New Granada.

Then, in mid-1541, Pérez de Quesada suddenly changed: he heard about El Dorado and immediately became obsessed to find the place before any rival. Two events changed his attitude. One was the arrival of Montalvo de Lugo, who came from Venezuela with tempting reports of the land so nearly conquered by Hohermuth. Then came news that Gonzalo Pizarro had left Quito to search for El Dorado and the land of Cinnamon, in roughly the same area. Pérez de Quesada wrote to the King: 'I had a report, not just from one source but from many, that behind some mountains which we call Western, there was the greatest wealth of gold and silver and emerald stones that had ever been heard about.' He had heard that in Quito, Popayán, Venezuela and Cubagua, 'in all these places they were preparing to make this discovery and expedition. Since I was in the province of Bogotá with so many men, so experienced in these parts of the Indies, and very well equipped in horses, weapons and other things needed for war, I decided . . . to go to explore, . . . for I was in the best location, closer and with less mountains to cross. So it was that . . . I left the New Kingdom [of Granada] on 1 September 1541 with 260 Spaniards and almost 200 horses, with all the other equipment needed for that expedition.' One important item of 'equipment' was native porters. Pérez de Quesada was later accused of rounding up 'over six thousand head of free Indians, men, women and children, all tied and imprisoned, removed by force and against their will . . . All of them died, without a single one returning to this kingdom.' It was said that the expedition's press gangs took only 'the most peaceful and secure' Indians. They particularly denuded Cocuy, leading off all its men in collar shackles, tied to Spaniards. Individual Spaniards were so excited by the expedition, and so convinced that they would settle in the rich land of El Dorado, that they ransacked their Muisca encomiendas, robbing their chiefs of all their possessions 'like men who thought they would never return to them'.

The town council of Tunja tried to dissuade Pérez de Quesada from this expedition. He was far too determined. He told the men of Tunja that 'if he failed to make that expedition, His Majesty could lose a great quantity of gold and silver,

Quimbaya warriors from the upper Cauca valley went into battle resplendent in gold armour: this may have been the origin of the 'golden Indian' captured by Benalcázar near Quito.

128

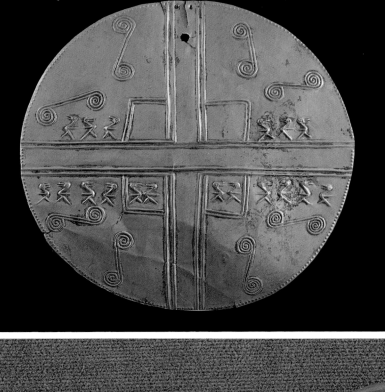

precious stones and many types of riches of which news has been received, as well as many lands and lordships that would fail to be discovered.'

The expedition had a galaxy of distinguished officers, headed by Lope de Montalvo de Lugo. There was no trouble recruiting men. All were delighted to follow Pérez de Quesada, because he was 'expert in the arts of easy persuasion; and the lure of self-interest was so effective at gripping human hearts . . . Men could rejoice in new fatigues, after their earlier labours and present idleness.'

The route began with a crossing of the frozen *páramo* of Fosca, the bleak highlands where Federmann's men had suffered so much. The expedition then had no particular difficulty in descending to the site of San Juan de los Llanos, or marching along the plans to the Guaviare and Papamene rivers. It was here that the forests of the Amazon basin began. There was much debate on whether to plunge into jungles that had ruined Hohermuth's expedition; but Lope de Montalvo argued that this must be done if they were to reach the promised rich land. So they started cutting, through to the Papamene and the land of the Waipis Indians, the people who were said to know El Dorado. They reached the forested hills of the Choques and had to fight off Choque attacks during ten days spent crossing the tribe's territory. They reached the Bermejo river, the farthest point of Hohermuth's advance. There were very few Indian villages in these forests. 'If they came upon a settlement of four huts it seemed to them they had found a sumptuous town. But turbulent rivers they encountered in great abundance, which caused them strenuous labour. And so Hernán Pérez [de Quesada] was losing his men every day, both Spaniards and Indians and horses.'

The splendid expedition was rapidly disintegrating. It advanced for a further thirty leagues through dense highland jungles. 'But considering that their lack of food was increasing hourly and many men were dying from hunger, from illness occasioned by hardship, and the bad climate of the land, they resolved to return to the lower land.' It was no better down there. The men marched for many days with no food apart from some roots. All were very weakened, scarcely able to cut a path. On some days they had to build ten or twelve bridges to cross rivers. 'These fatigues brought them to the height of misery and caused illnesses to spread throughout the army. Some soldiers and the majority of the Indian porters died.' Such hunger and constant physical struggle brutalized the Spaniards. When they came upon a native settlement slightly larger than usual, they named it Valladolid after the great Spanish city. Its inhabitants refused to give their food to the haggard adventurers who came crashing into their forests, so the invaders laid an ambush on an island. They counted it a notable victory when they caught a group of warriors off guard. 'Rushing out suddenly, they caused such surprise among the Indians that these were too confused to wield their arms. The rest of the Spaniards ran up and caught them in the middle of the river, where the horses could enter, and there made such a slaughter among them that very few escaped with their lives. The river was filled with dead bodies and was dyed with blood.' The spoils of this victory was the food stored by the natives of 'Valladolid'.

Pérez de Quesada's army explored blindly southwards and came upon the goal sought by Gonzalo Pizarro, Benalcázar and others before they had heard of El Dorado: endless groves of cinnamon trees. This South American cinnamon was

Quimbaya goldsmiths reproduced natural creatures in objects of great beauty: a pectoral disc with embossed pelicans and pendants in the shape of sea shells.

not the same as the oriental spice brought from India by the Portuguese. 'It is a little husk shaped like a small hat, of the same colour and taste as oriental cinnamon . . . The lands where that spice grows are unbelievably uninhabitable, full of swamps, rivers and quaking bogs, and above all sterile of fruits, roots, birds or fish, so that throughout them there is scarcely any food to be found.' Now that they had found the sought-after cinnamon, it was no help to them: they had to trudge across forty leagues of this nightmarish wilderness.

For a time the expedition emerged on to slightly better land where it fought many tribes. Search parties were sent for miles across the headwaters of the Caquetá and possibly also of the Putumayo. There was no sign of paths leading to richer lands, not even Indians to entice the men with tales of kingdoms to be conquered. The rains intensified. When Pérez de Quesada decided to turn back from one reconnaissance, it was found that two rivers had risen and flooded the expedition's path: a new trail had to be hacked through the undergrowth far upstream.

Perhaps the rich land lay in the mountains, as it had done with the Aztecs, Incas and Muisca? The expedition turned westwards and made its way up one of the headwaters of the Caquetá, into the valley of Mocoa. 'They captured some Indians who, by signs, gave good reports of the land that lay ahead.' Perhaps all their suffering would be rewarded. The tribes of these foothills put up a stiff resistance. Whenever the Spanish column entered a defile and the horses could not manoeuvre, the Indians attacked. At one place a man-eating tribe managed to seize five men in view of the rest of the column, and quartered them before anything could be done to save them. But this seemed a good sign. The tribes were doubtless defending the approaches to El Dorado. 'Our men advanced, continually on the alert, fighting at times, and not pausing for a single day because of the great news they had been given in Mocoa about a land called Achibichi.' Then came the anti-climax. 'When they entered it after such prolonged hardships, they found themselves in the valley of Sibundoy, in the district of the town of Pasto belonging to governor Benalcázar. Such was the ruinous end of . . . the much-vaunted conquest of El Dorado.' This great expedition, after all its desperate endurance and suffering, had hacked its way through to the main road from Quito to Popayán, an area already well known to Spaniards.

Hernán Pérez de Quesada already had plenty of enemies. There was now a royal inspector at Bogotá and, after the débâcle of his El Dorado attempt, he felt it was safer to avoid that part of Colombia. His brother tried to help. Jiménez de Quesada wrote to the King that he had 'discovered some two hundred leagues beyond that kingdom of New Granada; but in the part he was exploring he always found few settlements and bad land, a poor place with little food and few people. In the end, near those two hundred leagues, he found a province deserted and almost un-inhabitable, in which for many leagues there are an infinite number of cinnamon spice trees.' To save his brother's reputation, the conquistador hinted that a lucrative spice trade could be established if only this cinnamon could be carried out on convoys of native porters or pack animals. Hernán Pérez de Quesada himself wrote to the King, excusing his disaster by recording all the tempting siren songs of the Indians that had lured his men forward. First the Waipis: 'Such was

Pérez de Quesada's men considered it a notable victory to destroy a village on the upper Caquetá. A Makuna of the Caquetá with a diadem of egret feathers.

the news they gave, that it was considered quite certain that we had found a region where Your Majesty's . . . royal patrimony could be handsomely swollen.' Then came the Bermejo river where Montalvo de Lugo recalled that Hohermuth had 'turned back with great news' and the region of cinnamon where 'we thought for sure that we were in good land, according to some Indians born in Quito' who were with the expedition as guides. Turning inland to Mocoa, Indian prisoners gave enticing news. 'We marched with very great reports of a land they called Achibichi . . . A great part of the Spaniards and horses died here . . . but when we reached it with insufferable hardships, we found ourselves in the valley of Sibundoy near Pasto.' The leader did not disguise the fact that 'eighty Spaniards died on it and the rest emerged weak and ill-disposed.' He neglected to mention the loss of 110 horses or of the thousands of peaceful Muisca and Moxo Indians torn from their homes in the northern Andes.

Philip von Hutten was still hoping to conquer this same remote part of the Andean foothills. He was still obsessed with pursuing the reports of rich lands that Hohermuth had heard when they were together on the Bermejo river in 1537. Various problems delayed the young German. He went inland from Coro in August 1541; but it was not until early 1542 that he finally set out across the *llanos* with a smaller force than he would have wished. Hutten had probably not heard of El Dorado. He 'wanted to see the Papamene again and investigate the far corners of the Choques' territory.' He followed the customary route along the base of the Andes, but it came as a shock when his expedition reached the site of the future San Juan de los Llanos and saw fresh tracks of Pérez de Quesada's Spaniards heading south. 'He was perplexed for some time, undecided whether to pass forward following the tracks of Hernán Pérez.' In the end they decided to follow, reasoning that the brother of the conqueror of the Muisca would never have left his rich fief without a sure notion that he was going to find something better. Pedro de Limpias 'said that it was wise to follow the tracks of his old friend'.

So Hutten's men followed Pérez de Quesada's, south-westwards along the edge of the Andes. It was familiar ground and they moved fast. At the Papamene Philip von Hutten interrogated a friendly chief. 'The chief understood well what he was being asked. He answered that it was unwise to follow the route [Hernán Pérez] had taken, for in that direction there were no settlements of people who possessed gold. It was all jungles and very badly inhabited land, very dense and hilly. A certain number of Spaniards or people like them had passed by there a few weeks before. All of them were dying from not finding food to eat and from diseases they had caught. He understood by word from neighbouring tribes that all or most of them were now dead.' Hutten failed to heed this warning. He suspected that the chief might be trying to deflect him from the promised land. So he drove his men forward, sick and near-mutinous. He decided to veer to the left, eastwards towards the Vaupés, a tributary of the Negro.

At one stage Pedro de Limpias was sent off on an exploration that lasted three months. Years later, a soldier called Juan Martín del Albercón remembered that he had been with Limpias. After many days they had met large numbers of Indians. They were too few to enter the dense land ahead. The Indians 'had given [Limpias] such great skirmishes that they had made [the Spaniards] flee; but they had seen very large towns, of such an extent that they were astounded.' A Canoas Indian boy who was guiding Limpias said that he went down the Guaviare towards the rich lands of a ruler called Gualcaba, but was put to flight by his warriors. Limpias was back with the rest of the expedition in May 1543.

Limpias said that he had been offered two gold coronets, said to have come from the Amazons who lived down-river. Later that year, other Indians told Hutten that down a river called Manna was a place called Ocuarica where the Amazons lived on the far bank of the main Marañón or Amazon river. It was all reminiscent of the Amazons about whom Hutten had heard when he was with Hohermuth. He could not have known Orellana's tales of Amazons, since Hutten marched inland some months before Orellana's boats reached the Caribbean. The river called Manna sounds like the Manau tribe, who lived on the middle Negro: if Hutten was on the Vaupés, as is often thought, he would have been within range of the Manau, who moved far upstream in their trading missions.

The rains of 1543 were spent in 'a very sterile and pestilential land, with very few natives'. Such Indians as there were proved to be very primitive Pardaos,

Philip von Hutten's expedition may have reached the Vaupés tributary of the Río Negro. A Tukano boy from the Vaupés wears a headdress of feathers mounted on a basketry frame.

eating snakes, frogs and a mixture of soft maize and ants. Hutten's men caught a strange ailment that turned them a sickly orange. 'Their hair fell out, and in its place emerged a pestiferous scabies from which they died.' The horses were also covered in mange. The afflicted men grew desperate for salt and would jump on any old piece of sweat-soaked clothing to eat it.

After the rains at the end of 1543, the sick were taken back to the relative comfort of San Juan. But Hutten was not the man to give up so easily. 'This captain was so spirited and determined to emerge with some success that, despite all the hardships and calamities he had endured, he had lost none of the energy with which he had left Coro.' Now the Indians told him about a place called Guagua or Omagua: he was to seek a town called Macatoa on the banks of the Guaviare. So Philip von Hutten set off again, with only forty men, but including the formidable veteran and tribal linguist Pedro de Limpias. They reached the Guaviare and, after some adventures, moved up it to Macatoa. The Spaniards had by now acquired an evil reputation among the tribes of this remote part of South America. They were said to be 'terrible, ferocious, cruel men, opposed to any peace, friendship or concord: people who incited wars and spilled human blood, and whose entire happiness was to disturb the wretched peoples they passed, with a thousand variations of cruelty.' But Hutten managed to reassure the chief of Macatoa, a branch of the Guaiupe tribe, and the Indians responded with traditional hospitality, bringing maize, fish and venison.

The chief of Macatoa said that 'alongside a certain mountain range, which could be observed from there on clear days, there were enormous towns of very rich people who possessed innumerable wealth.' The trouble was that, to these stone-age forest tribes, any more advanced group seemed enormously rich: it was all a matter of degree. The men of Macatoa acted as guides for the Germans and Spaniards, across a deserted plain for nine days to the land of a friendly tribe. The attractive reports were confirmed. The rich people ahead were said to be clothed and kept animals similar to llamas—conquistadores always associated llamas with gold, possibly in an unconscious reference to the golden fleece, for the *Argonautica* of Caius Valerius Flaccus was revived as a popular renaissance book, recently translated into Spanish and published at Alcalá de Henares. 'What pleased our men most was the great quantity of gold they were said to possess, and very secluded towns.' It took five more days to reach what the Spaniards took to be the edge of Omagua territory—a village superior to most that they had seen recently, a place of fifty huts and extensive plantations.

In the distance was the first sight of Hutten's promised land. 'From this place, . . . both the General and all the rest saw a town of disproportionate size, quite close. Although they were quite near, they could not see the far end of it. It was compact and well-ordered and in the middle was a house that greatly surpassed the rest in size and height. They asked the chief they had as a guide: "Whose house was that, so remarkable and eminent among the others?" He answered that it was the house of the chief, called Qvarica. He had some golden effigies or idols the size of boys, and a woman all made of gold who was their goddess. He and his subjects possessed other riches. But a short distance beyond, there were other chiefs who exceeded that one in the number of subjects and quantity of riches.'

Hutten's men saw in the distance a rich town of many huts, 'compact and well-ordered and in the middle a house that surpassed the rest in size.' A village of the modern San Miguel of the Sierra Nevada de Santa Marta.

The next move was to try to capture some members of this rich Omagua people. Philip von Hutten and Captain Arteaga sallied forth on the two best horses in the expedition and soon rode down two Indians. But, instead of the usual reaction of terror, these two Omagua calmly turned and defended themselves with long lances. Each managed to wound one of the mounted Spaniards, striking up below their padded armour and piercing their ribs. This was unheard-of, a most alarming development. The Spaniards were shaken by this unexpected reverse. They could hear war drums and pipes, and in the distance they could see the assembly of Omagua warriors. If two Omagua could cause such havoc, wounding the expedition's tough young leader, what would happen in a serious attack? The small contingent of explorers, exhausted from years of arduous travel, felt that it could not possibly attempt an invasion of this powerful land. So they crept away in the darkness, with the two wounded officers carried in hammocks by friendly Indians.

Back in the forest Indian village, a Spaniard called Diego de Montes decided that he must try his hand at surgery if his commander's life was to be saved. He knew nothing about anatomy. So he took an aged Indian 'who had had a full life' and sat him on a horse, dressed in Hutten's armour. He then took a native lance and pushed it up through the hole in the armour. 'Dismounting him from the horse, [the Indian] was opened up by Diego de Montes and his anatomy explored. [Montes] saw that the wound fell above the innards. He then took the two sick men and tore open their wounds along the length of their ribs. He washed them in a certain way, swinging them from side to side in the way that wineskins are washed. They were cleansed of much corruption that they had inside; and were soon healthy. The Indians of the village were impressed.'

The Omagua or Omegua who had wounded Hutten evidently lived in the eastern foothills of the Andes, near the headwaters of the Caquetá or the more southerly Putumayo. They cannot have been the same as the Omagua seen by Orellana, who lived on the main Amazon, opposite the mouth of the Putumayo hundreds of kilometres to the south-east. There was a skirmish against a large force of this tribe, but they proved to be less formidable than the Spaniards had feared: a charge by the expedition's scrawny horses had the usual devastating effect. Despite this, even Philip von Hutten realized that he had too few men to attempt an invasion of the Omagua. He decided to return to Coro to recruit more men, and then return for the great conquest of which he had always dreamed. So early in 1545, three years after entering the *llanos*, Hutten's men turned for home.

The long, tedious journey back was uneventful for such seasoned explorers. They marched for month after month along the familiar trail, crossing known rivers, with the Andes always above them to the left. They wintered during the rains of 1545. As the expedition approached the mountains south of Coro, Pedro de Limpias persuaded Hutten to let him push ahead to start recruiting men for the return expedition. Limpias was a tough veteran, who disliked Germans and in particular the rich young Bartholomeus Welser, heir of the great merchant-banking family from Augsburg. Philip von Hutten naturally favoured this scion of the house that owned the government of Venezuela, and Limpias resented having this young non-Spaniard preferred to himself as second-in-command of the expedition.

When Limpias reached Coro he found that a Spanish legal official, Juan de Carvajal, had some impressive-looking papers and was claiming that *he* was the next governor of Venezuela. Limpias encouraged this Carvajal to defy the Germans, who reached Barquisimeto in February 1546. There was confused manoeuvring between the rival groups. Each side tried to outwit the other and capture its men or horses; there were mutinies; there was an apparent reconciliation, with the Germans in the ascendant; but in the end, through treachery, Juan de Carvajal managed to seize the two German nobles. Carvajal was still brandishing his documents, which were in fact forgeries. He was now gripped by the gold-rush fever, wanting to find the rich land described by Limpias—for unlike Hutten, who had been in the interior for almost five years, Carvajal must have known all about the El Dorado legend. There were wild scenes between the two rival commanders, with Hutten saying that he was going to report to the King and the Welser, and Carvajal shouting back that the Welser had nothing to do with this land. As the German explorer and the Spanish lawyer hurled defiance at one another, their men grew violent and passionate in the remote camp. On a later occasion, Carvajal's men charged into the Welser camp, cutting down any who opposed them. Hutten and Welser were captured and bound. Carvajal's soldiers incited him: ' "What are you doing?" "Do you think you are in Santo Domingo or Valladolid? Turn on them and cut off their heads!" ' Carvajal sent his negro slave to sharpen two machetes. He ordered his man to cut the heads off some followers of the Welser. Young Bartholomeus Welser protested that they had not received absolution. Carvajal turned on him: ' "Shut up, Bartolomé Welser, or I'll send you to the King to be punished!" ' At which his ensign said: ' "Your Honour is the king, and there is no other king here. Do what you must do!" ' Carvajal then ordered his slave: ' "Since I am the king, negro, cut off Bartolomé Welser's head!" ' This was done. Then came the turn of Philip von Hutten. The explorer asked for the priest to hear his confession, but Carvajal refused, saying ' "Let him confess in heaven." ' Aguado wrote that the execution was a clumsy business, with 'their heads cut off on the ground itself, with a blunt machete, with barbarous cruelty. . . . The worn machete could not cut anything: it hacked pieces off their necks, chopping and breaking the flesh and bones of which these were composed, so that they were given cruel and agonizing deaths.' The severed bodies lay beside the camp throughout that moonlit night and were given a shallow burial next morning. Carvajal seized the two Germans' belongings and distributed them among his men. He then fled inland with his followers, hoping to found a settlement in the interior of Venezuela.

There was a great outcry when the news reached Europe. The elder Bartholomeus Welser wrote to the King protesting about Carvajal's murder of his son, which he said was done 'from insatiable avarice, for he stole everything they had brought with them'. And Hutten's brother, the Bishop of Eichstedt, wrote begging the King to arrange the recovery of Philip von Hutten's treasure and the diary of his journey. Justice was done efficiently. A royal magistrate called Juan Pérez de Tolosa marched boldly inland with only 25 men. He managed to surprise and capture Carvajal at Tocuyo despite his larger force. Carvajal was given a trial, in which he defended himself by saying that he had freed Caquetió and other

Indians chained by Hutten, and that the German had been impaling Indians by the roadside. He claimed that Hutten and Welser were in revolt against royal authority. None of this could save Carvajal, particularly when his patents of office with forged signatures were found. Tolosa sentenced him to be dragged behind a horse to the gallows, and there hanged, and left hanging.

Philip von Hutten was much lamented by his contemporaries. Juan de Castellanos wrote that 'his brain, his valour and his prudence concealed his lack of years, and clearly showed the most generous descent from which he sprang. . . . [Hutten and Welser] were both Germans and excellent captains.' And Ruiz de Vallejo wrote to the royal audiencia that 'all the rest weep for him and will weep for as long as they are in the Indies, for they say that he was not just a captain-general, but was the father of them all.'

With the death of Hutten, the great German-led expeditions ceased. They had explored some of the most inaccessible parts of South America, had caused the deaths of hundreds of Europeans and thousands of natives, and had left no mark whatever on the map. Coro was a pathetic cluster of huts on the sands of the Caribbean shore. When Pérez de Tolosa arrived to punish Hutten's murderers, he was appalled by the poverty of the men of Coro. 'Had I not brought a little cloth and footwear I could not have had any men to take with me.' They had no gold or silver or other money, despite all their frenzied hunting for treasure, but were using 'little counters made from fish, which they trade with one another at a value of a real'. From now on, Spaniards started the permanent colonization of Venezuela; and it was not long before the royal grant of that territory to the Welser was revoked.

While Hutten and Pérez de Quesada were searching for El Dorado in the Andean foothills, another dogged old conquistador also hoped to find his fortune in that wilderness. Sebastián de Benalcázar had been deflected from his El Dorado expedition of 1542 by the need to help royal forces punish Francisco Pizarro's assassins. He remained convinced that the gateway to El Dorado lay in the hills behind his town Timaná. He set off in 1543 to punish the Páez Indians who had fought so effectively at Timaná. He took his young son Francisco, as well as some veterans of Orinoco and Venezuelan expeditions, and even some men who had wanted to join Pérez de Quesada's ill-fated expedition. Benalcázar's expedition was another disaster. It became entangled in the forested hills of the Páez. Many men were lost. Royal officials at Cali wrote to the King that 'had God not miraculously wished to favour him, [Benalcázar] himself and all the rest could not have escaped alive.'

Benalcázar had a lieutenant of great ability called Juan Cabrera who administered Popayán when the governor was away. The royal officials recommended that this Cabrera be sent to conquer the land of Cinnamon, La Canela, beyond the snowy mountains south of Timaná, 'for that is the entry by which one must enter on that conquest . . . In those lands there are such great reports of wealth, that they should be colonized, discovered and conquered.' Cabrera did go south, and started to explore those hills. But he was a more thorough and cautious explorer than his master Benalcázar. In 1544 he sent to Montalvo de Lugo in Bogotá, suggesting that they pool their resources in men and horses, 'to go well equipped on the El Dorado expedition, of which there are great reports that it contains much wealth.' Benalcázar sent his son Francisco, also with men and horses, to help Cabrera 'discover the provinces of Dorado and La Canela, in order to settle all the land that lay from sea to sea on this route.' But Cabrera then learned that Montalvo de Lugo had betrayed his friend Hernán Pérez de Quesada to the royal investigator in Bogotá. He hesitated to go exploring with such a companion.

Cabrera was then deflected, just as Benalcázar had been a few years earlier, and was ordered to go and help suppress another civil war in Peru. This time the rebel was the dashing Gonzalo Pizarro himself. After emerging from his ordeal in the land of Cinnamon, the handsome Pizarro returned to what is now Bolivia, to live in great luxury on his estates there. But when the Spanish government issued New Laws for the government of the Americas that were considered far too liberal towards the natives, the settlers, the conquistadores, rebelled. They summoned Gonzalo Pizarro to lead them in what amounted to a unilateral declaration of independence against the mother country. For four years, Pizarro was uncrowned king of Peru. He and his tough soldiers ran Peru in a brutal dictatorship, a time of great hardship for its natives. The Spanish Crown revoked the pro-Indian laws, and sent an administrator to reconquer Peru from the rebels. After a series of battles, Gonzalo Pizarro, the first to search for El Dorado, was defeated and hanged in 1548 outside the Inca capital, Cuzco.

The New Laws that had inspired Gonzalo Pizarro's rebellion were the product of an extraordinary anti-colonial movement in Spain itself. A great many people, particularly theologians, were worried about the morality of invading other lands —for Europeans had not yet embarked on their age of colonial expansion. There was also concern about the appalling treatment of American Indians by their Spanish conquerors. There was no lack of reports of abuse and atrocities. Cieza de León wrote that 'His Majesty was informed by many people from many sources of the great oppression the Indians suffered from the Spaniards.'

The leader of the reformers was Bartolomé de las Casas, himself once a colonial settler, but now an ecclesiastic and bishop of Chiapas in southern Mexico. Las Casas returned to Spain in 1539. He and his followers launched a sustained and highly successful campaign against the concept and institutions of colonial rule. They condemned encomiendas—the system whereby Indians were forced to provide food and tribute to Spanish masters—as 'contrary to the well-being of the Indian republic, against all reason and human prudence, against the welfare of our Lord and King, contrary to all civil and common law, against all rules of moral philosophy and theology, and against God's will and his Church'. They warned the King that his very soul was in jeopardy because of the unchristian outrages being done in his name. The first success of these eloquent reformers was the issue of the pro-Indian New Laws, at Barcelona on 20 November 1542. As we have seen, the Laws created such a furore when they were promulgated in the Americas, that Gonzalo Pizarro and many others risked their necks in rebellion. King Charles could not afford to rule without the flow of silver from the Indies; so he bowed to expediency and revoked the most humanitarian of the New Laws.

The next stage in the struggle for morality in the Americas was a great debate between Las Casas himself and Juan Ginés de Sepúlveda, an erudite humanist who argued that the superiority of Spanish civilization and religion justified the conquests. The debate was held in Valladolid during the hot month of August 1550. Bemused judges listened for days on end while the two protagonists read hundreds of pages of argument, in elegant Latin. Both debaters used the same sources—Aristotle and the Bible—to buttress their conflicting arguments. The debate was never properly resolved; but it did have an effect on the search for El Dorado. Prior to the debate, in April 1549, the King issued new rules for the conduct of expeditions, including the amazing order that all food consumed on them be paid for! Then, on 16 April 1550 a royal decree ordered the suspension of *all* conquests, expeditions and exploration, until the Las Casas-Sepúlveda debate could decide on their legitimacy. It was a most extraordinary move: the most powerful monarch in the world stopped his subjects from conquering new lands on his behalf. The ban lasted for a decade. It worked admirably, for no one could recruit or equip an expedition without permission, and there was no point in conquering new lands if the conquest would then be deemed to have been illegal. So for ten years the Indians of the Americas had a respite. Press gangs stopped rounding them up to march off as shackled porters. Forest villagers no longer had their seclusion broken by the arrival of packs of starving desperadoes, who stole their food and asked frenzied questions about rich lands over the horizon.

Bishop Bartolomé de las Casas, the anti-colonial reformer whose eloquence led to the law of 1550 forbidding all expeditions.

8 IN NOVEMBER 1549 THE INHABITANTS OF THE FRONTIER TOWN OF CHACHAPOYAS IN north-east Peru were startled by the arrival of 'some three hundred Indians who said they were from Brazil and had left it in far greater numbers. . . . They told great news of their journey continually up-river, in which they had spent ten years.' These Brazilian Indians had actually migrated *up* the Amazon, paddling for many hundreds of kilometres against the current. They were probably Tupinamba, trying to escape the oppression of Portuguese colonists who had invaded their lands on the coast of Brazil.

The first reaction of the Spaniards in Chachapoyas was to protect themselves against these fierce warriors. Once this was done, the Brazilians were dispersed to different parts of Peru, so that they could be used as slave labour without any danger of their uniting to escape again. They were also interrogated about their extraordinary adventure—an exploit more formidable even than the conquistadores' own expeditions. They reported 'marvellous things they had seen, diverse tribes against which they had fought, strange and intemperate climates they had discovered, and notable provinces where they had been. Of these novelties, they described none of greater splendour than the greatness of the Omaguas . . .: the inestimable value of their riches, and the vastness of their trading. This aroused the usual desire of Spaniards accustomed to exploring and conquering, to such an extent that in Peru they talked of nothing but this expedition.'

This glowing account reminded people of Orellana's description of the Omagua. When he passed their lands on the upper Amazon in 1542, he had noticed fine roads that appeared to lead to richer cities in the interior. A later Portuguese writer summed up current thinking about the Omagua: 'These rich people must be the inhabitants of Lake Dorado, in whose discovery infinite Spanish men and captains have been consumed and came to die in the forests of our Maranhão [Amazon].' Gómez de Alvarado, corregidor of Chachapoyas, sent four Brazilian Indians with their chief Uiraracu ('Big Bow') to see the president of Peru, Pedro de la Gasca. Alvarado begged to be allowed to go and conquer this land of the Omagua; but Gasca, who had just finished suppressing Gonzalo Pizarro's rebellion, felt that there had been enough expeditions lately, and refused.

There was now a new idea: that El Dorado might be further south, among the Omagua on the Amazon itself. It was inevitable that someone would go to investigate. Almost as soon as the royal ban on expeditions was lifted, a later Viceroy of Peru gave permission for a conquest of this province of 'Omagua and Dorado'. His choice as leader was Pedro de Ursúa, a well-connected man who had impressed the Viceroy with his exploits in Colombia—Ursúa had suppressed a number of Indian risings, notably among the gold-rich Tairona of the Sierra Nevada de Santa Marta. Ursúa reached Peru at the end of 1558 and received his patent as governor of the new expedition the following February. He spent 1559 recruiting men and gathering supplies for a great expedition. The Viceroy wanted to clear Peru of troublesome vagabonds, unemployed soldiers who had survived yet another civil war during the mid-1550s.

A Cuiva Indian from the southern llanos the area penetrated by Jiménez de Quesada in 1570.

There was no lack of recruits for Ursúa's venture. Excited men spent small fortunes equipping themselves and their followers; monks left monasteries to join; married men went with their wives and children. A flotilla of brigs, flatboats, rafts and canoes was built on the Huallaga, a tributary of the Amazon that was free of rapids and that flowed close to Chachapoyas. The expedition was a splendid affair, with 370 Spaniards and thousands of Andean Indians. It was the largest force of Europeans to embark on the Amazon in two centuries. But it was explosively thrown together. Ursúa himself was unknown. His men were the rabble of Peru, with no loyalty to their leader, often inexperienced in jungle expeditions, and frequently seething with discontent after being dispossessed in the recent civil wars. Pedro de Ursúa proved to be an ineffective leader; and he compounded his difficulties by taking his beautiful mestizo mistress doña Inéz de Atienza.

The expedition's purpose was to colonize the lands of the Machiparo or the Omagua, and explore their rich hinterland. It set sail on 26 September 1560 and reached its first objective easily enough. But the disorganized rabble was quickly disillusioned at finding themselves in a rain-soaked forest instead of a glittering new conquest. They took to massacring Indians, and the expedition was soon short of food and festering with revolt. Pedro de Ursúa spent more time in dalliance with the lovely Inéz than leading his men. The dissidents claimed that she was their real leader, and that they were liable to punishment at the whim of a whore.

Ursúa set his men to work building a town on the muddy banks of the Amazon. It was the rainy season, with its dismal skies, constant heavy rains, and incessant dripping from the trees of the forest. A Portuguese called López Vaz wrote an account of this notorious expedition, that is known only in its translation into Elizabethan English. He told how Ursúa's men contrasted the comforts of Peru with the misery of the Amazon, 'where because it raineth much, and withall is very hot, sickness and want of victuals began to prevaile amongst them, whereupon the soldiers fell a murmuring among themselves.' The unrest rapidly degenerated into mutiny. On the night of 1 January 1561, the rebels murdered Pedro de Ursúa in his hammock, near the mouth of the Putumayo. The mutineers elevated a Spanish noble, don Fernando de Guzmán, to be their figurehead. But the instigator of the rebellion was Lope de Aguirre, a man of unmitigated evil, cruel, psychopathic and gripped by an obsessive grievance against the whole of Spanish society. López Vaz described him as a Biscayan, 'a very little man of bodie and lame of one of his legs, but very valient and of good experience in the wars . . .'

Lope de Aguirre's dream was to return to conquer Peru, where he felt that he had been unjustly deprived of his deserts. For a time the expedition pursued its original objectives, under the leadership of Guzmán. On 2 June he and his friends divided the chief positions in the army among themselves: Lope de Aguirre became Camp Master, but he shocked his companions when he signed 'traitor' after his name. Aguirre then started to put his amazing plan into effect. He persuaded the expedition to build more boats and seek salvation by descending the mighty Amazon. Any thoughts of finding El Dorado were forgotten. Aguirre's greatest triumph was to induce Fernando de Guzmán into proclaiming himself 'Lord and Prince of Peru, the Main, and Chile'. All the leading men in the expedition kissed the hands of their new prince and were rewarded with great tracts of uninhabitable forest. Lope de Aguirre drew up a strange document, dated 23 March 1561 and signed by 186 of the 270 men remaining on the expedition. In it they declared that 'all present with one voice named and elected Fernando de Guzmán as prince and lord, in order that he would go to the kingdoms of Peru and conquer them, and remove and dispossess those who now hold them . . . and should remunerate and reward us in them for the labours we have had in conquering and pacifying the native Indians of those kingdoms. For although we won those Indians with our persons and effort, spilling our blood, at our expense, we were not rewarded . . . Instead the Viceroy . . . exiled us with deception and falsehood, saying that we were coming to the best and most populous land in the world, when it is in fact bad and uninhabitable . . .'

Prince Fernando's rule was a short one. He managed to persuade the beautiful Inéz to join him as consort of the expedition's new leader. Two large boats were finally completed, after three months' work, and everyone sailed off, down the Amazon, towards the reconquest of Peru itself. All of them were now rebels and outlaws. Aguirre managed to infect those around him with his own twisted passions. There was jealousy of Inéz's lover, mingled with mistrust of this bogus prince. So, on 22 May, on an island in the Amazon, Aguirre ordered his men to murder the expedition's leaders. Two men called Llamoso and Carrión went to kill doña Inéz: 'One stabbed at her and the other took her by the hair and gave her over twenty sword thrusts. Thus ended the poor lady who was the most tragic figure in the world. She was the most beautiful lady remaining in Peru, according to all who knew her.' Other killers went on to murder don Fernando, with a thrust that pierced him and his bed, as well as some of his close companions. After this massacre, the expedition became a bloodbath, with the paranoid Lope de Aguirre in full command. He surrounded himself with a loyal guard of fifty Basque arquebusiers, and he disarmed the rest of the expedition. He had no interest in exploration. He drove the men downstream day and night, as fast as the current and their sails and paddles could take them. He made sure that they avoided the lands of the Omagua, which might have tempted some on a diversionary conquest. It was not long before the boats had passed the narrows of Obidos, and felt the first movement of Atlantic tides.

During the descent of the Amazon there were a few skirmishes against riverine tribes. But the greatest danger was Aguirre's lust for blood. During those months on the Amazon, he reduced the expedition's Spaniards from 370 to 230. López Vaz said that 'he determined not to carry with him any gentleman or persons of qualitie, and therefore slew all such persons; and then departing onely with the common souldiers, he left behind him all the Spanish women and sicke men. If I should rehearse all the cruell murthers of this wicked man one by one, I should be over tedious unto you.' Aguirre was constantly in fear of his life. 'Had he seene at any time but two souldiers talking together, he would streight suspect that they were conspiring of his death . . .' He was equally cruel to his Andean Indians. Most had died, but to lighten the boats for the sea voyage, Aguirre ordered the remaining 170 men and women to be marooned on the banks of the Amazon, at the mercy of its tribes. These victims were *yanaconas*, Christian Indians who loyally served Spanish masters. They wept and complained bitterly at the injustice of their treatment. But when some Spaniards tried to intercede for them Aguirre immediately had these garrotted for insubordination.

Aguirre's boats sailed into the Atlantic at the beginning of July 1561. Winds and currents took them swiftly past the shores of Guiana, and on 21 July they reached the island of Margarita off the coast of Venezuela. Its inhabitants feared an attack by corsairs, but were relieved to find that the strange ships belonged to Spaniards. They allowed these compatriots to land, and it was not long before Aguirre's men had seized the island and murdered its governor. There were more murders and plots. Lope de Aguirre planned to capture Nombre de Dios and round up all the discontented soldiers of Panama for his great invasion of Peru. But in the end he sailed only to the mainland, landing at Borburata early in September. He then set off across country. His mad plan was to cross the Andes and the northern part of the continent to reach his goal. As his horses slipped on the mud, trying to climb into the hills in the rainy season, Aguirre screamed defiance at God: ' "Does God think that, because it is raining, I am not going to reach Peru and destroy the world? Then he does not know me!" ' The rebel force took a town called Valencia, and moved on to Barquisimeto, the place inland from Coro first seen by Nicolaus Federmann.

Aguirre's men were now deserting whenever they could find a chance to slip from his clutches. Overwhelming royal forces were marching to crush the rebels. It was at this point, in October 1561, that Aguirre wrote a famous letter, addressed to the King of Spain. It was an extraordinary document, a mixture of rebellious defiance, megalomania and self-pity. He told the King of his 24 years of service and two wounds, and then accused King Philip of being cruel and faithless towards his conquistadores. 'Consider, Lord and King, that you cannot, with any just royal title, take any income from these lands where you risked nothing, until those who have laboured and sweated for them have first had their reward.' He inveighed against corrupt friars and self-seeking lawyers. He boasted of killing Ursúa and Guzmán and all the others who were plotting against him. He ended by warning the King about the Amazon river. 'God knows how we escaped from such a fearful lake! I advise you, Lord and King, do not organize or permit any fleet to attempt this ill-fated river: for I swear to you, King, on my word as a Christian, that if a hundred thousand men came, none would escape. For the reports are false: there is nothing on that river but despair, especially for novices from Spain.'

Lope de Aguirre realized that his position in Barquisimeto was untenable. He planned to march back towards the coast. On 27 October 1561 he went to prepare his sixteen-year-old daughter Elvira for the journey. He found that yet more of his men had deserted. So he placed a crucifix in the girl's hand, grabbed his sword, and ran her through. He also killed her serving woman. He shouted that he was doing it to save them from rape by the royalists. He would not let his Elvira go through life as the daughter of a rebel! Aguirre's own men then rushed in and killed him with their arquebuses. His body was quartered; the sections hung for years at the gates of different towns, an awful reminder of the fate of rebels. But his mad odyssey had started with a refusal to join the search for El Dorado.

When Lope de Aguirre started marching across Venezuela, there was alarm, almost panic, far away in Bogotá. The civic authorities required all able-bodied

Quimbaya flasks from the middle Cauca valley have the elegant shapes of oriental pottery. The flasks held lime, used as a catalyst in chewing coca.

men to present themselves for possible military service. The man who was placed in charge of these defensive preparations was none other than Gonzalo Jiménez de Quesada.

The conqueror of the Muisca had emerged triumphantly from the morass of legal actions that confronted him on his return to Spain. He was belatedly granted the title of Marshal and, a few years later, the rank of Adelantado—the second highest rank awarded to successful conquistadores, but not as distinguished as that of Marquis, so far received only by Cortés and Pizarro. Jiménez de Quesada was also permitted to return to New Granada. He settled in the city he had founded, Santafé de Bogotá, and enjoyed the substantial income from his various encomiendas of tribute-paying Indians. He lived quietly, occasionally undertaking minor magisterial or administrative jobs for the colony's governors. It was therefore a proud moment for Quesada to organize the defence of Bogotá and review its troops. His ageing veterans marched in from their encomiendas and were pleased to see their old commander in action again.

The El Dorado legend was now discredited but by no means dead. The colossal efforts of earlier expeditions seemed to indicate that there must be substance to the quest: it was only bad luck and bad judgment that had produced such spectacular disasters.

The failure of Ursúa's attempt to conquer the land of the Omagua proved nothing, for Lope de Aguirre had sabotaged that venture. Three commanders from Chachapoyas—the town in Peru where the Brazilian Indians had ended their ascent of the Amazon—therefore undertook a land journey northwards from their city. By marching from Chachapoyas to the Marañón (Amazon) and then north along the eastern edge of the Andes, they felt sure of finding the rich heartlands of the Omagua. They would explore all the lands beyond the expeditions of Hohermuth, Gonzalo Pizarro, Pérez de Quesada and Hutten. The expedition left Chachapoyas in 1566, led by Captain Martín de Poveda and containing two notable explorers called Pedro Maraver de Silva and Diego Soleto. We know very little about the events of this expedition, which had no chronicler. But anyone who knows some of the land it traversed must be astounded by its achievement. For its members succeeded: they reached San Juan de los Llanos after great hardships and then moved up to Bogotá. It was an expedition far beyond the aspirations of any modern explorer. It somehow managed to cross many hundreds of kilometres of some of the most appalling country in the world: areas that had annihilated previous expeditions—hilly forests, tropical rivers and swamps that are still almost entirely uninhabited. This feat is so remarkable that it would be tempting to dismiss it as a fraud; but there could be no deception about an expedition that left Chachapoyas and was next seen, months later, near Bogotá, having traversed fifteen hundred kilometres of wilderness and lost most of its members.

Poveda's expedition performed two notable services: it finally established that there was no wealth in the hinterland of the Omagua, and it showed that El Dorado was not to be found east of Quito or south of Timaná, beyond the regions searched by Gonzalo Pizarro and Pérez de Quesada. But it opened a new field of speculation. Its interrogations of Indians indicated that the rich lands lay farther east, in the *llanos* themselves, towards the Orinoco. The location of El Dorado moved

Quimbaya goldsmiths used techniques that enabled them to create natural curves on human bodies or a feline head.

145

dramatically, back almost to the land of Meta, where Diego de Ordás had once sought wealth beyond the rapids of the Orinoco.

This shift in location of the legendary kingdom was confirmed by other sources. There were persistent reports that two hundred Spaniards, shipwrecked from Ordás' expedition, were living somewhere near the source of the Orinoco. An inquiry was held about this at Bogotá on 19 January 1560. One witness told about a half-caste morisco who had reached Margarita island in about 1548 and said that he had been among these Spaniards. They were living in pallisaded villages, subjects of a powerful ruler called Carivan.

In 1556 Captain Juan de Avellaneda went to found a town at San Juan de Los Llanos, an outpost at the edge of the great plains, on the site of the place where Hohermuth, Federmann and Hutten had all wintered during their explorations. People involved in that settlement swore that they saw Indians with gold jewellery, with golden figures of lizards, frogs, and other creatures. All the Indians said that they had obtained these from the interior of the *llanos* 'towards other mountains, where there was a great quantity of gold and people'. Juan Rodríguez asserted that 'From this I regard it as certain and proven that that land is the richest there could possibly be of any so far discovered: for these objects were of worked gold, and only smiths or people who understand [gold] could have made them.' A few years later an Indian trader appeared at San Juan and told its eager inhabitants about the rich land that contained Ordas' missing Spaniards—the land was now full of half-caste children and dogs that they had introduced into it. This was the land of Coarica (Hutten's Qvarica). It was eighty days' march from San Juan, and the Indian offered to lead an expedition to conquer it. He held up his hands thirty times, to show that it would take 300 Spaniards to conquer this last great empire . . .

The arrival of the Peruvian explorers, by such an appalling route, caused a justifiable sensation in New Granada. Gonzalo Jiménez de Quesada questioned the survivors with great care. He decided that they had shown the way to another conquest worthy of an old conquistador of his stature. He became as excited about the search for El Dorado as his brother had been almost twenty years before.

Although now in his late sixties, the Adelantado applied for a patent to explore and govern a broad expanse of the southern *llanos*. There were delays, but on 26 November 1568 King Philip sent an order to his audiencia in Bogotá to grant Quesada the governorship he wanted. On 21 July 1569 he was named as governor and commander-in-chief of the province of Pauto and Papamene, on the *llanos*, with an extension of 400 leagues east and south—an immense territory that would

Medallion heads of (left) Pedro de Ursúa, (centre) Sebastian de Benalcázar, (right) Nicolaus Federmann.

146

have stretched east into modern Guiana and south far beyond the Amazon. In return, Jiménez de Quesada undertook to go in person and to take at least 400 Spaniards, fully equipped and ministered to by at least eight ecclesiastics. He was to try to found new towns, taking artisans, cattle and negro slaves, but absolutely no Indians—royal decrees now forbade the use of Indians as porters, and the encomenderos of New Granada did not want to lose their tribute-payers. If his conquest was successful, Jiménez de Quesada would receive the title of Marquis that he coveted so greatly.

Everyone flocked to join the great old explorer on this second golden conquest. He organized the mightiest of all expeditions. There were three hundred Spaniards, 1,100 horses, 600 cows, 800 pigs and, of course, in complete disregard of the royal decrees prohibiting Indian porterage, 1,500 native Indians and imported negroes. It all cost 150,000 ducats: enough to pay the salaries of the governor and royal officials of New Granada for decades.

Jiménez de Quesada marched his huge column of conquerors and colonists down to the *llanos* and deep into those endless dusty plains. They left Bogotá in December 1569 and explored a great expanse of the southern *llanos*. The hardships were greater even than those of expeditions that stayed close to the Andean foot-hills. There was nothing but the silent solitude of the *llanos*. Baked dry in summer and drowned in the rainy season, this was a land of chest-high grasses, dismal swamps stretching to the horizons, little food and few nomadic Indians, and clouds of thirsty mosquitoes. After many months of misery, men started to desert. Jiménez de Quesada acted resolutely to prevent mutiny or disintegration: he hanged would-be deserters. The expedition was struck by swamp fevers, and even the tough old conquistador had to relent somewhat. He finally allowed the sickest of his starving men to leave. But the expedition was now so deep in the heart of the continent that it took Captain Juan de Maldonado six months to stagger back to the meagre comforts of San Juan. We know little about the detail of this tragic exploration. Jiménez de Quesada had taken the best contemporary historian of New Granada, the Franciscan Antonio Medrano, to record the conquest of El Dorado; but Medrano was one of the many who died, and his notes were lost.

The expedition roamed the *llanos* for two and a half years. It was not until June 1572 that the authorities in Bogotá heard about the disaster. A few men reached the town and reported that Quesada 'is lost, fifty leagues from this city. Of three hundred soldiers he took, fifty are returning; of fifteen hundred Indians, Christian natives and mestizos, thirty; and of fifteen hundred horses, another thirty to forty. He has made no settlement and has achieved nothing. Instead, there are tales of many complaints and cruelties.' When the crestfallen Jiménez de Quesada finally reached Bogotá with his shattered survivors, the royal officials wrote to the King rather smugly about the discomfiture of the old hero. They reported that his expedition ended badly, 'for he was defeated and lost everything; and there were many deaths of men who went there.' 'After three years he emerged, lost, leaving there almost all the Spanish men, who died of starvation, and all the natives he took as porters, and after losing all his baggage and horses, which were eaten out of hunger.' The old man recovered from the destruction of so many of his younger followers. He soon started planning another attempt on El Dorado. The authorities

had to distract him with punitive expeditions against native rebellions. He then contracted a skin complaint that his contemporaries described as leprosy; and finally died, aged almost eighty.

Two other captains had obtained patents to conquer El Dorado, both in 1568, the same year that the King authorized Jiménez de Quesada to be governor of Pauto and Papamene. Diego Fernández de Serpa became convinced that the elusive El Dorado lay farther east, east of the *llanos* where Quesada sought it, in the Guiana hills lying south of the mouth of the Orinoco. He applied for permission to conquer this region, and received a patent as its governor, as early as 3 August 1549. But just as he was about to march inland from the Caribbean, Serpa was ordered to stop: he was the first victim of the royal prohibition on expeditions that resulted from the Las Casas-Sepúlveda debate. It was not until

Indians of Cabruta annihilating the colonizing expedition of Diego Fernández de Serpa in 1570.

15 May 1568 that Serpa received another patent, this time as governor of a region between the Orinoco and Amazon, stretching 300 leagues along the Orinoco. He called his territory New Andalucía and marched inland from Cumaná to occupy it in October 1569. Fernández de Serpa took plenty of Spanish farmers with their wives and herds of cattle. The pioneers built a town on the coast and the men moved inland to explore before trekking with their families. Most were newly arrived in the Americas. So, on 10 May 1570, they walked into a highly successful native ambush near the Cabruta tributary of the Orinoco. Serpa himself was killed, with two of his captains and 74 men. The forty survivors fled to the coast, and Serpa's bid to colonize El Dorado collapsed.

The other aspirant for El Dorado was Pedro Maraver de Silva, one of the leaders of the remarkable expedition from Chachapoyas to Bogotá. He received his patent on the same day as Fernández de Serpa, for a territory also between the Amazon and Orinoco, but for 300 leagues beyond Serpa's New Andalucía. Maraver de Silva hoped that his concession included the lands of the Omagua. He called it New Extremadura. It certainly was 'extremadura': had Maraver de Silva ever reached it, he would have found that it lay far south of the Amazon, in still unexplored forests near Brazilian Acre and Bolivia. Maraver de Silva had no trouble recruiting men in his native Extremadura, the harsh part of Spain near the Portuguese border, home of the Pizarros and of many bold conquistadores. He reached Margarita in April 1569. Most of his men wanted to march inland from Maracapana, where there were no hills between them and the *llanos*; but the governor insisted on setting out from Burburata. His bullying manner ruined the attempt to reach New Extremadura. Within a few months each of his leading captains deserted, each taking a large part of his army. By the beginning of 1570 he was back in Barquisimeto with the rump of his force, and yet another attempt on El Dorado had failed. But the mirage persisted. Juan de Castellanos—a sober chronicler—wrote that there had been so many enticing reports, from so many sources, that 'it is impossible that there will not be some good lands found where the province of Guiana lies, in the extended region between the river Orinoco and that of Orellana [the Amazon].'

9

GONZALO JIMÉNEZ DIED WITHOUT ANY IMMEDIATE FAMILY BUT WITH GREAT ESTATES of tribute-paying Muisca. He remained obsessed by El Dorado and determined that his heirs should conquer the kingdom that had eluded him. He chose as his heir his niece María, who was married to an old soldier called Antonio de Berrío, veteran of many Spanish campaigns in Italy, Flanders and against the Moors. In his will Jiménez de Quesada wrote: 'Item: I declare as my successor in . . . the governorship [of El Dorado], Captain Antonio de Berrío, husband of my niece doña María . . .' He could not possibly have chosen a better successor. Berrío proved to be as stubborn a fanatic and as indestructible an old warrior as the Adelantado Jiménez de Quesada himself.

Within two years of learning about the legacy, the Berríos obtained permission to move to New Granada with their many children. They reached Bogotá in 1581 and by the end of the following year had, after a long legal wrangle, obtained the succession as governor of El Dorado between the Pauto and Papamene rivers. They settled in the village of Chita, high in the Andes near the Sierra Nevada de Cocuy, and started to amass the revenues from their many encomiendas. The Indians of Motavita had to produce 72 pesos of gold a year; those of Chita, 567 pesos and many cotton cloaks; those of Pueblo de la Sal, 180 pesos and salt 'baked into loaves'; Baganique, 597 pesos; Chiscas, cotton mantles; and Tamara, 'good, fine, white cotton mantles'. All this tribute went towards the equipping of Berrío's attempt on El Dorado. He wrote to the King in September 1583: 'May it please God to let this concealed province be discovered, and a great infinity of peoples be converted to the Catholic faith, and the royal patrimony be greatly increased, by the love of God!'

Antonio de Berrío finally descended on to the plains with only eighty men, but with five hundred horses and great quantities of cattle, pigs and food. His column moved in a cloud of fine dust. There was deep silence in the *llanos*, a region of impressive monotony where the far horizons are lost in heat haze. The dreary march was interrupted only by occasional marshes, which the horses forded with difficulty, or dense thickets of palm or pine near the water courses. By February 1584 the expedition reached the Meta river.

There were occasional villages of Achagua Indians, whose large thatch huts were tightly closed against the myriad mosquitoes. 'They are a tribe where Indian men and women go naked without wearing anything whatsoever. Their heads are shaven: they shave them with small canes that they grow for this purpose. . . . They sleep in hammocks of a cord they make from twisted palm hearts. Their barter consists of shells and beads, salt, and dogs, tools, and gowns that they obtain from peaceful Indians in exchange for Indian women and child slaves that they raid or obtain by barter from other tribes, jaguar skins, and birds they call caharos, macaws and parrots, and anatto dye. They seemed to me,' wrote Berrío's man Alonso de Pontes, 'a people of good disposition, who love knowing what we call all things and my name, and who are very shrewd traders.' The Achagua had plenty of food—manioc, ground maize, pineapples from which they made a spirit, and plenty of fat fish and guama fruit. They were generous in feeding the passing expedition. The Spaniards had a healthy respect for the Achagua, who knew the labyrinthine swamps of the *llanos* and who could creep up noiselessly to attack a

Berrío tried for fifteen years to penetrate the forests of the Orinoco and scale the Guiana cordillera. He wrote to the King: 'By the grace of God, I discovered the cordillera so ardently desired and sought . . .'

151

sleeping camp. Diego Pinto described them as 'a very bellicose people, cannibal and warlike, and they have a very fierce poison that takes only sixteen hours to finish off a person wounded by it.'

One group of Achagua described a community of Amazons who lived five days to the east. Their village was a daunting paradise for visiting men. 'When you arrive, they come out and each takes her Indian by the hand and leads him to her house. Next morning the men are paid, according to how well they laboured the night before, in arrows that the women make, very embellished with poison; but any Indian who did not perform well would be killed. They are very white and go naked; and they have much food, manioc and maize, sweet potatoes and fish, and they cook very well. [Indians] do not dare to stay there for more than one night, after which they immediately return.'

Other Achagua excited Berrío by telling him that 'within ten leagues there are ten thousand Indians.' He sent a message to the authorities in Bogotá from the banks of the Casanare river. He told them that the Indians were giving him fantastic reports. 'I have made great efforts to interrogate each one by himself, apart from the rest, and using great tricks and [interrogation] techniques; so that I believe that a great part of it is true.' So the expedition trudged forward across the plains. In April the rains set in: the hard dusty ground turned spongy and the rivers flooded. Berrío ordered his men to camp, four leagues from the Orinoco, to sit out the rains of 1584. Four thousand Achagua attacked but were driven off with some losses. Berrío questioned the prisoners. They told him to aim for the hills on the far side of the Orinoco—which was precisely where he was convinced he would find El Dorado. 'They say that on the far side of it are great settlements and a very great number of people, and great riches of gold and precious stones. I asked whether there were as many people as on the plains. They laughed at me: they said that in the cordillera there were many settlements, in each of which there were more people than in all the llanos!'

These mountains contained Lake Manoa, a vast saline lake, so large that it took

Tribes of the llanos told Antonio Berrío that he must seek rich lands in the hills of Guiana beyond the Orinoco.

the Indians three days to paddle their canoes across. 'They say that once this lake is crossed, the great provinces of Guiana stretch to the Marañón [Amazon]. The Indians say that it would take two moons to go from Manoa to the [Amazon].' In the language of the Achagua, Manoa actually means 'lake'. It was a return to the idea connecting El Dorado with a fabulous lake.

The hills beyond the Orinoco were now firmly established as the target for El Dorado seekers. Juan de Salas, governor of Margarita island, had already described this wonderful place: 'There is much news that there is gold in the province of Guiana, both from Aruak Indians who come to this island and also from Spaniards who go there to trade for slaves . . . Beyond a sierra, which is not very large, on the far side, are many settlements and a very mighty lake on that plain, over six leagues wide and as many long. Within it are many islands, of one or two leagues. There are great settlements within it and on the mainland beside it. On the mainland and on one of those islands is the smelting house where they do their melting. It is a very rich land. Lords who possess riches order that when they die all their treasures should be thrown into this lake; they also order that part of their treasure be placed beside them in their tombs.'

When Antonio de Berrío heard all this and gazed up at the cordillera, he knew that he was about to make a spectacular conquest. 'By the grace of God and his glorious Mother, on Palm Sunday in the year '84, I discovered . . . the cordillera so ardently desired and sought for seventy years past, and which has cost the lives of so many Spaniards. It is so high that I first sighted it from a distance of 28 leagues!' He was already calculating how easy it would be to ship treasure from his great conquest back to Spain: he reminded the King that the Orinoco flowed into the ocean opposite Trinidad, so that ships would have an easy passage from his El Dorado.

As soon as the rains ended, Berrío was off, across the Orinocco and plunging towards the 'ardently desired' cordillera. Most of the men had fallen ill 'from the vapours of the swamps and the fear that filled them'. So the white-bearded old governor had to explore, on foot, with only thirteen companions. He hacked his way up through dense wilderness as far as a crag far above the Orinoco and, by his reckoning, only two leagues from the cordillera itself. Back at the river, Berrío took a canoe downstream from his camp and came upon an island filled with Indian warriors. With characteristic courage, Berrío approached and made friends by means of gifts. The Indians told him that their island, near the great Atures rapids, was the point of contact between the plains and the mountains. Beyond lay the open road to the cordillera. With this 'certain knowledge' Berrío paddled back to his camp and was disgusted to find not a single man fit for duty. Even this don Quixote decided that he must return to replenish and refit his expedition. 'I decided that it would not be right, after having discovered the cordillera, . . . to venture further and to sacrifice my men, myself along with them, and the object of so many years' search, which by the grace of God I had found.' He reckoned that he would need three hundred men to enter El Dorado, 'and more than three thousand to finish the business, for the settlements and land stretch as far as the Marañón.' So he marched his men right back across the *llanos*. They found a good dry route, westwards up the Meta and its tributary the Casanare. Berrío was back with his family by April 1585. He boasted to the King that, although the expedition had cost him 30,000 ducats, he had lost only eight men during seventeen months of travel: three killed by Indians and five by disease.

Berrío rested only one month before going to Bogotá to start organizing another expedition. For a man in his middle sixties there was no time to be lost. He was well received, but there were frustrating delays. The authorities were preoccupied with native rebellions. Another governor, Francisco de Cáceres, was off seeking El Dorado in a different direction, south-eastwards to the lands that had ensnared Hutten and Limpias. So it was not until March 1587 that the intrepid Berrío entered the *llanos* again. He had managed to assemble 97 Spaniards (47 arquebusiers and 50 common soldiers), over five hundred horses and as many cattle on the hoof, and great loads of food, salt, maize, cheeses, hams, and six canoes. He was soon cruising down the Casanare with half the men and the serving Indians, while his lieutenant Alvaro Jorge and 47 horsemen drove the cattle across the plains. This Jorge was a Portuguese veteran as old as the governor himself: he had survived Hernán Pérez de Quesada's search for El Dorado, 46 years before. There is no chronicle narrative of Berrío's expeditions, apart from some passages in Pedro Simón: we must therefore piece together the events from Berrío's own letters to the King. The story that emerges is of hardship and endurance remarkable even for the sixteenth century.

On this second expedition, Berrío struck the Orinoco near the Atures rapids and took his expedition across on three rafts. Months were spent exploring the uninhabited forests on the far side. The expedition found a savannah with fresh grass for the horses, so they built a village of thirty thatch huts, a base for further explorations. But the natives were decidedly hostile. Every time someone went to

This sandstone and granite plateau of Pacaraima—Conan Doyle's lost world—has nothing but weathered rock on its summit.

the fields he risked being picked off in an ambush. It finally came to a pitched battle, with courageous fighting on both sides. Pedro Simón told about a horseman who pursued an Indian, but the warrior grabbed the horse by the neck and managed to force it to the ground. Another Spaniard rushed up and sliced open the Indian's stomach. The brave continued to fight, holding his entrails in with one hand and wielding his club with the other. Alvaro Jorge rode up and captured the valiant Indian; and managed to cure him within a week. In gratitude (or was it revenge?) the Indian told the camp great news about Lake Manoa.

The camp was again decimated by malarial fevers. Even the leathery old Berrío was 'very stricken with a disease of fevers'. So, when a contingent of reinforcements organized by Berrío's wife doña María reached the camp in May 1588, there was uproar. The mutinous men persuaded the commander of this relief force that they were in the grip of a mad fanatic. He agreed to lead them to safety down the Orinoco in a flotilla of canoes. Berrío was stranded. 'A large part of the men he had with him rebelled against him, so that he was forced to return . . .' He had to march back to New Granada, furious at the betrayal by this 'rebel'. An official told the King: 'Governor Berrío emerged from the El Dorado expedition in March of this year [1589]. It appears from most certain reports that he had arrived some eight leagues from settlements of innumerable Indians. He is lodging a complaint about a captain who made him miss this entry and who upset his men.'

Berrío had spent 30,000 ducats organizing his first expedition and 25,000 on the second. He now managed to raise a further 40,000—much of it supplied by the wretched Indians of his encomiendas. It took a year to organize the third expedition, but it was well planned. Berrío thought of everything: powder, shot, fighting dogs, savannah horses rather than elegant mounts, arquebuses, and even wine for mass. The expedition left in March 1590, with Berrío taking seventy men in a great flotilla of 44 canoes and rafts, and Alvaro Jorge on land again with the cattle and 42 horsemen. This time Berrío took his thirteen-year-old son and heir, Fernando. He later wrote to the King: 'It may seem a shame that so tender and rich a child should have experienced such hardship. But I consider it glorious that he should begin serving Your Majesty: so that he will know how to do it when he is a man.' Only by experience could the boy learn how to cross a river, how to sense an Indian ambush, how to attack a native village, how to lead tough backwoodsmen, and above all how to crush an incipient mutiny.

Berrío was steadily exploring all the right bank of the Orinoco, continually seeking the elusive pass into El Dorado. This time he started in the province of Aritaco, between the Parguaza and Suapure rivers well below the great cataracts. The first entry was blocked by an impenetrable belt of palm thickets and swamps. Then came the rains, which Berrío weathered in the fertile lands of the Amaipagoto tribe, possibly on the lower Cuchivero. Even during the rains, with leaden skies and dispiriting downpours, Berrío kept his men chopping inland, forever seeking the first outposts of the kingdom beyond the mountains. The land near the Orinoco was uninhabited because of regular raids by cannibal Caribs. Further inland the tribes had destroyed their homes and crops to repel the intruders. The expedition's supplies were exhausted: soon its sorties were merely to steal food, not to find roads to the fabulous kingdom. The starving expedition was struck by

155

a terrible illness, a form of madness that sffected men, dogs and horses alike. One by one, thirty soldiers and two hundred serving Indians died there. Men died raving of hunger, even when they had enough to eat; dogs and horses set upon one another. Nine men tried to escape down the river: it was later learned that they had been caught by Caribs, killed and eaten.

Nothing daunted by these disasters, Antonio de Berrío marched inland again as soon as the rains ended. With fifty men, he penetrated thirty leagues and emerged into better country. There were frequent paths and some food to steal. Plumes of smoke were visible in the distance: to an optimist as ardent as Berrío, these were a sure sign of dense population. When the expedition found Indian hearths, these were 'foundries' for melting gold. Berrío decided to explore a river. Everyone, himself included, wielded axes and adzes to build four dugout canoes. They loaded themselves into these and somehow managed to descend this wild river, surviving its many fallen logs, rapids and cataracts. These rivers flowing into the Orinoco from the Guiana highlands are still little known: to a modern explorer, this descent alone would be considered a notable expedition. Berrío's river was perhaps the Parucito and Parú. He was disappointed to find no traces of advanced civilization along it; and it led, not to Lake Manoa, but back to the Orinoco itself.

Berrío now made a historic decision, comparable to Cortés burning his boats on the shores of Mexico or Jiménez de Quesada sending his brigs back down the Magdalena when he marched up towards the Muisca. Berrío described his dilemma to the King: 'I had great reports, but was certain that it was impossible to cross the cordillera except by pushing in by a route downstream through the province of Caroní . . . I had endured the greatest calamities ever suffered in the Indies, with two-thirds of my men dead or fled, and the majority of those who remained determined to return to the kingdom [of New Granada]. I considered that if they did return this time, my aspirations would be totally finished. I therefore decided on a move of great daring. This was to descend the river to a place where logs were found for making boats. God, in a form of miracle, was pleased to send me five logs, all together—when for many leagues round about there were none at all—and they were the most beautiful and largest that I had ever seen in my life! When I found them, I decided to kill all the horses, so that the soldiers would lose any hope of returning to the kingdom. Using salt that we treated, we made jerked meat [from the horses] to eat there while the canoes were being made —which we needed very badly. With the meat that was left over, and almost no other food, I commended myself to God and to fortune, and cast myself off down the river. I sailed down it for almost 250 leagues to reach the Caroní river, which descends from the great and rich provinces that we call El Dorado . . .'

The Caroní river was quite well known to Spaniards. It was the largest tributary flowing into the Orinoco from the south, and its lower reaches had been investigated by various explorers during the course of the sixteenth century. Berrío was absolutely convinced that this river was the pass he had been seeking: 'The great river called Caroní comes down from Guiana and cannot be navigated because of a great waterfall; but a little higher up, where a chief called Morequito lives, the mountains end and the provinces of Guiana begin, behind which in turn come those of Manoa and El Dorado and many other provinces.'

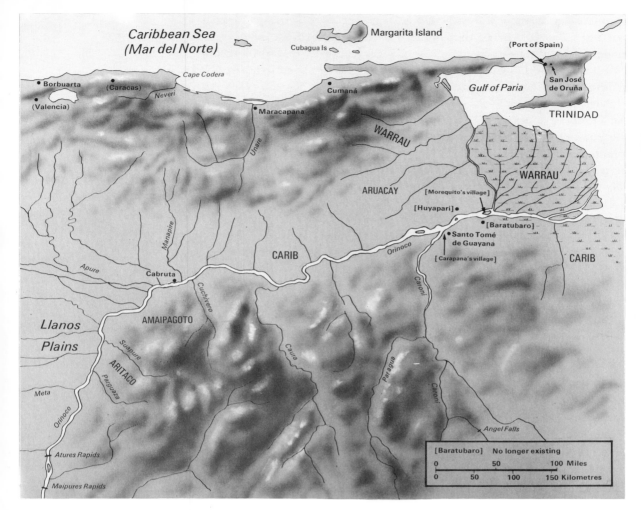

The lower Orinoco

OVERLEAF Captain Domingo de Vera marched along the Caroní and was sure that he had found the entrance to the hills of El Dorado.

During his descent of the Orinoco, Berrío made friends with some canoe loads of Caribs—normally bitter enemies of the Spaniards—and they confirmed his hopes. 'We had much friendship on this journey; two of their chiefs came into my canoe and I handed one Spaniard over to them. They revealed great secrets about the land, and confirmed all the information which I had received higher up. . . . I shall state my opinion in this matter. These great provinces lie between two very great rivers, the Amazon and the Orinoco.' Explorers on the Orinoco were deceived by seeing no rich settlements on its banks. 'But the Indians tell the truth, because the great towns and the riches are very much up from the border country of Morequito; but it is not possible to enter there, and the large towns begin more than sixty leagues inland. I have travelled down the streams and explored around the mountains—over 700 leagues by land and water—during my three expeditions, and have spent ten years in continuous labours, so that I am well informed and know the facts. From the mouth of the Amazon to that of the Orinoco the map indicates more than 400 leagues in latitude and over 1500 in longitude, in which there is not a single Spanish habitation. . . . I came across specimens of gold in every district during my journey of 700 leagues or more, skirting the mountains; and when I asked whence they brought it, they all said from the far side of the mountains; and they exaggerated the quantity so greatly that it is incredible. . . . I shall enter into Guiana without delay; and if it is one twentieth part of what is believed, it will be richer than Peru!'

Berrío sent a letter to the governor of Margarita, the island near the mouth of the Orinoco, begging for reinforcements. He had useful meetings with chief Morequito near the mouth of the Caroní. There was further confirmation of the wealth that lay near the source of that river. But the reinforcements did not arrive. Berrío had lost more of his men, and the majority of those who remained were afflicted by a form of blindness: doubtless a trachoma caused by a parasite that is still prevalent on the upper tributaries of the Orinoco. The dried horse meat was all consumed. So Berrío left a small garrison in the village of a friendly chief called Carapana, on an island a day's journey down the Orinoco from the mouth of the Caroní, and himself moved down to seek reinforcements among the men on the Caribbean.

It must have been terribly frustrating for a man of Berrío's conviction to face further delays and intrigues. He reached Trinidad in September 1591 and decided to establish a base on the island for his conquest of Guiana. He then moved to Margarita and set up a recruiting office in a small house, despite the coolness of the island's governor. Berrío attracted a number of followers, including one man who was to become his most valuable lieutenant, an amiable giant called Domingo de Vera e Ibargoyen. The first task for this faithful new supporter was to found a town on Trinidad. Domingo de Vera did this, with plenty of proclamations and some makeshift ceremonial, in May 1592. By the time Berrío arrived in January 1593 a flourishing town called San José de Oruña was being laid out and built, inland of Trinidad's modern capital Port of Spain. Domingo de Vera was also sent to recruit men in Caracas, and he proved to have a genius for promotion and publicity. His tales of the potential wealth of Guiana soon attracted a crowd of aspirants, despite the long history of failures to reach El Dorado. Berrío also sent a recruiting officer back to New Granada: his own son Fernando, aged fourteen.

Early in 1593 Captain de Vera was given a chance to investigate the approaches to El Dorado. Berrío sent him up the Orinoco with 35 men and by April he was unloading his canoes full of presents—red bonnets, glass beads, knives, machetes, combs and flutes—for the happy Indians of chief Carapana. On 23 April he was with Morequito at the mouth of the Caroní. Captain Vera was a tall man who looked most imposing in his cuirass and curved morrion helmet; but he was simple, warm-hearted and as easily influenced by Indian reports as was Berrío himself. He also loved pageantry. He decided that his first sight of the Caroní justified a speech, and declared to his men: 'Captains and soldiers! You know that our governor Antonio de Berrío discovered the rich provinces of Guiana and Dorado through eleven years' effort and the expenditure of over 100,000 pesos of fine gold, and he took possession of them for his government . . . He has now sent me to learn and discover the easiest roads to enter and settle those rich provinces, to find where cattle can be kept and armies can enter those plains.'

Captain Vera then marched along the banks of the Caroní, planting crosses at

159

each Indian village and taking possession of the land for the King of Spain and governor Berrío. The villages increased in size as Vera moved up the Caroní. The people were well fed and very hospitable, providing Vera's men with plenty of food. The women were 'healthy, tall, obliging and well-formed'. Back in Trinidad a few weeks later, Captain Vera gave his master a detailed, circumstantial description of El Dorado. Both explorers were convinced that Vera had entered the outer marches of the long-sought empire. It was now possible to state categorically that Guiana began 12 leagues from the Orinoco, beyond the lands of chiefs Ahuyacanare and Taruca. It consisted of some fifty leagues of densely populated savannahs, valleys and unforested hills. It was a richly-endowed land, with its own salt and spices. It was a cool, temperate place, supporting a population of two million in its many settlements. (A large population was as great an attraction to Spanish conquistadores as was gold: for the native population would provide labour and tribute after the land was divided into encomiendas.) There was, of course, gold in abundance. The natives wore it in their noses and ears, on their chests and arms. If Vera failed to see any of these ornaments, it was only because his guide, chief Morequito, had warned the Indians to hide their gold. 'Eleven days' journey from where the Spaniards reached, they say that there is a very large lake, which is called the land of Manoa, around which there is a vast number of clothed people and towns and lords.' Most of the people had pigtails, except for great warriors who allowed their hair to flow free.

There were two other elements in this new picture of El Dorado. One was that it was peopled by fugitive Incas. Pedro de Cieza de León, a most careful and excellent chronicler of Peru, wrote that when the Incas defeated the neighbouring Chanca tribe, the defeated leader Ancoallo migrated eastwards into Amazonia with many of his people. 'With the women in the van he set out and traversed the provinces of Chachapoyas and Huánuco and, having crossed the Andes mountains, they wandered through those sierras until, as they relate, they came to a great lake, which I believe must be the site of the legend that is told of El Dorado. They built their settlements there and multiplied greatly.' Pedro Maraver de Silva repeated this idea, although for him the fugitives were Incas escaping after Pizarro's massacre of their leaders at Cajamarca. For the visionary Berrío, Guiana was the place of *origin* of the Incas: 'There are many stories, with which everyone is acquainted . . . that the Inca kings of these provinces [of Guiana] went forth to conquer Peru, and afterwards, owing to quarrels arising between two brothers, the one returned, from fear of the other, fleeing to these provinces.' So Berrío was hardly surprised when Captain Vera reported that the richest people near Lake Manoa had arrived only about twenty years before and had subdued many of the original inhabitants. These newcomers were clothed and spoke a different language. They 'are a people of many trades and very rich in gold, which they dedicate to numerous shrines that they maintain in the hills and mountains.'

The other story concerned one Juan Martín de Albujar, a fugitive from Maraver de Silva's ill-fated expedition into the *llanos* to find El Dorado. Juan de Castellanos told this man's extraordinary story: 'The report which I give now was revealed by Juan Martín, a soldier who is now a citizen of Carora in Venezuela. He spent seven years living among people who never wear clothes: their ornament

Sinú chiefs evidently wore magnificent headdresses hung with gold plates. Pendants and a rattle shaped as human faces with nose and ear ornaments. One figure has cheeks full of coca cud.

and fashion consists of painting what nature gave them.' He was the sole survivor of one group of Silva's men. Captured by Indians, Juan Martín soon demonstrated his talent for leading them to victory in battle. He learned his tribe's language and lived as an Indian, naked and with several wives. He came to know much of the savannahs of Guiana and its 'numerous strong [tribes] in the midst of extensive provinces never seen or known up to now. . . . But all these lack treasures: they possess some gold mixed with copper, but in other respects are poor people.' Juan Martín in fact reported that he had seen no sign of El Dorado or of the mountains 'that run north to south across the plain, and in which we believe that news of Manoa or Guiana could be possible'. He had sometimes seen Aruak traders bring back gold objects from distant canoe trips. But he convinced Castellanos that El Dorado 'does not and never did have foundation . . .' Such objectivity was not what the believers wanted to hear. So Juan Martín's story was soon embroidered. He was said to have been taken, blindfold, to the city of Manoa, where he lived for seven months, saw a glimpse of its treasures, and conversed with its wise and powerful ruler.

Antonio de Berrío was overjoyed by Vera's success in finding the route into Guiana. It now remained only to organize the army that would enter the promised land. Poor Berrío was soon entangled in legal wrangles and intrigues more labyrinthine than the forests of the Orinoco. The governor of Margarita was sceptical and hostile: he sent a slave raiding party to seize Morequito's people. The governor of Cumaná, Francisco de Vides, appeared in Trinidad in October 1594 with a royal order confirming that Trinidad belonged to *his* jurisdiction. And the governor of Caracas, when Captain Vera reappeared with his wonderful stories about Manoa and Guiana, refused to let any men join Berrío—because he planned to invade Guiana himself. In New Granada, Berrío's devoted wife had died, and his many children were embroiled in legal actions. The old governor wrote, ruefully, 'I leave ten children, seven of them females; . . . but I have spent all the girls' dowries!' The only hope was to send that brilliant salesman, Domingo de Vera, back to Spain itself to raise three hundred men and additional money and equipment.

RIGHT It was believed that the Spaniard Juan Martín was taken, blind-folded, to the fabulous city of Manoa or El Dorado on the edge of the salt lake Parima.

OPPOSITE Spanish conquistadores melted down tons of golden objects from tombs in the Sinú valley, south-west of Cartagena. (Above) A staff head with crocodile ornament, (below) cast filigree nose clips and necklace.

10

IN APRIL 1595, WHEN BERRÍO WAS IN TRINIDAD, WAITING FOR SALVATION TO ARRIVE from Spain, two foreign ships were reported in the bay of Port of Spain. They were English, the ships of Queen Elizabeth's great courtier Sir Walter Ralegh. England and Spain were not technically at war; but relations were very strained between two countries opposed in religion. It was only a few years since the defeat of the Spanish Armada. The arrival of the famous 'Milor Guatarral' was therefore highly alarming.

According to Berrío, he received a letter from Ralegh, dated 4 April 1595, that said: 'I have arrived at this port with much desire to see you and to discuss with you my affairs, of service to His Majesty King Philip. I beg you on no account to refuse this visit . . . And so that you will be more trusting, I promise you on a gentleman's honour that it will be in all security . . .' The letter was accompanied by a ring as a token of good faith, and by effigies of the Virgin and Saint Francis to indicate Ralegh's Catholic sympathy.

Berrío did not agree to a meeting; but he sent his nephew as an envoy, with presents of fruit, chickens and venison. Then, on the night of 7 April, Ralegh landed with a hundred men and marched inland to surprise San José de Oruña in a dawn attack. Berrío later wrote his version of what he described as 'one of the greatest acts of treachery and cruelty ever witnessed in the world. For he ordered my nephew Don Rodrigo de la Hoz to be bound, with the other soldiers and the page who was with him; and when bound he ordered them killed by sword thrusts. When this was done, with the help of the Indians who all flocked to him, he went to where the sentries were; and that very night he surrounded and killed them. He came to the town, in which there were no more than 28 soldiers, and he captured me and eleven other soldiers. He ordered these to be bound hand and foot, and at night he ordered them to be taken out one by one and given sword thrusts. And when this was done, he burned the town.'

Ralegh's version of these events was somewhat different. He felt that any attack on Berrío was revenge for his having killed eight Englishmen serving Ralegh's captain Jacob Whiddon—these had landed at Trinidad the previous year, and been killed in an ambush after being assured of safe conduct while fetching water. Ralegh had heard reports of great cruelty against the Indians of Trinidad by Berrío's Spaniards. Ralegh wrote that Berrío 'made the ancient . . . Lords of the countrey to be their slaves, that he kept them in chains, and dropped their naked bodies with burning bacon, and such other torments, which I found afterwards to be true: for in the city after I entered the same there were 5 of ye lords or litle kings . . . in one chaine almost dead of famine, and wasted with torments. . . . Those five Capitaines in the chaine were called Wannawanare, Carroaori, Maquarima, Taroopanama, and Aterima.'

Ralegh's description of the attack tallied with Berrío's: 'Taking a time of most advantage I set upon the Corps du guard in the evening, and having put them to the sword, sent Captaine Calfield onwards with 60 souldiers, and my selfe followed with 40 more and so tooke their new City which they called S. Joseph by breake of day: they abode not any fight after a fewe shot, and all being dismissed but onely Berreo and his companion [Alvaro Jorge], I brought them with me abord, and at the instance of the Indians, I set their new citie of S. Joseph on fire.'

Sir Walter Ralegh with his son Wat painted in 1602 when Wat was aged eight. He was killed on the Orinoco sixteen years later.

What was Sir Walter Ralegh doing attacking a tiny settlement on Trinidad? Aged about 41, he was Captain of Queen Elizabeth's Guard and a member of the inner circle of English courtiers. He was the epitome of an Elizabethan: intellectually brilliant, inventive, witty, adroit in court intrigue, ambitious, ruthless when necessary, brave in battle (although not one of the greatest sailors), and above all adventurous. He was enormously energetic. Sir Robert Cecil once remarked, 'He can toil terribly.' His friend the Earl of Northumberland described his driving personality, his dominance of lesser men: 'He desired to seem to be able to sway all men's fancies—all men's courses.'

By the time of his arrival at Trinidad, Ralegh had risen very far and fast—and had begun to slip. The younger son of a good family of Devon gentry, he had attached himself to Queen Elizabeth's vibrant court after brief studies at Oxford and in the law. He managed to attract the Queen's attention, partly through his influential half-brother Sir Humphrey Gilbert and partly through his own tall good looks and charm. Ralegh wrote amorous poetry to the virgin Queen, and gained and held her affection. He soon had the reputation of an unruly gallant. He became known to the most important men in England: Walsingham was impressed by his analytical mind and restless energy. Ralegh thus gained entry to the inner circle of Elizabeth's favourites.

Ralegh's first foreign adventure was the command of a ship on an attempt with his brother Humphrey to colonize in North America in 1578–9. During the next two years, Ralegh commanded some troops in Ireland, and it was after this that he won his position as the Queen's intimate. For nine years, from 1583 to 1592, Ralegh enjoyed the Queen's favour, and she rewarded her 'Water' with a lucrative state monopoly and with estates that he coveted in Devonshire. He was a member of Parliament and, like so many distinguished Elizabethans, he financed privateering ships whose main victims were the Spaniards. His famous Virginia colony took place between 1584 and 1586—at the time when Berrío was searching for El Dorado—and this effort gained Ralegh his knighthood in 1585. Between 1586 and 1590 he was concerned with moving English settlers to a vast land concession in Ireland. He used his new wealth and influence to build up estates in Devon and Dorset, and his ships were involved in various adventures against the Spaniards, in the Armada, the Azores and the Indies. During this period of his ascendancy, Walter Ralegh dressed extravagantly and lived flamboyantly. He wrote powerful propaganda essays and gained the reputation of being a fine soldier, an adventurer, and a great English patriot.

Ralegh's first downfall came in 1592. A rival favourite, the younger and better-born Robert Earl of Essex, was supplanting him in Queen Elizabeth's affections. But what infuriated Elizabeth was an affair and clandestine marriage between Ralegh and one of the Queen's ladies of the bedchamber, the 27-year-old Elizabeth Throckmorton. On 29 March 1592 the bride's brother, Arthur Throckmorton, wrote in his diary, 'My sister was delyvered of a boye between 2 and 3 in the afternowne. I wrytte to syr Walter Rayley, and sent Dycke the footmane . . .' Two weeks later Arthur Throckmorton recorded that he and his wife were two of the godparents of Damerei Ralegh. And in August his diary entry was: 'Ma soeur s'en alla a la Tour, et Sir W. Raelly.' A spell in the Tower of London was a very public rebuke for Ralegh's disrespect to his sovereign. The marriage to Bess Throckmorton proved a most successful one, and the sojourn in the Tower was brief; but Ralegh never regained the Queen's affection. In despair at his fall from favour, he wrote to Cecil: 'My heart was never broken till this day, that I hear the Queen goes away so far of—whom I have followed so many years with so great love and desire, in so many journeys, and am now left behind her, in a dark prison all alone.'

As the years went by and Ralegh remained banned from Court, he decided that he must make a spectacular gesture to regain his place in the sun. Some years before, in 1586, one of his ships had captured an important Spaniard, don Pedro Sarmiento de Gamboa, a noted chronicler of Peru, a commander in the campaign to capture the last Inca Tupac Amaru, an admiral against Drake, and governor of a Spanish attempt to colonize the Straits of Magellan. Sarmiento and Ralegh had long conversations before the Spaniard was sent back to Spain, and he may have told the Queen's captain about the missing empire of El Dorado. Ralegh wrote in 1596: 'Many yeeres since, I had knowledge by relation, of that mighty, rich and beautiful Empire of Guiana, and of that great and golden city, which the Spaniards call El Dorado and the naturals Manoa.' Ralegh was convinced that this Guiana was the refuge of a son of the last Inca, fleeing from Francisco Pizarro's conquistadores. If there really was a fourth golden American empire to be conquered, then Ralegh wanted it taken by England rather than by Spain. He sent his captain Jacob Whiddon to investigate Trinidad in 1594 and to try to learn more about El Dorado. But the sensational information seems to have been won by another captain, George Popham, who captured some papers in a Spanish ship, also in 1594. He probably seized Domingo de Vera's amazing report of his trip up the

Caroní and glimpse of the edge of El Dorado itself. Ralegh certainly obtained that account either than or later, because his famous *Discoverie of the large, rich, and beautifull Empire of Guiana, with a relation of the great and golden citie of Manoa (which the Spaniards call El Dorado)* was based very closely on Vera's exuberant flight of fancy.

It was thus to find a personal and national El Dorado that Ralegh sailed to Trinidad. He captured a Portuguese ship with wine on board during the transatlantic crossing, and used this wine to ply the first Spaniards he met at Trinidad. 'Those poore souldiers having bene many yeeres without wine, a few draughts made them merrie, in which mood they vaunted of Guiana and of the riches thereof.' This confirmed Ralegh's hopes. He determined to capture Antonio de Berrío—the man who knew most about El Dorado—and to destroy his new town of San José de Oruña, for 'considering that to enter Guiana by small boats, to depart 400 or 500 miles from my ships, and to leave a garison in my backe interested in the same enterprize . . . I should have savoured very much of the asse.'

The attack on San José followed; and on the evening of 8 April 1595 the dejected old veterans Antonio de Barrío and Alvaro Jorge climbed aboard the English flagship. Ralegh treated his prisoners well, arranging banquets to mellow the Spanish governor. Other Spaniards were watching everything from an Indian canoe, and they reported that Ralegh wanted to get Berrío 'to explain the letters he was writing to His Majesty—for he had captured a copy of them among the papers of [Vera's] expedition and of the riches of Guiana—because [Ralegh's] Lady the Queen wanted to conquer them. And if not, it would go badly with him.' A battle of wits ensued. Poor Berrío did everything possible to dissuade Ralegh from attempting to reach Guiana: after his own twelve years of desperate effort it would be unthinkable to have El Dorado fall to these Lutheran heretics. He said that the streams of the Orinoco delta were too shallow for even small boats. The rains would soon begin, and the rivers would then be too strong for an ascent. The natives would flee at the foreigners' approach, burning their villages and food. But if they were contacted, they would refuse to trade their gold. Manoa was a very long way away, hundreds of leagues further than Ralegh imagined. Berrío dissimulated so effectively that Ralegh believed he was an uneducated man who confused east and west. But Ralegh was not deceived by Berrío's obvious attempts to discourage him. When Berrío saw the intruders press ahead with preparations to ascend the Orinoco, he could not conceal that he 'was stricken into a great melancholy and sadness'. Ralegh was impressed by the 75-year-old governor. 'This Berreo is a gentleman wel descended, and had long served the Spanish king . . . very valiant and liberall, and a gentleman of great assurednes, and of a great heart.' Captor and prisoner were kindred spirits: both adventurers and visionaries.

Ralegh appreciated that no seagoing ship could sail through the mudflats and sand banks of the Orinoco delta. He stripped his smallest vessel, removing the upper works and rebuilding the hull so that she could be rowed as a galley if the winds failed. Four other small boats were also prepared, with provisions for a hundred men for a month. Ralegh, the pampered courtier, was very frank about his dislike of the discomfort of the journey. He complained that the boats were packed with equipment and rotting meat. 'All driven to lie in the raine and weather, in the open aire, in the burning Sunne, and upon the hard bords . . . what with the victuals being most fish, with wette clothes of so many men thrust together, and the heat of the Sunne, I will undertake there was never any prison in England, that could bee found more unsavorie and loathsome—especially to my selfe, who had for many yeeres before bene dieted and cared for in a sort farre more difering.'

The tangle of channels of the Orinoco delta was appalling. 'I know all the earth doeth not yeelde the like confluence of streames and branches, the one crossing the other so many times, and all so faire and large, and so like one to another, as no man can tell which to take . . . and every island so bordered with high trees, as no man coulde see any further then the bredth of the river or length of the breach. . . . We might have wandred a whole yere in that labyrinth of rivers . . .' The expedition's first guide was an Aruak Indian. He was soon hopelessly lost: the boats kept running aground, and Ralegh wanted to hang the incompetent guide. Salvation came in the form of a Tivitiva pilot who soon steered them through the maze.

Whenever an ebb tide joined the river's current, the boats were swept downstream. 'We then had no shift but to perswade the companies . . . to take paines, every gentleman & others taking their turnes to row, and to spell one the other at the houres end.' The weather was extremely hot and the air close and sickly. The men began to despair. Rations were reduced, 'and our men and our selves so wearied and scorched, and doubtful withall whether wee should ever performe it or no, the heat increasing as we drew towards the [equator] line . . . The further we went on (our victuall decreasing and the aire breeding great faintnesse) wee grew weaker and weaker, . . . and we were brought into despaire and discomfort.'

Ralegh was delighted by the grasslands of the Orinoco; the only blemish was that the river was full of alligators.

Finally, towards the end of May, Ralegh's expedition emerged from the delta into the main stream of the Orinoco. Suddenly the scenery improved. Mangrove thickets gave way to open savannahs that reminded Ralegh of a landscaped English park. 'On both sides of this river, we passed the most beautifull countrey that ever mine eyes beheld: and whereas all that we had seene before was nothing but woods, prickles, bushes, and thornes, here we beheld plaines of twenty miles in length, the grasse short and greene, and in divers parts groves of trees by themselves, as if they had beene by all the arte and labour in the world so made of purpose: and still as we rowed, the deere came downe feeding by the waters side, as if they had beene used to a keepers call.' The only blemish was that the river was full of alligators.

It was Ralegh's policy to woo the native tribes. This was done partly from humanitarian principles—the Protestants of northern Europe were shocked by what they had heard about Spanish cruelty to American Indians. It was also a deliberate attempt to gain the alliance of the tribes. If they could be induced to rebel against their colonial oppressors, this might give the English a chance to move in as the new colonial power. When he was in Trinidad, Ralegh assembled the chiefs and made them a speech about the power and goodness of his Queen, a virgin who had more chiefs under her than there were trees on the island. She was opposed to Spanish tyranny and had sent men to free the Trinidadians and defend Guiana from Spanish conquest.

The tribes on the Orinoco were treated with similar deference. When Ralegh's men landed at Indian villages, the people feared that they would behave as badly as some Spaniards, 'who . . . tooke from them both their wives and daughters dayly, and used them for the satisfying of their owne lusts.' Ralegh was determined to stop his men committing such outrages. He believed that he succeeded, but it was not easy, since 'we saw many hundreds, and had many in our power, and of those very yong, and excellently favoured, which came among us without deceit, starke naked. Nothing got us more love amongst them then this usage.' He would not let his men take so much as a pineapple without payment, or touch any woman. 'But I confesse it was a very impatient worke to keepe the meaner sort from spoyle and stealing, when wee came to their houses.' Ralegh himself was not above temptation. He saw one chief's wife of such beauty that he exclaimed: 'In all my life I have seldome seene a better favoured woman: shee was of good stature, with blacke eyes, fat of body, of an excellent countenance, her haire almost as long as her selfe, tied up againe in pretie knots.' She conversed and drank with Ralegh's officers, 'and was very pleasant, knowing her owne comelinesse, and taking great pride therein. I have seene a Lady in England so like to her, as but for the difference of colour, I would have sworne might have bene the same.' English behaviour was in such marked contrast to the conduct of the Spaniards that the Indians were impressed by this new tribe of foreigners. They were even more impressed when they heard that Ralegh's men had slaughtered the Spaniards on Trinidad.

Ralegh, with his lively intelligence, was curious about this new world. He wanted to learn more about the curare poisons that caused such insufferable torment. He heard that men wounded by poisoned arrows had 'a most ugly and lamentable death, sometimes dying starke mad, sometimes their bowels breaking out of their bellies: which are presently discoloured as blacke as pitch and so

The aged chief Topiawari walked many miles to converse with Ralegh near the mouth of the Caroní. De Bry shows an ocean going ship on the Orinoco, but Ralegh had to travel up river in open ship's boats.

unsavoury, as no man can endure to cure, or to attend them.' The Indians told him that the sure remedy was to avoid all drink until the wound was dressed. He noted the names of the riverine tribes but disapproved of their heavy drinking. At one village he found the chiefs lying drunken in hammocks with their women ladling manioc spirit into their cups. Ralegh observed that at their feasts the Indians were 'the greatest karousers and drunkards of the world'. They loved the wine that Ralegh had pirated.

The expedition finally reached the village of Morequito near the mouth of the Caroní. Chief Morequito himself was dead. He had gone down to Cumaná at the invitation of its governor Vides, who hoped that Morequito would guide him to Guiana. But Berrío heard about this and insisted that Morequito be executed as a 'rebel' because his men had killed some Spaniards. The village was now run by Morequito's aged uncle Topiawari. This venerable chief (Ralegh said that he was aged 110) walked many miles to visit the English. His people brought presents of manioc bread and wine, small green parakeets, pineapples 'the prince of fruites that grow under the Sunne', and an armadillo 'all barred over with smal plates, somewhat like to a rinoceros' with a tail that could be used as a hunting horn. Ralegh conversed with chief Topiawari and interrogated him about Guiana. His answers tallied with Ralegh's preconceived ideas, culled from Domingo de Vera's account. 'He answered with a great sigh, as a man which had inward feeling of the losse of his Countrey and libertie . . .' and told about the invasion by a powerful tribe from the direction of the 'sleeping sun'. Ralegh naturally took this to be the arrival of the Inca exiles. Other details about the tribes of Guiana corroborated what Vera had been told. Ralegh was impressed by the proud and wise Topiawari. 'I marvelled to finde a man of that gravitie and judgement, and of so good discourse, that had no helpe of learning nor breede.'

The culmination of Ralegh's small reconnaissance was to look at the Caroní. The rivers were now rising with the start of the rainy season. An attempt to row up the Caroní was a failure: 'Wee were not able with a barge of eight oares to row one stones cast in an houre, and yet the River is as broad as the Thames at Wolwich' near its mouth. So they landed, and Ralegh took a few men overland to see the beautiful Macagua cataracts. Crossing the first hill 'we behelde that wonderfull breach of waters . . . There appeared some tenne or twelve overfals in sight, every one as high over the other as a Church-tower, which fell with that fury, that the rebound of water made it seeme, as if it had bene all covered over with a great shower of raine: and in some places wee tooke it at the first for a smoke that had risen over some great towne.' Ralegh, middle-aged and unfit, was content with a distant view of the falls, but his men insisted on walking up to them. Ralegh was lyrical about the scenery. 'I never saw a more beautifull countrey, nor more lively prospects, hils so raised here and there over the valleys, the river winding into divers branches, the plaines adjoyning without bush or stubble, all faire greene grasse, the ground of hard sand easie to march on, either for horse or foote, the deere crossing in every path, the birdes towards the evening singing on every tree with a thousand severall tunes, cranes and herons of white, crimson, and carnation pearching in the rivers side, the aire fresh with a gentle easterly winde, and every stone that we stouped to take up, promising either golde or silver by his complexion.'

Ralegh claimed that he did not pester the natives for gold because he did not want to jeopardize the eventual conquest of Guiana. For the same reason he desisted from a raid to attack outlying towns of the rich empire. This expedition was simply a reconnaissance. 'Till I had known Her Majesty's pleasure, I would rather have lost the sacke of one or two townes . . . then to have defaced or indangered the future hope of so many millions, & the great good, & rich trade which England may be possessed of thereby.' He did, however, load his boats with a few hundredweight of ore that might prove to contain gold. The Indians of one village told Captain Laurence Keymis about a gold mine; and Captain Alvaro Jorge told Ralegh that there was a silver mine on the Caroní. These riches would have to await a stronger expedition. For the present, Ralegh's men hurried down the Orinoco, and regained their ships in mid-June 1595 after an expedition of little over a month. It was a trivial affair compared to the great odysseys of the Spaniards or Germans, but it was the first English venture into the interior of South America. It inspired Ralegh to emulate the conquistadores. He was becoming another victim of the legend of El Dorado.

Back in the Caribbean, Ralegh's ships tried to win some treasure to finance their voyage. They sailed to Margarita island, but failed to attack. An attempt to take Cumaná on the mainland was repulsed with heavy losses, even though the English 'attacked with the impetus of the Devil'. Ralegh therefore sent his captain Amyas Preston along the north coast of South America; he obtained some spoils from the sack of Caracas, Río de la Hacha, and Santa Marta. Berrío and Jorge were set ashore near Cumaná, in the territory of the rival governor who was trying to oust them from Trinidad.

Ralegh himself decided that it was time 'to leave Guiana to the Sunne, whom they worshippe, and steare away towardes the North'. He was back at Plymouth at the end of August. Lady Ralegh, whose spelling was far worse than her husband's, wrote an ecstatic letter to their friend Sir Robert Cecil: 'Sur hit tes trew I thonke the leveng God Sur Walter is safly londed at Plumworthe with as gret honnor as ever man can, but with littell riches. I have not yet hard from him selfe. . . . In haste this Sunday. Your pour frind E. Raleg. . . . Pardon my rewed wryteng with the goodnes of the newes.'

The problem for Ralegh was to persuade Queen Elizabeth of the need to conquer Guiana. He wrote to Robert Cecil: 'The like fortune was never offered to any Christian prince. I know it will be presently followed both by the Spanish and

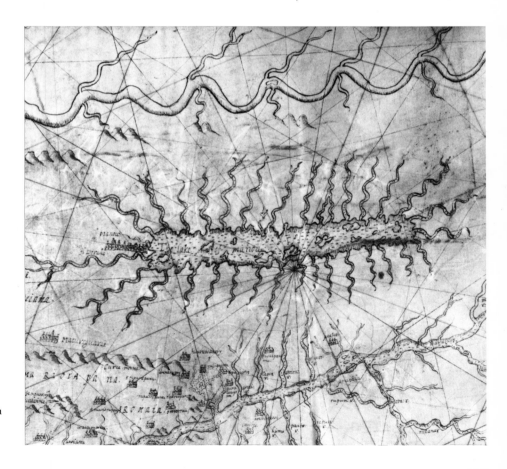

Ralegh had Thomas Hariot draw a map of Guiana. It showed Lake Manoa like a great caterpillar poised between the Amazon and Orinoco rivers.

French; and if it be foreslowed by us, I conclude that we are cursed of God . . .' He had Thomas Hariot prepare a map to be presented to the Queen. This showed Lake Manoa surrounded by tributary streams, like a great caterpillar poised between the Amazon and Orinoco. He pleaded: 'I hope I shall be thought worthy to direct those actions that I have at mine own charges laboured in; and to govern that country which I have discovered, and hope to conquer for the Queen without her cost.' Ralegh's friends tried to help. George Chapman wrote a poem in praise of the exploit, in which he predicted that the Queen would be delighted, 'And now she blesseth with her woonted Graces, Th'industrious Knight, the soule of this exploit . . .' He was quite wrong. The Queen showed no sign of interest in the fabulous kingdom. She completely ignored 'the industrious knight' and his proposed conquest. Detractors and personal enemies scoffed at the mirage, particularly when the ore and stones brought back from Guiana proved to be worthless. Some even hinted that Ralegh had never been to South America at all.

It was to save his reputation and publicize his achievement that Walter Ralegh wrote his famous *Discoverie . . . of Guiana*, published in 1596 and rapidly translated into other European languages. This book was an account of his own expedition; a survey of all that the Spaniards had learned about El Dorado; and eloquent recruiting propaganda for another expedition. Ralegh listed all the expeditions that had sought El Dorado. When he told the legend of El Dorado, the Golden Man, Ralegh blended all the different versions: in his El Dorado, *all* the Indians anointed themselves with gold, although they did not do so every day. He gave Vera's description of the legendary land, and unfortunately repeated some of the wilder fantasies. He speculated about the existence of Amazons and repeated the familiar stories about them. He even described the Ewaipanoma, a tribe in Guiana 'whose heads appear not above their shoulders: . . . they are reported to have their eyes in their shoulders, and their mouthes in the middle of their breasts, and a long traine of haire [growing] backward between their shoulders.' He asserted his conviction that Guiana was peopled by fugitive Incas of great wealth. This wonderful story, full of compelling detail and told in Ralegh's fluent prose, became a best seller throughout Europe. Shakespeare wrote, in *Othello*, of 'Cannibals that each other eat, the anthropophagi, and men whose heads do grow beneath their shoulders'. It was Walter Ralegh who popularized the legend of El Dorado.

Ralegh knew exactly how to appeal to all classes when selling the idea of a new Guiana venture. 'The common souldier shall here fight for golde, and pay himselfe in steede of pence, with plates of halfe a foote broad, whereas he breaketh his bones in other warres for provant and penury. Those commanders and chieftaines that shoot at honour and abundance, shall finde there more rich and beautifull cities, more temples adorned with golden images, . . . then either Cortez found in Mexico or Pizarro in Peru.' He ended with a description that no explorer could resist. 'To conclude, Guiana is a countrey that hath yet her maydenhead, never sackt, turned, nor wrought, the face of the earth hath not bene torne, nor the vertue and salt of the soyle spent by manurance, the graves have not bene opened for golde, the mines not broken with sledges, nor their images puld downe out of their temples.'

This same propaganda was being used to even greater effect in Spain itself. Captain Domingo de Vera e Ibargoyen had been sent back to the mother country to try to recruit men to save Berrío's Dorado venture. He was a big man and brilliant at promotion. He knew that he must look exotic and outlandish to attract attention. Domingo de Vera rode through the streets of Madrid on a huge horse. He wore a strange long cassock, closed in front and edged in satin, with four sleeves, two of which hung almost to the ground. His long brown hair flowed loose and he had a massive beard. All this was covered in a hat of vicuña cloth 'with a very large crown and brim'. People murmured as he passed: 'There is the Indianist of El Dorado and the rich lands!' He appointed no less than twenty veteran soldiers to move about Spain as his recruiting agents.

Domingo de Vera made the most of his wondrous tales. He told about Guiana's riches, its exotic tribes and fugitive Incas so often that he came to believe he had been there himself. He had a few gold objects, which were brandished at the appropriate moment in his speech. He cleverly made the Guiana expedition an exclusive enterprise: his recruiting officers were to accept only respectable Christians, each armed with his own weapons and ammunition, food, farming implements and harnesses. He harangued his audiences with good liberal sentiments: 'It must be understood that those who wish to go there should go to settle in those lands and not to depopulate them, to win but not to deceive them, to pacify but not destroy them. For any who does not do this, should be warned that the wrath of God will descend upon him!'

All this was absurdly successful. Farmers sold their holdings to join the venture; twelve Franciscans came under Father Luis de Mieses; the prebendary of Salamanca cathedral and the nephew of the President of the Council of the Indies signed on; men actually paid the recruiting officers to be allowed to go; and people came with their wives, children and wordly goods. In the end, instead of finding three hundred men, Domingo de Vera recruited a great mob variously estimated at between fifteen hundred and three thousand five hundred people. He even appeared before the Council of the Indies and convinced it that 'with prudence and good methods he had just discovered the true and easy entrance to the land of El Dorado. He entered and was within that land, which he affirmed to be most rich, high, agreeable, with great valleys, with many rich mines of gold and silver and some of iron, and a great saline lake . . .' It was many decades since the heroic era of the first discoveries, and the royal councillors were electrified by such talk. They advised King Philip not to stint in such a 'great and desired enterprise'. He authorized Vera to take a thousand families, himself provided six large ships, and even lent Vera 26,000 ducats. Vera was astounded by his own success. He boasted to a friend: 'I am taking the greatest complement of ships and people that any man has ever taken to the Indies, without [starting with] a copper or a farthing! I am amazed at what I negotiated in Madrid, and how those gentlemen councillors did not even inform themselves of what I had, but simply gave me everything I asked for . . .' In his elation, Domingo de Vera apparently gave no thought to the accommodation of his army of colonists in the New World—perhaps he genuinely believed that they would walk straight into El Dorado itself.

This colonial flotilla left Spain in February 1596 and reached Trinidad on 10 April. Vera found a changed situation. He knew that the English had destroyed his town of San José de Oruña and had captured his governor Berrío. He now found that Berrío was free and had made his way up the Orinoco to settle at the mouth of the Caroní with a handful of men. Some of Berrío's best officers had deserted to join the governor of Cumaná. These had confronted Berrío in his Orinoco fort and forced him to surrender his claims to the island of Trinidad. They then went and founded their own town on the ruins of the place Ralegh had destroyed the previous year. Their town was only two months old when Vera arrived with his boatloads of colonists. Hundreds of new arrivals swarmed into the few huts of the town and grabbed its few provisions. Its plantations were barely able to support eighty inhabitants: no one knew how to feed the thousands of new-comers—least of all their visionary commander Domingo de Vera. His solution was to send as many as possible up the Orinoco in canoes; but Berrío was quite incapable of feeding them when they reached his small settlement. Many fled to towns on the Venezuelan mainland. Luis de Santander said that 'It is a certainty that if God does not provide some remedy of food, they will surely all die of hunger . . . It is a great tragedy to see so many men, women and children dying of hunger.' People seized snakes, grubs or insects to feed their families. They addressed an angry petition to Captain Vera e Ibargoyen, accusing him of deceiving them with his Dorado speeches, of lying to the Council of the Indies, and of swindling the King.

The men who went up-river fared no better. They were all new to the Indies and ill-equipped for the hazards of the Orinoco delta. The first contingents sent by Vera arrived safely. They went under an experienced captain, who had plenty of trade goods to win Indian help. But another flotilla was tricked and massacred by Carib raiders from the Antilles islands of Grenada and Dominica. As Domingo

Indians saved Hugh Goodwin, left on the Orinoco by Ralegh, from capture by the Spaniards by saying that he had been killed by a jaguar.

de Vera said, 'This was the beginning of a long series of disasters.' Vera hurried with a hundred men to try to ambush the Caribs. He set out in good weather for the short crossing to the mainland, but was then struck by a freak storm. Forty-five men were drowned, together with all his food and munitions. The loss of this food was so terrible that Vera did not dare return to the starving people on Trinidad: he went up the Orinoco to join Berrío instead. The old governor was as bewildered as his lieutenant. He was furious that some 500 men had been sent up to his fledgling town of Santo Tomé de Guayana without a scrap of food. He had founded the town at the mouth of the Caroní the previous December, and there had not been time to grow even one harvest of manioc for its original inhabitants. So when Domingo de Vera arrived, Berrío's welcome was glacial. Vera was hurt that his recruiting triumphs were not acknowledged. He wrote to the King rather pathetically: 'During the three days I remained there, he did not even say in a civil manner, "I will supply His Majesty's wants" or anything else due in consideration of all my goodwill and labours.' So Vera returned to Trinidad and confronted his hungry and rebellious colonists. For eight months of 'illnesses, deaths and hardships' he had no communication with Berrío in Santo Tomé de Guayana. Every time he sent a canoe upstream, its men deserted him and fled to Cumaná.

Berrío, meanwhile, finally launched the great expedition to conquer Guiana itself. The old governor was too old to go, although he planned to follow triumphantly when his men were in Manoa. Alvaro Jorge—who had made his first expedition with Hernán Pérez de Quesada 55 years before—was leader of four hundred newly-arrived men. The expedition was not properly equipped in horses, food or porters; but it set off up the Caroní valley. In four months of painful marching it covered about 120 kilometres. The Indians were friendly enough, and kept the expedition fed as it passed their villages. Then the experienced old Alvaro Jorge, weak and near-blind, died. There was no obvious successor as leader. The expedition fragmented, with groups of men following rival leaders. Discipline collapsed, and the soldiers began to 'demand gold from the natives, to seize their daughters and wives, and to insult them in the presence of their sons'. As Vera correctly surmised, 'the Indians lost respect for them' and launched a brilliant pre-dawn attack. The Spaniards, new to the Americas, were caught off guard and annihilated in a rush of arrows and club-wielding warriors. One survivor, Bernabé de Brea, counted 250 Spanish corpses, and Domingo de Vera told the King that 350 were killed. The survivors were so 'cowed and devoid of plans' that Berrío had to send a fresh commander to lead them back to Santo Tomé. The return journey was an agonizing calvary. As the expedition's survivors left the scene of their defeat at the hill of Totumos, they watched the Indians destroy crosses that the Franciscans had erected over the dead. The returning expedition was a rabble of sick, unshod and hungry men, harrassed by Indians. Franciscan friars had to give absolution to each dying man who was abandoned by the side of the trail. In the end one of the friars assumed command, to bring the survivors back into Santo Tomé. There were nine days of requiem masses in the settlement's tiny church, culminating in a service by the survivors and the many widows and orphans on 3 August 1596. There was further grief a few weeks later when 36 more men died on an expedition sent to try to find food for the starving town.

The base of this Popayán figure may have been a ceremonial knife. The curves of its plumage and wing-like upper arms brilliantly complement the curve of the base. Height about 16 cm.

The final assault on El Dorado had been a 'timorous, dispirited and mindless' fiasco. Back at Santo Tomé, the men began to mutiny and 'rushed down the river in twenties and thirties . . . As they were inexperienced in the rivers, which divide into innumerable channels, and had little food, only three men out of all this great number emerged safely at the end of seven months.' There had to be a scapegoat for a catastrophe of such magnitude. It could not be Antonio de Berrío, for that old don Quixote died during 1597, a few days after his son Fernando finally reached Santo Tomé with food and reinforcements from New Granada. There was an attempt to punish Domingo de Vera. He went up to join Fernando de Berrío for a time, and somehow survived retribution for his over-enthusiastic recruiting. He was last heard of living in Caracas at the end of the century.

The initiative to search for El Dorado now lay with the English, who were as much victims of Domingo de Vera's hallucinations as were the Spanish peasants who sold their land to sail to the Orinoco. When he left Guiana, two of Sir Walter Ralegh's men chose to stay behind among the Indians. They were acting partly as hostages for a son of chief Topiawari, whom Ralegh took for education in England. They also hoped to locate gold mines and learn Indian languages as a prelude to the conquest of Guiana. Spanish spies who watched Ralegh's movements knew all about these two Englishmen and it was not long before they caught one of them, Francis Sparrey, when he was out in a canoe with his Indian friends. The Indians managed to hide the other Englishman, Hugh Goodwin, by claiming that he had been killed by jaguars: he lived in a tribe for twenty years and almost forgot his mother tongue. Sparrey was interrogated at Margarita on 25 February 1596 and then sent to prison in Spain. In 1598 he sent a plea to England by means of a fellow prisoner who was being repatriated. This prisoner reported that 'He found a sufficient [mine] which the Spaniard knoweth not. He gave me reason how & a map where to find it. I delivered it to Sir Walter . . .' Ralegh was of course pleased to have this map, but he could do nothing to help Sparrey leave his Spanish prison. Two years later, Sparrey tried to win release by claiming that he was a convert to Catholicism and was now ready to serve the King of Spain. In a petition to the King and subsequent interrogation, Sparrey tried to tempt his captors by saying that he had buried a million ducats worth of gold on the banks of the Orinoco. 'He was asked whether he could locate the place where he had buried it. He said that he could, and that it would be there without fail, for he buried it on the banks of the Orinoco river whereas the natives of those kingdoms had their dwellings far inland . . .' Sparrey never returned to Guiana, but he managed to escape from Spain and wrote his adventures in England in 1602.

Ralegh's men had told the Indians of the Orinoco that 'in the following year they would return with 1500 men to colonize the country. They also . . . left a shield or coat-of-arms of the Queen as a sign of possession, and [said] that within a year they would be lords of the Indies.' Back in England, Ralegh or one of his captains wrote a treatise, *Of the Voyage for Guiana*, that was a plan for the colonization of that part of South America. It recommended benign treatment of the ruler of Guiana so that he would be a willing subject of the English Queen—principles that were later to be fundamental in the administration of the British Empire. It sum-

Cast gold pendant from the Popayán region at the source of the Cauca river. This anthropomorphic figure has a bird's beak, a magnificent plumed helmet, and calves swollen by ligatures at the knee and ankles.

marized four 'offers to be made to the Guianians' as: 1. 'That we will defend them
. . . 2. That we will help them to recover their country of Peru. 3. That we will
instruct them in liberal arts of civility . . . 4. And lastly that we will teach them the
use of weapons', battle manoeuvre, armour, ordnance and the use of horses.

Although Ralegh was disappointed by his lukewarm reception in England, he
did try to organize further attempts on Guiana. He wrote to Cecil on 13 November
1595: 'I am sending away a bark to the country [of Guiana] to comfort and assure
the people, that they despair not.' Cecil helped him finance two ships that sailed
under Laurence Keymis, in January 1596, with orders to explore all the rivers
north of the mouth of the Amazon, to try to find another route to El Dorado.

Keymis made a very thorough reconnaissance of the mouths of the Guiana
rivers. He noted the size of each and listed the tribes and their languages. His most
exciting discovery was a report by Indians at the mouth of the Essequibo—the
great river that flows through the modern country of Guyana—that there was a
vast lake at the head of their river. The Indians said that it took them twenty days
to paddle up the Essequibo and, after one day's portage, they reached a lake which
the Iaos tribe called Rupununi and the Caribs called Parima. This lake was 'of
such bignesse, that they know no difference betweene it & the maine sea. There be
infinite numbers of canoas in this lake, and (as I suppose),' wrote Keymis, 'it is
no other then that whereon Manoa standeth.' Occasionally, during heavy rains,
there are floods on the Rupununi plateau and around modern Boa Vista on the
upper Rio Branco: these floods may have been the vast lake described by the

The Rio Branco near Boa
Vista. The flooding of this
plain may have given rise
to the idea of the great
lake of Parima.

Indians, which gave such dramatic corroboration to the legend of the lake of El Dorado and Manoa.

Keymis went from the Essequibo to the Orinoco. He managed to find an easier, deeper passage through the delta; but he was bitterly disappointed when he reached the Caroní. He found that their friend Topiawari was dead and the two Englishmen, Sparrey and Goodwin, gone. He saw Berrío's new town of Santo Tomé, 'a ranchería of some twentie or thirtie houses', and at the mouth of the Caroní 'a secret ambush, to defend the passage to those mines, from whence your ore and white stones were taken last yeere.' He learned about Domingo de Vera's arrival at Trinidad with a great flotilla of colonists from Spain. The only promising result of this second voyage was news given by an old Indian from Carapana's village. 'This old man shewed mee, whence most of their golde commeth, which is formed in so many fashions: whence their Spleene-stones & others of al sorts are to be had in plentie: where golde is to bee gathered in the sandes of their rivers.' Keymis was a firm believer in the existence of El Dorado. He left places he called Cape Cecil and Raleana on the Guiana coast; and he kept alive the hope of golden wealth from this hidden empire. The faithful Keymis echoed his master when he wrote, at the end of his report: 'My selfe, and the remaine of my few yeeres, I have bequeathed wholly to Raleana, and all my thoughts live onely in that action.'

Ralegh promptly followed up this promising report. On 27 December 1596 he sent his captain Leonard Berry with the pinnace *Watte* to explore the rivers of the Guianas. Berry investigated the Oyapock, Marowijne and Courantyne rivers (which are now the boundaries of French Guiana and Dutch Surinam), exploring each upstream to the first falls or rapids. He followed Keymis' example in trading with the Guiana tribes and informing them that their benefactors were Sir Walter

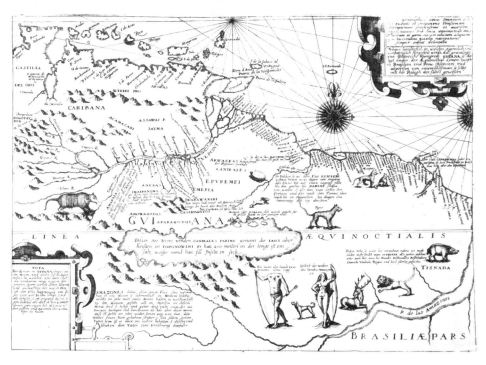

Laurence Keymis thought that Lake Parima and Manoa could be reached by ascending the Essequibo. His and Ralegh's reports influenced cartographers throughout the seventeenth century.

Ralegh and the Queen of England. Berry brought back confirmation that the Indians knew a great lake at the head of these rivers. Lake Parima was thus established, and it was therefore reproduced faithfully on maps.

While his captains were consolidating the exploration of Guiana, Ralegh himself was engaged on maritime enterprises against Spain, first as a vice-admiral of the great fleet that attacked Cádiz in 1596, and then on the unsuccessful Islands Voyage to the Azores in 1597. In 1598 Ralegh flirted with the idea of enlisting a Swedish prince as his financial backer in a fresh attempt on Guiana. But from 1597 to 1603 Ralegh had achieved his main purpose in trying to find El Dorado: he was restored to the confidence and counsel of the aged Queen Elizabeth. These were years in which he undertook public offices, consolidated his estates, and was again involved in colonial enterprises in Virginia.

Although he served his Queen, Ralegh failed to provide for his own future. Most of Elizabeth's ministers made secret overtures to King James VI of Scotland, who was her obvious successor. Ralegh failed to make any such contact, and was caught by surprise when Elizabeth died in March 1603. Ralegh tried to join in the welcome to King James when he marched south to become King of England. According to Aubrey, they met at Cecil's house at Burghley in Northamptonshire, and the new King made an ominous pun: ' "Ralegh. On my soul, mon. I have heard rawly of thee." ' Ralegh's enemies—his former friend Sir Robert Cecil among them—had been scheming against him behind his back. Everything about Ralegh, his dynamic character, his military prowess, his dislike of Spain, even his promotion of tobacco, was repugnant to King James. It was rumoured that Ralegh had been involved in a plot to put Arabella Stuart on the throne, possibly even with Spanish money. It was also said that he had spoken treasonably against the King and his children. In July 1603 Ralegh was interrogated before the Privy Council and then removed to the Tower on a charge of high treason. His trial took place in November. His old friend Lord Cobham implicated him in the Arabella Stuart plot, and there were tortuous conspiracies against him. By modern standards his trial was a sham, with the attorney-general Sir Edward Coke haranguing him from the bench, Francis Bacon as a malevolent prosecutor, and a series of dubious hearsay witnesses. But the verdict was guilty. King James hesitated to execute this great Elizabethan, who was now a national hero and would have become a popular martyr. So for twelve years Ralegh was imprisoned in the Tower of London, maintaining a household with some degree of comfort, conversing with prominent people including James's Queen Anne and his heir Prince Henry, and writing the first part of his monumental *Historie of the World* that was so admired by Cromwell.

While Walter Ralegh was ensnared, another heir of the search for El Dorado was active on the Orinoco. Antonio de Berrío's son Fernando reached Santo Tomé a few days before his father's death and he vowed to continue the quest that had obsessed the old man. English writers have accused Fernando de Berrío of being lazy and dilatory, but it appears from Spanish sources that he did seek El Dorado with great determination. He was not in any way daunted by his father's failures. For ten years from 1598 he laboured tirelessly, on no less than eighteen expeditions, to reach the elusive land.

Fernando de Berrío penetrated the upper Caroní, almost as far as Angel Falls, the world's highest waterfall.

Fernando de Berrío tried to advance up various tributaries of the Orinoco—the Caroní, Caura, Cuchivero—but ran into the inevitable rapids, cataracts and dense jungle on each of them. He was always blocked by the plateau, the scarp of ancient sandstone that forms the tablelands of Pacaraima and Roraima on top of the pre-Cambrian granite shield of the Guianas. He wrote to the King in 1604: 'In the 350 leagues that this first cordillera borders the Orinoco river, it seems that God erected a wall and fortress so great that it could be called impregnable: for it all grips the river at a distance of 30 or 35 leagues at the most.' In 1598 Berrío tried to found the town of Los Arias on fertile land up the Caroní; but the same tribes that destroyed Alvaro Jorge's expedition made this place untenable. At another time, Fernando de Berrío reached the deep valleys and high tablelands at the top of the Caroní, at the northern edge of the Gran Sabana and near Angel Falls, the world's highest waterfall. On another expedition, apparently in the land of Chimores Indians of the lower Caura river, Berrío managed to cross swamps and savannahs to enter dense hill forest. He found 'two very skilfully painted cloaks like Peruvian ones' and was told that these had been traded from the people of Manoa. A third expedition took him up the Caroní again. A hundred men with two hundred horses penetrated as far as a place called, for obvious reason, Province of the Crags. But no route could be found up the massive and forbidding cliffs; and the resistance of the courageous Panacayes Indians forced Berrío to turn back yet again.

Fernando de Berrío had his father's indomitable will. He tried again, sending Captain Martín Gómez up the Caura; and then himself tried up the Cuchivero and Guaynaima; but on each occasion Indian resistance and heavy rains defeated the explorers. Another attempt, with horses, up the Cuchivero was brought to a close by mutiny after Berrío himself fell ill and his men had to cross the hills without food. On an attempt up the Caroní, Berrío wanted to try to scale the wall of cliffs, but his men made him desist. And when he tried yet again up the Cuchivero, 'the most sure and short entry that is known' he suffered terrible hardships and had to build canoes and shoot rapids to return—just as his father had done on his second expedition in 1586. Fernando de Berrío was financially ruined by all this effort. He tried to recoup his fortunes by trading with foreign ships on the Orinoco. Such trade was considered a crime, and Berrío was denounced and disgraced in 1612. He had to go to Spain to beg for pardon in view of the great services of himself, his father, and his great-uncle Jiménez de Quesada. He was restored as governor of Guiana in 1619 and was soon off on more expeditions—now seeking a fabulous lake called Caranaca near the source of the Orinoco. He would doubtless have gone on stubbornly exploring until old age, as his father had done; but Fernando de Berrío was captured by Barbary pirates when sailing to Spain in 1622, and he died of plague, a captive in Algiers.

Domingo de Vera and Antonio de Berrío had remarked on the fact that Spain had no settlement anywhere in the extensive lands between the Amazon and Orinoco. Walter Ralegh publicized this vacuum in his popular *Discoverie . . . of Guiana*, which was eagerly studied in other European countries. It was therefore inevitable that there would be colonial attempts on the Guiana coasts. Henri IV of France authorized a Guiana colony in 1602 under the lord of Montbariot; and the Dutch repeated Ralegh's expedition up the lower Orinoco. Between 1602 and 1606 there was an attempt to plant an English colony on the Oyapock river—now the boundary between French Guiana and Brazil—by Ralegh's friends Sir John and Charles Leigh. This led to a more ambitious effort by Robert Harcourt. When he reached the Oyapock in May 1609 Harcourt assumed that its Indians were friends of Walter Ralegh (who had never been that far south) or at least of Keymis or Berry. He summoned the chiefs and made an appropriate speech: 'First, I brought to their remembrance the exploits of Sir Walter Ralegh in their Countrie. Then, I excused his not returning according to his promise, by reason of imployments imposed on him by the late Queene.' The main purpose of Harcourt's colony was trade and peaceful farming; but he was not above searching for Manoa. After the rains, in July 1609, he 'beganne to travell abroad in search of those golden mountaines . . .' Harcourt later tried to ascend the Marowijne in search of Manoa but was driven back by rapids and waterfalls. Two years later, Sir Thomas Roe made a thorough exploration of this part of the Guianas. He started at the Amazon and worked his way north, attempting each river in turn. After surmounting no less than 32 rapids, 'he found a level and uniform country without any more rapids, and afterwards a very deep and broad river. They would have travelled onwards along it, and by it arrived at the great city of Manoa, of which there is so great fame', but the local Aruak Indians had fled and the expedition's food was exhausted. All this exploration revealed no trace of Manoa or El Dorado. The legendary land was becoming discredited in England, and we hear little more about it.

In a letter to Robert Cecil, now Earl of Salisbury, Thomas Roe described another expedition that Fernando de Berrío was planning in his perpetual quest to reach El Dorado from Santo Tomé de Guayana. Roe remarked that 'the river and Towne is infinite ritch and weake, and may easily be taken away, and as easily held.' He was clearly contemplating an invasion of Spanish territory on the Orinoco, for he went on to tell about a renegade Spaniard who could be of use to the English. All this coincided with the rise of an anti-Spanish faction in England; and it involved Ralegh, who had invested £600 in Thomas Roe's exploration.

As he languished in the Tower for months and years on end, Ralegh naturally longed for another attempt on Guiana. His *Discoverie . . . of Guiana* had been too strident, and his enemies ridiculed its wilder fantasies: Ralegh therefore concentrated on the gold mines that he and Keymis had heard about near the Caroní. In 1607 he proposed to Salisbury and the Council that he and Keymis should go together to try to find the mine. The Council insisted that Keymis must go first, and must bring back some gold before an expedition could be sanctioned; which offer Ralegh refused, on the grounds that this would hand Keymis' discovery to the Spaniards. Ralegh had had some of his ore from the Orinoco assayed, and it showed traces of gold. He made the most of this in conversations with Queen Anne and her son Prince Henry. He repeated his offer to the Council in 1611; and now agreed to their condition that Keymis go alone. He even offered to pay for the entire expedition, if Keymis failed to bring back half a ton of 'slate gold'. The Council demurred. Ralegh begged eloquently to be allowed to go. 'To die *for* the King, and not *by* the King, is all the ambition I have in the world.'

Ralegh's release finally came in March 1616. There had been a change of faction at Court; the new favourite George Villiers and the new Secretary, Sir Ralph Winwood, disliked the King's subservience to Spain. Ralegh was released on probation, but with a keeper and solely to plan his Orinoco venture. He had always argued that he had formally annexed Guiana for England in 1595, so that an attempt to mine gold there would not infringe Spanish sovereignty. This argument undoubtedly influenced King James, who was strongly dominated by the Spanish ambassador Count Gondomar. When Ralegh received his patent for the Guiana expedition on 26 August 1616, it was issued to him 'under the peril of the law' and he was required to promise to inflict no injury of any kind on subjects of the King of Spain. King James even promised Gondomar that Ralegh would be sent to Spain for trial if he damaged any Spanish property. He also gave the Spanish ambassador exact details of Ralegh's plans and charts, with his proposed ports of call and dates. The King was to receive one fifth of any gold or jewels brought back by the expedition; he risked nothing and could only gain. Ralegh, on the other hand, had to find the finance and to succeed in the difficult undertaking—but if he failed he had everything to lose. He pledged his life on the outcome.

Ralegh acknowledged that 'from anie territory confessed to be the King of Spaines itt is noe more lawfull to take gould, then lawfull for the Spaniards to take tinne out of Cornewall.' But he insisted that King James's title to Guiana was 'the best and most Christian, because the natural lords did most willingly acknowledge Queene Elizabeth to be their sovran . . . I made no doubt butt that I might enter the land by force, seeinge the Spaniard had noe other title butt force . . .'

Despite this argument, there were two curious aspects about the planning of Ralegh's second Guiana voyage. One was that King James allowed it to go. For a king so concerned not to trespass on Spanish property, it was rash to send a large armed expedition to a river controlled by the busy little port of Santo Tomé. We can only conclude that he did not know that this town was so near the mines; or that he was swayed by Ralegh's argument of a prior English claim. The other curious aspect was that Ralegh could have seriously imagined he could find and mine gold, at a place about which he and Keymis had heard vague reports over twenty years before, and all within a few miles of a Spanish town. The idea of Guiana gold had developed during his years of captivity into a reckless conviction. It was a terribly dangerous gamble.

Walter Ralegh was now in his sixties, grey haired, stooped from ague and rheumatism, short of breath and walking with a stick. He attracted attention as he explored London again after so many years of confinement, for he was the last of the great Elizabethan sea-dogs. Although his legs and lungs were weak, he still had his energy and enthusiasm. He organized a splendid expedition. He himself contributed some £10,000 by selling or pledging most of his remaining possessions. A further £20,000 was raised, with difficulty, from private subscribers. A fine ship, *Destiny*, was built for Ralegh and delivered to him on the Thames in December 1616 by her designer Phineas Pett.

There were delays during part of 1617, so that the fleet did not leave Plymouth until June and was forced by bad weather to shelter at Cork until August. There were thirteen vessels in all, led by the 440-ton *Destiny* and 240-ton *Star* (or *Jason*), and almost a thousand men. Some of the officers were experienced or distinguished men—the tall, thin Laurence Keymis who had a cast in one eye, Ralegh's son Wat and nephew George, William Herbert, Edward Hastings, Captain North and Sir William St Leger, all well connected. But other captains were former pirates, and Ralegh himself described most of his men as the scum of the world, drunkards, blasphemers and vagabonds. Ralegh issued stern and sensible instructions to his fleet, dealing with military drills, discipline, divine service daily, and no swearing, stealing, gambling, smoking below decks, or eating between meals. Once in the Americas, Ralegh's men were to avoid eating unsalted meat or over-fat hogs or turkeys. They should swim only where they saw Indians swimming, for fear of alligators; and 'you shall not take anything from any Indian by force . . . but you must use them with all courtesie.'

The fleet reached the Cayenne river in what is now French Guiana on 12 November. There had been two severe illnesses during the voyage that left 42 dead on the flagship alone. Ralegh wrote to his wife: 'Sweet Heart, I can yet write unto you but with a weak hand, for I have suffered the most violent calenture for fifteen days, that ever man did, and lived.' He felt that God was strengthening his indomitable spirit 'in the hell-fire of heat'. The welcome given by the Indians was a great consolation. He wrote to Bess: 'To tell you I might be here King of the Indians were a vanitie; but my name hath still lived among them. Here they feed me with fresh meat, and all that the countrey yields; all offer to obey me.' Now that he was in the Americas, Ralegh began to be apprehensive about the magnitude of the undertaking. He was about to defy the Spanish American empire with a force of men already depleted by the Atlantic crossing. But he remained resolute. 'Howsoever, we must make the adventure; and if we perish, it shall be no honour for England nor gain for his Majestie to loose, among many other, one hundred as valiant gentlemen as England hath in it.'

The fleet sailed on, and anchored off the mouth of the Orinoco in December 1616. Ralegh remained with the ships, to provide a strong command in case of Spanish attack, and because he was not sufficiently fit for the expedition up the river. The two obvious leaders for this venture were dead or ill, so Ralegh appointed Laurence Keymis to lead it, together with his young son Wat. Keymis was a curious man, a scholar of Balliol who composed elegant Latin verse and wrote eloquent protestations of loyalty to Ralegh. It was his information about the gold mine that had nourished Ralegh's illusions during the years in the Tower. There were in fact *two* supposed mines. One was a few miles from Morequito's village, the site of Berrío's town Santo Tomé de Guyana, where Ralegh had picked up gold-bearing ore during the walk to the Caroní cataracts. The second mine was near a mountain called Iconuri or Aio. It lay inland of Carapana's village, which was on an island some 32 kilometres downstream or east of Santo Tomé. Ralegh had heard about this mine from chief Putijma in 1595 and started to walk towards it, up rivers he called Mana and Cumaca, possibly the modern Supamo and Tipurua which enter the Orinoco opposite Tortola island. Keymis was with Ralegh on that walk, and he investigated the place again when he was there the following year. 'I sawe farre off the mountaine adjoyning to this gold myne.' Keymis reckoned that it was fifteen miles away. He recalled how Putijma had

Ralegh had the 440-ton *Destiny* built for his last voyage. A design for an Elizabethan ship from Mathew Baker's *The Ancient Art of Shipwrightary*.

pointed to it and indicated that Keymis should go there. 'I understood his signs and marked the place, but mistook his meaning, imagining that he would have shewed me the overfall of the River Curwara from the mountaines.' The Indian in fact showed Keymis how his people panned for gold in the streams beneath that mountain.

Ralegh issued careful instructions to his lieutenants for the Orinoco journey. They were to locate and try to work the mine, if possible without involving the Spaniards. They should fight only in self-defence. 'If you find the Mine royal, and the Spaniards begin to war upon you, You, George Ralegh, are to repel them, and to drive them as far as you can.' There was another plan in case a rich mine could not be located. Ralegh desperately needed evidence of gold, so he wrote: 'If you find the Mine be not so rich as may persuade the holding of it, and draw on a second supply, then you shall bring but a basket or two, to satisfy His Majesty that my design was not imaginary, but true, though not answerable to his Majesty's expectation.' If the expedition found the river heavily defended, they were to land only with great prudence, 'for,' Ralegh admitted, 'I know, a few gentlemen excepted, what a scum of men you have. And I would not, for all the world, receive a blow from the Spaniards to the dishonour of our nation.' Ralegh wished his men well and promised to remain at the mouth of the river, dead or alive. 'And if you find not my ships there, you shall find their ashes. For I will fire with the galleons, if it come to extremity; run will I never.'

The expedition had the usual difficulty penetrating the shallow channels of the Orinoco estuary. Keymis set off on 10 December with 250 soldiers and 150 sailors in five vessels of shallow draught, but only three of these reached Santo Tomé at the beginning of January 1618. Keymis had sailed right past the lower mine near mount Iconuri. He landed his men a few miles from Santo Tomé itself, apparently intending to find the mine near the Caroní. The landing was made at four in the afternoon of 2 January; but in the early hours of that same night the English stormed into the town of Santo Tomé, led by young Walter Ralegh. Such an attack on a Spanish town was the most flagrant breach of the older Ralegh's royal patent.

There are various versions of what may have happened and, as with Ralegh's earlier attack on San José on Trinidad, we have descriptions of the battle by both sides. One possibility is that Laurence Keymis was determined to destroy Santo Tomé immediately, to remove this threat before he began to search for the mines. This was the view of Captain Roger North, who later testified that 'Keymis said that he would not discover the mine until they had taken the Town.' According to North, Keymis felt that it would be folly to open a gold mine in full view of a town full of Spaniards. Some writers have speculated that Ralegh gave Keymis secret instructions to destroy Santo Tomé; but this seems highly unlikely in view of the royal prohibition. Another possibility is that the English planned to contact a group of malcontents within Santo Tomé, and hoped that its gates would be opened to them by treachery. We know from Spanish sources that there was friction within the town. Many of the inhabitants had established good relations with foreign traders who visited the Orinoco before Fernando de Berrío's disgrace in 1612. These potential rebels hated the new governor Diego Palomeque de Acuña. But it seems impossible for such clandestine contact to have been made between the English and Spanish dissidents during the few hours before the assault.

A third, and more probable, explanation was that Keymis landed his men and stationed his boats for a blockade of Santo Tomé: this was roughly in accord with Ralegh's instructions. It was thus the Spaniards who launched the first attack. Pedro Simón admitted that the Spanish governor ordered that a mortar fire stone shot at the English ships. Simón also said that a Spaniard called Jerónimo de

LEFT Ralegh's fleet reached the Cayenne river in November 1617. One of his men sent back '*Newes of Sir Walter Ralegh*' that was published before his return.

RIGHT A contemporary Spanish drawing shows Berrío's town of Santo Tomé de Guayana, with ships on the Orinoco in the foreground. It was the attack on this town in 1618 that led to Ralegh's execution.

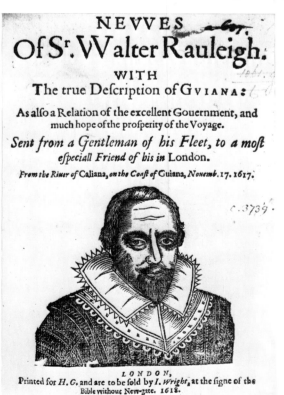

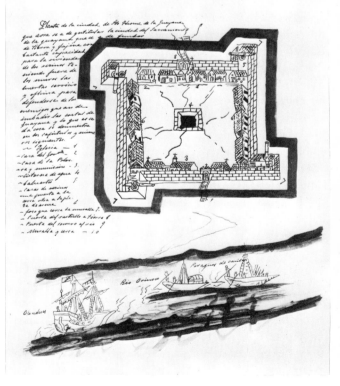

Grados prepared an ambush beside the town and 'gave the enemy his first shower of bullets'. Captain García de Aguilar Trujillo recalled that Grados then ran to the governor and said: ' "Mister Governor, the enemy has broken up our ambush, and is coming with the main body ot his men" ' into the town itself.

The English apparently marched right up to the town wall in the darkness. When fired upon, there was confusion and near panic. Young Wat Ralegh rallied the men and led them forward in a charge right into Santo Tomé. Different witnesses gave slightly different versions of why this happened. William Herbert said that the English officers 'went to consultation whether they should sett upon the Town or go forward' to the mine. Captain Charles Parker said bluntly that 'we landed within a league of St. Thomé, and about one of the clocke at night we made an assaulte.' He severely condemned Wat Ralegh's 'unadvised daringness' in leaving his company of pikemen and rushing forward to lead an assault. Even Keymis indirectly criticized Wat Ralegh to his father: 'Had not his extraordinarie vallor and forwardnes . . . ledd them all on, when some begann to pause and recoyle shamefully, this action had neither bene attempted as it was, nor performed as it is . . .' It was thus Ralegh's own son who forced the attack that was to ruin his father.

A contemporary Spanish drawing of Santo Tomé showed that it was very small. It was square, with a bastion for cannon projecting at each corner of its rampart. There was a large water cistern in the middle of the sand square. The houses were built around the square, just within the ramparts, which were in turn surrounded by a moat. There were two gates, a church, governor's house and powder magazine. In the foreground, the drawing shows a Dutch ship and two large Carib canoes. During the English attack in January 1618, the Spaniards fired their arque-buses from loopholes in the houses. A popular later version of the attack had Wat Ralegh shouting ' "Come on my hearts! This is the mine you must expect: they that look for any other are fools!" ' Charles Parker said, simply, that when Wat Ralegh heard the Spaniards attack the English van, he 'indiscreetely came from his commande to us, wher he was vnfortunately welcomed with a bullett, which gave him no tyme to call for mercye to our hevenly father for his sinfull lyfe he had ledde.' Pedro Simón wrote that 'one Englishman, getting ahead of the rest, came along singing "Victory". Coming up to him, Jerónimo de Grados gave him such a sword thrust on the left side of his gullet that he sent the heretic to re-echo his song in Hell!' This was Mr Harington, a relative of the Countess of Bedford. On the Spanish side there were also two dead, and one of these was the governor Palòmeque de Acuña himself. He was missing when the Spaniards abandoned their defence and fled into the night. Next day an Indian woman said she was taken into Keymis' house in the captured town. She saw 'many of his soldiers standing round in a circle, contemplating the naked corpse of Governor Palomeque, the left side of whose head was split open down to the teeth with a sword slash.'

Having captured Santo Tomé, Keymis lost his resolve. He did not know where to begin to look for the mine in the midst of the Guiana wilderness. The men were bewildered: he was the one man who had always known where the mine lay. 'Every man's expectation looked hourly for the discovery of the mine, while Captain Kemis minded rather the tobacco, apparel, household stuff, and other pillage;

often saying these would help if all failed.' Keymis did not dare to begin his hopeless search in full view of his expectant men. He crept off one night with a few friends and brought back some ore, 'which he cheerfully shewed Captain Thornhurst; but being tried by a refiner, it proved worth nothing, and was no more spoken of.' Captain Charles Parker, who hated Keymis, said that he 'trifeled up and downe some 20 dayes keepinge us in hope still of findinge it, but at last we found his delayes meere illusiones and him selfe a mear Machevill . . .'

Keymis made no attempt to look for the other mine, the one he had described so glowingly in his *Relation of the Second Voyage to Guiana*. He did not even try very diligently to find the mine near the Caroní. A few excursions in search of it were ambushed or driven back by the Spaniards. There was little attempt to contact the tribes who had been so friendly twenty years before. The English were virtually besieged in the town by a handful of its former citizens. The only positive action was a voyage by three launches commanded by George Ralegh, who went up the Orinoco for a few hundred kilometres to a place called Guarico near the mouth of the Apure. They took frequent soundings—a futile exercise on a river that rises and falls as violently as the Orinoco—and urged any Indians they met to rise against the Spaniards in preparation for the arrival of the English. It was supposed to be a prelude to a future attack on New Granada. Such was the last move in Ralegh's dream of an Anglo-Guianian alliance that would drive the Spaniards out of South America.

After 29 days Keymis admitted failure. The Spaniards refused to parley. The plunder was therefore loaded on to the ships and Santo Tomé was set on fire. Everyone was terrified that Spanish reinforcements would arrive at any time: the boats therefore hurried down the Orinoco without stopping at Carapana's village to inquire about the second mine. Keymis had already sent a letter to tell Ralegh about the death of his beloved son and the equally terrible news of the attack on the Spanish town. The expedition reached him on 2 March and confirmed its utter failure. Keymis came to Ralegh's cabin to ask his forgiveness and his support in reporting the failure to English backers. But, in Ralegh's own words, 'I told him that he had undone me by his obstinacie, and that I woiuld not favour . . . in any sort his former follie. He then asked me, whether that were my resolution; I told him it was; he then replyed in these words, "I knowe then, Sir, what course to take", and went out of my cabin upp into his owne, into which he was noe sooner entered but I heard a postol goe of. I sent up (not suspecting any such thing as the killing of himselfe) to knowe who shott the pistoll; Kemish himselfe made answere, lyeing on his bedd, that he had shott it of(f) because it had bene longe charged, with which I was satisfied. Some halfe an hower after this, his boye going into his cabbin, found him dead, haveing a longe knife thrust under his lefte pappe through his heart, and the pistol lyeing by him, with which it appeared he had shott himselfe; butt the bullett, lighting upon a ribb had but broken the ribb, and went noe further.' It was a situation of great tragedy: Keymis was full of remorse at his failure and the obvious jeopardy to the life of the man he had served for many years; Ralegh, distraught at Wat's death and glumly aware of his own predicament, refused to endorse Keymis' excuses, although he had no idea that Keymis was contemplating suicide. He heard later that Keymis had mentioned the second mine as he passed Carapana's village but had failed to try to find it. This made it impossible for Ralegh to forgive his lieutenant. Charles Parker vented his fury in a letter to a friend. He condemned Keymis as 'false to all men and moste odious to him selfe, for moste vngodly he butchered himselfe lothinge to live since he could doe no mor villany; I wil speke no more of this hatefull fellow . . .'

Walter Ralegh had to tell his wife about the loss of their beloved son. He wrote to her from Saint Kitt's island on 22 March: 'I was loath to write because I know not how to comforte you. And God knowes, I never knewe what sorrow meant till now. All that I can say to you is, that you must obey the Will and Providence of God . . . I shall sorrow for us both; and I shall sorrowe the lesse because I have not long to live.' He could not bring himself to describe the disastrous failure of the expedition. He told her to learn about it from Secretary Winwood, 'for my braines are broken, and tis a torment to mee to write, and especially of Miserie. . . . The Lord blesse you, and Comfort you, that you may beare patientlie the death of your valient Sonne.' Ralegh then added a long postscript. He said that he would gladly die heartbroken, as Drake and Hawkins had done after similar failures, but for his wish to care for his wife. He confirmed his belief in the gold mine. 'It is true, that Kemish might have gonne directly to the myne, and meant it.' But Keymis had made trivial excuses and 'left it unfound. When hee came backe I told him that hee had undone mee, and that my creditt was loste for ever.' Ralegh then described Keymis' suicide. He ended the letter to his wife by saying that he knew, from captured documents, that all his plans had been betrayed to the Spanish ambassador—it was quite obvious by whom. 'There was never poore man soe exposed to the slaughter as I was; for being commanded upon my allegiance to sett downe, not onely the country, but the very river by which I was to enter it, to name my shipps, number my men and my artillery'; every detail had been sent by Gondomar to King Philip. The Spanish King had written to his colonies about it, on 19 March 1617, 'when I had not yett lefte the Thames'.

Ralegh's fleet was disintegrating. Some captains went off to prey on Spanish shipping. They advised Ralegh to join them, for if he returned to the mercy of King James he was a dead man. Ralegh thought of wild schemes. He learned from captured documents that there really *was* a gold mine near the Orinoco: he tried to persuade his men to follow him back up the cursed river. He talked of selling the tobacco from Santo Tomé in Newfoundland; or of attacking the Spanish plate fleet. He wrote desperate apologies to Secretary Winwood, begging him not to believe the 'scumme of men' returning from the fleet and vilifying its commander. All Ralegh's captains deserted him and he set out towards Newfoundland in the *Destiny*. But, when he learned that half his men planned to seize the ship and take to piracy, he turned reluctantly for home. The *Destiny* sailed into Plymouth on 21 June 1618.

Count Gondomar stormed into King James, repeating the one word, 'Pirates! Pirates! Pirates!' but the King was already incensed. The order to arrest Ralegh was issued on 11 June, and Sir Lewis Stukeley was sent to bring him to London. The arrest and march to London were very slow, almost as if Ralegh was expected to escape. He passed his former estate at Sherborne, long since confiscated by the King. He feigned illness, in order to gain time to write an appeal for royal clemency.

Ralegh's entourage were his devoted wife Bess, his faithful captain Samuel King, and two apparent agents provocateurs, a French doctor called Manourie and his captor Stukeley—later known as 'Sir Judas' Stukeley. When they reached London, Ralegh was approached by two French agents who suggested that he would be welcome iu France. He decided to attempt a flight across the Channel—a course he could so easily have adopted when he still had the *Destiny* or during the weeks before his arrest. A bogus escape was arranged, with Ralegh entering a small boat to row down the Thames, dressed in a large hat and a ludicrous false beard; but when the boat reached Greenwich, Stukeley revealed his true colours and arrested Ralegh again.

Walter Ralegh entered the Tower for the third time on 10 August. During the ensuing weeks he put up a determined defence. In a letter to the Privy Council on 24 September, he argued that he had refrained from attacking any part of the Spanish Indies with his powerful fleet: he concentrated on the mine in Guiana, 'where, without any direction from me a Spanish village was burnt'. Other English captains had done far worse damage and remained unpunished. He had voluntarily surrendered himself by returning to England. 'My mutineers tould me, that if I returned for England I should be undone; but I beleeved more in your Majesty's goodnes then in their arguments.'

There was a legal dilemma on how to proceed. King Philip III of Spain refused the offer that Ralegh be sent there for trial. King James could always execute him under the 1603 conviction for treason, for which he had never been pardoned; but it would look vindictive to kill an old man after thirteen years' imprisonment. He could be punished for his crimes in Guiana; but this would involve a second trial, in which the case against Ralegh was not conclusive. In the end, it was decided that Ralegh should appear before a committee of six, headed by Sir Francis Bacon. The King insisted that this be a private hearing, to avoid any public compassion for the aged prisoner: Ralegh could easily have shown himself as the victim of the King's unpopular policy of alliance to Spain.

Ralegh appeared before the Commission on 22 October. Members of the Guiana expedition had testified to alleged crimes by its leader. There was talk of French plots. We have no full record of the closed proceedings, but Bacon evidently informed Ralegh that the commissioners were satisfied of his guilt and that he must die. He was taken, weak with ague, before the Justices of the King's Bench on 28 October. He tried to argue that his patent to lead the Guiana expedition, with power of life and death, was equivalent to pardon of the previous conviction. This was rebutted; and his attempts to excuse the conduct of the recent voyage were cut short as irrelevant. Ralegh threw himself on the King's mercy; but the Lord Chief Justice intervened: 'Sir Walter Ralegh, you must remember yourself; you had an honourable trial, and so were justly convicted; and it were wisdom in you now to submit yourself.' Ralegh was reminded that he had legally been a dead man ever since his conviction for treason fifteen years before. The King had then spared him from execution. But 'new offences have stirred up his Majesty's justice, to remember to revive what the law hath formerly cast upon you. I know that you have been valiant and wise, and I doubt not but you retain both these virtues, for now you have occasion to use them.' He ended his sombre

Ralegh's magnificent
composure on the scaffold
gained him great 'honour
and reputation in the
opinion of men'.

address with the words: 'Execution is granted.' Ralegh replied: 'Here I take God
to be my judge, before whom I shall shortly appear, I was never disloyal to his
Majesty, which I will justify where I shall not fear the face of any king on earth.
And so I beseech you all to pray for me.'

Emotional appeals for clemency from Ralegh's family and friends, and from the
Queen herself, were ignored. The execution was fixed for 29 October. There was
official fear of a public demonstration, for it was obvious that the old Elizabethan
was being sacrificed to please Spain. Ralegh spent his last night in the gatehouse
opposite Westminster Hall. He left a note in which he denied the various shabby
accusations against him. One item of this was: 'My true intent was to goe to a Mine
of Gold in Guiana. Itt was not fained, but is true that such a Mine there is, within
three miles of St Tomé.' He was attended by Dr Robert Tounson, Dean of West-

minster, who wrote to a friend a few days later: 'He was the most fearless of death that ever was known, and the most resolute and confident, yet with reverence and conscience. When I began to encourage him against the fear of death, he seemed to make so light of it that I wondered at him . . .' Ralegh was cheerful and merry, and said that he 'hoped to persuade the world he died an innocent man'. He ate a hearty breakfast and smoked tobacco.

Ralegh was led across Westminster yard, on the morning of 29 October 1618, in an escort of sixty guards, wearing a black gown over a brown satin doublet, black waistcoat and breeches, and grey silk stockings. He wore a ruff, and a night-cap under his hat. Ralegh was suffering from a bout of tertian fever and worried that if he trembled from this it might be taken for fear. He need not have worried. He showed complete composure, smiling and greeting friends, taking a drink from a bystander, and delivering a magnificent 45-minute oration from the scaffold to the crowd that packed the yard. He made a profession of his Christian faith. He denied a rumour that he had exulted over the death of Essex many years before. He then rehearsed his innocence of the recent accusations against him; he exposed Stukeley's duplicity but then pardoned him. He reiterated his belief in American gold for the last time: 'There was a report that I meant not to go to Guiana at all, and that I knew not of any Myne, nor intended any such matter, but only to get my Liberty, which I had not the Wit to keep. But it was my full intent to go for Gold, for the Benefit of his Majesty and those that went with me, with the rest of my Country men.'

After the speech, Ralegh embraced his friends 'with such courtly compliments of discourse as if he had met them at some feast. They then cleared the scaffold, which being done, he takes up the axe, and feels the edge, and finding it sharp for the purpose, "This is that," saith he, "that will cure all sorrows", and so kissing it, laid it down again.' Ralegh tested his head on the block; the executioner asked forgiveness and Ralegh embraced him. He asked the executioner to strike when he raised his hand, ' "And then fear not," saith he, "but strike home." . . . After he had lain a little while upon the block, conceiving some prayers to himself, he gave the watchword, and the executioner, it seems, not minding it, he called aloud unto him, asking him why he did not strike. "Strike, man" said he; and so, in two blows, was delivered from his pain.' His head was held up on each side of the scaffold and then put into a red leather bag. 'The large Effusion of Blood, which proceeded from his Veins, amaz'd the Spectators, who Conjectured he had stock enough left of Nature, to have surviv'd many Years, though now near Fourscore Years old.' 'His end was, by the general report of all that were present, very christian like, and so full of resolution as moved all men to pity and wonder. . . . nay, the beholders seemed much more sensible than did he. So that he hath purchased here, in the opinion of men, such honour and reputation . . . which is like to turn so much to his advantage.'

This was the end of the last visionary seeker of El Dorado. That elusive place was never found. The searches for it cost many lives and terrible suffering, particularly among the American natives. But the legend of the Golden Man inspired more sustained exploration, of some of the wildest parts of South America, than any comparable idea, anywhere else in the world.

Appendix

The Draining of Lake Guatavita

ONCE THE SPANIARDS LEARNED THAT THE MUISCA MADE OFFERINGS IN THEIR SACRED lakes, a conviction grew that great wealth awaited anyone who could plumb those mysterious waters. Cieza de León, who wrote in Peru in the 1550s, spoke of 'a very large lake in the province of Bogotá from which, if His Majesty would order it to be drained, he would remove a quantity of gold and diamonds [emeralds] that the Indians threw into it in ancient times.'

Lázaro Fonte, Jiménez de Quesada's captain who was in trouble for his outrages against the Indians, may have attempted to drain Lake Guatavita, which lay within his encomienda. Pedro Simón said that Lázaro Fonte did try but soon desisted for lack of funds—which seems improbable since Fonte had plenty of subject Indians, and since he left Bogotá soon after the abortive El Dorado expedition of 1541 and went to live in Quito.

The first documented attempt on Lake Guatavita was by Antonio de Sepúlveda, who obtained a royal licence to drain the lake, issued on 22 September 1562. He returned to New Granada and built huts alongside the lake and a boat for soundings. He assembled many Indians and set them to work, laboriously cutting a trench through which to drain the water. Pedro Simón said that he had to provide quantities of wine to keep his men working on that cold páramo. Sepúlveda managed to lower the lake level slightly and found some gold discs and emeralds in the mud at the edge of the lake. Further efforts took him deeper, towards the lake's centre, which was where everyone supposed that the valuable offerings were dropped. Juan Rodríguez Fresle wrote that Sepúlveda's cuttings could still be seen in his day in the 1630s. He wrote that 'a long time later [Sepúlveda] continued to want to make another drainage, but could not. In the end he died poor and exhausted. I knew him well and often conversed with him, and I helped bury him in the church of Guatavita.' Pedro Simón said that Sepúlveda extracted 5–6,000 pesos of gold objects from Guatavita: Rodríguez Fresle said 12,000 pesos; but the original record of 22 June 1576 has now been found, and it records only '232 pesos and 10 grams of good gold'. In 1625 twelve people from the mining camp of Santa Ana applied for permission to search for treasure in the lake. They obtained the usual elaborate legal documents, with permission to use as many Indians as they needed, 'paying them as they must be paid'. But nothing came of this, or of any other attempt during the centuries of colonial rule.

There was a far more serious effort in 1823, soon after Colombia achieved independence from Spanish rule. An enthusiast called José Ignacio 'Pepe' París formed a company to drain Guatavita, with sixteen shareholders subscribing $8,000. He hired an overseer called Ramírez and started cutting a trench on the north-east edge of the circular lake. His drain lowered the lake waters; but no treasure was found. He told a friend that the original investment was gone: ' "I thought it would be sufficient; but unfortunately it has now cost me $20,000 and there are still 35 feet of water left." '

A British naval captain called Charles Stuart Cochrane visited Colombia at this time, and made friends with 'Pepe' París. Cochrane amazed the Colombians by demonstrating how a syphon could drain a water tank; but when he reached Guatavita he realized that it was too large to be emptied by this means. Cochrane was struck by the eerie beauty of the lake: 'Picture to yourself a lovely autumnal

Lake Guatavita.

195

day on the lakes of Westmoreland,—such had we; not a breath of wind disturbed the glassy surface of the lake, which reflected back the thick woods that studded its shores, rising in tiers on tiers to the height of 127 feet; and above all was seen a calm reflected sky; nought living moved, save a few water-fowl, that gently glided away from us . . .' Cochrane happily settled down among the Colombian Indians, living in their cold hut, huddled over the camp fire at night, but with plenty of excellent game to eat. He saw that the trench passed through slate and grey sandstone, so that the water undermined its sides. He arranged for it to be shored. On 25 October 1823 Cochrane reckoned that the trench was ready. 'I determined on opening an embouchure, sufficient to let two square feet of water keep running out during the night. This I did, and retired to rest with the pleasing noise of the roar of the water dashing through the canal, and winding its way to the plains below.' But, by the next morning, the lake was lowered only about six inches and the trench was crumbling. Cochrane ordered hundreds of planks to be cut for more shoring, and then moved on in his travels. His friend Pepe continued the work, with the dogged determination of a Berrío. Seven successive trenches caved in. Colonel J. P. Hamilton, a British diplomat who visited the lake in 1826, wrote that 'as his design had no chance of success this way, he was advised to dig a subterraneous channel, about 30 feet lower than the bed of the lake, in the same direction he had taken in making the first fissure . . . I heartily wish he may succeed at last; he deserved to possess a good fortune, being a most liberal good-natured man, particularly attentive to foreigners and a great friend of Bolívar's . . .' But another disaster occurred. Indian labourers perished when the tunnel collapsed, and 'Pepe' París was left as disillusioned and destitute as all his predecessors.

The lure of hidden gold still had powerful attraction. Captain Cochrane quoted someone called 'Monsieur de la Kier, of the Royal Institute, Paris' who calculated that the lake ought to contain gold and precious stones worth 'one billion one hundred and twenty millions sterling'. Colonel Hamilton was more sceptical. He doubted whether the lake would ever yield enough to repay the cost of draining it. He reasoned that the Muisca, with no gold mines of their own, would never have thrown much treasure into these waters.

The next attempt was made, not on Lake Guatavita, but on Siecha, another round lake on an isolated moorland to the south of the village of Guatavita. Siecha was 220 metres in diameter and at an altitude of 3,673 metres. It was reasoned that Siecha might have been the lake of the Muisca ceremony or that it might contain treasure of the chief of Chía, thrown into it to escape the conquistadores. The first company formed to drain Lake Siecha failed, but the second attempt, in 1856, dug a channel three metres deep and 50 metres long, and managed to lower the lake by a full three metres. Its reward was to find some Muisca objects, including the famous golden figure of the chief and ten attendants on a raft. Liborio Zerda said of this raft: 'In our opinion this piece represents the ceremony of El Dorado.' This success inspired a later attempt on Lake Siecha. In 1870 two men called Crowther and Urdaneta drove a shaft for 187 metres towards the western wall of the lake. They were within a short distance of completing their perforation when, on 9 October 1870, they both died of asphyxiation, from the lack of air in their tunnel and from fumes from the lake mud.

At the end of the century there was renewed interest in Lake Guatavita. Three unmarried ladies who owned the hacienda that contained the sacred lake gave a concession to an entrepreneur to drain Guatavita. In September 1899 this concession passed to an Englishman called Hartley Knowles who floated an enterprise called Contractors Limited, with himself as administrator at a salary of £25 a month. Quantities of equipment were carried up to Guatavita on muleback, including the pride of the English engineers: a steam pump. The work progressed slowly. In 1908 a Colombian engineer called Hernando de Villa joined Contractors Limited and, with drainage channels and steam pumps, the lake was almost drained. A German traveller called Konrad Beissmanger visited Guatavita in July 1910 and actually took a photograph of the drained lake—a mass of mud, rivulets and pools of water. He found an Englishman called W. Cooper in charge of the operation, and visited a 400-metre tunnel that was being used to drain the lake's mud. It was supported by wooden pit props near its entrance, but otherwise ran through solid limestone. Cooper said that he had worked at Guatavita for eight years. He had a dozen Indian labourers scouring the mud of the lake's floor, prodding with sticks and occasionally finding Muisca objects.

The treasures from Guatavita were sent to London, where Contractors Limited put them on exhibition in August 1911, prior to auction at Sotheby's on 11 December 1911. The sale consisted of 62 lots, 22 of which contained gold and the rest were ceramics or other Muisca artefacts. The finest pieces were pectorals, neck and nose ornaments, a gold snake and a goddess, a golden helmet, pendants and pins. One breastplate weighed over eight ounces and the helmet weighed almost six ounces; otherwise the objects were typical small Muisca pieces weighing between one and two ounces.

The exhibition catalogue revealed that Contractors Limited had had initial capital of £40,000 to which £37,500 of rights and additional issues had been added. It said that 'the Lake was successfully drained dry in 1904 in spite of many drawbacks and the long revolution [in Colombia]. Great difficulties have been encountered in dealing with the mud and sand at the bottom, a five years' drought causing a great scarcity of water. Work, although slowly, has been going on steadily all the time. A depth of 30 feet has been obtained in the centre and along the ditch to the tunnel, through which all the mud is being washed. Although the surface is now fairly hard and solid, the mud below is in a semi-liquid state, and is always pressing in from the sides to the centre. The bottom, perfectly flat when drained, is now cup-shaped.' The mud of Guatavita hardened like cement. The First World War brought an end to Contractors Limited. Spring waters refilled the lake. And visionaries remained convinced that the cup-like centre of Guatavita contained the important treasures.

An Irishwoman called Dorothy Warren floated a company to drain Guatavita in 1920; and in 1932 Americans led by a marine diver called Jonessen floundered about in the lake's mud wearing heavy diving suits, and recovered a few more objects. In 1949 Gustavo Jaramillo Sánchez formed a company that designated Guatavita as a mine called El Dorado—to avoid a government prohibition on draining natural lakes. He declared: 'I had a great idea. There is no need to drain the lake to reach its bottom. By mounting a type of dragline called Clamshell everything can be extracted from the Lake.' An American diver called Timperly arrived in 1953 and scoured the lake with 'a steel ball with movable claws . . . and the very latest metal–detecting equipment'; but all in vain.

Twelve years later, in 1965, Jaramillo Sánchez was still able to declare: 'I am completely certain that the fabulous treasure of the Chibchas [Muisca] is to be found in the bottom of Lake Guatavita. I am an old miner and I know why I am saying this.' He was convinced that, since precious objects had been found at the edges of the lake, 'it is logical that the veritable Dorado is at its bottom.' His conviction spread. Successful American treasure hunters heard about it through an item in the Wall Street Journal. So, in 1965, Colombian Exploration Inc. was formed in Miami, with one Colombian and four American partners. The formidable diver Kip Wagner, whose Real Eight Corporation had found the treasure of a Spanish plate fleet wrecked off Florida, was involved. The team arrived in Colombia in a blaze of publicity. It declared that the cold of the lake's waters ruled out skin divers: it intended to use strong suction pumps instead. A preliminary reconnaissance began. But the Colombian Institute of Anthropology and the Council of Monuments intervened and declared that inexpert excavation would be illegal: any work on Guatavita could be done only by its own archaeologists. So Lake Guatavita now has a respite, no longer drained, dragged or pumped. But it is unlikely to contain any further Muisca treasure.

Chronology

25 September 1513 Vasco Núñez de Balboa crosses Darien, discovers Pacific Ocean.

1519 Panama founded.

1519–20 Hernán Cortés conquers the Aztec empire in Mexico.

27 March 1528 King grants Welser licence to govern Venezuela.

24 February 1529 Ambrosius Dalfinger reaches Coro as governor of Venezuela.

26 July 1529 Francisco Pizarro receives licence to conquer Peru.

August 1529 Dalfinger leaves Coro for exploration of Maracaibo.

13 September 1530 Nicolaus Federmann leaves Coro to explore southward.

27 December 1530 Francisco Pizarro leaves Panama on third expedition.

17 March 1531 Federmann returns to Coro from first expedition.

23 June 1531 Diego de Ordás starts to explore Orinoco river.

1 September 1531 Dalfinger leaves Coro on second expedition.

6 January 1532 Dalfinger sends Captain Vascuña back with expedition's gold.

June 1532 Dalfinger sends Esteban Martín back to Maracaibo.

1532 Ordás dies on journey back to Spain.

16 November 1532 Pizarro captures Inca Atahualpa at Cajamarca in Peru.

May–June 1533 Dalfinger killed.

26 July 1533 Execution of Inca Atahualpa at Cajamarca.

25 October 1533 Jerónimo Dortal's patent as governor of Paria.

2 November 1533 Survivors of Dalfinger's expedition reach Coro.

15 November 1533 Pizarro enters Cuzco.

5 December 1533 First Inca treasure reaches Seville.

June 1534 Sebastián de Benalcázar occupies Quito.

October 1534 Dortal reaches Paria, sends Herrera up the Orinoco.

May–June 1535 Survivors of Herrera's attempt on Meta reach Paria.

15 May 1535 George Hohermuth leaves Coro on expedition south-west across llanos.

May 1535 Federmann leaves Coro to settle Cabo de la Vela.

February–March 1536 Skirmishes between Dortal and Sedeño near Maracapana.

6 April 1536 Gonzalo Jiménez de Quesada leaves Santa Marta to explore Magdalena.

August 1536 Sedeño expedition inland from Maracapana.

September 1536 Federmann returns to Coro from Cabo de la Vela expedition.

October 1536 Jiménez de Quesada reaches La Tora on Magdalena river.

14 December 1536 Federmann leaves Coro, ostensibly to help Hohermuth.

28 December 1536 Jiménez de Quesada leaves La Tora towards mountains.

December 1536 Benalcázar founds Popayán and Cali.

3 March 1537 Jiménez de Quesada reaches first Muisca town.

21 April 1537 Jiménez de Quesada reaches Muisca capital, Bogotá.

June 1537 Jiménez de Quesada at Somondoco emerald mine.

13 August 1537 Hohermuth's expedition decides to turn back from Choques territory.

20 August 1537 Jiménez de Quesada captures the chief of Tunja.

September 1537 Spaniards sack Muisca temple of Sugamuxi (Sogomoso).

October 1537 Spaniards kill Zipa of Bogotá.

December 1537–February 1538 Jiménez de Quesada investigates Neiva.

March 1538 Benalcázar leaves Quito to escape arrest.

27 May 1538 Survivors of Hohermuth expedition reach Coro.

12–15 June 1538 Jiménez de Quesada's men divide Muisca booty.

c. February 1539 Fire at Bogotá. Torture and death of Sagipa.

March 1539 Federmann and Benalcázar reach Muisca lands.

27 April 1539 Foundation of Santafé de Bogotá.

May 1539 Jiménez de Quesada, Federmann and Benalcázar descend Magdalena.

November 1539 Jiménez de Quesada and other captains reach Seville.

early 1540 Jerónimo Dortal explores llanos rivers leading to Orinoco.

11 June 1540 Death of Georg Hohermuth. Bishop Bastidas interim governor of Venezuela.

1 December 1540 Gonzalo Pizarro reaches Quito as lieutenant governor.

late February 1541 Gonzalo Pizarro leaves Quito for La Canela and El Dorado.

March 1541 Benalcázar returns to Cali as governor of Popayán.

26 June 1541 Francisco Pizarro assassinated.

1 **August 1541** Philip von Hutten leaves Coro to continue Hohermuth's exploration.

1 **September 1541** Hernán Pérez de Quesada leaves Bogotá to search for El Dorado.

26 December 1541 Francisco de Orellana leaves Gonzalo Pizarro's expedition, sails down Napo.

12 February 1542 Orellana enters Amazon river.

February 1542 Hutten leaves Barquisimeto, enters llanos.

24 June 1542 Gonzalo Pizarro returns to Quito from El Dorado expedition.

26 August 1542 Orellana leaves Amazon, enters Atlantic ocean.

9–11 September 1542 Orellana's two boats reach Margarita.

end December 1542 Hernán Pérez de Quesada's survivors reach Mocoa and Pasto.

May 1543 Hutten explores upper Vaupés.

December 1544 Hutten wounded by Omagua, turns back.

April 1546 Hutten and Welser murdered by Carvajal.

9 April 1548 Gonzalo Pizarro defeated and executed at Cuzco.

October 1549 Brazilian Indians ascend Amazon, reach Chachapoyas.

16 April 1550 Royal decree suspends all expedition activity.

August 1550 Debate between Las Casas and Sepúlveda at Valladolid. Prohibition on expedition activity.

1556 Juan de Avellaneda founds San Juan de los Llanos.

15 July 1559 Royal decree again permits expeditions.

September 1559 Pedro de Ursúa sets off down Huallaga and Amazon.

1 **January 1561** Lope de Aguirre murders Pedro de Ursúa.

22 May 1561 Lope de Aguirre murders Fernando de Guzmán.

21 July 1561 Lope de Aguirre's boats reach Margarita after descending Amazon.

27 October 1561 Lope de Aguirre shot at Barquisimeto.

1566 Martín de Poveda and Pedro Maraver de Silva expedition from Chachapoyas to Bogotá.

15 May 1568 Patents as governor of El Dorado territories for Diego Fernández de Serpa and Pedro Maraver de Silva.

21 July 1569 Gonzalo Jiménez de Quesada named governor of Pauto and Papamene.

December 1569 Jiménez de Quesada leaves Bogotá to explore llanos for El Dorado.

10 May 1570 Fernández de Serpa expedition destroyed by Indians near Orinoco.

July 1572 Jiménez de Quesada returns to Bogotá with few survivors.

1579 Jiménez de Quesada dies, names Antonio de Berrío as heir.

3 January 1584 Antonio de Berrío leaves Chita for El Dorado.

1585 Berrío explores to Orinoco, returns to New Granada.

1585–8 Berrío's second expedition from New Granada to explore right bank of Orinoco.

March 1590 Berrío leaves New Granada on third expedition.

1 **September 1591** Berrío reaches Trinidad after exploring Orinoco and Caroní.

May 1592 Domingo de Vera e Ibargoyen founds San José de Oruñ on Trinidad.

March–May 1593 Domingo de Vera explores lower Caroní.

8 April 1595 Sir Walter Ralegh sacks San José, captures Berrío.

May–June 1595 Ralegh enters Orinoco and Caroní.

December 1595 Berrío founds Santo Tomé de Guayana at mouth of Caroní.

1596 Ralegh publishes *The Discoverie . . . of Guiana.*

1596 Laurence Keymis explores Guiana coast.

10 April 1596 Domingo de Vera's colonists from Spain reach Trinidad.

December 1596 Captain Leonard Berry explores Essequibo towards Lake Parima.

1597 Death of Antonio de Berrío. Fernando de Berrío succeeds as governor of Guayana.

1598–1606 Repeated expeditions by Fernando de Berrío seeking El Dorado.

July 1603 Ralegh imprisoned in the Tower.

1609 Robert Harcourt's colony on the Oyapock.

1612 Fernando de Berrío accused of trading with foreigners on Orinoco.

March 1616 Ralegh released from Tower to plan Guiana expedition.

19 August 1617 Ralegh leaves England, reaches Orinoco 11 November.

3 January 1618 Keymis captures Santo Tomé de Guayana. Wat Ralegh killed.

2 March 1618 Keymis rejoins Ralegh at mouth of Orinoco. Keymis' suicide.

21 June 1618 Ralegh returns to Plymouth.

29 October 1618 Ralegh beheaded.

1622 Death of Fernando de Berrío in Algiers.

Notes

Chapter 1

5 *countries at present.*' Paolo dal Pozzo Toscanelli to Fernão Martinez de Roriz (confessor to King Alfonso V of Portugal), Florence, 25 June 1474, in Björn Landström, *Columbus*, London, 1967, 19–20.

5 *covered in gold'.* Idem, 20.

5 *Great Khan . . .'* *The Journal of Christopher Columbus*, entry for Sunday, 21 October 1492, trans. Cecil Jane, Hakluyt Society (London, 1960), 41.

5 *something about theirs.*' Landström, *Columbus*, 144.

5 *great river . . .'* Idem, 145.

6 *was a marvel'* Columbus, *Journal* for 8 January 1493.

7 *rivers of Darien.* Las Casas, *Historia de las Indias*, bk 3, ch. 40, ed. Lewis Hanke, 3 vols (Mexico, 1951), 3 36.

7 *or even dreamed!'* Bernal Díaz del Castillo, *Conquista de Nueva-España*, ch. 87, BAE 26 (Madrid, 1947), 82; trans. Alfred Percival Maudslay (5 vols, Hakluyt Society, London, 1890), 2 37. Amadis of Gaul was a romance of medieval chivalry composed in thirteenth-century Spain and republished in Zaragoza in 1508. It was a favourite book in renaissance Spain.

8 *to go there.*' Bernal Díaz, idem, ch. 157, 201.

9 *behind their backs.*' Girolamo Benzoni, *History of the New World* (1572), bk 1, trans. W. H. Smyth, Hakluyt Society 21 (London, 1857), 6–7.

9 *the pearl fishery'.* Francisco López de Gómara, *Hispania victrix, La historia general de las Indias . . .* (1552) in Kirkpatrick, *The Spanish Conquistadores*, 295.

9 *especially silver.*' Diego de Ordás to his friend Francisco Verdugo, 12 September 1529, in Enrique Otte, 'Nueve cartas de Diego de Ordás', *Historia Mexicana*, nos 53–4, Mexico, 1964.

11 *who wanted it.*' José de Acosta, *Historia natural y moral de las Indias*, bk 4, ch. 2, BAE, 73 (Madrid, 1954), 90.

11 *to seek food.*' Aguado, *Historia de Venezuela*, bk 4, ch. 12, 1950 edn, 420–1.

11 *of that coast'.* Fernández de Oviedo, pt 2, bk 24, ch. 3, 1852 edn, 2 216.

11 *on his face'.* Fernández de Oviedo, idem, 220. American Indians grow very little facial hair, and normally pluck any that does grow.

12 *wine from Castile.*' Fernández de Oviedo, idem, 220–1.

12 *everything is revealed.*' Fernández de Oviedo, idem.

12 *the new acquaintance.*' Fernández de Oviedo, idem, 222.

12 *taken as prisoners.*' Fernández de Oviedo, idem, 217.

12 *of [Ordás'] King.*' Aguado, bk 4, ch. 15, 1950 edn, 431.

12 *the river upstream'.* Aguado, bk 4, ch. 14, 428; Castellanos, Elegía 9, canto 2, verse 2, 1847 edn, 85.

12 *considered certain'.* Juan Ruiz, interrogation on behalf of Ordás, Seville, November 1533, in Florentino Pérez-Embid, *Diego de Ordás* (Seville, 1950), 116–45.

13 *intolerable rigour'.* Castellanos, Elegía 9, canto 1, verse 51, 83.

13 *desire he nourished'* Castellanos, idem, verse 24.

15 *go up it.*' Fernández de Oviedo, pt 2, bk 24, ch. 3, 1852 edn, 2 217. The first craft to descend these formidable rapids was a British hovercraft, on 3 May 1968. The eleven men inside compared the experience to going over Niagara Falls in a barrel – and living. Brian Branston, *The last great journey on earth*, (London, 1970), 242.

15 *with that metal.*' Aguado, bk 4, ch. 16, 1950 edn, 436.

16 *land of Meta.*' Fernández de Oviedo, pt 2, bk 24, ch. 3, 2 218.

16 *of guava trees.*' Fernández de Oviedo, idem.

16 *into the river.*' Fernández de Oviedo, idem, 219.

16 *a bad outcome.*' Fernández de Oviedo, pt 2, bk 24, ch. 4, 1852 edn, 2 222.

Chapter 2

18 *lions or monkeys'.* Bernal Díaz, *Conquista de Nueva España*, ch. 39, BAE, 26 (Madrid, 1947), 34.

18 *those distant lands.*' Dürer's *Journal*, quoted in Victor von Hagen, *The Germanic People in America*, 25, or *The Golden Man*, 13–14. Some of this treasure may still be seen in the Museum für Völkerkunde in Vienna.

19 *herbs and spices'* The Welser licence was negotiated between the Emperor Charles V and the Welser agents Heinrich Ehinger of

Constanz and Hieronymus Sailer of Sanct Gallen. It has been published fairly often, for instance by Jerónimo Bécker in his edition of Pedro de Aguado, *Historia de Venezuela* (Madrid, 1950), 37–48.

21 *wives and property*.' Aguado, pt 2, bk 1, ch. 4, *Historia de Venezuela*, 55.

21 *there is none*'. Esteban Martín, *Relación de la expedición de Ambrosio Alfinger*, in Gabaldón Márquez, *Descubrimiento y conquista de Venezuela*, 272; Federmann, *Historia indiana*, 168.

21 *with Federmann*.' Castellanos, *Elegías de varones ilustres*, pt 2, elegía 1, canto 1, elegía 2, canto 2, BAE 4, 1847, 186, 222.

21 *the South Sea*.' Federmann, *Historia indiana*, 178.

21 *us very well*'. Federmann, *Historia indiana*, in Gabaldón Márquez ed., *Descubrimiento y conquista de Venezuela* 2, 170.

21 *and bearded people*'. Idem, 171.

24 *their small size*.' Idem, 178–9.

24 *given to devils*.' Idem, 180; the royal officials Antonio de Naveros and Alonso Vázquez de Acuña wrote to the Emperor from Coro, 6 October 1533, that Federmann brought back two dwarf females, who were perfectly proportioned but were only as high as an average man's waist, Gabaldón Márquez, *Descubrimiento y conquista de Venezuela* 2, 285.

24 *alliances between them*.' Idem, 182.

25 *is least expected*.' Idem.

25 *to be immortal*.' Idem, 183.

25 *with us had fled*.' Idem.

25 *spend the night*.' Idem, 185.

25 *defending themselves*.' Idem, 186.

25 *in the Indies*'. Idem, 188.

26 *of our journey*.' Idem, 189.

26 *slaughter among them*.' Idem, 190.

26 *of the Ladies*.' Idem, 225.

26 *and sell gold*' ; Idem, 191.

26 *precious stones . . .* ' Idem, 192–3.

27 *hunted by horsemen*.' Idem, 198.

27 *arquebus shots wide*'. Idem, 202. Juan Friede doubted that this was the modern town of Acarigua, since this is not on a river 150 metres wide. He thinks it was probably near the modern town of Cojedes on the Cojedes (ancient Coahery) river. Friede,

'Itinerario de la expedición', in *Descubrimiento y conquista de Venezuela*, 240–50.

27 *the South Sea*.' Idem, 205.

27 *hands of enemies*.' Idem, 207.

27 *of the enemy*.' Idem.

27 *this city [Coro]*!' Antonio de Naveros and Alonso Vázquez de Acuña to Emperor, Coro, October 1533, in *Descubrimiento y conquista de Venezuela*, 2 287.

28 *than fighting men*.' Federmann, *op cit.*, 217.

29 *with the rest . . .* ' Idem, 218.

29 *who were fleeing*.' Idem, 219.

30 *to serve them*'. Idem, 220.

30 *cold and hot*' Idem, 221.

30 *on my horse*.' Idem, 226.

30 *flee from it*.' Idem, 227.

30 *we had there*'. Idem.

30 *all the rest*.' Idem, 228–9.

32 *especially of water*.' Idem, 230.

32 *have reached Coro*.' Idem, 232.

32 *sea to sea*'. Fernández de Oviedo, pt 2, bk 25, ch.1, 1852 edn, 2 270.

32 *trust us much*.' Esteban Martín, *Relación*, 254.

32 *truthful people*.' Martín, idem.

33 *off as prisoners*.' Martín, idem, 255. The river leading northwards through this pass, towards the Magdalena, is still called César, after an explorer from Santa Marta called Francisco César who first penetrated it. The other river that forms this pass is still called the Ranchería, after some early settlement, while the town at its mouth is Riohacha, 'Axe River', because an early sailor lost his axe here. The valley was also known as the Upar or Valledupar. Dalfinger was not the first explorer to try to reach the South Sea by this route. In 1526 Juan de Ampíes had asked for the governorship of Venezuela 'as far as the other sea which is called the South Sea', and in 1528 Alvárez Palomino hoped to march from Santa Marta to the land of Peru sighted by Pizarro. He attempted an expedition along the Upar valley, but died on it. Anon, *Relación del descubrimiento . . . de Santa Marta*, 83–4; Demetrio Ramos, *El mito del Dorado*, 64–6.

33 *black paintings*' Martín, idem; Gonzalo Fernández de Oviedo reminded his readers

that Julius Caesar had described ancient Britons tattooing themselves in this way: pt 2, bk 25, ch. 1, vol. 2, 272.

33 *of their horses*.' Martín, 256.

33 *castellanos on them*.' Martín, 257–8; Fernández de Oviedo, pt 2, bk 25, ch. 2, 1852 edn, 2 274.

35 *and the Chimila*.' Castellanos, *Elegías de varones ilustres*, pt 2, elegía 1, canto 3, BAE 4, 1847, 203.

35 *on its far side*.' Pedro Aguado, *Recopilación historial*, pt 2, bk 1, chs 6–7, *Historia de Venezuela*, 71–2; Castellanos, idem, 203–4.

35 *town of Maracaibo*.' Letter from royal officials Antonio de Naveros and Alonso Vázquez de Acuña to King, Coro, 6 October 1533, in Gabaldón Márquez, *Descubrimiento y conquista de Venezuela*, 2 289.

36 *to mend myself*. Martín, 256–7.

36 *its great current*'. Martín, 259.

36 *extract the gold*'. Martín, idem.

36 *finest quality*'. Martín, idem.

37 *of their bodies*.' Aguado, idem, ch. 10, 85.

38 *your fault . . .* ' The Requirement (Valladolid, 1513), trans. Lewis Hanke, in his *History of Latin American Civilization* (Boston, 1973), 95.

39 *to eat from it*.' Martín, 264.

39 *need of porterage*.' Martín, idem.

39 *and frostbitten*.' Martín, 265.

39 *many sick men*.' Martín, 266.

39 *their own people*.' Martín, idem.

39 *to carry them*.' Martín, 266–7. Johann Kasimir from Nuremberg had been with Cabot on the Plate and Paraguay.

40 *a dozen went.*" ' Fernández de Oviedo, pt 2, bk 25, ch. 5, 1852 edn, 2 284; Martín, 268.

40 *in the mountains*.' Martín, 268–9.

40 *down that valley*.' Martín, 269.

42 *Christian's relief*.' Fernández de Oviedo, pt 2, bk 25, ch. 2, 2 286; Martín, 271.

42 *lost their way*.' Martín, 271.

42 *which were broken*.' Oviedo, pt 2, bk 25, ch. 6, 2 288.

42 *later ate them*.' Fernández de Oviedo, pt 2, bk 25, ch. 6, 2 289; Pedro de Aguado, pt 2, bk 1, ch. 8, *Historia de Venezuela*, 1 78.

42 *was left there.*' Idem, 290.

43 *for their journey.*' Idem, ch. 7, 292.

43 *along seated*'. Idem.

43 *highly regarded.*' Idem, 293.

43 *thanks to her.*' Idem.

43 [*184 kilos*] *of gold.* The weight of gold brought by the expedition was noted in a letter to the Emperor from the three royal officials in Coro, Alonso Vázquez de Acuña, Antonio de Naveros and Pedro de San Martín, 17 January 1534, and these same officials mentioned Vascuña's disappearance in an earlier letter of 6 October 1533, in Gabaldón Márquez ed., *Descubrimiento y conquista de Venezuela*, 2 289, 315–7; Licentiate Juan Pérez de Tolosa, *Relación de las tierras . . . de Venezuela* (1546) in A. Avellano Moreno, *Relaciones geográficas de Venezuela*, 8–9; Fernández de Oviedo clearly obtained a copy of Francisco Martín's story, which he told in detail, pt 2, bk 25, chs 6–7, 1852 edn, 2 286–94; Esteban Martín described the meeting with Francisco Martín, 271; Aguado, *Compendio historial*, pt 2, bk 1, chs 8–9, *Historia de Venezuela*, 77–83, 96–100, 105–6; Castellanos, *Elegías de varones ilustres*, pt 2, elegía 1, canto 3, BAE 4, 1847, 204–6; Oviedo y Baños, *Historia de la conquista . . . de Venezuela*, 1885 edn, 1 52–3.

Chapter 3

45 *with such might.*' Francisco de Xerez, *Verdadera relación de la conquista del Perú* (Seville, 1534), BAE (Continuación), 26 333.

45 *vast proportions!*' Pedro Pizarro, *Relación del descubrimiento y conquista de los reinos del Perú* (1571), *Colección de documentos inéditos para la historia de España* 5 (Madrid, 1844), 230.

45 *from a dream.*' Gaspar de Espinosa to King, Panamá, 10 October 1533, in Raúl Porras Barrenechea ed., *Cartas del Perú* (Lima, 1959), 3 66.

45 *now in Peru.*' García de Lerma to King, Santa Marta, 9 September 1532, DIHC 2 318.

45 *land of Peru*'. Town council of Santa Marta to King, 20 August 1533, DIHC 3 72.

45 *and restless.*' Royal officials to King, Santa Marta, 2 November 1533, DIHC 3 78–9.

45 *on their return.*' Idem, 79.

46 *are tied down.*' Officials of Puerto Rico to King, San Juan, 26 February 1534, in Porras

Barrenechea, *Cartas del Perú*, 100; Francisco Manuel de Lando to King, Puerto Rico, 2 July 1534, idem, 118.

46 *dismembered cow*'. Francisco de Xerez, *Verdadera relación de la conquista del Perú*, BAE (Continuación), 26 345–6.

46 *exhibited in Seville*' Cieza de León, *Crónica del Perú*, pt 1, ch. 94, trans. Harriet de Onis, Norman, Oklahoma, 1959, 255.

46 *of cosmographers*' Informe by Audiencia of Santo Domingo, 10 December 1533, in Demetrio Ramos Pérez, *El mito del Dorado*, 96.

46 *secrets and riches!*' Audiencia of Santo Domingo to King, 20 October 1533, in Ramos, *El mito del Dorado*, 97.

46 *the land contains*'. Dortal, Memorial, January 1533, in Guillermo Morón, *Los orígenes históricos de Venezuela*, 488–9. The Capitulación making Dortal governor of Paria was issued on 25 October 1533.

47 *ever left Spain*'. Jerónimo Dortal to King, Cubagua, 24 December 1534, in Avellano Moreno, *Documentos para la historia económica de Venezuela*, 106.

47 *to guide me.*' Dortal to King, idem, in Aguado, *Historia de Venezuela*, ed. Jerónimo Bécker, 1950 edn, 643. Dortal wrote about himself in the third person, but I have changed this to the first person for greater clarity. Dortal's reckoning was that Ordás and he had reached 2°N, whereas Pizarro captured Atahualpa at 7°S: hence the distance between them was only 150 leagues or about 800 kms. Cajamarca is in fact 7°S, but the Maipures rapids reached by Ordás are 5°N, not 2°N. Also, Dortal did not realize that Cajamarca was a full 10° west of his exploration up the Orinoco. The distance between them was in fact 1,900 kms, and the journey would still be quite impossible even today.

47 *from this region.*' Idem.

47 *under the equator,*' Idem, 644.

47 *caring for them.*' Gonzalo Fernández de Oviedo, *Historia general y natural*, pt 2, bk 24, ch. 7, 1852 edn, 2 236.

48 *in such cases.*' Pedro de Aguado, *Recopilación historial*, pt 2, bk 5, ch. 3, *Historia de Venezuela*, 1950 edn, 1 512; Castellanos, *Elegías de varones ilustres*, elegía 11, canto 2, BAE, 1847 edn, 105.

48 *there for food.*' Aguado, idem, ch. 5, 521.

48 *tasty to eat*'. Aguado, idem, ch. 7, 532.

48 *paradise itself!*' Fernández de Oviedo, pt 2, bk 24, ch. 8, 1852 edn, 2 238; Aguado, *Recopilación historial*, pt 2, bk 5, ch. 7, *Historia de Venezuela* 1 533–4.

49 *from a tree.*' Oviedo, idem, 239.

49 *of their horses.*' Oviedo, idem, 240; Aguado, pt 2, bk 5, ch. 8, vol. 1, 538; Castellanos, elegía 11, canto 3, 107–8.

49 *on their arrows.*' Oviedo, idem.

49 *who come here.*' Fernández de Oviedo, pt 2, bk 24, ch. 4, 1852 edn, 2 222–3.

50 *and Portuguese . . . *' Idem.

50 *and to command!*' Las Casas, quoted in Juan Friede, *Descubrimiento y conquista del Nuevo Reino de Granada*, 139.

52 *treasures of Quito*'. Herrera, *Historia general*, decada 5, bk 6, ch. 12, vol. 11, 72. Alvarado may have heard about the wealth of Quito from agents sent by Benalcázar to recruit reinforcements in Nicaragua.

52 *told the route.*' Testimony of Pedro Brabo to an inquiry held at San Miguel, 12 October 1534, in José Toribio Medina ed., *Colección de documentos inéditos para la historia de Chile*, 4 (Santiago de Chile, 1891) 244.

53 *many of them.*' Ibid.

53 *find in Quito.*' Herrera, decada 5, bk 6, ch. 1, vol. 11, 11.

53 *his first impression*' Herrera, decada 5, bk 7, ch. 14, vol. 11, 172–3.

53 *to be discovered.*' *Probanza de méritos* of Luis Daza, Popayán, 3 October 1542, quoted in Demetrio Ramos Pérez, *El mito del Dorado*, 216–7. This book by Ramos Pérez brilliantly analyses the motives of the various exploring expeditions, and explodes the myth that they all set out to search for El Dorado. The soldier who captured Rumiñavi after a struggle was Miguel de la Chica. John Hemming, *The Conquest of the Incas*, 166–7.

53 *North Sea* [*Caribbean*]'. Herrera, decada 5, bk 10, ch. 13, vol. 11, 376. Herrera used a detailed source, probably a missing work by Cieza de León. In his son's record of service it was claimed that Benalcázar 'continued his conquests . . . to this province of Popayán, of which he had been told by a great chief from it'. *Relación de méritos y servicios de Sebastián de Benalcázar y de su hijo Don Francisco*, in José Manuel Groot, *Historia eclesiástica y civil de la Nueva Granada* (Bogotá, 1889), vol. 1, 477–83, quoted in Demetrio Ramos Pérez, *El mito del Dorado*, 218.

Chapter 4

56 *Federmann had discovered*' Royal officials Antonio Vázquez de Acuña, Antonio de Naveros and Pedro de San Martín to King, Coro, 11 September 1535, in Avellano Moreno ed., *Documentos para la historia económica de Venezuela*, 83. Köler's account of his journey to South America is in British Museum Addington Ms. 15,217. Victor von Hagen, *The Golden Man*, 70–1, 106. Licentiate Juan Pérez de Tolosa gave the date of Hohermuth's arrival at Coro as January 1535, in his *Relación*, quoted by Bécker in the 1950 edition of Aguado, *Historia de Venezuela*, pt 1, ch. 1, 121; Aguado said that Hohermuth arrived late in 1534, pt 1, bk 2, ch. 2, 117.

56 *the [gold] mines*'. Royal officials to King, Coro, 11 September 1535, idem, 84. Federmann had been exiled from Coro for four years by Ambrosius Dalfinger, who was furious that he had not authorized his young lieutenant to undertake his southern exploration.

56 *in Indian wars*' Aguado, *Historia de Venezuela*, pt 1, bk 2, ch. 2, 118. Aguado described these experts as 'islanders' meaning that they were from Cubagua—and hence well aware of the Meta theories.

56 *full of gold!*' Tito Neukomm of Lindau to his mother and brother, Coro, 6 September 1535, letter quoted in the Chronicle of Augsburg by his uncle Ulrich Neukomm, ed. F. Joetze, *Forschungen zur Geschichte Bayerns* 15, 1856, 271–8, and trans. Juan Friede, in Joaquín Gabaldón Márquez ed., *Descubrimiento y conquista de Venezuela*, 2 408. Neukomm said that Hohermuth left on 12 May with 310 men; the royal officials wrote to the King on 11 September that he left on 15 May with 400 men. Aguado said that Hohermuth sent 200 men without horses due south across the hills while he himself took 'the rest of the men' with 80 horses along the coast to Borburata before turning the expedition inland.

56 *in those days*.' Castellanos, *Elegías de varones ilustres*, pt 2, elegía 2, canto 1, 213.

56 *their great thirst*', Philip von Hutten, *Zeitung aus India*, in *Johann George Meusels Historisch-Litterarisches Magazin* 5 (Bayreuth and Leipzig, 1785) 52, or trans. Frederica de Ritter, in Gabaldón Márquez ed., *Descubrimiento y conquista de Venezuela*, 2 351.

56 *Christians were wounded*.' Hutten, idem, 350. Hutten was from one of the noblest families of Franconia. Born in Birkkenfeld in 1511, he was 24 when the expedition set out. He had been in the Court of Emperor Charles V as a young man and was a playmate of the future Emperor Ferdinand II. Friedrich Ratzel, *Notizen zur Biographie Philipps von Hutten* (Munich, 1880), 153.

56 *legitimate peace*.' Hutten, idem, 351.

56 *and devastated them*.' Hutten, idem, 352.

57 *among the Christians*.' Hutten, idem, 353; Aguado, pt 2, bk 2, ch. 3, 124; José de Oviedo y Baños, *Historia de la conquista y población... de Venezuela*, bk 1, ch. 11, 1885 edn, 1 74–5.

57 *was all lies*.' Hutten, idem, 353.

57 *they soon fled*.' Hutten, idem, 354.

57 *not in courage*.' Aguado, bk 2, ch. 3, 122–3.

57 *the next camp*.' Hutten, idem, 355.

57 *with his own hand*.' Hutten, idem, 356; Aguado, bk 2, ch. 5, *Historia de Venezuela*, 1 134–5.

58 *with many sick*.' Hutten, idem, 356.

58 *horses could pass*.' Hutten, idem, 359.

58 *from which many died*.' Hutten, idem, 360; Aguado, pt 2, bk 2, ch. 5, *Historia de Venezuela*, 1 136.

58 *our Indian slaves*'. Hutten, idem, 359.

58 *of the dead . . .* ' Hutten, idem.

58 *but would rest*.' Hutten, idem, 362.

58 *from their hands*.' Aguado, pt 2, bk 2, ch. 6, *Historia de Venezuela*, 1 147.

59 *the pole star*.' Hutten, idem, 363; Castellanos, pt 2, elegía 2, canto 2, verse 30. The expedition was still north of the Ariari river, and must therefore have been at $3\frac{3}{4}°$N rather than $2\frac{3}{4}°$N. The expedition was on one of the headwaters of the Meta, and the Indians told them that Christians had already been on that river—either Ordás' men in 1531–2 or Herrera's in 1535.

59 *the confined maidens*.' Aguado, bk 2, ch. 11, 168–9.

60 *to the right*.' Hutten, idem, 363.

60 *[llamas] and gold*' Hutten, idem, 364.

61 *province called Choques*.' Aguado, pt 2, bk 2, ch. 12, 174.

61 *with these weapons*' Licentiate Juan Pérez de Tolosa, *Relación de las tierras y provincias de . . . Venezuela*, in Antonio Avellano Moreno ed., *Relaciones geográficas de Venezuela*, 12; Aguado, pt 2, bk 2, ch. 12, 174–5.

61 *of the village*.' Aguado, bk 2, ch. 13, 180.

61 *lose heart . . .* ' Aguado, idem, 184.

61 *type of warfare*.' Aguado, idem, 187.

61 *lessened their labour*'. Aguado, idem, 190.

61 *to treat them*.' Hutten, *Zeitung*, 365.

61 *and much hunger*.' Hutten, idem.

62 *the Spaniards themselves*.' Aguado, bk 2, ch. 14, 190.

62 *previously suffered*.' Hutten, *Zeitung*, 365–6.

62 *far from our route*.' Hutten, idem, 366.

62 *and many died*.' Hutten, idem.

62 *height of a man*.' Hutten, idem, 367.

63 *save our lives!*' Hutten, idem, 367–8.

63 *we can reach*.' Hutten to his father Bernhard von Hutten, Coro, 20 October 1538, in Gabaldón Márquez ed., *Descubrimiento y conquista de Venezuela*, 2 369.

63 *leagues from it . . .* ' Hutten to Georg Geuder of Nuremberg, Coro, 20 October 1538, idem, 370.

63 *seen these Indies*.' Hutten to his father, Coro, 31 March 1539, *Johann Georg Meusels Historisch-Litterarisches Magazin* 5 (Bayreuth and Leipzig, 1785), 81.

63 *to that place*.' Jorge de Espira (Hohermuth) to King, Coro, 15 January 1539, Gabaldón Márquez ed., *Descubrimiento y conquista de Venezuela*, 2 327–30. Hohermuth's determination to return was confirmed in a letter from Licentiate Fuenmayor and other officials to the Emperor, Santo Domingo, 31 December 1538, *Colección de Documentos Inéditos . . . del Archivo de Indias*, 1 (Madrid, 1864) 555.

63 *been depopulated*.' Antonio de Naveros and Pedro de San Martín to King, Coro, 1536, Gabaldón Márquez ed., *Descubrimiento y conquista de Venezuela*, 2 324. The letter said that there had originally been a hundred populous villages of Caquetió near Coro, but by 1536 there were only ten half empty villages.

64 *not bury them . . .* ' Aguado, pt 2, bk 2, ch. 6, *Historia de Venezuela*, 1 140.

64 *self-important, and dead*.' Aguado, idem, ch. 10, 160.

64 *titles and rewards*. Audiencia of Santo Domingo to Crown, 12 February 1536, DIHC, 4 57–8. Ramos Pérez, *El mito del Dorado*, 122, 129.

64 *two hundred men died.'* Bastidas to King, Coro, 2 April 1538, DIHC, 4 298–9.

65 *deceive one another.'* Fernández de Oviedo, pt 2, bk 24, ch. 9, 1852 edn, 2 244.

65 *knives and mirrors.'* Fernández de Oviedo, pt 2, bk 24, ch. 10, 1852 edn, 2 247.

65 *namely, gold.'* Fernández de Oviedo, pt 2, bk 24, ch. 9, 2 244.

65 *him much better!'* Fernández de Oviedo, idem, ch. 10, 248.

66 *with some blow.'* Fernández de Oviedo, idem, ch. 11, 251. This diligent author talked to survivors of the expedition in Santo Domingo in February 1537, and he later became a close friend of Dortal himself.

66 *which was rich.'* Juan Fernández de Alderete's report to the King, included in a royal decree addressed to the Bishop of Venezuela, 16 April 1538, DIHC, 4 307–9. The mutiny took place at Chapaure, 50 leagues from the sea; Residencia of Jerónimo Dortal, *Boletín del Archivo General de la Nación*, 57, no. 213 (Caracas, 1967), 290–1. Fernández de Oviedo, pt 2, bk 24, ch. 11. Aguado, bk 6, ch. 9, *Historia de Venezuela*, 1 688.

66 *news of Meta'.* Aguado, bk 2, ch. 15, *Historia de Venezuela*, 1 208. Federmann had written secretly to the authorities in Coro to arrest Alderete, who had gone there to take his gold. Federmann did not want his expedition to contain a man who had led the mutiny against Dortal. The other leader of that mutiny, García de Aguilar, had died before reaching the Welser lands. Philip von Hutten also wrote to his brother that Federmann had gone inland 'to the Meta river and the House of the Sun'. Hutten letter to his brother, Coro, 16 January 1540, *Descubrimiento y conquista de Venezuela*, 2 380.

67 *in the world'*; Pedro Simón, *Noticias historiales*, pt 1, noticia 5, ch. 1.

67 *of the llanos.'* Aguado, bk 2, ch. 17, *Historia de Venezuela*, 1 207.

67 *to the south-east'* Testimonies sworn before Antonio de Aragón, Cartagena, 4 July 1539, DIHC, 5 203.

67 *than in food'.* Federmann to Francisco Dávila, Jamaica, 1 August 1539, paraphrased in Fernández de Oviedo, bk 25, ch. 17, 1852 end, 2 317.

67 *lack of food.'* Idem, 318.

67 *that harsh winter.'* Idem.

67 *rich land ahead'.* Idem.

Chapter 5

70 *from sea to sea'.* Official documents of Pedro Fernández de Lugo quoted in Ramos Pérez, *El mito del Dorado*, 142.

70 *blood on them . . .'* Instructions to Gonzalo Jiménez de Quesada, revealed in response to a Petition by Licentiate Diego Gutiérrez Gallego, Cartagena, 3 June 1539, DIHC, 4 76.

70 *and eight hundred.* Jiménez de Quesada himself said that he led 600 overland, with a further 200 going up-river in five ships: *Epítome de la conquista* (of 1550), 44, and Fernández de Oviedo, *Historia general y natural*, bk 26, ch. 18, 1852 edn, 2 379. But his officers Juan de San Martín and Antonio de Lebrija wrote in 1539 that he had 'almost 500 men' on land and sea: in Oviedo, bk 26, ch. 11, 2 357. Jerónimo de Lebrón said 600 men: Lebrón to Audiencia of Santo Domingo, Santa Marta, 9 May 1537, DIHC, 4 195. In his testimony before Antonio de Aragón, Jiménez de Quesada declared that he left Santa Marta with 500 men, but he may have referred only to the land force: Interrogation, Cartagena, 4 July 1539, DIHC, 5 210–11. Aguado, following the *Epítome*, said there were 600 men on land and 200 more in the boats: pt 1, bk 2, ch. 5, *Recopilación historial*, 1 210. Castellanos said 500 by land and 460, including sailors, by water: pt 2, elegía 4, canto 3.

70 *in their stomachs.'* Aguado, pt 1, bk 2, ch. 6, *Recopilación*, 1 213.

70 *water and gold'.* Aguado, pt 1, bk 2, ch. 5, *Recopilación*, 1 211.

70 *such a death.'* Aguado, pt 1, bk 2, ch. 4, *Recopilación*, 1 205.

71 *in this way.'* Aguado, pt 1, bk 2, ch. 2, 1 195.

71 *Indian settlement.'* Aguado, pt 1, bk 2, ch. 7, 1 219; Fernández de Oviedo, bk 26, ch. 18, 2 379.

72 *in heavy rains.'* Fernández de Oviedo, bk 26, ch. 18, 2 381; Castellanos, pt 2, elegía 4, canto 3, BAE 4, 1847, 304–5. The soldier who saved the raft was called Juan Sánchez de Toledo: his Probanza is in the Archivo de Bogotá, encomiendas 24, Raimundo Rivas, *Los fundadores de Bogotá*, 1921 edn, 305. This incident was on the Serrano or on the Lebrija river, which had first been discovered in 1529 by Captain Lebrija who was now with Jiménez de Espada. Dalfinger had also seen it and its Pemeos Indians.

72 *on top of them.'* Aguado, bk 2, ch. 8, *Recopilación*, 1 225.

72 *up that river.'* *Epítome de la conquista*, 45. The Epítome was written by Jiménez de Quesada in the third person, but I have changed this to the first person for greater clarity.

74 *of the South.'* Fernández de Oviedo, pt 2, bk 26, chs 11, 19, 2 358, 382. Información by Bartolomé Camacho Zambrano, Santafé, August 1565, and by his son Rodrigo Sánchez Zambrano, Santafé, August 1584, in Raimundo Rivas, *Los fundadores de Bogotá*, 1921 edn, 54. Jiménez de Quesada had apparently sent an earlier reconnaissance under Cardozo and Juan de Albarracín: this had investigated the lower Opón and Carare rivers where they entered the Magdalena. Daniel Ortega Ricaurte, *Ruta de Gonzalo Jiménez de Quesada*, 420–1.

74 *Río Grande [Magdalena].'* *Epítome de la conquista*, 44; Demetrio Ramos Pérez, *El mito del Dorado*, 145.

74 *so greatly desired'.* Aguado, pt 1, bk 2, ch. 10, 1 231.

74 *sleep at night'.* Aguado, idem, 232.

74 *most tender lamb.'* Aguado, idem, 233.

74 *Christians ate it.'* Jerónimo Lebrón to King, Santa Marta, 10 August 1537, DIHC, 4 232. Lebrón was the interim governor of Santa Marta following the death of Pedro Fernández de Lugo soon after Jiménez de Quesada's departure. This report was the first news of the expedition's attempt to reach the mountains: it was based on information brought down the river by boat.

74 *valued his friendship.'* Aguado, pt 1, bk 2, ch. 11, *Recopilación*, 1 237.

75 *to the ground.'* Aguado, idem, 238.

75 *and steep path'* Aguado, idem, 239.

75 *no small one.'* Aguado, idem, 238.

75 *on a horse.'* Oviedo, pt 2, bk 26, ch. 20, 2 384.

76 *without pause.'* Castellanos, *Elegías de varones ilustres*, pt 2, elegía 4, canto 4, BAE 4, 1847, 311.

76 *always greater'.* Fernández de Oviedo, bk 26, ch. 22, 1852 edn, 2 386. Various Colombian historians have retraced the conquistadores' route: Daniel Ortega Ricaurte in 1938, Juan Friede in various works, notably his *Descubrimiento del Nuevo Reino de Granada* (1951) and *Gonzalo Jiménez de Quesada a través de documentos históricos* (1960), and Alberto Ariza in 1967.

76 *weighed and graded.* Juan de San Martín, Baltasar Maldonado and Gil López, *Libro de lo que se ha habido en esta jornada y descubrimiento del Río Grande . . .* , 13 June 1538, DIHC, **4** 79–91. The chests of gold and box of emeralds were described by Jiménez de Quesada himself, as part of his defence against an accusation that he had enriched himself with this treasure: *Petición . . . del proceso de don Gonzalo Jiménez de Quesada con el fiscal*, Madrid, 15 February 1546, in Friede, *Gonzalo Jiménez de Quesada a través de documentos históricos*, 85, 281.

77 *meaning "sun-moon" '*, Fernández de Oviedo, bk 26, ch. 21, **2** 387.

77 *fortune would dispose.'* Idem, 386.

77 *type of food.'* Idem, 387; Jiménez de Quesada, *Epítome de la conquista*, 49.

77 *for a short time.'* Idem.

78 *guinea-pigs a day.'* Idem, ch. 23, 389.

79 *the modern system.'* R. B. Cunninghame Graham, *The horses of the Conquest* (London, 1930), 10–11; John Hemming, *The Conquest of the Incas*, 112.

80 *throwing sticks'.* Federmann testimony to Antonio de Aragón, Cartagena, 4 July 1539, DIHC, **5** 215.

80 *had seen before.'* Fernández de Oviedo, bk 26, ch. 22, **2** 388; Aguado, *Recopilación*, pt 1, bk 3, ch. 5, **1** 271.

80 *in the Indies.'* Letter from Juan de San Martín and Antonio de Lebrija to King, 6 April 1536, in Fernández de Oviedo, pt 2, bk 26, ch. 11, **2** 359.

80 *to their lords . . .* ' Jiménez de Quesada's notebook, quoted in Fernández de Oviedo, bk 26, ch. 23, **2** 389; *Epítome de la conquista*, 52.

81 *great treasures . . .* ' Fernández de Oviedo, idem, 386.

82 *punishment by God.'* Idem, ch. 23, 390.

82 *an emerald mine]!'* Idem, ch. 25, 393. The invaders called Turmequé the Valley of the Trumpets because they made four trumpets there from old metal pans.

83 *to be inhabited.'* Idem, chs 11, 25, **2** 360, 394; Aguado, *Recopilación*, pt 1, bk 3, ch. 7.

83 *where Tunja resided.'* Idem, ch. 26, **2** 396.

83 *where Tunja was.'* Idem.

83 *outbreak might occur.'* Idem.

84 *palace itself.'* Idem.

84 *delicate figures.* A. M. Barriga Villalba, 'Orfebrería Chibcha y su definición científica', 207–8; Luis Duque Gómez, *Historia extensa de Colombia*, vol. 1, pt 1, *Prehistoria: etnohistoria y arqueología*, 298.

85 *forty thousand ducats.'* Pedro de Cieza de León, *La crónica del Perú, primera parte*, ch. 11, BAE **26**, 1947, 364.

85 *burials sacked . . .* ' Cieza de León, idem, ch. 14, BAE **26**, 367.

85 *from a river.'* Idem, ch. 15, 368.

85 *foot in gold . . .* ' Idem, ch. 18, 371.

85 *after death.'* Idem, ch. 21. 373.

86 *from nothing else.'* Report from Fray Francisco de Carvajal, Madrid, 6 February 1560, FDNRG, **4** 56. Abuse by Pedro de Ursúa on Buriticá led to revolt of 400 villages: Royal decree, Valladolid, 10 May 1554, FDNRG, **2** 153.

86 *[mines] do exist.'* Anon, *Descripción de la ciudad de Tunja* (c. 1610), CDIA **9**, 1868, 393.

86 *at Sogamoso.* Juan de San Martín and Antonio de Lebrija to King, 20 September 1539, in Oviedo, pt 2, bk 26, ch. 11, **2** 360; Juan de San Martín, Baltasar Maldonado and Gil López, *Libro de lo que se ha habido en esta jornada*, DIHC, **4** 88.

87 *off in sacks'*, Federmann to Francisco Dávila, Jamaica, 1 August 1539, in Oviedo, pt 2, bk 25, ch. 17, **2** 321.

87 *their idolatries.'* Jiménez de Quesada, *Gran cuaderno*, in Fernández de Oviedo, pt 2, bk 26, ch. 27, **2** 399.

87 *innumerable riches!'* Idem.

87 *from that stockade.'* Idem.

87 *or seeing him.'* San Martín and Lebrija letter to King, 20 September 1539, in Oviedo, pt 2, bk 26, ch. 11, **2** 361.

88 *demanded of him.'* *Acta del escribano Juan Rodríguez de Benavides*, Santafé de Bogotá, November 1538, in Friede, *Jiménez de Quesada a través . . .* , 172.

88 *session of torture . . .* ' Idem, 173.

88 *cut off his head.'* Testimony of Gil López, in Interrogatório of Jiménez de Quesada, Calzadilla, Spain, 2 June 1546, in Friede, *Gonzalo Jiménez de Quesada a través de documentos históricos*, 306.

88 *not kill him.'* Friede, idem, 43.

88 *severe tortures.'* Probanza organized by Hernán Pérez de Quesada, Santafé, 8 April 1539, DIHC, **5** 141.

88 *to his feet . . .* ' Probanza by Jerónimo de Lebrón against the Quesadas, Santa Marta, 7 April 1541, in Friede, *Jiménez de Quesada*, 249.

88 *camp, he died.'* Probanza of 8 April 1539, DIHC, **5** 141. In reply, Captain Juan de San Martín admitted that he and his men had tortured Sagipa, but he pointed out that only one foot had turned because of the burning. He also noted that no uprising occurred after this death: idem, 143.

89 *die from it . . .* ' Idem, 140.

89 *maimed by it'.* *Petición del proceso de don Gonzalo Jiménez de Quesada con el fiscal*, Madrid, 10 February 1546, idem, 284.

90 *send into battle.'* Fernández de Oviedo, pt 2, bk 24, ch. 10, 1852 edn, **2** 247. Cortés' letter of 1524 is in BAE **22**, 1946, 102. Philip von Hutten spoke about Amazons on the Papamene, *Diário*, 364.

91 *that of Tunja.'* San Martín and Lebrija letter to King, 20 September 1539, in Fernández de Oviedo, pt 2, bk 26, ch. 11, **2** 362; also bk 26, ch. 29, **2** 404.

91 *lances and maces.'* Idem, 363–4.

92 *towards [the east].'* *Relación* of Pascual de Andagoya, c. 1541, *Anuário de Estudios Americanos* **17** (Seville, 1960), 603–8. The dispute in the Quito town council is in *Libro primero de cabildos de Quito* (Quito, 1934), **1** 293–4. Gaspar de Espinosa's appointment as governor of the Río de San Juan (Southern Colombia) was in a royal decree, Valladolid, 11 September 1536, CDIA, **22** 452–71. The events and intrigues of this period are brilliantly set out in Demetrio Ramos Pérez, *El mito del Dorado*, 230–52.

92 *many other groups." '* Castellanos, *Elegías de varones ilustres*, pt 3, Elegía a Benalcázar, canto 4, BAE **4**, 1847, 463.

92 *much suffering'.* Probanza of Cristóbal de Segovia, Island of Margarita, October 1542, in Gaspar de Carvajal, *The Discovery of the Amazon*, trans. Bertram T. Lee (New York, 1934), 267–8. Benalcázar testimony before Licentiate Antonio de Aragón, Cartagena, 4 July 1539, DIHC, **5** 206–7.

92 *and bad Indians'.* Puelles testimony, Cartagena, 4 July 1539, DIHC, **5** 213.

93 *land, and marshes'* Castellanos, BAE **4**, 463.

93 *horses and Christians'* Gonzalo de la Peña testimony, Cartagena, July 1539, DIHC, **5** 209.

93 *killed every day'.* Puelles testimony, Cartagena, 4 July 1539, DIHC, **5** 214.

93 *North Sea [Caribbean]*' Aguado, *Recopilación historial*, pt 1, bk 4, ch. 1, 1 324.

93 *anything from Spain*.' Aguado, idem, 325.

94 *who it could be*.' San Martín and Lebrija letter of 20 September 1539, in Oviedo, pt 2, bk 26, ch. 11, 2 365.

94 *provided with natives*'. Aguado, pt 2, bk 2, ch. 9, *Historia de Venezuela*, 1 223.

94 *his neck shackles*'. Aguado, idem.

94 *was roasted there*.' Aguado, idem, 226.

94 *frozen to death*'. Federmann to Francisco Dávila, Jamaica, 1 August 1539, in Fernández de Oviedo, pt 2, bk 25, ch. 17, 2 318–9.

94 *restore themselves . . .* ' San Martín and Lebrija to King, in Fernández de Oviedo, pt 2, bk 26, ch. 11, 2 365.

95 *from the sea!*' San Martín and Lebrija, idem.

96 *more Indians dead!*' Idem, ch. 12, 369.

96 *be a Lutheran!*' Fernández de Oviedo, idem.

Chapter 6

99 *on top of it*.' Fernández de Oviedo, bk 49 (pt 3, bk 11), ch. 2, BAE cont. 121, 1959, 236.

99 *what is said*.' Idem.

100 *from biting them*', Gumilla, *El Orinoco ilustrado*, pt 1, ch. 7 (Caracas, 1963), 116, 121.

100 *of El Dorado*.' Cieza de León, *The War of Chupas*, ch. 18, trans. C. R. Markham, Hakluyt Society, 2 series, 42 (London, 1918), 55.

100 *in the expedition*.' Idem, 55–6.

100 *and explore it*.' Gonzalo Pizarro to King, Tomebamba (Cuenca), 3 September 1542, in Bertram T. Lee trans., Gaspar de Carvajal, *The Discovery of the Amazon* (New York, 1934), 245.

100 *of the Muisca*.]' Jiménez de Quesada, *Epítome de la conquista*, 44.

101 *big as pitchers*.' Jerónimo Lebrón letter, Santa Marta, 9 May 1537, DIHC, 4 195.

101 *lost for ever*.' Jiménez de Quesada, *Epítome*, in Demetrio Ramos Pérez, *El mito del Dorado*, 331.

101 *innumerable routes*.' Castellanos, *Elegías de varones ilustres*, pt 3, Elegía to Benalcázar, canto 2, verses 37–9, BAE 4, 1847, 453.

101 *any rich land*.' Castellanos, idem, 454.

102 *seems an enchantment*'. Herrera, decada 5,

bk 7, ch. 14, 11 173–4. Luis Daza's *Probanza*, held at Popayán, 3 October 1542, is in Ramos Pérez, *El mito del Dorado*, 470. It clearly states that the report given by the 'Indian called Dorado' led to the discovery of Popayán 'and the news of El Dorado'. Herrera seems to have based this part of his history on a missing work by Cieza de León.

102 *this sacred lake*. Pedro Simón, *Noticias historiales de las conquistas de Tierra Firme . . .*, pt 2, noticia 3, ch. 1, 1953 edn, 163–4. This famous chapter was first published by Edward King, Viscount Kingsborough, in his translation of Augustine Aglio, *Antiquities of Mexico* (9 vols, London, 1830–48), 8 221–38. However, it was not until 1891 that Father Simón's complete work was published by Medardo Rivas at Bogotá.

102 *and fortunes . . .* ' Rodríguez Fresle, *Conquista y descubrimiento del Nuevo Reino de Granada*, ch. 2.

102 *investiture ceremonies*. Fernández Piedrahita, *Historia general de las conquistas . . .*, pt 1, bk 4, ch. 1, and bk 6, ch. 3, 1688 edn, 109, 204.

102 *him El Dorado*.' Basilio Vicente de Oviedo, *Cualidades y riquezas del Nuevo Reino de Granada* (Bogotá, 1930).

104 *these two regions*. Garcilaso de la Vega, *Comentarios reales de los Incas*, pt 1, bk 7, ch. 23 (Lisbon, 1609), BAE cont. 133 (Madrid, 1960), 325–6. Federmann also noted the difference between Ecuadorean and Colombian emeralds in his letter to Francisco Dávila, Jamaica, 1 August 1539, in Fernández de Oviedo, pt 2, bk 25, ch. 17, 2 321. José Pérez de Barradas, *Los Muiscas antes de la conquista* (Madrid, 1950), 1 147. Ramos Pérez, *El mito del Dorado*, 302–9.

104 *infamous sanctuaries . . .* ' Castellanos, *Elegías de varones ilustres*, pt 4, canto 1 (Bogotá, 1955 edn), 155.

106 *gold and jewels*'. Peña testimony, Cartagena, 4 July 1539, DIHC, 5 208.

106 *their sacrifices*'. Peña testimony, idem.

107 *of the Muisca*. Federmann to Francisco Dávila, Jamaica, 1 August 1539, in Fernández de Oviedo, pt 2, bk 25, ch. 17, 2 320.

107 *contemporary sources*. Demetrio Ramos Pérez established this ingenious and convincing explanation of Castellanos' remark, in *El mito del Dorado*, 134–20. One of Dr Ramos' research students, María de las Mercedes Velasco Fito, found Francisco de Benalcázar's application to search the Council of

Indies' papers, in the Archivo General de Indias, Seville, Justicia, box 1122. The Probanza of the merits of the Benalcázars was published by José Manuel de Groot in his *Historia eclesiástica y civil de la Nueva Granada* (Bogotá, 1889), 1 477–83.

107 *reports by Añasco*. Cieza de León, *War of Chupas*, ch. 18, Hakluyt Society, 2 series, 42 55. Cieza said that the report also came from Benalcázar; but he could not have brought it, for he did not return to Quito until late 1541, after Gonzalo Pizarro had gone to seek El Dorado.

107 *rich settlements*'. Puelles testimony, Cartagena, 4 July 1539, DIHC, 5 213–4.

108 *close to it . . .* ' This anonymous fragment was found by Demetrio Ramos Pérez in the Archive of the Indies in Seville, Patronato, legajo 27, ramo 1: *El mito del Dorado*, 366–7.

108 *of El Dorado*' Cieza de León, *War of Chupas*, ch. 18, Hakluyt Society, 55.

108 *horse and foot . . .* ' Cieza de León, *War of Chupas*, ch. 18, Hakluyt Society, 2 series, 42 56; Fernández de Oviedo, pt 3, bk 49, ch. 2, 1852 edn, 4 383.

108 *at least cinnamon*'. Royal grant, Louvain, 31 May 1540, CDIA 23, 1875, 33–5.

108 *from many Indians*.' Fernández de Oviedo, pt 3, bk 49, ch. 1, BAE cont. 121, 1959, 235.

108 *lands, beyond there*.' Benalcázar to King, Cali, 30 March 1541, DIHC, 6 132–3. In this letter, Benalcázar worried that a rival governor, Pascual de Andagoya, had also written to the King about the wealth beyond Timaná. He poured scorn on the unadventurous Andagoya, who acted only on reports from his officers: 'He learned about it, seated, with papers going and papers coming, and sleeping in a very soft bed.'

109 *in such quantity*.' Benalcázar to King, Cali, 20 September 1542, DIHC, 6 298. Soon after reaching Cali, Benalcázar had welcomed a royal emissary, Cristóbal Vaca de Castro, who was going to Peru to try to resolve the quarrel between Francisco Pizarro and the heirs of his former partner Diego de Almagro. Then came news that Pizarro had been murdered, in his palace in Lima, on 26 June 1541. Vaca de Castro sent to order Benalcázar to march south to help him suppress a rebellion in Peru led by Almagro's young son. Benalcázar went down to Quito, but was eventually sent back to Popayán when Vaca de Castro decided that he was too sympathetic to Pizarro's murderers.

Chapter 7

111 *food beneath it.*' Cieza de León, *War of Chupas*, ch. 19, Hakluyt Society, 57.

111 *to cross rivers.*' Gonzalo Pizarro to King, Tomebamba, 3 September 1542, in Carvajal. *The Discovery of the Amazon*, 245.

111 *of much substance.*' Cieza de León, *War of Chupas*, ch. 19, 59.

111 *in the negative.*' Cieza de León, idem, 60.

112 *made it worse.*' Cieza de León, idem.

112 *Spaniards died.*' Pizarro letter of 3 September 1542, in Carvajal, *The Discovery of the Amazon*, 51, 246.

112 *this expedition.*' Cieza de León, *War of Chupas*, ch. 20, 61–2.

112 *invaded his country.*' Idem.

113 *all to be true.*' Idem.

113 *crossing many streams.*' Gonzalo Pizarro letter of 3 September 1542, in Carvajal, *The Discovery of the Amazon*, 53, 246.

113 *besought Our Lord.*' Cieza de León, *War of Chupas*, ch. 20, 64.

113 *North Sea [Atlantic]*'. Pizarro letter of 3 September 1542, in Carvajal, 247.

113 *boat was built.*' Gaspar de Carvajal, *Descubrimiento del río de las Amazonas*, trans. Bertram T. Lee (New York, 1934), 169.

113 *all been eaten.*' Cieza de León, *War of Chupas*, 65.

114 *whole expedition.*' Pizarro letter to King, 3 September 1542, Carvajal, *Discovery*, 248.

114 *without sense.*' Carvajal, *Descubrimiento*, 172.

114 *emptied into it . . .*' Ibid, 171.

114 *were too strong . . .*' Probanza of Cristóbal de Segovia (one of Orellana's men), Margarita island, October 1542, question 17, in Carvajal, *Discovery*, 269.

116 *fruitful land*'. Carvajal, *Discovery*, 202.

116 *very fine highways*'. Ibid, 200.

116 *into one another*'. Toribio de Ortigüera, *Relación verdadera de todo lo que sucedió en la jornada de Omagua y Dorado*, BAE cont. 15 317.

116 *and gold objects.* The expedition of 1538 was led by Captain Alonso de Mercadillo. It reached the Huallaga, and Mercadillo then sent some men to explore further ahead. Their discovery of the Machiparo was reported by a

Portuguese member of the group called Diogo Nunes. This report could well have influenced Gonzalo Pizarro in attempting his Cinnamon and Dorado expedition. See 'Apontamentos de Diogo Nunes das suas viagens na America' (c. 1554), in Carlos Malheiro Dias ed., *História de colonizacão portuguesa do Brasil*, 3 vols (Porto, 1924–6), 3 367–8; Marcos Jiménez de Espada, 'La jornada del capitán Alonso de Mercadillo a los indios Chupachos e Iscaicingas', *Boletín de la Sociedad Geográfica* 38 (Madrid, 1895), 217–18; Carlos Drumond, 'A carta de Diogo Nunes e a migracão tupi-guaraní para o Perú', *Revista de História* 1 (São Paulo, 1950), 95–102; Ladislao Gil Munilla, *Descubrimiento del Marañón* (Seville, 1954), 167–8.

116 *largest family.*' Cristóbal de Acuña, *Nuevo descubrimiento del gran río de las Amazonas* (Madrid, 1641), trans. Clements R. Markham, *Expeditions into the Valley of the Amazons*, Hakluyt Society 24 (London, 1859), chs 26, 39, pp. 70, 82.

116 *detains them.*' Acuña, idem, ch. 36, 80.

119 *of the Amazons*'. Carvajal, *Discovery*, 212.

119 *the end of me.*' Carvajal, *Discovery*, 214.

122 *with [that breast].*' López de Gómara, *Historia general de las Indias* (Saragosa, 1552), BAE 22, 210, trans. in Carvajal, *Discovery*, 26. Herrera, decada 6, bk 9, ch. 4; Fernández de Oviedo, bk 50, ch. 24.

122 *of the Amazons*''.' Idem.

122 *suffering or pain.*' Carvajal, *Discovery*, 216.

123 *miraculous event*'. Fernández de Oviedo, *Historia general*, bk 50, ch. 24, trans. in Carvajal, *Discovery*, 405.

123 *camp could pass.*' Cieza de León, *War of Chupas*, ch. 21, Hakluyt Society, 67.

123 *look upon them.*' Cieza de León, *War of Chupas*, ch. 21, 70.

123 *not get dry.*' Idem, 73.

123 *in his hand*'. Gonzalo Pizarro letter of 3 September 1542, in Carvajal, *Discovery*, 250.

123 *gone to seek . . .*' Benalcázar to King, Cali, 20 September 1542, DIHC, 6 298.

124 *better than Peru*'. Royal officials of Cubagua to King, 20 June 1538 (AGI Santo Domingo, legajo 149), quoted in Demetrio Ramos Pérez, *El mito del Dorado*, 408.

124 *that lieutenant.*' Fernández de Oviedo, pt 2, bk 24, ch. 14, 2 264.

124 *of geography*'. Idem.

124 *of his life*', Idem, ch. 16, 265.

124 *richer than Peru.*' Letter to Georg Geuder of Nuremberg, Coro, 20 October 1538, in Gabaldón Márquez ed., *Descubrimiento y conquista de Venezuela*, 2 370–1.

125 *to come here!*' Hutten to his brother, Bishop Moritz of Eichstedt, Coro, 16 January 1540, idem, 375.

125 *a long time . . .*' Hutten to his father, Bernhard von Hutten, Coro, 31 March 1539, idem, 373.

125 *for his effort!*' Hutten to his brother, Coro, 16 January 1540, idem, 375–6.

126 *all the soldiers*' Castellanos, pt 2, elegía 2, canto 3, verses 51–2, BAE 4. In his will, Hohermuth had bidden Montalvo de Lugo to 'enter and colonize the land in the interior': Letter by Licentiate Pérez de Tolosa, Coro, 8 July 1548, in José de Oviedo y Baños, 1885 edn, 2 255. Both Pedro de Aguado and Pedro Simón said that when Limpias reached Coro in November 1540, he brought news of El Dorado which inspired Hutten. This cannot have been so, since El Dorado was not yet known outside Quito. Hutten needed no encouragement to go exploring (his private letters are full of reports of rich lands, and he wrote about Amazons in his *Zeitung*) but he never once mentioned El Dorado about which he was ignorant. Also, in Bogotá itself, Hernán Pérez de Quesada was not yet aware of El Dorado: he spent 1540 on minor enterprises, including a journey *northwards* to seek the House of the Sun. Demetrio Ramos Pérez, *El mito del Dorado*, 418–9.

126 *such crimes . . .*' Jiménez de Quesada, *Indicaciones para el buen gobierno*, para. 8 (c. 1547), BHA 14, no. 162 (Bogotá, 1923), 349.

126 *off small children.*' Denunciation by Jerónimo Lebrón against Juan de Arévalo, Santa Marta, 30 March 1541, item 4 and testimony of Blasco Romero, DIHC, 6 121, 128.

126 *in the Indies*'. Idem, testimony of García de Valmaseda, 127.

127 *quantity of Indians.*' Idem, testimony of Antón de Aguilar, 126.

127 *below the crag.*' Idem.

127 *innocent people.*' Idem, Denunciation, 6, 122.

127 *punishment of impaling*'. Probanza of Lope Montalvo de Lugo, Madrid, 14 January 1552, BHA 26, 1939, 320; also *Proceso del capitán Hernán Vanegas con el Adelantado de Canaria*, idem, 316–7; *Residencia y pesquisa secreta*, by

Licentiate Miguel Diez de Armendáriz against Martín Pujol, 4 February 1547, idem, 318–9; Residencia of Licentiates Juan de Galarza and Beltrán de Góngora, idem, 743, etc.

127 *at the head'*. BHA **26**, 1939, 751.

127 *against their will'*. Accusation by city of Tunja against Lázaro Fonte, 11 December 1543, DIHC, 7 133; Friede, *Jiménez de Quesada a través de documentos*, 270.

128 *sleep with her!'* Idem, testimony of Simón Díaz, 134.

128 *been heard about.'* Hernán Pérez de Quesada to King, Cali, 16 May 1543, DIHC, 7 13.

128 *for that expedition.'* Hernán Pérez de Quesada to King, idem.

128 *to this kingdom.'* Residencia secreta, by Licentiate Miguel Diez de Armendáriz against Hernán Pérez de Quesada, 16 May 1547, charge 14, in Ernesto Restrepo Tirado, 'Residencias que se tomaron a los primeros gobernadores . . .', BHA **26**, nos 295–6, 1939, 311; Probanza against Jiménez de Quesada and Hernán Pérez de Quesada, Santafé (Bogotá), 28 June 1543, DIHC, 7 25–6.

128 *return to them'*. Probanza of 28 June 1543, idem, 25.

129 *to be discovered.'* Minutes of Cabildo of Tunja, 21 June 1541, in Nicolás García Samudio, *Crónica del muy magnífico capitán don Gonzalo Suárez Rendón*, 130–1.

129 *present idleness.'* Lucas Fernández Piedrahita, *Historia general de las conquistas del Nuevo Reino de Granada*, pt 1, bk 9, ch. 3, 357.

129 *Indians and horses.'* Aguado, *Recopilación historial*, pt 1, bk 4, ch. 12, 1 382.

129 *the lower land.'* Piedrahita, pt 1, bk 9, ch. 3, 359.

129 *Indian porters died.'* Idem.

129 *dyed with blood.'* Aguado, *Recopilación*, pt 1, bk 4, ch. 12, 1 384.

130 *food to be found.'* Piedrahita, pt 1, bk 9, ch. 3, 359.

130 *that lay ahead.'* Piedrahita, idem, 360.

130 *called Achibichi.'* Idem.

130 *of El Dorado.'* Idem. Father Marcellino de Castellví has worked out the probable route of the expedition: from the Papamene and Macos Indians (probably Guahibo-speaking tribes) to the Choques (Carib-speaking?), past a mountain spur the Spaniards called Finesterra to the Bermejo (Red) river in the region of the upper Yarí and

Caguán, a tributary of the Caquetá. Then a reconnaissance into the Sierra Yágueza of the Cordillera Oriental and down into the low forests and swamps between the Caguán and El Pescado rivers; through the present region of Los Canelos to the land of the Muisca or Chibcha-speaking Andaki, through the lands of the Palenques (also Andaki?) to the region of La Fragua after crossing the Fragua and Caquetá. Valladolid was probably on the Caquetá, on the side of modern Puerto Limón. Thence up the Mocoa river and valley and its tributaries the Patoyaco and Minchoy rivers; across the ridge of Portachuelo to the valley of Sibundoy; then over the páramo of El Bordoncillo to the town of La Laguna (now El Encano), and over the páramo of Tábano to the Spanish municipality of Pasto. Castellví, 'Los descubridores del Caquetá y del Mocoa', 789–90.

130 *cinnamon spice trees.'* Gonzalo Jiménez de Quesada to King and Council of Indies, 1547, in Friede, *Gonzalo Jiménez de Quesada a través de documentos*, 359; BHA **14**, no. 162, 1923, 348.

130 *handsomely swollen.'* Pérez de Quesada to King, Cali, 16 May 1543, DIHC, 7 13.

132 *with great news'* Idem.

132 *born in Quito'* Idem.

132 *Sibundoy near Pasto.'* Idem.

132 *and ill-disposed.'* Idem, 15.

132 *Choques' territory.'* Castellanos, pt 2, elegía 3, canto 1, verse 3, BAE **4**, 1847, 226. Before leaving Coro, in March 1541, the leaders of this expedition had set out their plans in a notarized statement. They declared that they intended to 'pass forward along the route and trail taken by Georg [Hohermuth] on the discovery and conquest of the great riches that he had gone to seek and of which he had considerable news'. Fernández de Oviedo, pt 2, bk 25, ch. 21, 2 327–8; Demetrio Ramos Pérez, *El mito del Dorado*, 423.

132 *of Hernán Pérez.'* Aguado, pt 2, bk 3, ch. 1, *Historia de Venezuela*, 1 243.

132 *his old friend'*. Castellanos, pt 2, elegía 3, canto 1, verse 25, BAE **4** 227.

132 *were now dead.'* Aguado, pt 2, bk 3, ch. 2, *Historia de Venezuela*, 1 248.

133 *they were astounded.'* Report by Juan Rodríguez and others, Santafé, 24 October 1576, testimony of Juan Martín del Albercón, FDNRG, 7 121.

133 *by his warriors.* Idem, testimony of

Antonio Alexandre de Castilla, talking about an Indian called Hernandillo, 123–4.

133 *very few natives'*. Aguado, pt 2, bk 3, ch. 2, *Historia de Venezuela*, 1 249.

134 *which they died.'* Aguado, idem, 250.

134 *had left Coro.'* Aguado, idem, 251.

134 *variations of cruelty.'* Aguado, idem, ch. 4, 260.

134 *innumerable wealth.'* Aguado, idem, 262.

134 *secluded towns.'* Aguado, idem, ch. 5, 264.

134 *quantity of riches.'* Aguado, idem, 266. Chief Qvarica entered the list of legendary places for a time. In 1548 Licentiate Juan Pérez de Tolosa wrote to the King about the 'wealth of such renown of Ocoarica': Tolosa to King, 8 July 1548, in Oviedo y Baños, 1885 edn, 2 257. This was where Hutten was told that the Amazons lived. Castellanos said that news of the fabulous Ocuarica was obtained during Hohermuth's expedition. Antonio Alexandre de Castilla spoke, in 1576, of Coarica as 'a lord of such majesty that all were humiliated by him . . . He had towns of such great power that one could not see the far end of them, and much riches of gold, for his table service was made of it. . . . [Also in Coarica's land was] an animal with much wool that appears to be sheep of Peru.' Testimony, Santafé, 27 October 1576, FDNRG, 7 123–4.

135 *a full life'* Aguado, idem, 268.

135 *were impressed.'* Idem.

136 *off their heads!"'* Carvajal's confession, in Friede, *Los Welser en la conquista de Venezuela*, 399. Información by Licentiate Tolosa, in José de Oviedo y Baños, *Historia de . . . Venezuela*, Cesareo Fernández Duro ed. (Madrid, 1885), 2 259.

136 *to be punished!"'* Idem, 400.

136 *agonizing deaths.'* Aguado, pt 2, bk 3, ch. 8, 1 284. Castellanos, pt 2, elegía 3, canto 2, BAE **4**, 238. Oviedo y Baños, bk 3, ch. 3, 1 189.

136 *brought with them'*. Bartolomé Welser to King, in Gabaldón Márquez ed., *Descubrimiento y conquista de Venezuela*, 2 396.

137 *excellent captains.'* Castellanos, pt 2, elegía 3, canto 2, BAE **4**, 238.

137 *father of them all.'* Diego Ruiz de Vallejo to the Audiencia of Santo Domingo, 28 June 1546, in Friede, *Los Welser*, 408.

137 *value of a real'*. Letter from Licentiate Pérez de Tolosa, Coro, December 1546, in Oviedo y Baños, 1885 edn, 2 236.

137 *escaped alive.*' Royal officials to King, Cali, 2 February 1544, in Demetrios Ramos Pérez, *El mito del Dorado*, 440.

137 *discovered and conquered.*' Idem.

138 *contains much wealth.*' Cieza de León, *La guerra de Quito*, ch. 108 (Madrid, 1877), 114–5.

138 *on this route.*' Probanza organized by Francisco de Benalcázar, Popayán, in Groot, *Historia eclesiástica y civil de la Nueva Granada*, I 481.

138 *from the Spaniards.*' Cieza de León, *War of Chupas*, 338.

138 *and his Church*'. Miguel de Salamanca sermon, quoted by Las Casas, *Historia de las Indias*, bk 3, ch. 135, trans. Lewis Hanke, *The Spanish struggle for justice in the Conquest of America* (Philadelphia, 1949), 86.

Chapter 8

141 *spent ten years.*' Marquis of Montesclaros, Viceroy of Peru, to King, Callao, 12 April 1613, in Marcos Jiménez de la Espada, *Relaciones geográficas de Indias* 4, BAE cont. 135 233. Pedro de Cieza de León said that 200 Indians had arrived: *Crónica del Perú*, pt I, ch. 78.

141 *this expedition.*' Diego de Aguilar y Córdoba, bk I, ch. 6, in idem, BAE cont. 135 238.

141 *Maranhão [Amazon].*' Simão Estácio da Silveira, quoting Magalhães de Gandavo, *Relacão sumária das coisas do Maranhão* (Lisbon, 1624), BAE cont. 135 237.

142 *among themselves.*' López Vaz, *A Discourse of the West Indies and South Sea* (1587), in Richard Hakluyt, *Principall Navigations of the English Nation* (London, 1589), Everyman's Library 338 (8 vols, London, 1962), 8 167.

142 *in the wars . . .*' Idem, 167.

143 *and unihabitable . . .*' Election of Fernando de Guzmán as Prince of Peru, Machifaro, 23 March 1561, in Emiliano Jos, *La expedición de Ursúa al Dorado . . .*, 77.

143 *all who knew her.*' Custodio Hernández, *Relación de todo lo que acaeció en la entrada de Pedro de Orsúa . . . y de la rebelión de don Hernando de Guzmán . . .* (Ms. in Biblioteca Nacional de Madrid), in Emiliano Jos, *La expedición de Ursúa al Dorado . . .*, 87.

143 *tedious unto you.*' López Vaz, *Discourse*, in Hakluyt, *Principall Navigations*, 8 169.

143 *of his death . . .*' Idem.

144 *does not know me!*' ' Aguado, *Recopilación historial*, pt 2, bk 10, ch. 78, 4 369; Pedro Simón, *Noticias historiales*, 6th Notice, in William Bollaert trans., *The Expedition of Pedro de Ursúa and Lope de Aguirre in search of El Dorado and Omagua*, Hakluyt Society, 28 (London, 1861), ch. 43, 184; Oviedo y Baños, *Historia de Venezuela*, bk 4, ch. 5, I 311. The bloody story of Lope de Aguirre was a favourite in its day, so that there are a great many chronicle versions of it. These include: Toribio de Ortigüera, *Jornada del Marañón*; Captain Altamirano of Chachapoyas in Antonio Vázquez de Espinosa, *Compendio y descripción*, bk 4, chs 10–16; Garcilaso de la Vega; Diego de Aguilar y Córdoba; Juan Meléndez; Antonio de Herrera; Juan de Castellanos; Francisco Vázquez; Manuel Rodríguez; Juan Rodríguez Fresle; Lucas Fernández de Piedrahita; Pedrarias Almesto; Francisco López de Caravantes.

144 *had their reward.*' Lope de Aguirre to Philip II, Barquisimeto, October 1561, in Emiliano Jos, *La expedición*, 297.

144 *novices from Spain.*' Idem, 200.

146 *could have made them.*' Report by Juan Rodríguez and others, Santafé, 24 October 1576, FDNRG, 6 117.

147 *and cruelties.*' Dr Venero de Leyva, President of Audiencia of New Granada, to King, Santafé, 1 June 1572, FDNRG, 6 174. Antonio Medrano's great history was completed by his fellow Franciscan Pedro de Aguado; but the *Recopilación historial* contains almost nothing about Jiménez de Quesada's expedition of 1569–72. There are a few details in Pedro Simón, *Noticias historiales*, noticia 7, chs 27–8; Oviedo y Baños (1885 edn), 274 ff.; Joaquín Acosta, *Compendio histórico del descubrimiento y colonización de la Nueva Granada*, ch. 18 (Paris, 1848), 345–8.

147 *men who went there.*' Dr Venero de Leyva and other officials to King, Santafé, 10 March 1573, FDNRG, 6 207.

147 *out of hunger.*' Anon, *Descripción de la ciudad de Tunja* (1610), CDIA 9, 1868, 436.

149 *Orellana [the Amazon].*' Castellanos, pt 3, Elegía to Benalcázar, canto 2, BAE 4 453. Also, *Relación del camino y viaje que siguió Pedro Maraver de Silva a la Nueva Extremadura llamado Eldorado, para donde salió en 12 de julio de 1576*: AGI Patronato, legajo 26, ramo 28. Pedro Simón, 1963 edn, 2 520 ff. Elena Ruiz, *La búsqueda de Eldorado por Guayana*,

39–42; Jerónimo Martínez-Mendoza, *La leyenda de El Dorado*, 32–3; Demetrio Ramos Pérez, *La leyenda del Dorado*, 458–60; V. T. Harlow, in Ralegh's *Discoverie . . . of Guiana*, lxv–lxvii.

Chapter 9

151 *niece doña Maria . . .*' Most of Jiménez de Quesada's will is lost. This fragment was found by the Jesuit historian Pablo Ojer and published in his *La formación del oriente Venezolano* I, or *Don Antonio de Berrío, Gobernador del Dorado*, 28.

151 *white cotton mantles*'. Pleito of doña María de la Hoz y Berrío, in Archivo Nacional de Bogotá, Ernesto Restrepo Tirado, 'Repartimientos del Adelantado', BHA 45, no. 473, 1954, 251.

151 *the love of God!*' Berrío to King, Santafé de Bogotá, 8 September 1583, in Ojer, *Don Antonio de Berrío*, 44.

151 *shrewd traders.*' Alonso de Pontes, *Relación de su jornada al río Meta*, in Ojer, *Berrío*, 184.

152 *wounded by it.*' Diego Pinto testimony, Información of Pedro Fernández, Santafé, 30 September 1566, FDNRG, 4 50.

152 *immediately return.*' Alonso de Pontes, Relación, in Ojer, *Berrío*, 181.

152 *it is true.*' Berrío to Juan Prieto de Orellana, inspector of New Granada, 4 February 1584, in Ojer, *Berrío*, 47.

152 *all the llanos!*' Berrío to King, Santafé, 24 May 1585, in Ojer, *Berrío*, 52; Berrío to President and oidores of Audiencia of New Granada, Banks of Casanare, 1 April 1587, idem.

153 *means 'lake'.* Gumilla, *Historia natural, civil y geográfica . . . del río Orinoco*, I 356. This is a more convincing derivation of the name Manoa than to relate it to the Manau tribe, who lived on the middle Río Negro and whose name is recorded in the modern city of Manaus.

153 *in their tombs.*' *Relación de lo que Juan de Salas hizo y descubrió en la isla de Margarita . . .* (after 1570), in Martínez-Mendoza, *La leyenda*, 39–40. The spelling of Guiana presents a problem. In Spanish it is Guayana, which is the spelling of the south-eastern province of modern Venezuela. In English it is Guiana, as in the name of the British colony east of Venezuela, which since independence has become the republic of Guyana.

153 *of 28 leagues!'* Berrío to King, 24 May 1585, trans. Harlow, in Ralegh, *Discoverie . . . of Guiana*, 92.

153 *that filled them.'* Idem, 93; Ojer, *Berrío*, 53.

153 *I had found.'* Idem, 93.

153 *as the Marañón.'* Berrío to Audiencia, Casanare, 1 April 1587, Ojer, *Berrío*, 55.

155 *disease of fevers'.* Información on the banks of the Barraguán (Orinoco), 30 March 1588 (Archivo Nacional de Bogotá, Civil xiv, folio 3), in Ojer, *Berrío*, 63. Simón, *Noticias historiales*, pt 2, noticia 7, ch. 36. Información at La Asunción, 11 October 1591.

155 *forced to return . . . '* Información at La Asunción, 11 October 1591, question 4, in Ojer, *Berrío*, 65.

155 *upset his men.* Licentiate Ferráez de Porras to King, Santafé, 18 June 1589, in Ojer, *Berrio*, 66. The captain was the future governor of Venezuela, don Gonzalo de Piña Ludueña. Berrío letters to King, 1 April 1587 and 1 January 1593 (AGI Patronato 254, ramo 1 and Escribanía de Cámara, 1011–A, piece 8).

155 *he is a man.'* Berrío to King, Trinidad, 2 December 1594, in Ojer, *Berrío*, 197.

156 *call El Dorado . . . '* Idem.

156 *other provinces.'* Berrío to King, Margarita, 1 January 1593, in Harlow ed., Ralegh, *Discoverie*, 99.

158 *richer than Peru!'* Berrío to King. Idem, 99–100, 102–4.

158 *enter those plains.'* Rodrigo Carranza, *Traslado bien y fielmente sacado de una escritura de posesiones que parece tomó Domingo de Vera Ibargoyen . . .* (AGI Escribanía de Cámara, 1011–A, piece 6), in Ojer, *Berrío*, 95.

160 *and well formed'.* Report on the discovery of Guayana, by Vera e Ibargoyen and Berrío, Trinidad, 1593, in Harlow ed., Ralegh, *Discoverie*, 107.

160 *towns and lords.'* Idem.

160 *multiplied greatly.'* Cieza de León, *Crónica del Perú*, pt 1, chs 78, 90, trans. de Onis, 100, 131.

160 *these provinces.'* Berrío to King, Margarita, 1 January 1593, in Harlow ed., Ralegh, *Discoverie*, 103.

160 *hills and mountains.'* Report by Berrío and Vera e Ibargoyen, Trinidad, 1593, in Harlow ed., Ralegh, *Discoverie*, 108.

161 *nature gave them.'* Castellanos, pt 3, Elegía to Benalcázar, canto 2, BAE 4 453.

161 *are poor people.'* Castellanos, idem.

161 *could be possible'.* Idem.

161 *have foundation . . . '* Idem.

161 *girls' dowries!'* Berrío to King, Margarita, 26 October 1591, in Ojer, *Berrío*, 82.

Chapter 10

163 *in all security . . . '* Ralegh's letter quoted in Berrío to King, Margarita, 11 July 1595, in Ojer, *Berrío*, 113–4.

163 *burned the town.'* Berrío to King, Idem, 115.

163 *and Aterima.'* Ralegh, *The Discoverie . . . of Guiana* (Everyman edn), 284.

163 *S. Joseph on fire.'* Idem.

164 *all men's courses.'* Aiken, *Memoirs of King James*, 1 58; Harlow, in Ralegh, *Discoverie*, xix, xxiv.

165 *Dycke the footmane . . . '* Arthur Throckmorton's diary, in John Winton, *Sir Walter Ralegh* (London, 1975), 113; A. L. Rowse, *Ralegh and the Throckmortons* (London, 1962).

165 *et Sir W. Raelly.'* Idem, 117.

165 *prison all alone.'* Ralegh to Cecil, Tower of London, July 1592, in Winton, *Ralegh*, 119.

165 *naturals Manoa.'* Ralegh, *The Discoverie of the large, rich and beautifull Empire of Guiana*, in Hakluyt, *The English Voyages*, 7 273–4.

166 *the riches thereof.'* Ralegh, idem, 283.

166 *of the asse.'* Idem, 284.

166 *badly with him.'* Report by Pedro de Salazar, governor of Margarita, of events up to 12 June 1595 (AGI Santo Domingo, 180), Ojer, *Berrío*, 122.

166 *of a great heart.'* Ralegh, *Discoverie*, 285.

167 *farre more difering.'* Idem, 305.

167 *labyrinth of rivers . . . '* Idem, 307.

167 *the houres end.'* Idem, 310.

167 *despaire and discomfort.'* Idem, 311.

168 *a keepers call.'* Idem, 313.

168 *their owne lusts.'* Idem, 316.

168 *then this usage.'* Idem, 316.

168 *to their houses.'* Idem, 316.

168 *bene the same.'* Idem, 318.

169 *to attend them.'* Idem, 321.

169 *of the world'.* Idem, 318.

169 *under the Sunne',* Idem, 322.

170 *to a rinoceros'* Idem, 323.

170 *and libertie . . . '* Idem, 323.

170 *learning nor breede.'* Idem, 325.

170 *Thames at Wolwich'* Idem, 325.

170 *some great towne.'* Idem, 326–7.

170 *by his complexion.'* Idem, 327. There is now a new city at the mouth of the Caroní, called Santo Tomé de Guayana in memory of a town built there by Berrío. One of its activities is the refining of iron ore from the open-cast Cerro Bolívar mine; and there is an aluminium plant powered by electricity from the Macagua hydroelectric scheme harnessing the cataracts viewed by Ralegh.

170 *possessed of thereby.'* Idem, 335.

171 *of the Devil'.* Francisco de Vides, governor of Cumaná, *Relación de lo sucedido en la ciudad de Cumaná . . .* (AGI Santo Domingo, 184), in Ojer, *Berrío*, 128. There were plenty of reports of this Spanish victory, by Berrío in his letter to the King, Margarita, 11 July 1595, and in reports and letters by Governor Pedro de Salazar of Margarita.

171 *towardes the North'.* Ralegh, *Discoverie*, 342.

171 *goodnes of the newes.'* Elizabeth Ralegh to Sir Robert Cecil, in Winton, *Sir Walter Ralegh*, 174–5.

172 *cursed of God . . . '* Ralegh to Cecil, Sherborne, 13 November 1595, in Quinn, *Ralegh and the British Empire*, 148.

172 *without her cost.'* Idem.

172 *of this exploit . . . '* George Chapman, *De Guiana, Carmen Epicum*, in Winton, *Sir Walter Ralegh*, 177.

173 *betweene their shoulders.'* Ralegh, *Discoverie*, 328.

173 *Pizarro in Peru.'* Idem, 345.

173 *of their temples.'* Idem, 347.

173 *crown and brim'.* Pedro Simón, *Noticias historiales*, pt 1, noticia 7, ch. 10.

173 *the rich lands!'* Domingo de Vera, *Memorial del descubrimiento del Dorado*, CDIA, 6 563.

173 *descend upon him!*. Vera, Memorial, CDIA, 6 563.

174 *saline lake . . .* ' Council of the Indies, consulta al Rey, 7 September 1595, CDIA, 2 series, 14 88.

174 *I asked for . . .* ' Información held at Cumaná, 5 July 1596, in Ojer, *Berrío*, 142.

174 *dying of hunger.*' Luis de Santander testimony, *Información de testigos*, Cumaná, 5 July 1596, in Ojer, *Berrío*, 151.

176 *series of disasters.*' Vera to King, Trinidad, 27 October 1597, in Harlow ed., Ralegh, *Discoverie*, 109.

176 *goodwill and labours.*' Idem, 110.

176 *deaths and hardships*' Idem.

176 *of their sons*'. Idem, 109.

176 *respect for them*' Idem.

176 *devoid of plans*' Idem, 109; *Información de servicios de Bernabé de Brea*, Héctor García Chuecos, ed., *Encomiendas* (Archivo General de la Nación, Caracas, 1947), 5 277.

176 *dispirited and mindless*' Idem, 110.

176 *of seven months.*' Idem, 110.

177 *to Sir Walter . . .* ' Captain Joseph Stanley petition to Sir Robert Cecil, 22 September 1598, Marquis of Salisbury, *Hatfield papers*, 8 358, in Harlow ed., Ralegh, *Discoverie*, xc; Licentiate Pedro de Liaño to King, 25 March–12 April 1596, idem, 122; Roque de Montes Colmenares to King, Cumaná, 18 April 1596, idem, 136.

177 *dwellings far inland . . .* ' *Interrogatorio a que fué sometido Francisco Esparrei*, presented to Licentiate Benavides de Benavides, late 1600, in Demetrio Ramos Pérez, *El mito del Dorado*, 677. Sparrey's own account was published as *The Discription of the Isle of Trinidad, the rich Countrye of Guiana, and the Mightie River of Orenoco* (1602), in *Purchas, His Pilgrimes* (1625), Glasgow, 1906, 16 301.

177 *of the Indies.*' Pedro de Salazar to King, Margarita, July 1595, in Harlow ed., Ralegh, *Discoverie*, 120.

178 *use of weapons*', *Of the Voyage for Guiana*, in Harlow ed., Ralegh, *Discoverie*, 146; Quinn, *Ralegh and the British Empire*, 151.

178 *they despair not.*' Ralegh to Cecil, 13 November 1595, in Quinn, *Ralegh and the British Empire*, 151.

178 *Manoa standeth.*' Laurence Keymis, *A relation of the second voyage to Guiana*, 1596, in Hakluyt, *The English Voyages*, 1962 edn, 7 368.

179 *taken last yeere.*' Keymis. *Relation*, idem, 373–4.

179 *of their rivers.*' Idem, 380.

179 *in that action.*' Idem, 386.

182 *at the most.*' Fernando de Berrío to King, 4 January 1604 (AGI Santo Domingo, 208), in Martínez-Mendoza, *La leyenda de El Dorado*, 48.

182 *Peruvian ones*' Vázquez de Espinosa, *Compendium and description of the West Indies* (c. 1620), ch. 13 (Washington, 1968), 63.

182 *that is known*' Fernando de Berrío to King, 1610, in Martínez-Mendoza, *La leyenda de El Dorado*, 50.

183 *the late Queene.*' Robert Harcourt, *Relation of a Voyage to Guiana* (1613), in *Purchas, His Pilgrimes* (Glasgow, 1906), 16 364.

183 *golden mountaines . . .* ' Idem.

183 *food was exhausted.* John Stow, *The Annals of England*, revised by Edmund Howes (London, 1615), 946; Sir Thomas Roe to Robert Cecil, Earl of Salisbury, Port of Spain, Trinidad, 28 February 1611, *Colonial Calendar 1574–1660*, 11; J. A. Williamson, *English Colonies in Guiana . . .* (Oxford, 1923), 55.

183 *as easely held.*' Sir Thomas Roe to Cecil, Earl of Salisbury, Port of Spain, 28 February 1611, idem.

183 *in the world.*' Ralegh to Privy Council, 1611, in Winton, *Ralegh*, 296; Harlow, *Ralegh's Last Voyage*, 112–3; Ralegh to Sir Ralph Winwood, c. 1615, idem, 114.

184 *out of Cornewall.*' Ralegh to George, Lord Carew, 1618, in Harlow, *Ralegh's Last Voyage*, 38, 250.

184 *title butt force . . .* ' Idem.

185 *with all courtesie.*' Ralegh, *Orders to be observed by the commanders of the fleete and land companies*, Plymouth, 3 May 1617, in Harlow, *Ralegh's Last Voyage*, 125–6.

185 *did, and lived.*' Ralegh to Elizabeth Ralegh, Cayenne river, 14 November 1617, in Harlow, *Ralegh's Last Voyage*, 158.

185 *offer to obey me.*' Idem, 159.

185 *England hath in it.*' Idem, 158.

185 *this gold myne.*' Kemis, *Relation*, in Hakluyt, *Voyages* (1599 edn), 3 679.

186 *from the mountaines.*' Idem. There has been much confusion about the location of these mines and of the town of Santo Tomé. Sir Robert Schomburgk made a contorted effort to resolve this, in his notes to Ralegh's *Diary* (Hakluyt Society 3, 1848, 206). Professor Harlow corrected Schomburgk's mistake by demonstrating that: (a) Spanish documents clearly showed that Santo Tomé in 1617 was just below the mouth of the Caroní, where Berrío had founded it in 1596; it was moved much later down river some 45 kms to a place now known as Santo Tomé de Guayana la Vieja, and (b) there were two mines in Ralegh's and Keymis' thinking. But Professor Harlow himself was then confused by a remark of Ralegh's that his men in 1617 found a Spanish town or village 'twentie miles distance from the place where Anthoneo Berreo the first Governor by me taken in my first discovery had attempted to plant'. Harlow wondered why Ralegh should have falsified his narrative'. What Harlow did not realize was that Berrío's first settlement was in fact in his friend Carapana's village: that was the only Spanish presence on the Orinoco when Ralegh was there in 1595. It was only in 1596 that Berrío founded Santo Tomé 20 miles from where he first 'attempted to plant'. Harlow, *Ralegh's Last Voyage*, 61–3.

186 *far as you can.*' Ralegh, *Instructions for Captaine Kemish*, in *Sir Walter Raghleys Large Appologie for the ill success of his enterprise to Guiana*, 1618, in Harlow, *Ralegh's Last Voyage*, 325.

186 *Majesty's expectation.*' Instructions to Laurence Keymis, idem.

186 *of our nation.*' Idem.

186 *will I never.*' Idem.

187 *taken the Town.*' Examination of Captain Roger North, Whitehall, 17 September 1618, in Harlow, *Ralegh's Last Voyage*, 258.

188 *shower of bullets*'. Pedro Simón, *Noticias historiales*, pt 1, noticia 7, ch. 24, trans. Harlow, *Ralegh's Last Voyage*, 167.

188 *body of his men*" ' Testimony by Captain García de Aguilar Trujillo before Captain Diego Martín de Baena, Santo Tomé de Guayana, 29 August 1618, in Harlow, idem, 194.

188 *or go forward*' William Herbert deposition, idem, 76.

188 *made an assaulte.*' Charles Parker to Captain Alley, 1618, in Schomburgk, *Raleigh's Discoverie*, Hakluyt Society 4, 217–8.

188 *as it is . . .*' Keymis to Sir Walter Ralegh, Santo Tomé, 7 January 1618, in Harlow, *Ralegh's Last Voyage*, 60.

188 *other are fools!"* ' Winton, *Sir Walter Ralegh*, 313.

188 *he had ledde.*' Charles Parker to Captain Alley, Trinidad, 1618, in Harlow, *Ralegh's Last Voyage*, 231.

188 *song in Hell!*' Simón, *Noticias historiales*, pt 1, noticia 7, ch. 24, in Harlow, idem, 167.

188 *a sword slash.*' Simón, ch. 25, idem, 171.

189 *if all failed.*' Rev. Samuel Jones, *A true and brief Relation of Sir Walter Raleigh his late voyage to Guiana*, in Harlow, *Ralegh's Last Voyage*, 235.

189 *more spoken of.*' Idem.

189 *mear Machevill . . .* ' Parker to Alley, Trinidad, 1618, in Harlow, idem, 231.

189 *went noe further.*' Ralegh to Sir Ralph Winwood, 21 March 1618, Harlow, idem, 242, 80.

190 *hatefull fellow . . .* ' Parker to Alley, 1618, idem, 231.

190 *long to live.*' Ralegh to his wife, St Kitts, 22 March 1618, in Harlow, idem, 243.

190 *valient Sonne.*' Idem.

190 *loste for ever.*' Idem.

190 *my artillery' ;* Idem.

190 *lefte the Thames'.* Idem, 245.

191 *their arguments.*' Sir Walter Ralegh to King, Tower of London, 24 September 1618, in Harlow, *Ralegh's Last Voyage*, 278.

191 *submit yourself.*' Hargrave's *State Trials*, 8, appendix 4, in Harlow, idem, 303.

191 *to use them.*' Idem.

193 *pray for me.*' Idem, 304.

193 *of St Tomé.*' Winton, *Sir Walter Ralegh*, 335.

193 *wondered at him . . .* ' Dr Tounson to Sir John Ishan, idem, 336.

193 *innocent man'.* Idem.

193 *my Country men.*' Sir Walter Ralegh's Speech immediately before he was beheaded, in Harlow, *Ralegh's Last Voyage*, 309.

193 *it down again.*' Thomas Lorkin to Sir Thomas Puckering, idem, 313.

193 *from his pain.*' Idem.

193 *Fourscore Years old.*' Sir Walter Ralegh's Speech . . . , idem, 310.

193 *to his advantage.*' Lorkin to Puckering, idem, 311, 313–4.

Appendix

195 *in ancient times.*' Cieza de León, *The War of Las Salinas*, ch. 82, in Demetrio Ramos Pérez, *El mito del Dorado*, 348.

195 *church of Guatavita.*' Juan Rodríguez Fresle, *Conquista y descubrimiento del Nuevo Reino de Granada* (1638) (1859 edn), 52.

195 *of good gold'.* Delivery by Añtonio de Sepúlveda to royal treasurer, Bogotá, 22 June 1576, in Eduardo Posada, 'La Laguna de Guatavita', BHA 8, no. 88, 1912, 238.

195 *must be paid'.* Licence by Governor Juan de Borja to Alonso Sánchez de Molina and others, Santafé de Bogotá, 15 July 1625, *Archivo Nacional de Bogotá, Miscelánea Colonia*, vol. 92, folios 848–51.

195 *of water left."* ' Captain Charles Stuart Cochrane R.N., *Journal of a residence and travels in Colombia during the years 1823 and 1824* (2 vols, London, 1825), 2 204–5.

196 *away from us . . .* ' Idem, 200.

196 *the plains below.*' Idem, 257.

196 *Royal Institute, Paris'* Idem, 203.

196 *twenty millions sterling'.* Idem.

196 *of El Dorado.*' Liborio Zerda, *El Dorado: estudio histórico, etnográfico y arqueológico de los Chibchas . . .* (Bogotá, 1883), 10. This raft belonged to one Salomón Koppel, who sold it to the Imperial Museum of Berlin. It apparently disappeared from Berlin after the 1914–18 War. The gold raft now in the Museo del Oro in Bogotá was found by farm workers near the town of Pasca: they may have discovered a Muisca workshop. The Museum bought it for 200,000 Colombian pesos in 1970.

197 *is now cup-shaped.*' *Description and details of articles recovered from the Sacred Lake of Guatavita, Republic of Colombia, South America, through the operations of Contractors Ltd, 65 London Wall, E.C.* (London, 1911), 5. *Catalogue of Antique Gold Ornaments and Pottery recovered from Lake Guatavita, in the Republic of Colombia, South America . . .* sale by Messers Sotheby, Wilkinson & Hodge (London), 11 December 1911. Agreements between the Señoritas Urbina and Daniel Villa and others, 24 February 1898; between Daniel Villa and Ricardo de la Torre, with the approval of Señoritas Urbina, 7 May 1898; formation of Compañía Explotadora de la Laguna de Guatavita by de la Torre brothers, 2 June 1898; Hartley Knowles acquires 59 per cent of rights from Eustacio and Ricardo de la Torre, 16 September 1899; Hartley Knowles' agreement with Contractors Ltd, 11 June 1900, all in *Libro de Protocolo, Notaria Segunda de Bogotá*. Konrad Beissmanger, *Im Lande der heiligen Seen. Reisebilder aus der Heimat der Chibcha Indianer (Kolumbien)* (Nürnberg, 1911), 288. Jesús Emiliano Ramírez, S. J., 'El lago de oro', *Publicación del Instituto Geofísico de los Andes Colombianos, Serie C—Geología*, 15 (Bogotá, 1972) 10–11.

197 *from the Lake.*' Gustavo Jaramillo Sánchez, *La verdad sobre la Laguna de Guatavita* (Bogotá, 1949), and registration of his mine, Sesquilé, 27 January 1949.

197 *metal-detecting equipment',* Hans Roden, *Treasure seekers* (New York, 1963), 52.

198 *am saying this.*' Hector Muñóz, 'Las exploraciones en la Laguna de Guatavita', *El Espectador*, Bogotá, 10 December 1965.

198 *at its bottom.*' Idem.

Bibliography

ABBREVIATIONS

AGI: *Archivo general de Indias*, the immense Archive of the Indies in Seville.

BAE: *Biblioteca de Autores Españoles desde la formación del lenguaje hasta nuestros dias*, ed. Manuel Rivadeneira, 71 vols (Madrid, 1846–80); *Continuación*, ed. M. Menéndez-Pelayo (Madrid, 1905–).

BANH: *Biblioteca de la Academia Nacional de la Historia*, (Caracas).

BHA: *Boletin de Historia y Antiguedades*, Academia Nacional de Historia, (Bogotá, 1908–).

BHN: *Biblioteca de Historia Nacional*, Academia Colombiana de Historia, (Bogotá, 1902–).

BolANH: *Boletin de la Academia Nacional de la Historia*, (Caracas, 1912–).

CDIA: *Colección de documentos inéditos relativos al descubrimiento, conquista y colonización de las posesiones españolas en América y Oceania sacadas en su mayor parte del Real Archivo de Indias*, ed. Joaquín F. Pacheco, Francisco de Cárdenas and Luis Torres de Mendoza, 42 vols (Madrid, 1864–84).

DIHC: *Documentos inéditos para la historia de Colombia*, ed. Juan Friede, 10 vols (Bogotá, 1955–60).

FDNRG: *Fuentes documentales para la historia del Nuevo Reino de Granada* (1550–90), ed. Juan Friede, 8 vols (Bogotá, 1975–6).

HSAI: *Handbook of South America Indians*, ed. Julian H. Steward, Bureau of American Ethnology, Smithsonian Institution, Bulletin 143, 6 vols (Washington, D.C., 1946–63), vols 2, *The Andean civilizations*; 3, *The tropical forest tribes*.

Early sources

ACOSTA, Joaquín, *Compendio histórico del descubrimiento y colonización de la Nueva Granada en el siglo décimo sexto* (Paris, 1848).

AGUADO, Pedro de (and Antonio Medrano), *Recopilación historial* (Lisbon, 1581), ed. Juan Friede (4 vols, Bogotá, 1956); pt 1, *Historia de Santa Marta y del Nuevo Reino de Granada* (Bogotá, 1906); pt 2, *Historia de Venezuela*, ed. Jerónimo Bécker (2 vols, Madrid, 1950).

ALMESTO, Pedrarias de, *Relación verdadera de la jornada de Omagua y Dorado que el gobernador Pedro de Ursúa fue a descubrir . . .*, Nueva BAE 15, 1909, 423–84.

ANON, *Descripción de la ciudad de Tunja* (1610) in CDIA, 9 (Madrid, 1868), 393–448.

ANON (perhaps by Antonio Cardozo), *Relación del descubrimiento y población de la provincia de Santa Marta* (c. 1545) in M. Serrano y Sanz ed., *Relaciones históricas de América, primer mitad del siglo XVI* (Madrid, 1916), 76–135.

BENALCÁZAR, Sebastián de, Testimony to Antonio de Aragón, Cartagena, 4 July 1539, DIHC, 5 206–8.

–Letter to King, Cali, 30 March 1541, DIHC, 6 132–3.

–Letter to King, Cali, 20 September 1542, DIHC, 6 292–302.

–*Relación de méritos y servicios de Sebastián de Benalcázar y de su hijo Dn. Francisco*, Popayán, in José Manuel Groot, *Historia eclesiástica y civil de la Nueva Granada* (2 vols, Bogotá, 1889), 1 477–83.

BERRÍO, Antonio de, Letter to King Philip, Santafé, 24 May 1585, trans. in V. T. Harlow ed., Sir Walter Ralegh, *The Discoverie of Guiana*, 91–5.

–Letter to King, Margarita, 26 October 1591, in Harlow, idem, 95–7.

–Letter to King, Margarita, 1 January 1593, in Harlow, idem, 98–105.

–*Relación de lo sucedido en el descubrimiento de Guayana y Manoa* (Trinidad, 1593), in Demetrio Ramos Pérez, *El mito del Dorado*, 665–7; trans. in Harlow, idem, 106–8.

–*Carta-relación* to King, Trinidad, 2 December 1594, in Pablo Ojer, *Don Antonio de Berrío*, 187–98.

–Letter to King about his capture by Ralegh, Margarita, 11 July 1595, in Ojer, idem, 199–204.

CARVAJAL, Gaspar de, *Descubrimiento del río de las Amazonas*, ed. José Toribio Medina (Seville, 1894); trans. Bertram T. Lee and ed. H. C. Heaton, *The Discovery of the Amazon* (New York, 1934).

CASTELLANOS, Juan de, *Elegías de varones ilustres de Indias* (Madrid, 1589); ed. Caracciolo Parra (2 vols, Caracas, 1930–2); ed. Miguel A. Caro (4 vols, Bogotá, 1955).

–*Historia del Nuevo Reino de Granada* (2 vols, Madrid, 1886).

CIEZA DE LEÓN, Pedro de, *Primera parte de la crónica del Perú* (Seville, 1553), BAE 26 (*Historiadores primitivos de Indias* 2), Madrid, 1947, 354–458; partly trans. C. R. Markham, Hakluyt Society 33 (London, 1864); trans. Harriet de Onis, ed. V. W. von Hagen (Norman, Oklahoma, 1959).

–*La guerra de Quito*, trans. C. R. Markham, Hakluyt Society, 2 series, 31, 1913.

–*La guerra de Chupas*, trans. C. R. Markham, Hakluyt Society, 2 series, 42, 1918.

DAZA, Luis, *Probanza (sobre el indio dorado)*, Popayán, 3 October 1542, in Demetrio Ramos Pérez, *El mito del Dorado* (Caracas, 1973), 467–76.

FEDERMANN, Nicolaus, *Indianische Historia, eine schöne kurtzweilige Historia, Nicolaus Federmann des Jüngers von Ulm* (Hagenau, 1557); ed. Karl Klüpfel, *Bibliotek des Literarischen Vereins in Stuttgart* 47 (Stuttgart, 1859); trans. Juan Friede, in Joaquín Gabaldón Márquez ed., *Descubrimiento y conquista de Venezuela*, 2 155–250 (Caracas, 1962).

FERNÁNDEZ PIEDRAHITA, Lucas, *Historia general de las conquistas del Nuevo Reyno de Granada* (Antwerp, 1688).

GARCILASO DE LA VEGA, *Comentarios reales de los Incas* (Lisbon, 1609, Córdoba, 1617), BAE cont. 134–5, 1960; trans. Harold V. Livermore (London and Austin, 1966).

GUMILLA, José, S. J., *El Orinoco ilustrado y defendido* (Madrid, 1741), ed. Demetrio Ramos Pérez, Biblioteca de la Academia Nacional de la Historia 63 (Caracas, 1963).

–*Historia natural, civil y geográfica de las naciones situadas a las riveras del río Orinoco* (Barcelona, 1791).

HERRERA TORDESILLAS, Antonio de, *Historia general de los hechos de los castellanos en las islas y Tierrafirme del Mar Océano* (Madrid, 1610–15), ed. Antonio Ballesteros Beretta and Miguel Gómez del Campillo (17 vols, Madrid, 1934–55).

HUMBOLDT, Alexander von, *Vues des cordillères et monuments des peuples indigènes de l'Amérique* (Paris, 1810).

–*Personal narrative of travels to the equinoctial regions of the New Continent during the years 1799–1804*, trans. Helen Maria Williams (6 vols, London, 1826).

HUTTEN, Philip von, *Zeitung aus India* (1539), *Historisch-Litterarisches Magazin von Johann Georg Meusel*, 5 51–117 (Bayreuth and Leipzig, 1785); trans. Frederica de Ritter, in Joaquín Gabaldón Márquez ed., *Descubri-*

miento y Conquista de Venezuela 2 (Biblioteca de la Academia Nacional de la Historia 55), 339–402 (Caracas, 1962).

JIMÉNEZ DE QUESADA, Gonzalo, *Reparto del botín* (Santafé de Bogotá, 15 June 1538), in Friede, *Gonzalo Jiménez de Quesada . . .* (Bogotá, 1960). 136–61.

–*Interrogatorio*, Madrid, 24 April 1546, in Friede, idem, 292–316.

–(attributed to) *Epítome de la conquista del Nuevo Reino de Granada* (c. 1550), ed. Manuel Lucena Salmoral, *Jiménez de Quesada* 3, no. 13 (Instituto Colombiano de Cultural Hispánica, Bogotá), December 1962, 43–60.

–*Memoria de los descubridores y conquistadores que entraron conmigo a descubrir y conquistar este Nuevo Reino de Granada* (c. 1566), in Joaquín Acosta, *Compendio histórico . . .* (Paris, 1848), 398–404; trans. C. R. Markham, *The Conquest of New Granada* (London, 1912), 203–9.

–*Indicaciones para el buen gobierno*, BHA 14, no. 162 (Bogotá, 1923), 345–61.

KEYMIS, Laurence, *A Relation of the Second Voyage to Guiana, performed and written in the year 1596*, in Richard Hakluyt, *The Principall Navigations of the English Nation* (London, 1589), Everyman's Library 338, 8 vols (London, 1962), 7 358–400.

LEÓN PINELO, Antonio de, *El Paraíso en el Nuevo Mundo, comentario apologético, historia natural y peregrina de las Indias Occidentales, Islas y Tierra Firme del Mar Océano* (Madrid, 1656); ed. Raúl Porras Barrenechea (Lima, 1948).

LÓPEZ DE VELASCO, Juan, *Corografía de la gobernación de Venezuela y Nueva Andalucía* (1571–1574), in Antonio Avellano Moreno ed., *Relaciones geográficas de Venezuela* (Biblioteca de la Academia Nacional de la Historia 70) (Caracas, 1964), 95–109.

MARTÍN, Esteban, *Relación de la expedición de Ambrosio Alfinger* (Coro, 18 August 1534), in Joaquín Gabaldón Márquez ed., *Descubrimiento y conquista de Venezuela* 2 (Biblioteca de la Academia Nacional de la Historia 55) (Caracas, 1962), 253–74.

MERCADO, Pedro, de S. J., *Historia de la provincia del Nuevo Reino y Quito de la Compañía de Jesús* (1683), ed. Juan Manuel Pacheco (4 vols, Bogotá, 1957).

NAVARRETE, Martín Fernández de, *Colección de los viajes y descubrimientos que hicieron por mar los españoles desde el fin del siglo XV . . .* (5 vols, Madrid, 1829–59); Biblioteca de Autores Españoles 75–7 (Madrid, 1955).

OCÁRIZ, Juan Flórez de, *Genealogías del Nuevo Reino de Granada* (3 vols, Madrid, 1672–4).

ORTIGÜERA, Toribio de, *Jornada del río Marañón con todo lo acaecido en ella . . .* (c. 1585), ed. M. Serrano y Sanz, BAE cont. 15, *Historiadores de Indias* 2 (Madrid, 1909).

OVIEDO, Basilio Vicente de, *Cualidades y riquezas del Nuevo Reino de Granada*, ed. L. A. Cuervo, Biblioteca de Historia Nacional 45 (Bogotá, 1930).

OVIEDO Y BAÑOS, José de, *Historia de la conquista y población de la provincia de Venezuela* (Madrid, 1723), ed. Cesáreo Fernández Duro (2 vols, Madrid, 1885); BAE 107 (Madrid, 1958).

OVIEDO Y VALDÉS, Gonzalo Fernández de, *Historia general y natural de las Indias, islas y Tierra-firme del Mar Océano* (Seville, 1535–47), ed. José Amador de Los Rios (4 vols, Madrid, 1852); ed. Juan Pérez de Tudela Bueso, BAE (continuation) 117–21 (Madrid, 1959).

PONTES, Alonso de, *Relación de su jornada al rió Meta* (1583), in Pablo Ojer, *Don Antonio de Berrío, Gobernador del Dorado*, 177–86.

RALEGH, Sir Walter, *The discoverie of the large, rich, and beautifull Empire of Guiana, with Manoa (which the Spaniards call El Dorado) . . .* (1595), ed. Richard Hakluyt, *The Principall Navigations of the English Nation* (London, 1589), Everyman's Library 388 (8 vols, London, 1962), 7 272–350, ed. V. T. Harlow (London, 1928).

–*Sir Walter Raghleys Large Appologie for the ill successe of his enterprise to Guiana* (1618), in Harlow, *Ralegh's Last Voyage*, 316–34.

RODRÍGUEZ FRESLE, Juan, *El Carnero de Bogotá: Conquista y descubrimiento del Nuevo Reino de Granada* (1636), ed. F. Pérez (Bogotá, 1942); trans. William C. Atkinson, *The Conquest of New Granada* (London, 1961).

SAN MARTÍN, Juan de (and Baltasar Maldonado and Gil López), *Libro de lo que se ha habido en esta jornada y descubrimiento del Rio Grande . . .* , 13 June 1538, DIHC, 4 79–91.

–(and Antonio de Lebrija), *Carta missiva a Su Magestad, dando relación del subcesso de su camino*, Santafé, 20 September 1539, in Gonzalo Fernández de Oviedo, *Historia general y natural de Indias*, pt 2, bk 26, ch. 11 (Madrid, 1852), 2 357–68.

SIMÓN, Pedro, OFM, *Noticias historiales de las conquistas de Tierra Firme, en las Indias Occidentales* (Cuenca, 1627); part trans. William Bollaert, *The Expedition of Pedro de Ursúa and Lope de Aguirre in search of El Dorado and Omagua in 1560–1*, Hakluyt Society 28 (London, 1861); (5 vols, Bogotá, 1882–92); ed. Demetrio Ramos Pérez, Biblioteca de la Academia Nacional de la Historia 66–7 (2 vols, Caracas, 1963).

SPARREY, Francis, *Memorial del servicio que haze . . . a su Majestad* (c. 1600), in Demetrio Ramos Pérez, *El mito del Dorado* (Caracas, 1973), 671–7.

–*The Discription of the Isle of Trinidad, the rich Countrye of Guiana, and the Mightie River of Orenoco* (1602), in Samuel Purchas, *Hakluytus Posthumus or Purchas, His Pilgrimes* (1625), Hakluyt Society, 20 vols, (Glasgow, 1906), 16 301–9.

TOLOSA, Licenciado Juan Pérez de, *Relación de las tierras y provincias de la Gobernación de Venezuela, que es cargo de los alemanes* (1546), in Antonio Avellano Moreno ed., *Relaciones geográficas de Venezuela*, 1–14.

–*Relación breve . . . de las personas que se han hallado en Venezuela, desde el principio que se vino a poblar por los Velzares . . .* , Coro, 8 July, 1548.

VÁZQUEZ, Francisco, *Relación verdadera de todo lo que sucedió en la jornada de Omagua y Dorado*, BAE cont. 15 (Historiadores de Indias 2) (Madrid, 1909).

VÁZQUEZ DE ESPINOSA, Antonio, *Compendio y descripción de la Indias Occidentales* (1629); trans. and ed. Charles Upson Clark (Washington, D.C., 1942).

Modern works

ALBUQUERQUE PÉREZ, Antonio, *Orellana: al margen del corriente* (Madrid, 1975).

ARCINIEGAS, Germán, *Jiménez de Quesada* (Bogotá, 1939).

–*Los alemanes en la conquista de América* (Buenos Aires, 1941); trans. Angel Flores, *Germans in the Conquest of America: A Sixteenth Century Venture* (New York, 1943).

ARIZA, Alberto E., O.P., 'Itinerario cronológico y geográfico de Jiménez de Quesada a la conquista de los Chibchas', BHA 54, nos 627–9 (Bogotá, 1967), 101–20.

ARMELLADA, Cesárea de, *Por la Venezuela indígena* (Caracas, 1960).

BANDELIER, Adolph F., *The Gilded Man (El Dorado) and other pictures of the Spanish occupancy of America* (New York, 1893).

BARRIGA VILLALBA, Antonio María, 'Orfebrería Chibcha y su definición científica', *Revista de la Academia de Ciencias Exactas, Físicas y Naturales* 11, no. 43 (Bogotá, 1961), 199–214.

BAYLE, Constantino, *El Dorado fantasma* (Madrid, 1943).

BEISSMANGER, Konrad, *Im Lande der heiligen Seen. Reisebilder aus der Heimat der Chibcha Indianer (Kolumbien)* (Nürnberg, 1911).

BRAY, Warwick, 'Ancient American metalsmiths', *Proceedings of the Royal Anthropological Institute* (London, 1971).

–'Gold working in ancient America' and 'The organization of the metal trade', in *El Dorado, the gold of ancient Colombia*, The American Federation of Arts (New York, 1974).

–*The gold of El Dorado* (London, 1978).

BRITISH GOVERNMENT, *British Guiana boundary: Appendix to the case on behalf of the Government of Her Britannic Majesty, 1898–99* (London, 1899).

BROADBENT, Sylvia M., *Los Chibchas: organización socio-política* (Bogotá, 1964). 'La fundación de Santafé', BHA **54**, nos 630–2 (Bogotá, 1967), 189–207.

BUARQUE DE HOLANDA, Sérgio, *Visão do paraíso* (Brasiliana 333) (São Paulo, 1969).

BUSTO DUTHURBURU, José Antonio del, *Francisco de Orellana. Lope de Aguirre* (Lima, 1965).

CASTELLVÍ, Marcellino de, 'Reseña crítica sobre el descubrimiento de la región de Mocoa y fundaciones de la ciudad del mismo nombre', BHA **29**, nos 330–1, 1942, 367–90.

–'Los descubridores del Caquetá y del Mocoa', BHA **31**, nos 357–8 (Bogotá, 1944), 755–90.

COCHRANE, Captain Charles Stuart, R.N., *Journal of a residence and travels in Colombia, during the years 1823 and 1824* (2 vols, London, 1825).

COHEN, Jack M., *Journeys down the Amazon* (London and Tonbridge, 1975).

CONTRACTORS LIMITED, *Description and details of articles recovered from the sacred Lake of Guatavita, Republic of Columbia, South America* (London, 1911).

CORTESÃO, Jaime, 'A lenda do lago Dourado e das Amazonas', *Boletim Geográfico Brasileiro* **47**, February 1947.

CUERVO, Antonio B., ed., *Colección de documentos inéditos sobre la geografía y la historia de Colombia* (4 vols, Bogotá, 1891–4).

CÚNEO VIDAL, Rómulo, 'Las leyendas geográficas del Perú de los Incas: El Dorado, las Amazonas, Jauja', *Boletín de la Academia de la Historia* (Madrid, Oct.-Dec. 1925).

DUQUE GÓMEZ, Luis, *Colombia: monumentos históricos y arqueológicos* (Mexico, 1955).

–*Prehistoria: etno-historia y arqueología*, in Luis Martínez Delgado ed., *Historia extensa de Colombia* 1, pts 1–2 (Bogotá, 1965).

EFRÉN REYES, Oscar, *Descubrimiento y conquista del Ecuador* (Quito, 1948).

FEBRES CORDERO, Julio, *Los Dorados y el Parime* (Caracas, 1947).

FERRANDIS TORRES, Manuel, *El mito del oro en la conquista de América* (Valladolid, 1935).

FRIEDE, Juan, 'Descubrimiento del Nuevo Reino de Granada', BHA **38**, nos 435–7 (Bogotá, 1951), 524–31.

–*Los Andaki, 1538–1947: historia de la aculturación de una tribu selvática* (Mexico/Buenos Aires, 1953).

–'La expedición de Sebastián de Benalcázar a Santafé', BHA **42**, nos 493–4, 1955, 723–30.

–*Documentos inéditos para la historia de Colombia*, Academia Colombiana de Historia, 10 vols (Bogotá/Madrid, 1955–60) (=DIHC).

–'Geographical ideas and the conquest of Venezuela', *The Americas* **16** (Washington, D.C., 1959), 145–59.

–*Nicolás Federmann, conquistador de Venezuela, 1506?–1542* (Caracas, 1959).

–*Vida y viajes de Nicolás Federmann, 1506–1542* (Bogotá, 1960).

–*Gonzalo Jiménez de Quesada a través de documentos históricos*, BHN **95** (Bogotá, 1960).

–*Descubrimiento del Nuevo Reino de Granada y fundación de Bogotá (1536–1539)* (Bogotá, 1960).

–*Los Welser en la conquista de Venezuela* (Caracas/Madrid, 1961).

–*Los Quimbayas bajo la dominación española. Estudio documental, 1539–1810* (Bogotá, 1963).

–'Historia de Sebastián de Benalcázar, escrita por su hijo, don Francisco', *Boletín Cultural y Bibliográfico* **7**, no. 4 (Bogotá, 1964), 573–80.

–*Descubrimiento y conquista del Nuevo Reino de Granada. Introducción* (Historia Extensa de Colombia 2) (Bogotá, 1965).

–*Invasión del país de los Chibchas, conquista del Nuevo Reino de Granada y fundación de Santafé de Bogotá* (Bogotá, 1966).

GABALDÓN MÁRQUEZ, Joaquín, ed., *Descubrimiento y conquista de Venezuela*, BANH **54–5** (2 vols, Caracas, 1962).

GANDÍA, Enrique, *Historia crítica de los mitos en la conquista americana* (Madrid, 1929; Buenos Aires, 1946).

GARCÍA, Casiano, *Vida del Comendador Diego de Ordaz, descubridor del Orinoco* (Mexico, 1952).

GARCÍA SAMUDIO, Nicolás, *Crónica del muy magnifico Capitán don Gonzalo Suárez Rendón*, BHN **61** (Bogotá, 1939).

GIL MUNILLA, Ladislao, *Descubrimiento del Marañón* (Seville, 1954).

GOODMAN, Edward J., *The Explorers of South America* (New York/London, 1972).

GRAHAM, R. B. Cunninghame, *The conquest of New Granada, being the life of Gonzalo Jiménez de Quesada* (London, 1922).

HAGEN, Victor Wolfgang von, *The Golden Man: the Quest for El Dorado* (Farnborough, Hampshire, 1974).

–*Der Ruf der neuen Welt: Deutsche bauen Amerika* (Munich/Zurich, 1970); The Germanic People in America (Norman, Oklahoma, 1976).

HAMILTON, Col. J. P., *Travels through the interior provinces of Columbia* (2 vols, London, 1827).

HARLOW, Vincent T., ed., Sir Walter Ralegh, *The Discoverie of the large and bewtiful Empire of Guiana* (London, 1928).

–*Ralegh's Last Voyage* (London, 1932).

HEMMING, John Henry, *The Conquest of the Incas* (London, 1970).

–*Red gold, the conquest of the Brazilian Indians* (London, 1978).

HERNÁNDEZ DE ALBA, Gregorio, 'Tribes of North-western Venezuela', HSAI, **4** 469–74.

HUMBERT, Jules, *L'occupation allemande du Vénézuela au XVIeme siecle* (Bordeaux/Paris, 1905).

JIJÓN Y CAMAÑO, Jacinto, *Sebastián de Benalcázar* (2 vols, Quito, 1936–8).

JIMÉNEZ DE LA ESPADA, Marcos, 'Primeros descubrimientos del país de la canela', *El Centenario* **2** (Madrid, 1892).

–'La traición de un tuerto', *La Ilustración Española y Americana* (Madrid, 1892).

–'Noticias auténticas del famoso río Marañón', *Boletín de la Sociedad Geográfica de Madrid*, 1880–93.

JOS, Emiliano, *La expedición de Ursúa al Dorado, la rebelión de Lope de Aguirre y el itinerario de los 'Marañones'* (Huesca, 1927).

–*Ciencia y osadía sobre Lope de Aguirre el Peregrino* (Seville, 1949).

KIRCHHOFF, Paul, 'Food-gathering tribes of the Venezuelan llanos', HSAI, **4** 445–68.

KIRKPATRICK, F. A., *The Spanish Conquistadores* (London, 1934).

KROEBER, Alfred L., 'The Chibcha', HSAI, **2** 887–909.

LATHRAP, Donald W., *The Upper Amazon* (Ancient Peoples and Places 70) (London, 1970).

LEVILLIER, Roberto, *El Paititi, El Dorado y las Amazonas* (Buenos Aires, 1976).

MARKHAM, Clements R., *The Conquest of New Granada* (London, 1912).

MARTÍNEZ DELGADO, Luis, ed., *Historia extensa de Colombia* (23 parts, Bogotá, 1965): 1 Luis Duque Gómez, Prehistoria; 2 Juan Friede, Descubrimiento y conquista del Nuevo Reino de Granada.

MARTÍNEZ-MENDOZA, Jerónimo, *La leyenda de El Dorado* (Caracas, 1967).

MORENO, Antonio Avellano, *Fuentes para la historia económica de Venezuela* (Caracas, 1950).

–*Documentos para la historia económica de Venezuela* (Caracas, 1961).

–*Relaciones geográficas de Venezuela*, BANH **70** (Caracas, 1964).

MORÓN, Guillermo, *Los orígenes históricos de Venezuela* (Madrid, 1954).

NAIPAUL, V. S., *The loss of El Dorado. A History* (London, 1969).

OJER, Pablo S. J., *Don Antonio de Berrío, Gobernador del Dorado* (Caracas, 1960).

–*La formación del Oriente venezolano* (Caracas, 1966).

ORAMAS, Luis R., *En pos del Dorado* (Caracas, 1947).

ORTEGA RICAURTE, Daniel, 'Ruta de Gonzalo Jiménez de Quesada', BHA 25, nos 285–6 (Bogotá, 1938), 409–52.

PANHORST, Carl Heinrich (Carlos), *Los alemanes en Venezuela durante el siglo XVI: Carlos V y la casa Welser* (Madrid, 1927).

PÉREZ DE BARRADAS, José, *Los Muiscas antes de la Conquista* (2 vols, Instituto Bernardino de Sahagún, Madrid, 1950–1).

–*Orfebrería prehispánica de Colombia: estilos Tolima y Muisca* (2 vols, Madrid, 1958).

PÉREZ-EMBID, Florentino, *Diego de Ordás, compañero de Cortés y explorador del Orinoco* (Seville, 1950).

PLAZAS DE NIETO, Clemencia, and FALCHETTI DE SAENZ, Ana-María, 'El territorio de los Muiscas a la llegada de los españoles, *Cuadernos de Antropología* 1, Universidad de los Andes (Bogotá, 1973).

–*El Dorado Colombian Gold* (Melbourne, 1978).

POSADA, Eduardo, 'La Laguna de Guatavita', BHA 8 (Bogotá, 1912), 235–40.

–*El Dorado: l'Homme Doré* (Liège, 1925); Spanish edn (Bogotá, 1936).

QUINN, David B., *Ralegh and the British Empire* (1947) (Harmondsworth, 1973).

RAASVELDT, H. C., *Los enigmas de la Laguna de Guatavita* (Bogotá, 1954).

RAMÍREZ, Jesús Emilio, S. J., 'El lago de oro', *Publicación del Instituto Geofísico de los Andes Colombianos, Serie C—Geología* 15 (Bogotá, 1972), 3–18.

RAMOS PÉREZ, Demetrio, 'Examen crítico de las noticias sobre el mito del Dorado', *Revista de Cultura Universitaria* 41 (Caracas, 1954), 19–58.

–*Ximénez de Quesada, cronista, y el Epítome de la conquista del Nuevo Reino de Granada* (Escuela de Estudios Hispano-Americanos, Seville, 1972).

–*El mito del Dorado. Su génesis y proceso* (BANH 116) (Caracas, 1973).

RATZEL, Friedrich, 'Notizen zur Biographie Philipps von Hutten', *Jahresbericht der Geographischen Gesellschaft in München* 8 (Munich, 1880), 153–6.

REHM, Bruno, *Die schrecklichen Pferde: der Welserzug nach Eldorado* (Berlin, 1934).

REICHEL-DOLMATOFF, Gerardo, 'Los indios Motilones', *Revista del Instituto Etnológico Nacional* 2 (Bogotá, 1945).

–*Colombia* (Ancient Peoples and Places 44) (London, 1965).

–*San Agustín: a culture of Colombia* (London, 1972).

REIMERS, Erich, *Die Welser Landen in Venezuela* (Leipzig, 1938).

RESTREPO, Vicente, *Los Chibchas antes de la conquista española* (Bogotá, 1895).

RESTREPO TIRADO, Ernesto, *Los Quimbayas* (Bogotá, 1912).

–*Descubrimiento y conquista de Colombia* (2 vols, Bogotá, 1917).

–*De Gonzalo Ximénez de Quesada a don Pablo Morillo: Documentos inéditos sobre la historia de la Nueva Granada* (Paris, 1928).

–*Historia de la provincia de Santa Marta* (2 vols, Seville, 1929).

–'Documentos del Archivo de Indias. Papeles de justicia. Residencias que se tomaron a los primeros gobernadores de las provincias del Nuevo Reino de Granada', BHA 26 (Bogotá, 1939), 237–74, 293–335, 484–98, 679–765.

RIVAS, Raimundo, *Los fundadores de Bogotá* (1921) (2 vols, BHN 57–8) (Bogotá, 1938).

RIVET, Paul and ARSANDAUX, Henri, 'L' orfèvrerie de Chiriqui et de Colombie', *Journal de la Société des Américanistes de Paris*, n.s. 15 (Paris, 1923).

–'La métallurgie en Amérique précolombienne', Université de Paris, *Travaux et Mémoires de l'Institut d'Ethnologie* 39 (Paris, 1946).

ROOT, William Campbell, 'Metallurgy', HSAI 5, 1949, 205–25.

–'Pre-columbian metalwork of Colombia and its neighbours', in Samuel K. Lothrop ed., *Essays in pre-columbian art and archaeology* (Cambridge, Mass., 1964).

ROSA, Moisés de la, 'Los conquistadores de los Chibchas', BHA 22, nos 249–50 (Bogotá, 1935), 225–53.

ROSALES, José Miguel, 'El Dorado', BHA 12 no. 138, 1919, 354–61.

RÖTHLISBERGER, Ernst, *El Dorado: Reise- und Kulturbilder aus den südamerikanischen Columbien* (Bern, 1898).

RUIZ, Helena, *La búsqueda de Eldorado por Guayana* (Seville, 1959).

SALAS, Julio César, *Tierra-Firme (Venezuela y Colombia): Estudios sobre etnología e historia* (Mérida, Venezuela, 1971).

SCHAUWECKER, Heinz, *Auf der Suche nach dem Goldland El Dorado* (Nürnberg, 1925).

SCHOMBURGK, Sir Robert H., ed., Sir Walter Ralegh, *The discoverie of the large, rich, and beautifull Empire of Guiana . . .*, Hakluyt Society 3, 1848.

TAYLOR, Eva G. R., 'Hariot's instructions for Sir Walter Ralegh's voyage to Guiana, 1595', *Journal of the Institute of Navigation* 5 (London, 1952).

TORRE Y DEL CERRO, José de la, 'Gonzalo Jiménez de Quesada', BHA 22, no. 258 (Bogotá, March 1936).

TRIANA, Miguel, *La civilización chibcha* (Bogotá, 1970).

TRIMBORN, Hermann, 'La política en "El Dorado" ', *Investigación y Progreso* 5 (Madrid, 1934), 152 ff.

VALLEJO, Alejandro, *La cita de los aventureros: gesta de don Gonzalo Jiménez de Quesada* (Bogotá, 1973).

VILA, Marco Aurelio, 'El primer viaje de Federman visto por la geografía', *Revista Nacional de Cultura* 140–1 (Caracas, May–August 1960).

WILLIAMSON, James A., *English colonies in Guiana and on the Amazon, 1604–1668* (Oxford, 1923).

ZAPATA GOLLÁN, Agustín, *Mito y superstición en la conquista de América* (Buenos Aires, 1963).

ZERDA, Liborio, *El Dorado, estudio histórico, etnográfico y arqueológico de los Chibchas* (Bogotá, 1883, reprinted 1972).

Illustration Acknowledgments

Archiv für Kunst und Geschichte, Berlin: 19 (right)

Bibliothèque Nationale, Paris: 8

By permission of the British Library, London: 6 (plate 4, from 'Travels', Vol. 5, by L. Hulsius, 1599), 7 (left) (plate 69, from *Historia de las Indias de Nueva España*, by Fray Diego Duran, *c*. 1560–80), 7 (right) (plate 71, from *Historia de las Indias de Nueva España*, by Fray Diego Duran, *c*. 1560–80), 24, 52 (from *Historia General Hechos de los Castellanos*, by Antonio de Herrera Tordesillas, 1601–15), 55 (from Codex Köler, Add. 15217), colour plates opp. 56 (from Codex Köler, Add. 15217), 161 (from 'Travels', Vol. 5, by L. Hulsius, 1599), 171, 172 (from 'Travels', Vol. 5, by L. Hulsius, 1599), 179 (from 'Travels', Vol. 5, by L. Hulsius, 1599), 187 (left), 187 (right) Add. MSS 36321, F66

Mario Carrieri: colour plates on half-title, frontispiece and opp. 16, 17, 32, 33, 48, 49, 57, 64, 65, 80, 81, 89, 96, 97, 113, 128, 129, 144, 145, 160, 161, 176, 177

Bruce Coleman: colour plate opp. 112 (top right)

Dr M. J. Eden: 4, 13, 29, 120 (above)

Galeria Cano, Bogotá: 105

Germanisches Nationalmuseum, Nürnberg: 21

Susan Griggs Agency: colour plate between 56–7 (below, RIGHT)

Robert Harding Associates, London: 7 (left), 7 (right), 8, 31, 46, 54 (from *Vom Amazonas und Madeira*, by Keiler-Leuzinger), 167 (from *Vom Amazonas und Madeira*, by Keiler-Leuzinger)

John Hemming: 22 (below left), 22 (below right), 26, colour plates between 56–7 (above and below, LEFT), 59, 60, colour plates between 88–9 (above and below, LEFT) and (above left, above right, below left, RIGHT), 90 (above and below), 99 (above left, above right and centre), 117, 121, 122

Historia General y Natural de las Indias, by Gonzalo Fernández de Oviedo, 1852 edition, Vol. 2: 36, 125

Courtesy London Editions Ltd: 37 (from *America . . .*, by Theodore de Bry, 1654), 97 (from *America . . .*, by Theodore de Bry, 1654), 148 (from *America . . .*, by Theodore de Bry, 1654), 164 (from *America . . .*, by Theodore de Bry, 1654), 169 (from *America . . .*, by Theodore de Bry, 1654)

The Mansell Collection, London: 17, 19 (left), 28 (above left, above right and centre), 139, 192

By permission of the Master and Fellows of Magdalene College, Cambridge: 186

Marion Morrison: 34 (above), colour plate between 56–7 (top right, RIGHT)

Tony Morrison: 34 (below), 194

Moser/Tayler Collection: 22 (above left), 33 (left), 33 (right), 38, 41, 62, colour plate opp. 88 (top), colour plate between 88–9 (below right, RIGHT), 98, 99 (bottom), 120 (below), 131, 133, 134

Brian Moser, Disappearing World, Granada T.V.: colour plate opp. 88 (below), 140

Museo Nacionale, Bogotá: 70, 76

The Museum of Natural History, 'Mammalia', by T. Spencer Cobbold, published by William Mackenzie: 119 (plate 26)

The National Portrait Gallery, London: 162

The Royal Geographical Society, London: 44, 178

Photo Rudolf: 70, 76, 105

Shell: 31

David Smithers: 14, 15

Times Newspapers Ltd: 70, 76, 105

Tratase de la Trimeras conquistas de Santa Marta, Libero Tercero, by D. L. Fernández Piedrahita: 146

Vues des Cordillères et Monument des peuples indigènes de l'Amerique, by Alexander von Humboldt, Paris 1810: endpapers (plate 5), 25 (plate 68), 36 (plate 55, fig. 9), 68 (plate 4), 82 (plate 6), 103

Adrian Warren/Ardea London: colour plate between 56–7 (top left, RIGHT), 110, colour plates opp. 112 (top left and below), 118, 150, 152, 154, 159, 175, 181

The Zoological Society of London: 78

Index